An Economy of Want

Donald Power

May 2024

To my parents

Disclaimer

This book is the result of almost thirty years of puzzling over economic questions. It has been written piecemeal and largely alone. Any errors are therefore mine alone.

Acknowledgements

Where images are not my own, I have used mainly unrestricted public domain images; I'm grateful to those who generously made them available. My heartfelt thanks to family and friends who have supported me in this endeavour with suggestions, practical help, and most of all, encouragement.

Images and References

I have endeavoured to cite faithfully and correctly the sources consulted. Citing any other work or source, and the use of images, does not imply any endorsement by their author or affirmer, of my work, or any connection with it. Image sources are indicated as follows:

WMC - *Wikimedia Commons, no restrictions, creative commons CC0 1.0 Deed CC0 1.0 Universal https://creativecommons.org/publicdomain/zero/1.0/.*

OGL - *UK Open Government Licence. To view this licence, visit http://www.nationalarchives.gov.uk/doc/open-governmentlicence/version/3/.*

geograph - *https://www.geograph.org.uk, stamped image file used with credit added (to comply with Creative Commons licence).*

Met - *The Met New York, under Creative Commons Zero (CC0), see https://www.metmuseum.org/about-the-met/policies-and-documents/open-access.*

Auth - *author.*

Front cover drawing: Lemming – *from archives of Pearson Scott Foresman [WMC].*

iv

Contents

CONTENTS

CONTENTS

CONTENTS

List of Figures

LIST OF FIGURES

List of Tables

Preface

Why would anyone want to write a book about economics if it is not their trade? And more to the point, why would anyone want to read it? I had better start with the first question and perhaps that may also supply an answer of sorts to the second.

The motivation is straightforward enough. Since childhood I have been conscious of both gross inequalities of wealth and of dangers to the environment, thanks to my parents who were very engaged in these issues. They helped run a local World Development Movement[1] group which met in our house. They were also alarmed by the risk of nuclear war – a very present risk in the 1960s, and still so today although we tend to ignore it.

Environmental poster drawn by author's father, c1970.

My father was interested in the intermediate technology ideas described in the book 'Small is Beautiful' by E F Schumacher, and he bought early books analysing environmental limits, such

---

[1]WDM focussed on poverty in the Third World; it is now renamed 'Global Justice Now'.

as: 'Population Resources Environment', published in 1970, and 'The Limits to Growth' commissioned by the Club of Rome and published in 1972.[1, 2, 3] My parents did not press their views on me, but rather the material itself was convincing. At university I joined a group called Third World First[2] and looked to various socialist alternatives to solve these problems; subsequently once in work, I involved myself in my spare time in the British trade union and labour movement.

"It's the economy stupid"[3]

While my political views have evolved since then, those early concerns about inequality and the environment, seem just as valid as when my parents' activities inspired my initial interest some 50 years ago, and indeed even more so. The constant root of those problems appears to be the economy, which astonishingly even in wealthy countries and despite ever more sophisticated technology, continues to leave a substantial part of the population struggling to make ends meet, and likewise is unable to protect our planet's ecosystems if doing so threatens profit or 'growth'. The ambition of this book is to spell out why this is so, working from basic principles of what an economy is and why it works the way it does. Then in a second part to the book, there are some suggestions for what we might do to improve things.

By profession I am an engineer and have always loved designing and building things. In my teens I experimented with electronics and simple computer circuits: this was 1970 when nobody had a home computer and trying to build your own seemed like the only way to acquire one! I began my working career as a mechanical engineer, but after a few years switched to digital electronics and software, generally working in what is called 'research & development', which in practice has meant designing things and getting them to work. Engineers are used to studying how systems work, and we base our understanding on the physics of the real world: my

---

[2]Third World First is now known as 'People and Planet'.

[3]A campaign slogan used by US president Clinton.

hope is that this approach is also applicable to gaining an under-standing of the economy.

At work, early career.

All my UK employments have been in private industry – usually large companies. Many of the great British engineering firms of my childhood have disappeared over the last 30 years – broken up, with the bits that remain now in different and often foreign hands. Names like ICI, GEC, British Leyland, Lucas, British Rail, British Steel, Cadbury's, EMI, BOC. In the 1970s if you bought a car, TV, radio, or washing machine in the UK, it was likely to have been made here by a British-owned company. Observing Britain's de-industrialisation, on occasion first hand when my own job was affected, raised questions about why it was happening and whether it was inevitable or should be resisted.

From 1987 in mid-career, I worked for five years for a UK aid agency, teaching in the national engineering university of Nicaragua.[4] Nicaragua was then the second-poorest country in the Americas. It was fighting a counter-insurgency war in its border areas and the USA refused to trade with it. Nicaragua had support from some western European countries, from a great many develop-ment charities, and from the Soviet Bloc. The socialist Sandinista government fell in the 1990 elections, ending the war and blockade, and was replaced by a centre right government. Throughout all of

---

[4]Universidad Nacional de Ingeniería, Managua.

those years, economics was a continuous source of debate and there were frequent dramatic policy changes. There were periods of rampant inflation and two changes of currency: one of these went from 10 Cordobas to the dollar at its introduction to something like 50 million to the dollar, before being replaced.

Hyperinflation: 1,000 Cordobas overprinted to be a million.

A constant question was: in a small Third-World country, what can you hope to manufacture locally? My electronics engineering students and my colleagues needed experience and some paid work to top up salaries. Seeking work and placements for them, I visited many local industries, both private and in state hands. In factories and in daily life I came across the products of the Soviet Bloc which were interesting to compare with their western equivalents: machine tools, vehicles, domestic goods such as soap, fridges and canned food, and the medical equipment in a hospital donated to Nicaragua by East Germany[5] – seen as a patient, undergoing an urgent appendicectomy which saved my life. I had the opportunity to make a working visit to a Cuban university, and also managed a three-day stopover in the Soviet Union when flying with Aeroflot to the UK; in both countries fascinated by the economic and technological differences.

One of the results of my years in Nicaragua was that I returned to the UK with a strong respect for private enterprise and the difficulties of state management of businesses, particularly where the state is weak or inexperienced. That experience, combined with my

---

[5]Following the Second World War, East Germany, or the 'DDR', became a separate country and part of the Soviet Bloc, until its reunification with West Germany in October 1990.

working life in the UK being entirely in the private sector, means that despite an interest in socialism I am not 'anti-market'. My aim is to understand why the economy behaves as it does, and hopefully, based on that understanding, some changes might suggest themselves - though almost certainly not a totally planned economy. Furthermore, I began to write the notes that led to this book in the early 1990s not long after Eastern Europe had eagerly thrown off communist rule and the system in the Soviet Union itself had spectacularly self-destructed.

Concern for the environment was brought into sharp focus in Nicaragua where I saw both the rain forest and adjacent degraded land where the forest had been cut down. During my stay I met a number of biologists working there, who taught me more about the natural world and our place in it. Concern that we are well on the way to making our planet uninhabitable has made me a supporter of Friends of the Earth and Greenpeace, and is another motivation for examining the economy and its effect on our planet.

These then are the experiences I bring to the task. Naturally, I have also studied a number of conventional economics texts and found much to learn and a great deal of interest in them – so it is with a good deal of nervousness that I share these writings, for fear of being mocked for challenging the experts. There are however numerous books published purporting to give various alternative views of economics, so possibly one more is not putting one's head too far above the parapet.

Part I

Understanding the Economy We Have

Chapter 1

Introduction – not for lemmings

Lemmings are small furry animals famous in folklore for mass migrations during which they sometimes jump to their deaths over the edge of cliffs or into rivers too wide to cross. Why on earth do they do that? Couldn't at least one or two of them stand up and say "Listen everyone, you're going the wrong way: do a U-turn and run back uphill <u>now</u>!"? Perhaps it would help if they had a handy little book explaining how to do a U-turn? Maybe the difficulty for the lemmings is actually knowing when they are heading for a cliff edge: as they stumble along from one tuft of grass to the next, they probably see only the tails of the ones in front of them plus the grass itself, not an overview of the scene. As well as not having that physical overview, they don't have language or books to hand down the history of past disasters. Even if you could call out to a lemming "cliff ahead" he or she would probably reply: "Scaremonger – in all my years I've never seen anyone fall of a cliff." "This downward slope is just a normal fluctuation in terraaaain .... aaaaarrgh .... thump."

So at the end of the day, writing a U-turn guide for lemmings is probably a waste of time. However, there is another animal which often shows the lemming-like behaviour of going careering off as a group without thinking too much about where it is heading. This new creature is fairly closely related to lemmings being also mammal. Of a sociable disposition it is larger, less furry and has the advantage that it can read. I hazard a guess dear reader that you are one of these animals (as of course am I), and unfortunately we humans are facing a cliff edge of our own. Plenty of humans have indeed stood up and warned us in the strongest terms. In the words of the United Nations General Secretary: "The world must wake up. We are on the edge of an abyss — and moving in the wrong direction".[4] He refers to a "cascade of crises" – disastrous climate change, glaring inequalities, and more. Yet it is proving very hard to heed these warnings – the reason almost certainly being that at the root of many of the problems is the operation of the economy. So understanding our economy is key to achieving the change of direction we urgently need, and that is what this book is about.[1]

Beginning an economics book talking about animals may be a little unusual. Yet economics is about ordinary activities that all creatures do: getting or producing the things we need to stay alive, sharing them out, and cooperating with others of our species in the process. Keeping in mind that we are one animal amongst many, allows us to compare ourselves with our cousins and thus gain a better perspective.

The knowledge that we are only one of many animals that live or have lived on this planet, also helps us to be more realistic about ourselves, about our place in the world, and about what the future might bring. When modern economics emerged the 18th and 19th centuries, European society was deeply Christian and Christianity then placed us centre-stage: God had a human appearance and

---

[1]There is a further reason to direct this book towards humans: despite the folklore, it is a myth that lemmings jump en masse to their deaths. In fact, out of the two of us, they may prove to be the more sensible.

created us in his image; the world itself was created for us and the other animals put in it for our benefit.

> "In the beginning God created the heaven and the earth."
> "And God said, Let us make man in our image, after our likeness: and let them have dominion over the fish of the sea, and over the fowl of the air, and over the cattle, and over all the earth, and over every creeping thing that creepeth upon the earth." – *The Bible, Book of Genesis.*

By Giovanni di Paolo, 1445. [WMC]

Figure 1.1: The Creation of the World and the Expulsion from Paradise.

Religions also offer hope for the future. However bad things may be now, life has purpose and direction, leading for example to heaven for the individual and judgement for the whole Earth. Much economics theory seems similarly optimistic: the world's resources have been placed here for our use and the operation of the free market will lead to the betterment of mankind.

Nor is it only free-marketeers who see the operation of the economy as leading to a 'happy end' for humanity. Karl Marx for example, believed that economic development would eventually lead to a sort of heaven on earth in which there was no obligation to work and all needs were met – and that this would inevitably come about. Even though Marx was an atheist and his heaven had to be an earthly one, his vision remains curiously similar to the religious belief that humans are special and that the human story leads to a future paradise.

First edition, 1848. [WMC]

Figure 1.2: The Communist Manifesto by Karl Marx and Frederick Engels.

"... as the exploitation of one individual by another will also be put an end to, the exploitation of one nation by another will also be put an end to. ... as the antagonism between classes within the nation vanishes, the hostility of one nation to another will come to an end." – *The Communist Manifesto, Karl Marx and Friedrich Engels.[5]*

"In a higher phase of communist society, after the enslaving subordination of the individual to the division of labour, and therewith also the antithesis between mental and physical labour, has vanished; after labour has become not only a means of life but life's prime want; after the productive forces have also increased with the all-around development of the individual, and all the springs of co-operative wealth flow more abundantly – only then can the narrow horizon of bourgeois right be crossed in its entirety and society inscribe on its banners: From each according to his ability, to each according to his needs!" – *Critique of the Gotha Programme, Karl Marx.[6]*

In the 19th century however, science began to remove humankind from our pedestal and place us firmly back among the other animals. Charles Darwin published the Origin of Species in 1859 introducing the theory of evolution and making it plain that we share common ancestors with all other animals. Nineteenth century English society was said to be shocked by the suggestion that they were 'descended from apes'! For me the extraordinary thing about evolution is not that we evolved from an ape like creature that was also the great great great ..... great grandmother of chimpanzees (the resemblance between us and chimps is after all pretty obvious) but that if you go even further back, our ancestors were furry little rat like creatures that scurried around under the feet of dinosaurs, and before that, reptiles, and before that fish, and so on back to the very origins of life on earth.

In recent years genetics has complemented evolutionary theory by allowing us to see how many genes we share with other life forms. The results are startling we share roughly 98% of our genes with chimpanzees, 85% with mice, 60% with fruit flies and 50% with bananas. Yes, the banana is a distant cousin, and all mammals are close relatives – little wonder that we like to drink the milk that our near cousins cow, sheep and goat make for their babies.

Once we accept that lemmings and other animals are our cousins, it is less surprising that like them, we are also focused on what is just in front of us for most of the time, and we find it hard to step back and see where we are going. It is natural for us to find it hard to tackle big world-wide problems. Like most other animals we are mainly interested in our own patch of ground and family, friends (and enemies) who live near us. We should not be too hard on ourselves if we find it a struggle to forget the concerns of our day-to-day existence and survey the wider scene, let alone

Lycoptera Fish Fossil. [WMC]

Figure 1.3: Our ancestors were fish.

take effective action based on what we see there. Yet, the wonder of being human is that we do have the ability to look out from the small part of space and time allotted to us and contemplate the immensity of the universe, study the distant past and gaze into the future.

That we are a small and recent branch on the immense family tree of creatures that have lived on this planet, must also lead us to another conclusion: that we are not the heroes of the story of life on earth that everything else has been leading up to. There is no guaranteed future for us any more than there was for dinosaurs or dodos in the past or there is today for polar bears and pigeons.

Having said all that, if you hold a religious faith that includes the belief that humans are created by God, please don't stop reading here. Though from a different starting point, you may well arrive at similar conclusions regarding the need to accept human limitations and that (given free will) there is no guarantee of a bright future for us.

The motivation then, behind this book, is that our economy appears to be leading us to an environmental and economic disaster; a future paradise for the human race is not guaranteed and probably not even likely. It is therefore up to us to have more foresight than lemmings, to understand and modify our economic system, to spot the precipices and turn away before we go over them. This has become more urgent than ever before because the human economy has grown to an extraordinary size. So what is economics and why does the economy matter?

1.1   What Is Economics

Economics is typically defined as a 'social science concerned with the production and consumption of goods and services'. So we can define the 'economy' as being *the system by which people produce and consume goods and services*. At the very least, we need our human economy to produce what we need to be able to survive. And just like other animals, to survive we need to:

- **Find food**;

- **Find shelter** – including clothing in our case;

- **Reproduce** – find a mate and rear young;

- **Keep safe** – avoiding being eaten by other animals.

Our economy produces food, drink, houses and clothing in abundance to cover the first two needs. Our desire to reproduce is provided for by an enormous variety of products that are supposed to make us more attractive or enhance our status – from fashion items and skin creams to fast cars and yachts. To keep safe we make locks and guns and pay for police, soldiers and health care.

Since all animals produce goods and services to cover their needs, do the other animals also have economies? It seems to me obvious that they do. If an animal is solitary and produces what it needs by itself for most of its life, then its 'economy' is admittedly a very simple one because it does not cooperate with others of its kind, in for example producing food or shelter. However, many animals do live socially and cooperate with one another, some in complex societies where individuals have different types of job and cooperate to survive; bees are one such example. Of all these social creatures, it is probably safe to say that we humans cooperate more extensively and widely than any other, having a myriad of professions and a web of relationships that spans the globe. For many of us, almost everything we consume is made by other people who we have never met and may well live thousands of miles away. Because our human economy involves such extensive cooperation, economics is a social science.

1.2   Why the Economy Matters

We live in exciting times economically speaking. One economic 'system' – free-market capitalism – has triumphed and is now dominant throughout most of the world. The talk is of globalisation in a world shrunk by modern transport and telecommunications. At the same time we are confronted by a number of major economic problems, or problems that at any rate have an economic component. Some of these are:

- **Environmental destruction.** We are living through one of the world's mass extinction events; the greatest loss of species since the death of the dinosaurs sixty million years ago, destroyed by a huge asteroid that struck the earth. This frighteningly fast degradation of our planet is directly due to human activity: economic development and population growth. So great is the impact, that scientists are calling for our period in the Earth's history to be named the 'Anthropocene' – the age of humans.

- **Poverty in the midst of plenty.** The persistence of unemployment, deprivation and a so called underclass in countries that are considered wealthy and 'developed'. In the USA the official poverty rate in 2020 was 11.4% – about 37 million people.[7]

- **Poverty of the Third World.**[2] The majority of the world's

---

[2]The term 'Third World' was used to refer to countries that are poorer and less-industrialised. I occasionally use it in this book since more recent terms like 'Global South' are also not very satisfactory or precise.

population live in what would be considered extreme poverty by first world standards. A billion live on less than $1.90 a day (about €1.71 or £1.24); nearly half live on less than $5.50 a day (about €4.96 or £3.60).[8]

- **Insecurity.** Prosperity and development have not brought security even for the better-off citizens of the world. Public services are under threat with insufficient money for essential infrastructure and cut backs in facilities we could formerly afford. At work there is growing pressure to work harder and for longer hours, because otherwise automation and foreign competition may take the jobs away.

Until the last two hundred years or so, human productivity grew only slowly (if at all) and much of what was produced were merely life's basic necessities: food, shelter, clothing, and so forth. But in these last two centuries the industrial revolution and sophisticated forms of organisation have made possible a growth in productivity such that in developed countries it is now only necessary for a small part of the population to be engaged producing those basics. The rest are either working to produce an ever-growing range of additional goods and services – many of which are new – or they are not producing at all (e.g. they are studying, retired or unemployed).

With these advances in productivity, why should the residents of the richer, more 'developed' countries, like the UK where I live, ever perceive the economy as a problem? No natural disaster or famine afflicts us, and while there may be ecological and resource problems visible on the horizon, for the moment there is no crisis. Yet in the UK there are over a million unemployed, insufficient money for essential infrastructure and cut backs in facilities we could formerly afford.[9] Those in work are expected to work ever harder if automation and foreign competition are not to take their jobs away.

At the same time, despite the problems of unemployment and poverty affecting some, overall levels of consumption have never been so high. We have become the *consume and throw away* society, damaging the environment and possibly leading to future resource shortages. But almost the only answer to poverty commonly proposed, is <u>more</u> economic growth – more production, consumption, and environmental damage. Apparently our economic system only works well with the accelerator pressed firmly to the floor. Paradoxically the technological advances which should in principal make life easier, seem to be making it more difficult.

Many 'alternative' books on economics move quickly to describing the economy that they would like to see, such as a more environmentally sustainable one. By contrast I want to first understand our existing economy. For example: 'Why does our economy suffer slumps when no-one in charge seems to want them?' Therefore, Part 1 of the book is aimed at analysing and understanding the economy as a neutral observer, without judging anything or anyone – the science approach, if you like. You could read it with no intention of changing anything.

However, like many people, I believe that we need changes if we are to avoid environmental disaster and if we want a fairer world. So there is a Part 2 which is not neutral. Based on the analysis in Part 1, it looks at what changes we would have to make to move towards a fairer and more sustainable economy.

So Part 1 – the 'science' part – sets out to tackle the questions *'Why does the economy behave as it does?'* and *'Where is our economic system taking us?'*.

I believe that you will struggle to find a straightforward answer to these questions in conventional economics text books. It could be argued that this is because there aren't any 'straightforward answers' – it maybe that the economy is so complex that it can only be understood by trained economists using sophisticated maths, or alternatively perhaps it's so complex that it can't be understood at all. Let's consider those two possibilities:

1. **'Economies <u>are</u> very complex, but trained economists <u>do</u> understand them'**. Whether or not economies are complex, it certainly seems unlikely that economists fully understand them since they often disagree amongst themselves. A lack of confidence in economists is illustrated by the fact that while political leaders do not generally try to design their own

bridges or aircraft as the results would make them look foolish, they frequently dream up their own economic policies.

2. **'Economies are so complex that <u>no-one</u> can understand them'.** This seems more plausible, i.e. that economies are so huge, complex and chaotic that there is no hope understanding or predicting their behaviour. Yet we can observe that many national economies behave in rather similar ways, despite differences of culture and geography. This suggests that there may be some basic underlying rules that govern all of them.

The approach I shall follow is to focus on the fundamentals of our economic system, i.e. our needs & wants, the physical resources available to us, and the work we do to turn those resources into the things that we want. By doing that I believe that we can get an understanding of the economy that will allow us to answer the two questions above – why it behaves as it does and where it's heading. We *shall* be able to understand why there is high unemployment and a lack of care for the environment, but we shall *not* however be able to predict the price of corn at any given moment.

In the course of answering these questions we shall also see that some of the claims made by economists are little more than ideology dressed up as science. In order to protect the interests of the superrich, economic theories are used to justify the indefensible: the impoverishment and marginalisation of a large part of humankind and the destruction of the environment.

1.3 Questions Part 1 Aims to Answer

To wet the appetite, these are the sorts of things that I have often puzzled over and that I hope in Part 1 to answer.

- What limits the maximum output of an economy?

- What is the source of growth and development?

- Why do economies have a boom and bust cycle?

- Why is there unemployment when there is obviously much work that needs to be done? *Such as unmet needs for food, housing and medical care of a significant part of the population in rich countries and even more in poorer ones?*

- Why is so much economic activity dedicated to supplying petty consumerist wants, when there are people going hungry?

- Why are there extreme and growing differences in wealth? *Eight men now own the same amount of wealth as the poorest half of the world; the richest 1% owns more wealth than the rest of the planet.[10]*

- Why the decline in or struggle to finance things that we used to be able to afford? *Decrepit railway stations, closed libraries, reduction or loss of universal benefits such as earnings-related unemployment pay & pensions, and public squalor in the middle of plenty.*

- Why the pressure on those in employment to work harder for longer hours and sometimes for less pay?

So let's get started by considering the simplest economy possible – that of a single isolated individual – and building from there.

Chapter 2

Economy Fundamentals

In the last chapter, we defined the 'economy' as being *'the system by which people produce and consume goods and services'*. We said that the primary purpose of those goods and services is to enable us to do the same things that other animals need to do in order to live:

- **Find food**   - **Reproduce**
- **Find shelter**   - **Keep safe**

In this chapter we are going to look at the fundamentals underlying all economies, whether human or of other animals: the essential ingredients that must be present for production to occur, what sets the level of production at any point in time, why production may fluctuate in the short term, what sets the maximum production possible and how that maximum can grow over time.

All animals have to 'produce' goods and services to cover their needs, often engaging in quite elaborate activities to produce food and/or shelter. Many species live socially and cooperate with one another, some in complex societies where individuals have different types of job and cooperate to survive; bees are one such example. If however an animal is solitary and produces what it needs by itself for much of its life, then its 'economy' can be a simpler one because it does not involve cooperation with others of its kind.

Figure 2.1: Food, shelter, reproduction, and safe in a tree. [WMC]

2.1 The Ingredients of Production

There are three essential ingredients required (or if you prefer 'conditions that must be met') for an economy to produce; if any are missing there won't be any production. There must be:

- **Want** – the needs and desires of the animal whose economy it is;

- **Resources** – the materials and energy available;

- **Work effort** – the available capacity the animal has to work.

Let's take as an example a polar bear. Adult polar bears tend to live solitary lives except in the mating season or if a mother with cubs. Seals make up most of their diet. So 'production' for our bear consists of a successful seal hunt. The number of seals she catches will depend on which of the three production ingredients is the most limiting: how much she wants to eat seal (hunger), the seal resources available (abundance of accessible seals); and how much work effort she is able to put into the task (more if she is young and fit, less if she is old or sick). Sometimes the limit might be zero production, if she is not hungry, or there are scarcely any seals to be had, or she is not strong enough to hunt.

Figure 2.2: A largely solitary economy. [WMC]

Thinking now in human terms, let's take a closer look at each of these three ingredients:

1. **Want – the needs and desires of humans**

   Human beings want things; most of all they want the necessities of life: food, shelter, safety, a mate. Indeed, all animals want these things – Why? – Because any creature that evolved not to want the necessities of life and couldn't be bothered to eat or reproduce, would quickly die off as a species. Wanting things is the first essential ingredient of an economy because quite plainly if nobody wanted anything, no-one would do any work at all. Whether the things that are wanted are essential needs or desired for other less obviously essential reasons is not our concern at this stage.

2. **Resources – the materials and energy available**

   Once we want things, where are we going to get them from? Our planet earth provides a wide variety of environments where it's possible for animals to obtain the things they want. Some animals are adaptable and can live and find what they want in many different environments, while others have become specialists, adapted to just one. Of course it's not chance that the earth fulfils our needs: we have evolved to be able to

17

take advantage of what the earth offers. The Earth's resources are the second ingredient of any animal's economy.

3. **Work Effort – the available human capacity to work**
   The Earth's resources don't just drop out of trees into our open mouths (well very occasionally). To obtain the things they want animals must 'work', i.e. they must expend energy moving around to find the 'raw materials' they need and to 'process them' usually to produce food or to build shelter. Work Effort, the amount of available labour, is therefore our third ingredient. Note that for humans, how effective that work effort is in producing things, depends a lot on the current level of human knowledge and technological development.

The three input ingredients for production are illustrated in Figure 2.3. Unless all three ingredients – *want, resources* and *work effort* – are present, production will not occur. Production is limited by whichever one is in shortest supply.

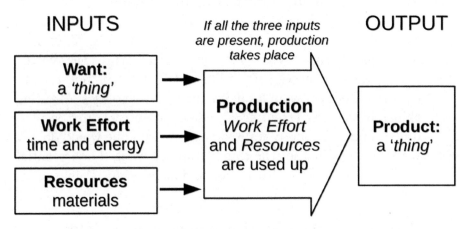

Figure 2.3: The three inputs necessary for production

2.2   Level of Production

The three-ingredient model tells us that the *level of production* – how much gets produced at any point in time – depends on which

of the three ingredients runs out first (reaches its limit): *Want,
Resources* or *Effort*. The level has to be somewhere between zero
and the maximum that the person or people whose economy it is
could produce if they worked as hard as possible and had abundant
resources available. To illustrate this we will first look at what limits
how much is produced in the simplest case: a *one-person economy*
in which that person has to produce everything for him or herself.

Imagine a woman cast away on a small island who has to do
everything for herself. Such a situation (but with a man as the
castaway) is described in the famous novel Robinson Crusoe by
Daniel Defoe: Crusoe is shipwrecked on a remote tropical island and
has to survive alone for some years. The example of a castaway on
an island also makes it easy to imagine a situation of finite resources,
e.g. the amount timber to build with or burn on a cooking fire is
limited to the number of trees on the island.

Figure 2.4: Alone on an island – a one-person economy.

In our castaway's economy, how much gets produced depends
on which of the three ingredients – Want, Resources, Work – runs
out (reaches its limit) first. So the three possibilities are:

a) Want (i.e. desire or appetite) runs out first: If our
castaway doesn't want very much, then she may well leave resources
unused and work only part of the time. Perhaps she spends part of
the day picking fruit but then has had all that she wants and prefers
to rest, even though plenty more fruit is available to be picked.

b) Resources run out first: If our castaway wants more than
can be made with the island's resources, she may again work for

only part of the time that she could, because before the day has ended she has already done all the work that there is to do, e.g. picked every ripe fruit there is. Note that our castaway behaves as if she owns everything on the island, so she can use any resource that exists.

*c) **Working Effort runs out first:*** If our castaway wants a lot and resources are abundant, she will work all day and the amount she produces is limited only by the amount of work she is physically capable of. For example, she has been picking and eating fruit all day, but picking it is hard work so she is tired out and has to stop and rest, even though there is no shortage of fruit, and she'd still like to eat more.

Many non-human creatures actually do pass most of their lives much like our human castaway. They work alone most of the time – as spiders and polar bears do – or they work in the company only of a mate, as many birds do. Like our castaway, they have relatively simple economies, and it's easy to see that how much they produce is limited by the same three factors, how much they want/desire the produce, the resources available and their capacity to work.

2.3 Fluctuations in the Level of Output

In human economies we are very interested in how the level of production fluctuates over the short term. We observe that economic output seems to go up and down in a cyclical manner, varying from 'boom' to 'slump' and back again over periods of months or years. Politicians and economists are keen to understand these cycles and to learn how to avoid or minimise the slumps.

We said that how much gets produced depends on which of the three ingredients – Want, Resources, Work – runs out first. So a variation in one or more of these three ingredients, is the cause of any fluctuation in output. The one responsible is the ingredient that is already in shortest supply (i.e. at its limit) or that has now become so. To illustrate this, let's go back to our castaway.

- A probable cause of fluctuation in production is a change in how much output she **wants**. While there will be small tasks that have to be done every day, fetching water for example, other jobs once completed will satisfy the want that was her motive to do them, for many months or years. An example could be the construction of a shelter: our castaway works hard to build her first shelter (an economic boom), but once it is completed is content to work less, only gathering food (an economic slump) until such time as the shelter needs maintenance or re-building (another boom).

- A fluctuation in the availability of **resources** could also affect our castaway. Perhaps the trees on the island produce less fruit because of poor weather, a plague of insects or disease. Agricultural work often varies with the seasons.

- The amount of **work effort** our castaway can expend would hopefully remain more or less constant over many years. But a period of illness could force her to work less than usual, making work effort the limit to how much she can produce.

Note that for our castaway, a lower level of production (a 'slump') is not a problem if the cause is that she wants less and is therefore working less. It's merely a choice: she prefers time for leisure or a rest to the extra output she could have generated had she worked for that time. Similarly, slumps in real economies would not be a problem if they occurred because everyone in society had chosen to work a bit less and consume a bit less – but unfortunately in our human economies reductions in consumption tend to be very unevenly distributed.

The peaks and troughs (booms and slumps) that we see in the levels of production of a human or other animal's economy, do not necessarily tell us what the maximum output is, that the animal could produce if it chose to work flat out and had bountiful resources available. It may be able to produce more than the peak levels we observe, but simply doesn't need or want to, or is constrained by insufficient resources.

2.4 Maximum Production Possible

What determines the *maximum possible output* that an animal or group of animals can produce? The maximum output will be generated if they all work as hard as they can and resources are abundant. What that maximum is, depends on the capabilities of the animal concerned – qualities like strength, knowledge, skill and intelligence.

You might well ask: "If an animal's '*capabilities*' decide the maximum it can produce, why don't we include it in the list of 'ingredients' that set the level of production, along with *want, resources* and *effort*?" The reason for not doing so is that at any point in history, an animal's capabilities are fixed. Those capabilities, such as its physical and mental abilities and its level of scientific and technical development, are not something that 'run out' – a recession doesn't occur because we've used up all the scientific knowledge. Furthermore, we don't experience our capabilities as a limiting factor because we take them for granted. Imagine a farmer one thousand years ago who has hired ten men to dig a trench. Dissatisfied with progress he asks them how it can be done faster. The men are not likely to suggest delaying the job some 800 years until mechanical excavators get invented, nor waiting for millions of years for evolution to produce a stronger worker; they'll say he needs to increase effort by employing more men or paying them to work longer hours.

2.5 Growth in the Maximum

For most animals, their capabilities change only slowly with evolution and adaptation to changing environments. If you go back far enough in time, the ancestor of dolphins was a four-legged mammal living on dry land.[1] Dolphins acquired the knowledge of how to swim, along with a body suited to swimming, by evolving over millions of years: small genetic changes accumulated over many generations until they were a very different animal to their furry ancestor, and far far better at catching fish. But genetic change is slow (particularly in large, long-lived animals). An ants nest or a lion from Roman times two thousand years ago would look much the same as one from today. However, the other way to pass on knowledge is simply to teach it to the next generation – no genetic change is required.

Humans can pass on a huge body of learnt knowledge to our children through our complex spoken and written language over the course of what nowadays may be twenty years or more of education. So it is that humans have gone from catching next to no fish a few thousand years ago to hoovering up vast (and unsustainable) quantities, not by any change to our bodies through evolution but by developing ever more sophisticated technology and passing on the knowledge to our children.

Many other animals also teach their young but cannot match us in the sheer volume of knowledge passed on. A few non-human primates, have learnt to make use of stones as tools. The long-tailed macaques of Thailand use simple stone tools to smash open shellfish on the seashore, and in recent years have begun using stones to crack open oil palm nuts on the plantations inland. As this behaviour is limited to certain populations, it would appear to be an example of a learnt skill that is passed on from one generation to the next.

Amazingly, some conventional economics books don't always make it clear that growth is the direct result of technical advance. In one standard economics textbook, a section that purports to

---

[1]Dolphins like whales, are not fish but mammals, whose ancestors were land animals. Much further back in time, all land vertebrates evolved from fish.

analyse growth begins with the assertion that 'In an economy with no technical progress growth will occur because there will always be investment in capital goods which are long-lived and so will accumulate, thus making labour more productive'. This is nonsense because:

Figure 2.5: Concrete cancer: capital wears out.

1. **Capital does wear out.** The word 'capital' is only a convenient distinction between things which last a longish time (like a tractor or a building) and things which last a shortish time (like a tankful of diesel). Imagine an economy that chose to build more and more capital goods but made no technical advances: eventually it would have more than it could maintain and the rate of loss would equal the rate of gain – all work would be replacement or maintenance. Only by increasing the level of technology and thus productivity could it increase its wealth further.

2. **Accumulation without technical advance does not imply ever-increasing productivity.** Given fixed technology there will be some level of capital at which, if more is added, the extra only gets in the way or cannot be used. How many spades, horses, etc. can one person use!

24

These points are easy to understand if we return to our castaway. She might find that clearing a short track to the beach she visits daily to collect shellfish is a worthwhile capital investment that increases what she can produce, because the saving in time spent maintaining it is less than the time she used to have to spend picking her way through the undergrowth. But building more and more tracks all over the island does not make sense because at some point maintaining them would be more work than any saving. To obtain the best economic performance she needs to apply the technology she knows in the most effective combination, not pile up 'capital goods' – whether they be tools or jungle tracks – that require more effort to build and maintain that the saving they offer. The only way to improve on that best performance is by technical advances: if she develops a better way to fish, hunt or collect food, that produces more for the same effort, then her maximum output increases.

2.6 Summary

The level of an animal's economic output is determined by which of the three ingredients required for production runs out first: *wants*, *resources*, or *work effort*. Fluctuations of output in the short term, are due to changes in the amount of one or more of those three ingredients. Long-term change to the maximum an animal can produce are due to changes in its *capabilities* thanks to its evolution or, and especially in the case of humans, thanks to its acquisition of learnt knowledge that it is able to pass on to its children.

Short term and long term are relative to the animal concerned. For an animal whose capabilities depend mainly on evolutionary change, 'short term' may be many thousands of years if it evolves only slowly. For humans, 'short term' may be as little as a few months or years as human capabilities are changing rapidly year by year due to our ability to learn and pass on what we have learnt to our descendants.

So far we have used simple examples like a castaway or a single-animal economy to illustrate economic fundamentals. But humans along with many other animals – bees, ants, lions, wolves, etc. – are social beings and usually work in groups, with different individuals specialising in different types of work. So we shall need next to consider a 'social' economy. But the basic *wants, resources, work effort* model considered in this chapter gives us some general pointers:

- Growth in human capabilities does not explain the cyclical behaviour of the economy that includes periods of recession (when output is clearly below the maximum) even though technical progress is continuing. For that explanation we need the three ingredient model.

- When we consider the economy of a whole society, the three-ingredient model enables us to understand the real-world limits to production. We can see that economies at different times in history and in different places, may be constrained by different limits. For example, we can guess from the massive amount spent on advertising, that running out of wants/desires is an issue for modern economies.

Lastly, we've got this far without any reference to money – and deliberately so. Can that be right – isn't economics all about money – is there an economy without it? Of course there is! If it were otherwise, no other animal would have an economy since no other animal uses money; we humans wouldn't have had an economy either for almost all of our 200,000 years existence as Homo sapiens, since the use of coins dates back less than 3,000 years.[2]

---

[2]The first use of coins is believed to be during the first millennium BC, though before that some societies used 'commodity money' – goods like peppercorns, shells, barley or gold, that had their own value but could also be used for payment.

Chapter 3

Rules for a Social Economy

In the last chapter we used single-animal economies as examples, like that of a castaway living alone on an island. For our castaway *there are no rules*: she can go anywhere, do anything, use anything. That allowed us to see what is fundamental to any economy: for production to occur you need the *desire* to produce, *resources* and *work-effort*. Now we will turn to consider the economies of societies: 'social economies'.

Figure 3.1: A social economy: leaf-cutter ants. [WMC]

Humans – along with bees, ants, monkeys, wolves and many other animals – are social beings and usually work in a group, with the potential for different individuals to specialise in different types of work. This is a much more complex situation than a single-

27

animal economy, because we have to think about what the group or
'society' wants, not just the individual. By contrast to the unusual
situation of having no rules like our castaway, in normal human
economies there are a myriad of rules that we live by. They are so
ingrained in us that we largely take them for granted. You <u>cannot</u>
go anywhere, do anything or use anything. Some of the rules are
formalised in law and others are norms or customs. What these
rules are, decides very largely how the economy functions.

Figure 3.2: In a social economy, you can't go anywhere you want
or use anything you like. [WMC]

While other social animals do not write down their rules, we can
see that they do have rules and customs, especially if they work co-
operatively. Where do the rules come from in the first place? Many
of them are I assume instinctive: in the complex social organisation of insects such as bees, termites and ants, biological evolution
would select for rules advantageous to the species concerned. In the
human world we know that apart from whatever rules come with
our biology, we also have rules that are part of our culture and have
to be learnt. These cultural rules also evolve over time as societies
discover new or better rules that make them more effective, with
the more effective societies then being likely to displace societies
with ill-functioning rules; such concepts are discussed in books like
Jared Diamond's fascinating 'Guns, Germs and Steel'.[11]

Let's now look at a rule that is fundamental to our human economy – the notion of '*ownership*' – and at what that rule makes
possible: the ability to trade and the concept of value.

3.1 Ownership

The concept of ownership is essential to our modern economy – buying and selling would be meaningless if things couldn't belong to anybody – but what does it really mean to own something?

Human societies have a strong sense of 'ownership' or 'property': to be allowed to use a resource you have to own it or at least have some temporary right over it, e.g. by rental. The idea of property is so familiar to us from childhood that it is easy to think of ownership as something clear-cut (it's either yours or it isn't). In practice there are shades of grey: If something is 'yours' it means that the rest of society recognise your control over it: your right to determine who uses, consumes or destroys it ... but only up to a point!

Perhaps you have a piece of paper somewhere that says you own your house: a title deed. If so, could you build a factory or a rocket testing site on the land? Almost certainly not: ownership is an agreement amongst humans to allow someone certain rights over property, but those rights are not unlimited. For example most city councils won't permit you to do whatever you like to your house, and may well take it away from you if they need the ground for a new road.

Suppose that you wave that title deed at the ants in your garden, will they take notice and clear off your property? Not likely! Your rights over that land are accepted only by human society – and then not by all of it. Yet many other animals do have notions of ownership, asserting their rights over territory, prey, food, and mates.

"In order to attract a female to mate with him, a male bird has to obtain and defend a territory. This territory will help determine his breeding success by providing him, and his mate, with food. Males claim a territory by singing in it, which tells other males to stay away. They leave gaps in their song to listen to replies, so they can discover where any rivals are and focus their defensive efforts on strangers looking to take over the territory."[1]

Figure 3.3: Ownership: it's his garden! [WMC]

"Aha" we might say. "Those other animals are just fighting for stuff, that's not recognising ownership". Well maybe they do fight sometimes when the moment is opportune, but in between fights they may recognise the status quo. Rather like we humans, who recognise the status quo for lengthy periods but now and then are tempted to go to war and seize other people's property.

Also, a fight between animals isn't necessarily physically violent, as with the bird described above that defends its territory by singing ... sort of more like a court case. *By the way, if there is a bird singing in your garden, please note that as far as he's concerned, it's not your garden at all, it's his!*

Why discuss rules, where rules come from, and whether other animals have them too? Well apart from curiosity, it could be important to distinguish which rules are part of the human psyche (we've evolved to have them, and they'd therefore be hard to override), and which are more arbitrary, and although they may seem 'natural' if we have lived with them for many years, could nevertheless be modified.

3.2 Trade

Once society recognises property, then '*trade*' or '*exchange*' become possible: you can swap things with other people. A trade is an

---

[1]From a BBC Nature web article, about the dawn chorus.

exchange of ownership/control – what was yours becomes theirs and in return what was theirs is now yours: buying and selling would be meaningless if things couldn't belong to anybody.

The existence of trade makes it possible for individuals to specialise in something: if your job is shoemaker, you'll have to swap (or 'exchange' or 'trade') most of the shoes you produce for the other things you need such as food. Money makes this swapping easier and more flexible – first you swap the shoes for money, and then you swap the money for food.

3.3   Value

When exchanging goods, what decides how much they are 'worth'. Suppose you own something that you have produced – let's call it stuff A – and you would like to trade it for something else that you don't or can't produce – let's call that stuff B. The classic economics problem is "How much of A should you swap for a given quantity of B?" Or if you like, "How many kilograms of A is a kilogram of B worth?" More familiarly, this is a question about prices: we are asking why is the price of a kilogram of one thing (such as cheese), different from the price of a kilogram of another thing (say potatoes). A moment's thought tells us that prices are not related to the true value of things: food and water are essential to survival, yet they are cheap compared to luxuries we could perfectly well do without.

Marx amongst others, believed that what decided how much a thing was worth was how much work or 'labour' it took to make it. Thus if it takes six times as much work to produce 1kg of cheese as it does to produce 1kg of potatoes, then in the market, the cheese to potato swaps will be at a rate of 1kg of cheese for 6kg of potatoes – in other words cheese will be six times the price of potatoes. The concept is known as the *labour theory of value*. Marx believed that labour was the source of <u>all</u> value – which was a convenient conclusion for a revolutionary who sided with the working class – but he struggled to explain how things like land can have value when no human labour has gone into producing it. Today he would also have to explain how heavily-promoted branded goods can be so much more expensive than unbranded equivalents that took the same amount of labour to manufacture.

Figure 3.4: A kilo of cheese takes more labour to make than a kilo of potatoes, and so costs more.

Personally I think that there is little point in looking for some universal underlying source of value that can be applied to all things, such as Marx's idea that it is the labour that went into making them. There are so many reasons why people may want things that it's better to accept that things have market value only because people want them: the value that they have is then simply how many other things people are willing to offer in exchange for them. Classical economists draw supply and demand curves to illustrate this, which roughly speaking tell you that: (a) if something is scarce and a lot of people want it, then it will be expensive; whereas, (b) if something is in plentiful supply compared to the number of people who want it, then it will be cheap.

It is clear however, that the amount of labour that goes into making products <u>does</u> affect their prices. This is because *although at any given moment in time*, supply and demand determine prices, *in the longer term* the level of prices feeds back into what producers do. So if something is in short supply, producers will tend to switch to making that because a day's work producing that earns them more than a day spent producing other goods. Accordingly, for manufactured goods, the amount of labour required to make them often does decide their relative prices (i.e. how much of one you exchange for another).

One might suppose that the cost of materials – the steel, copper and plastics that go into our gadgets – would be a major part of their price. But all these materials can in turn be costed in terms of the labour required to extract them. Essential to understanding this is the fact that from an economics point of view, the world's resources are free until they actually begin to run out. So when you buy metal to make into a car, what you pay for the metal is related mainly to the amount of work required to dig it up, process it and transport it.

Figure 3.5: We don't pay the environment for the resources we take from it. [WMC]

Resources taken from the environment are 'free' because the environment isn't a human being and asks for nothing in exchange. Of course a human might own the land where the resource is found, such as a mine; however in a world market (and excepting cases where a monopoly can be established), the owning company or country cannot charge more than the labour cost of extraction because a competitor could undercut them. The fact that there may be only thirty years supply of the mineral left on the planet is irrelevant. If the mineral becomes harder to find, it increases the amount of labour required to prospect for, mine and process what are likely to be poorer ores, and as a result the cost increases to reflect the increased labour. Only when it becomes impossible to produce more of a resource through extra labour, will the price go up beyond the labour cost and reflect scarcity instead of just the labour required to extract it. An example of this would be the last tree on the planet: it won't be harder to find or cut down than any other tree, but assuredly the sale value of the wood will be a great deal more than the cost of that labour.

Accordingly, examples of market scarcity (where the price of something isn't just determined by the work required to make it) are harder to find than one might think. However, when there is genuine scarcity, such as in the paintings of famous artists or desirable houses in central London, or hiring top class footballers, then prices bear no relation to any labour involved and are limited only by how much buyers want these things and how rich they are.

Note that when there is scarcity in the supply of something other than labour, then the prices of things made out of it will be related by how much of it they use, in just the same way as the prices for most manufactured goods are related by how much labour they use. For example, land is a scarce resource in London, so the prices of houses in central London are strongly related to the area of land they take up: a house that occupies twice the area will tend to cost twice the price, other things (such as quality of the building, neighbourhood, views, etc.) being equal.

3.4 Government

The castaway living alone on an island has no rules and so needs no government. But in the social economies we live in we have lots of rules that regulate how we interact, and there's no point in rules unless they are kept. In small groups this might be possible by mutual consent. Among children in the same family for example, young John may well accept that the book his sister Mary bought with her pocket money is hers, and Mary accept that the toy John was given for his birthday is his; no written documents are involved, though there is a level of governance (their parents) should a dispute arise. For bigger groups we need more formal governance to enforce the rules.

Most of us live under multiple layers of governance, not just

Figure 3.6: No rules for a castaway alone on an island.

the national government of your country, but also layers of local government such as a town council. It doesn't stop there: schools have governance and rules, so do employers, so do clubs and societies, churches, political parties, and any place that we might go that is managed by an organisation – the transport system or local supermarket for example. There's also a level of international governance, through agreements reached under the auspices of the United Nations or any one of numerous other bodies such as the EU or NATO.

Why accept so many rules? We do so – most of us – because the obligations they place on us are also placed on others. I cannot take other people's property, but they cannot take mine either. I'm not allowed to physically assault people who annoy me, but neither can others assault me. Modern governments don't only enforce such basic rules, they also provide a whole range of services: education, healthcare, transport networks, parks, and much more.

Of course all of these government functions do not come for free. If we are to have police to protect us from violence and our property from theft, then those of us working to produce goods and services have to accept that the government takes some of what we produce to provide to those working for the police force. In other words, we have to accept some form of taxation.

So it sounds like the deal is: 'we give up a bit of the cake we've

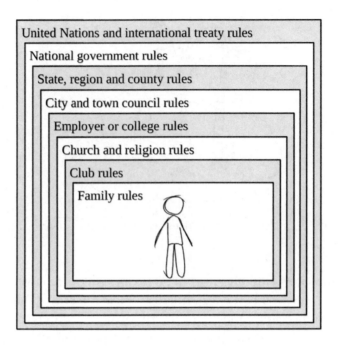

United Nations and international treaty rules
National government rules
State, region and county rules
City and town council rules
Employer or college rules
Church and religion rules
Club rules
Family rules

Figure 3.7: Lots of rules in modern society.

produced to the government and in return we get security and some other benefits'. But good government is far more valuable than that because it enables us as a society to produce **a far bigger cake**. The development of sophisticated industries requires a stable business environment, a trained workforce, good infrastructure, and so forth. Governments can also finance scientific research and technological development. It's quite common to meet people who've always lived under and benefited from relatively strong and stable governments, who are nevertheless very ready to complain about high taxes – but you don't notice many of them migrating to semi-lawless countries with weak governments. The migration is in the opposite direction: into countries where taxes are higher and more effectively collected but where people hope to feel safe and see their children educated.

3.5 Degree of Government Control

Governments vary considerably in the rules they set and the degree to which they try to direct the economy. At one extreme you have governments that try to plan economic activity, directly telling some or all businesses what they should do – so called 'command economies'. As example of such planning, we typically think of communism as it was practised in the former Soviet Union[2] and still is at the time of writing in North Korea. During wartime, capitalist countries may also choose to direct their economies to a far greater extent than they do normally; notably the USA and UK during the Second World War (WW2).

At the other extreme is the 'light-touch' free-market philosophy that the job of governments is only to provide a police and army, and enforce clear rules regarding property and trade. Apart from that, businesses should be free to make their own choices, with the direction of the economy being set by the operation of the market.

Our current world is now dominated by countries that have free-market economies – although they usually also have larger and more influential state sectors than light-touch free-market purists would like. In most industrialised western countries for example, the state provides free education and healthcare; both things that the purists believe should be left to the market (i.e. they believe that the public should instead have to pay to use private schools and hospitals). Meanwhile, the communist parties of China and Vietnam also allow private business and a market. China calls their system a 'socialist market economy' and accepts that private capitalists and entrepreneurs can co-exist with public and collective enterprise.

Private-sector businesses operating in market economies therefore determine to a great extent what gets produced and the level and conditions of employment. So to understand how our economies work we need to understand markets.

---

[2]The Union of Soviet Socialist Republics (USSR), created in 1922 following the 1917 Russian Revolution and dissolved in 1991.

3.6   Summary

Human economies are social economies which are governed by extensive rules that affect how the economy functions. Governments set and enforce many of these rules. The cost of good government is generally accepted because of the benefits it offers in terms of protection of individual rights and property, and other services such as health care. The concept of property enables trade and the operation of markets.

While governments can choose to suppress markets and plan economic decisions, as the former Soviet Union did under communism, almost all industrialised countries currently allow markets to operate, with private sector businesses therefore having extensive influence on employment levels and what gets produced. Therefore, we will next look at markets in more detail.

Chapter 4

Markets

In a free-market economy, production is carried out by independent businesses who offer their goods for sale in the market, and consumers are free to choose what and from whom they buy. To survive, businesses have to sell their goods and are therefore under pressure to produce goods that consumers want and at a price and quality that matches or is better than competitors.

Markets are places where we exchange goods or services with one another. In principle, we could directly exchange one thing for another – bread for shoes say – which is known as bartering. However, it's more convenient to exchange goods for money and at some later time exchange the money for other goods, or in other words, sell and buy. It's easy to see that money makes markets much more flexible than if the only way to exchange goods and services was through barter.

When we talk about a 'market' we are not thinking only of a traditional market in a public space where buyers and sellers come together – a familiar arrangement being small stalls set out in a hall or market square that buyers can walk among as pictured in Figure 4.1. Rather we mean all ways and forums in which sellers can offer goods for sale to buyers, including:

- High street shops and supermarkets

- On-Line shopping

- Catalogue sales

- Trade fairs

- Door to door salesmen

- Traditional street and covered markets.

Figure 4.1: A vegetable market. [WMC]

In the markets listed above, something that has been produced is being sold to an individual or business who will use or consume it. There are also *commodity markets* where large volumes of products such as oil, gas, coffee, gold, cotton and wheat, are traded – but typically between businesses, not with the final consumer. Then there are markets where what is sold are not products but *ownership* – especially of businesses (shares) and land. Beyond that are markets in foreign exchange and a complex range of '*financial products*' from insurance to options to buy something in the future. These financial products are not 'products' in any real sense, but rather services and agreements; if you buy fire insurance you get not a product but a promise ... that i̲f̲ your house burns down, you will be given the products and services to rebuild it. We talk a little more about the financial sector in Chapter 22.

The important feature of a 'market economy' is not sales outlets, but **the freedom to enter the market as a producer**, i.e. for individuals or groups to establish private businesses producing goods and services and offering them for sale. The producers are free to choose what to make and adjust their prices as they think fit without regulation, and buyers are free to choose which seller to buy from.

4.1 Market Operation

Classical economics praises the market as being the most effective way of ensuring that the right things get produced – the things that people want. The mechanism operates as follows:

> If demand for a good exceeds supply, its price rises, e.g. if more people want to buy eggs (and have the money to do so) than there are eggs being produced, then the price of eggs will rise. This means that the income of egg producers will go up compared to average incomes. Egg production then becomes a more attractive trade, so people will tend to move into it, increasing egg production. The extra production will cause egg prices to fall until egg producers' incomes are approximately average again. Adam Smith called this the *'invisible hand'*. The same free-market mechanism will favour reputable producers over those whose products are of inferior quality.

Free markets do indeed match supply to demand, as described above, provided that we understand that by *'demand'* economists mean the wants of people who have enough money to pay the asking price. But free markets do nothing for the starving in a famine stricken country: their demand for food is considered not to exist because they have no money to pay for it; charity and state aid are their only recourse. However notwithstanding such drawbacks, free markets have proved themselves to be a very good way to decentralise economic decision-making and through competition encourage producers to improve prices and quality.

The most idealistic exponents of the free market, argue that the best outcome will be obtained by having a totally unregulated market with 'perfect competition'. To have perfect competition however, certain assumptions must be met. Critics of the model point out that these assumptions are seldom met in reality. In practice all free markets have to operate in a legislative environment that restricts and regulates their operation.

In today's world, legislation outlaws the trading of slaves, and typically restricts or bans trade in certain classes of drugs, limits who can buy dangerous weapons, and forbids the sale of alcohol or tobacco to children. Regulation imposes standards that must be met in quality, safety and hours of work.

Periodically there are campaigns to reduce regulation, referring to it disparagingly as 'red tape' but the trend seems to be the other way. This is because as products become more technically complex it is increasingly difficult if not impossible for the consumer to control quality and safety: often long-term research is required into the effects of chemicals or additives that the consumer may not realise are present in the product and even if they do know, may be unaware of the implications.

Figure 4.2: A list of ingredients – how many of us would read and understand it before eating? [WMC]

So in the vegetable market of a medieval village, a consumer may be very nearly *'perfectly informed'*, as is required for the perfect competition model. But in the age of pesticides, GM crops and highly processed foods, this is less and less achievable even if we restrict ourselves to foodstuffs, let alone consider other technological products.

Another claim made by some market purists is that 'free markets always clear'. This assertion means that the market mechanism will ensure that there are no unsold goods. While the market does usually work this way, there are cases when it won't. Usually the market does clear, because producers will either lower prices until they are able to sell all their produce, or reduce or stop production if they cannot sell the products at a price which at least covers their costs of production: it makes no sense to spend more producing something than you can earn by selling it. Note however that sometimes a producer may sell even at below cost price, at least for a while – for example:

1. The decision to produce was made and the costs of production incurred, quite a long time before the goods were ready for sale. It may then make sense to sell the goods even at a price that is currently below the costs of production, to at least partly cover those costs. This is typical of farming where you have to commit to growing the produce long before you discover what the sale price will be when it is harvested, and if you don't sell, then the produce will spoil and be lost.

2. The producer cannot (or doesn't want to) escape some or all of the costs of production. For example if the costs are just the producer's own board and lodging, or the maintenance of premises they don't want to give up such as a farm or workshop. In these circumstances it may make sense to produce and sell goods at below cost to at least partly cover those fixed costs, since they are going to be incurred anyway. It wouldn't make sense however if the extra cost ('marginal cost' in economics terms) of producing the goods was greater than they could be sold for.

But the market does not always clear. In case (1) above, if the extra cost incurred in taking a product to market is greater than the price it can be sold for, then it may be cheaper just to dump the product or leave it to rot – as for example, if there is a glut of apples for sale and prices have fallen, it could cost an orchard owner more to pick their apples and transport them to market than the price they will fetch. A more important exception to market clearing is the labour market since workers cannot 'un-produce' themselves if their labour isn't selling. In Chapter 7 we shall examine in more detail the 'free markets always clear' claim as applied to labour markets.

4.2   Market Idealism

Belief that promoting the free operation of markets and private business will lead to the best economic outcomes is famously described in Adam Smith's book The Wealth Of Nations, published in 1776.[12]

> "Every individual... neither intends to promote the public interest, nor knows how much he is promoting it... he intends only his own security; and by directing that industry in such a manner as its produce may be of the greatest value, he intends only his own gain, and he is in this, as in many other cases, led by an invisible hand to promote an end which was no part of his intention." – *The Wealth Of Nations, Book IV, Chapter II.*

> "It is not from the benevolence of the butcher, the brewer, or the baker, that we expect our dinner, but from their regard to their own interest. We address ourselves, not to their humanity but to their self-love, and never talk to them of our necessities but of their advantages." – *The Wealth Of Nations, Book I, Chapter II.*

Many organisations and think tanks exist today to promote free-market, neoliberal ideas. One such in the UK has named itself the 'Adam Smith Institute', although having been founded only in the 1970s, some two hundred years after The Wealth Of Nations was published, I'm not sure if it has any particular claim to Smith's mantle. Such organisations go far beyond promoting markets as practical and useful; rather they are the perfect system and 'work for everyone, particularly the poorest' (according to the Institute). To give a flavour of these beliefs, here is an extract from the Adam Smith Institute's website (as it was in August 2023):

"Fighting Big Government"

"Today the Adam Smith Institute faces new challenges. The industrial landscape has changed beyond recognition since the 1970s. Communism has fallen. And most politicians at least pay lip service to the free market ideas of choice, competition and enterprise. And yet in many ways government is bigger and more intrusive than ever, whether it is regulating businesses, interfering with lifestyle choices, or undermining historic civil liberties. Meanwhile public spending has grown out of control, and Britain faces a fiscal crisis unprecedented in peacetime. In short, there are many battles still to be won." – *[13]*

Reading the above paragraph, what strikes me is the fundamentalism: a viewpoint that appears to be almost the mirror opposite of communism. It seems that:

- For free-market fundamentalists, perfection is an economy that is based almost entirely on private business and markets;

- For communist fundamentalists, perfection is an economy that almost entirely eliminates private business and markets.

Surely we can value choice, competition and enterprise, without making the 'free market' into some sort of pure and perfect goal. The curse of economics is that it so often turns into a religion. I prefer to approach it as an engineer: let's first simply try to understand how the economy operates, and then see what we think we could improve.

4.3 Summary

Free-market economies have an extensive 'private sector' of independent businesses, producing goods and services. Consumers can choose who they buy from. Such economies decentralise economic decisions. Producers move into fields where there is more demand and thus more profit, and consumer choice incentivises better quality and lower prices. Markets do match supply to demand but only to financial demand; those without money have to rely on charity. The increasing complexity and variety of products available means that consumers cannot easily judge quality and safety, and therefore need regulation to protect them from potentially harmful products. The promotion of the largest possible role for private business and free markets in the economy, is a cause of the political right, particularly in the USA and UK.

In the next chapter (Chapter 5) we attempt to visualise the exchanges or 'swaps' that are going on when goods or services are traded in the market. And in the chapter after that – given that free-market economies now dominate the world – we will consider what it's like to live in one.

Chapter 5

Market Exchanges

Markets are places where we exchange goods and services with one another. However usually we don't experience markets like that: for most of us for most of the time, markets are where we exchange *goods or services* for **money** – either buying something or selling something. Nevertheless, what is going on underneath is the exchange of goods and services with other people or businesses, even if it is not visible to us; money is just a sort of lubricant that makes complex swaps easier.

This chapter is an attempt to visualise those exchanges or 'swaps' that are going on underneath, and to explore some of the consequences of the market being essentially a set of many swaps. The chapter is illustrated with some numerical examples; should they be hard to follow, the Summary (5.7) gives the general idea in plain English.

In a free market, goods are exchanged by <u>mutual</u> preference between actors in the market. I swap product 'A' for your product 'B', because I'd prefer to have B instead of A <u>and</u> you would prefer to have A instead of B. These exchanges often involve long, complicated and interconnected chains of swaps. For trade to occur, complete closed chains of swaps must exist; missing elements can break the whole chain. We don't see these extraordinary swap chains because in a real economy we use money as an intermediate good: I swap A for dollars (or euros or gold coins ...), and then use the dollars to buy B. Provided money is flowing properly in the global economy (without building up huge trade imbalances), it really is the case that if I as say a computer programmer working in the UK, buy a pineapple from Costa Rica, then a few minutes of my work writing software, have somehow been swapped for the work of a pineapple farmer. Of course the farmer doesn't end up with my bit of software (heaven forbid!) but a chain of swaps passes it to someone who does want it, and results in the farmer getting some quite different product that he or she wants (or more realistically, a contribution towards buying it). Clearly such complex swaps would be very difficult to organise, perhaps impossible, without money as an intermediary.

We'll start by trying to visualise an economy that works only by barter with no money involved at all, and consider the implications of trade being by a series of swaps. Later we'll re-introduce money.

5.1   A Simple Exchange Economy

The diagram in Figure 5.1 explores the exchanges that occur in a very simple imaginary economy. We shall suppose that it operates based only on barter with no use of money, by people swapping things.

Explanation of the barter or 'swap' economy in Figure 5.1:

- There are eight people in the economy, all of them both **produce** and **consume**. The four at the corners shown in rectangular boxes are also '**resource owners**'– as well as working, they own the physical resources (farms, a forest, a mine) which are the inputs to our economy from the natural world. The other four, at the centre, are artisans who make things but don't own the sources of the raw materials they use – they have to 'buy' the materials through swaps with the resource owners.

- A swap is always 2-way, so arrows in both directions are shown.

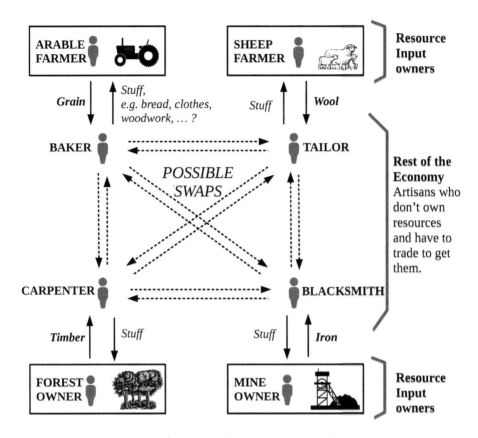

Figure 5.1: A simple barter or 'swap' economy.

- The swaps between the four artisans in the middle are shown with dashed arrows as they don't all need to occur; for example the carpenter could swap woodwork with the baker to get bread and swap some of the bread with the blacksmith to get nails – that way the blacksmith can get bread without swapping directly with the baker who perhaps doesn't need any ironmongery.

- You might think all the dashed arrows leading away from say the baker, should be labelled 'Bread' but that's not necessarily the case: at least some of them must be bread, but the baker can have other goods obtained in previous swaps that he then swaps again, so the arrows can be a different product or even a mix of products. An example of a mix is shown in what is swapped with the arable farmer in exchange for grain.

- The resources (raw material) used by this economy come from the four resource owners. I've put the swap arrows in solid (not dashed) lines because I've assumed the raw material must be going to the artisan it's used by, and of course they must be giving something back, though not necessarily just their own produce as it could be other things they've obtained in swaps. This assumption – that the resource owners only swap with the artisan that uses their raw material – is made for the sole reason of simplifying the diagram; in practice they could swap with any of the other resource owners or artisans, if they and the other person wanted to do so.

The purpose of this model is to allow us to visualise how an economy works without referring to money. It illustrates that:

1. In a market economy where people (or businesses) specialise, they have to swap some of their produce in order to obtain the other goods that they want/need.

2. Swaps only happen if both parties want to swap – they want the other thing more than what they are offering in exchange.

3. Exchange of goods proceeds until at most all possible exchanges which are perceived as beneficial by both parties involved have been carried out.

4. Thus in any given time period, there are a finite number of swaps.

5. If nobody wants the product you are offering, you cannot participate in the swaps.

6. The artisans in the diagram all obtain the raw material they use to make their products from someone else. So in this example, if you are an artisan and nobody wants the product you make, you cannot even make it for your own consumption because you cannot obtain the raw materials needed, e.g. if

nobody wants bread apart from the baker himself, the baker cannot obtain grain and so cannot make any.

7. There is no guarantee that the swaps will leave everyone fully employed and supplied with what they want. Suppose that the arable farmer has obtained all the things she wants supplying only a small amount of grain, this may leave the baker with insufficient to make the bread he would have liked to swap with the others for more of their products.

8. Lastly, we observe that this swapping rapidly gets complicated. In a real economy it would require complicated swap chains with people obtaining goods not because they wanted them for themselves but in order to swap them on for something else.

5.2 Effects of a Change in Demand

Modelling the economy as a series of swaps, we can explore why economies can easily operate at below their full potential if some of the actors run out what they regard as advantageous swaps before others do. In these examples we assume that products are exchanged on the basis of how long it takes to make them, e.g. when swapping bread for shoes, you expect to swap the quantity of bread made in time X for the quantity of shoes that can be made in the same amount of time. As described in Chapter 3 in the discussion of value and the 'labour theory of value', this tends to happen in a real economy because of competition. If tailors are getting very favourable swaps (or in real life, high prices) because there is a shortage of clothes, then other artisans will be tempted to retrain as tailors, the shortage will diminish, and the swaps revert to being in the ratio of the labour required to make the products involved. We also noted in Chapter 3, that the labour theory of value can apply to resource owners as well, provided that they don't have a monopoly of the resource concerned.

We'll now look at an example of how a reduction in what one

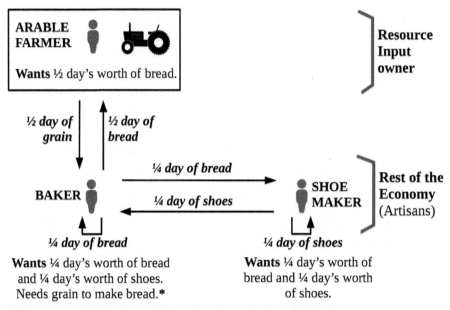

Figure 5.2: A set of swaps between a farmer, baker and shoemaker.

actor in the economy wants to consume, has wider effects. The starting situation for our example is shown in the diagram in Figure 5.2. The farmer wants $\frac{1}{2}$ day's worth of bread and nothing else. The grain she supplies for that is sufficient to satisfy the wants of both artisans, earning the baker some shoes in the process.

But now consider what happens if the farmer's desire for bread drops to a $\frac{1}{4}$ day's worth. The result is shown in the diagram in Figure 5.3. The small 'change in demand' has had a surprisingly large effect: it has rippled through the economy denying the shoemaker bread and the baker shoes. Total production (the same as total work) has slumped from 2 days to 1 ... by far more than the $\frac{1}{4}$ day's reduction in the farmer's work that was the cause. Table 5.1 shows the difference in production before and after the drop in the farmer's bread consumption.

We can easily imagine reasons why the farmer might choose to produce less grain than the farm is capable of growing. Perhaps

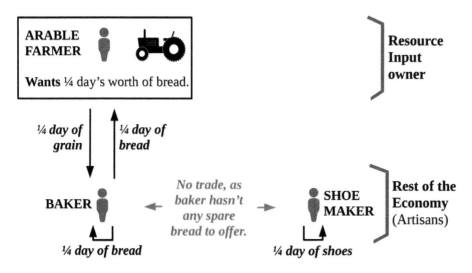

Figure 5.3: A drop in demand by the farmer for bread, lowers production of other goods too.

as well as its grain fields, the farm has extensive pasture where the farmer's children's ponies graze. The farmer and his family could plough up the pasture to plant more grain, but they have no incentive to do so if the grain they already produce is sufficient to earn them what they want. Similarly, in the real economy people who own resources can choose to keep them rather than expend or utilise them, if that is what they prefer. If an artisan isn't producing as much as the rest of the economy wants, other people can set up in that trade; but if a resource owner isn't producing as much as the rest of the economy wants, the shortfall cannot be made up unless there are competing owners of the same type of resource who step in (or in extremis, by taking the resources against the owner's will – a government might nationalise them, or in wartime, requisition them). All inhabitable land is already owned, and by relatively few people; most of us – even if we own a house with a garden or yard – have only a negligible amount. Some resource owners are able to achieve a degree of monopoly allowing them to charge more for their product than the value of the labour it took to produce – the Organization of the Petroleum Exporting

If the farmer wants ...	Farmer works	Baker works	Shoe-maker works	TOTAL WORK
$\frac{1}{2}$ *day's* *worth of* *bread:*	$\frac{1}{2}$ day	1 day	$\frac{1}{2}$ day	2 day
$\frac{1}{4}$ *day's* *worth of* *bread:*	$\frac{1}{4}$ day	$\frac{1}{2}$ day	$\frac{1}{4}$ day	1 day

Table 5.1: Drop in production when the farmer wants less bread.

Countries (OPEC) is a cartel of oil producers who cooperate to adjust production levels and thus maintain prices. Yet it does not follow that all resource owners are in a strong position. They may find themselves competing with each other to try to swap what they produce for all the other goodies the world's economy produces and thus driving down the prices they receive – think of the fluctuating fortunes of the world's coffee producers.

Of course the starting position could be the second diagram, and the farmer's desire for bread grows by a $\frac{1}{4}$ day's worth, resulting in the first diagram. Then that increase of $\frac{1}{4}$ day in the farmer's work ripples through the economy increasing total production (total work) from one day to two days. This phenomenon of a small increase in spending having a larger knock on effect was described as the multiplier by the economist John Maynard Keynes. In our example the multiplier is 4 because an increase of $\frac{1}{4}$ day in the farmer's work results in an increase of 1 (i.e. four times more) in the total work in the economy. Observe that the size of the multiplier depends on the length of the chain of swaps: if in the increase of demand case (going from the second scenario to the first one), the baker simple ate the extra $\frac{1}{4}$ day's worth of bread that she produces instead of trading it for shoes, then those shoes would never have been produced. The real economies that we live in, with their millions of products, may have some very long chains!

5.2.1   Resource shortages

We have supposed that the amount of grain the farmer supplies drops from $\frac{1}{2}$ day's worth to a $\frac{1}{4}$ day's worth, because her desire for bread has dropped to a $\frac{1}{4}$ day's worth and to get that she only needs to trade $\frac{1}{4}$ day's worth of grain. This is a drop in demand or 'wants'.

Another possibility is that farmer supplies less grain not because she wants to but because of a resource shortage – perhaps there is a drought and the farm is no longer capable of growing a $\frac{1}{2}$ day's worth of grain, and can only manage to produce a $\frac{1}{4}$ day's worth. There is still a knock on effect on the rest of the economy but for a different reason.

5.3   Effect of a New Product

Next we will consider how adding in a new 'want' – a product that wasn't there before – can create more economic activity. Look at the diagram in Figure 5.4 which shows swaps between two artisans.

Shoes are traded for shirts. The tailor would actually like a whole day's worth of shoes, but the shoemaker is only interested in trading for half a day's worth of shirts and will only offer half a day's worth of shoes for them. However, the shoemaker would like half a day's worth of music if only it were available.

Figure 5.4: Initial level of production before musician arrives.

Hey presto! A musician has arrived in the village – a singer. She offers music in exchange for the shirts that she wants. The diagram in Figure 5.5 shows what happens. To get the music he'd like, the shoemaker has to offer her shirts and to get those he has to offer more shoes to the tailor.

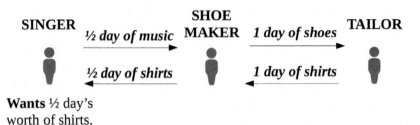

Figure 5.5: The availability of something new to want (music) also increases production of existing goods.

She works only $\frac{1}{2}$ day but the total production has grown by $1\frac{1}{2}$ days, more than doubling as the effect ripples through the economy. We can imagine that something similar happens in the real economy when a desirable new product like the motor car, television or smartphone gets released onto the market. We can also imagine the converse: the drop in production that occurs if people don't want those products any more – though manufacturers are careful to try to avoid such a situation by releasing endless new models. The change in the production figures with the arrival of the musician are shown in Table 5.2.

	Singer works	Shoe-maker works	Tailor works	TOTAL WORK
Without the singer:	-	$\frac{1}{2}$ day	$\frac{1}{2}$ day	1 day
With the singer:	$\frac{1}{2}$ day	1 day	1 day	$2\frac{1}{2}$ day

Table 5.2: Production before and after the singer arrives.

Notice again how the increased production due to the addition of the singer, depends on the length of the chain of swaps that it creates. If she wanted not shirts but shoes, then she could just do a single swap with the shoemaker who still has to produce an extra $\frac{1}{2}$ day's worth of shoes, but as these are swapped directly with the singer instead of to get shirts, no extra shirts are produced.

We can quantify this rather easily. If someone produces an extra X day's worth of goods just for their own consumption (and without any exchanging anything with others to obtain raw materials either, so zero swaps), then total production grows by X. If they exchange all the extra goods for something else (one swap), then total production grows by 2X, and so on. We can see that 'multiplier' is given by the length of the chain (or in other words, the number of swaps). In the case of our example, the chain is 3 long, so the multiplier is 3. The new production X is $\frac{1}{2}$ because the singer has introduced an extra $\frac{1}{2}$ day's worth of goods (music), and thus total production grows by 3X which is: *$3 \times \frac{1}{2} = 1\frac{1}{2}$*.

However, these are simple examples; in a real economy, the singer would want a whole range of goods in exchange for her music, and the chains of swaps would fan out and also diminish with the number of steps. Even with our simple example you can see how they might diminish: suppose the singer wants both shoes and shirts in equal quantities, so the shoemaker can supply part of what she wants directly and needs less from the tailor, and thus the total increase in production is lower, being: *singer $\frac{1}{2}$ + shoemaker $\frac{1}{2}$ + tailor $\frac{1}{4}$ = $1\frac{1}{4}$* (instead of the $1\frac{1}{2}$ we had before).

5.4 Employment

Viewing the economy as a set of swaps makes it obvious that there is no guarantee of full employment. Even assuming that all mutually desired swaps are made, that's no guarantee that everyone will be fully employed, particularly if they don't have much to offer at the outset – perhaps only unskilled labour. We can state the condition that must be met for full employment that applies to a swap economy, as follows:

For full employment to be reached, we need the following to be true for all levels of employment from the starting level of employment up to the employment of the last unemployed person: *'That there exists a chain of mutually desired exchanges that links the ultimate consumer(s) of what is produced by additional labour, with the extra people employed to carry it out.'*

Expressing that in more normal English, what this says is: 'for every worker we add to the workforce right up to full employment, we need people in the economy who are willing to offer what that worker wants (food, housing, etc.) in exchange for his/her labour, because they want the product of that labour.'

While this sounds a very demanding condition, we should remember that humans are adaptable and will actively try to find a product or service that they can offer that others will want.

5.5 Effects of Using Money to Carry Out the Swaps

Real economies normally use money as an intermediate good, which makes swapping much easier. Taking our original 8-person exchange economy, let's suppose that all of those 8 are given a sum of money – 100 silver coins each perhaps. Now they don't have to exchange their products by arranging complicated chains of swaps with each other – they can sell what they produce (swap it for money) and then buy what they want (swap the money back for produce from one of the others). The diagram in Figure 5.6 shows the same 8-person exchange economy that we saw earlier in Figure 5.1, but now redrawn to show money being used as the way to trade instead of barter.

If they continue to exchange products in the same quantities and proportions as before (the prices reflecting the same relative values they placed on the products when they swapped without

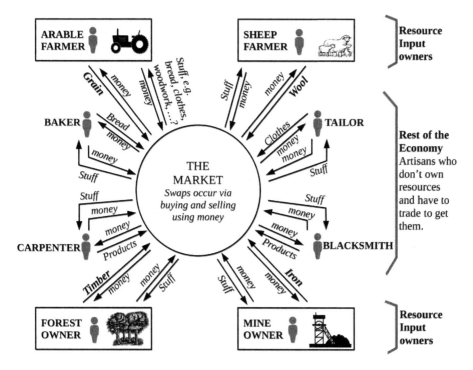

Figure 5.6: Using money to carry out swaps.

using money), then nothing really changes: money moves to and fro in a symmetrical way so that no-one gets any richer or poorer in cash terms over time.

If instead someone decides that now that they have money they can buy things without having to sell anything, they will obviously pretty soon run out of money.

What about the opposite: someone is producing and selling but doesn't spend all the money they are earning? Money then piles up with this person, which means that one or more of the others is running out of money. Eventually those others can no longer buy anything, production in the economy drops off, and the sales our frugal saver was making will dry up.

Thus while introducing money into the economy does mean that we can have temporary imbalances in trade (someone can sell something and then keep the money from the sale for a while before spending it again), nevertheless over time trade must balance, just as it does in our imagined barter economy that operates without money by swapping goods directly. That means that eventually in an economy with money, everyone needs to spend as much as they save. If they don't do so, then the effect is the same as someone in the barter economy no longer wanting to swap: they will reduce production to the level of the swaps in the economy that are still mutually desired. This conclusion is standard macroeconomics but sometimes surprises the wider public since we are always being advised to save.

The need for trade to balance over time does not mean that there cannot be large inequalities in wealth. In our example 8-person economy, the mine owner could spend less than he earns for a period until most of the 100 silver coins that each of the eight people in the economy had at the start, have ended up with him, and the other seven have only a handful of coins left. As they run low on money, the others will have to adjust their spending to match their earnings, and trade will adjust to a level at which it is balanced. However, the economy could simply bump along at that level, the mine owner remaining cash rich compared to the others.

While trade needs to balance over time, that may be quite a lot of time. At an individual level, this may be a lifetime: it's common for people to save through much of their adult life and then spend in old age (especially on medical expenses and personal care), finally leaving an inheritance that gets spent by the next generation. Countries can also run balance of trade deficits for many years which are balanced by foreigners bringing money in to buy up land or businesses. At some point however, there will be no more land or businesses to sell – though that might be decades into the future.

5.5.1 Inequality, trade imbalances and loans

In the real world, inequality is so high that it is very easy for even the moderately affluent, let alone the mega-rich, to accumulate savings. To maintain economic activity we need them to spend what they earn on consumption of the goods and services the economy produces. Investing money in buying things that already exist from other rich people – such as houses, company shares or paintings by old masters – doesn't cause any new production, it just shuffles the money to another rich person.

So here's an idea: if the rich person's savings are gumming up the economy, why not lend some of that money to poorer working-people to spend? Consider our 8-person economy above: we gave each person 100 silver coins to use for trade, but let's suppose that the mine owner has been spending less than he earns and has ended up with the lot, all 800 silver coins! No problem: he lends all the others 100 coins each at the 'modest' interest rate of 1 coin per trading day. However, if nothing else changes and the mine owner continues to spend less than he earns, all the money will just end up back with him again but this time even faster because of the interest he's being paid.

The economy is now gummed up again but the mine owner doesn't want to lend to the others a second time because they still all owe him the 100 silver coins he lent them before and now cannot even pay the interest. A new wheeze occurs to him: he will buy the houses the others live in from them for 100 silver coins each – that way they will have some money to spend, can resume paying interest on the 100 he lent them, and they can rent their houses back from him so that they still have a place to live. The deed is done, but ... if the mine owner continues to spend less than he earns, all the money will just end up back with him again and this time yet faster still because he's now being paid interest and rent!

What next? Maybe he could lend them money to buy their houses back, secured against the house if they fail to keep up inter-est payments. Does this sound sort of familiar? Think sub-prime mortgages. And in any case, such a scheme still won't give them any spending money to maintain economic activity. Perhaps the mine owner should use his political connections to call for a gov-ernment bailout to repay the bad debts: a bailout paid for by taxes – but taxes on incomes of course, not wealth because that would annoy rich and powerful people like ... well himself for one.

To keep the economy moving, financial tricks like those outlined above, can at best only give us a stay of execution but ultimately cannot work. The rich have to be persuaded to part with their money, either by tempting them with an Aladdin's cave of consumer goods – much of our economy is dedicated to that – or by taxation.

5.5.2   The value of money

We said in the barter examples in this chapter that the relative value of products was set mainly by the hours of labour that went into them. When money is introduced to replace barter, we assumed that prices would settle to the same relative values. But what sets the absolute value, the general level of the prices to be charged?

Money originated when people found that they could escape the complexities of barter by finding some generally desired and reasonably portable intermediate good, like silver or gold. The candidate needs to be valuable in its own right and take a significant amount of effort to find or produce; the two things go together because if it were easy to create money, then people would do so, and it would lose its rarity and thus its value.

When you use as money something that is intrinsically valuable like gold, then there is a clear mechanism for how to set the prices of goods – shoes, shirts, bicycles, whatever. The gold can simply be traded in the ratio of the amount of work it took to make the product, compared to the amount of work to mine and smelt the gold used in the gold coins that are offered in exchange. When paper banknotes were introduced they were initially just a note of ownership or IOU (I Owe You) for gold held by the bank, which in theory at least, the bearer of the note could retrieve, so a link to gold remained. Thus the use by countries of precious metals to back their money continued – with gaps - until fairly recent times: the UK leaving the gold standard in 1931 and the USA in 1971.

Nowadays, banknotes and their digital equivalents in bank computers, have no intrinsic material value and are not linked to precious metals. Yet modern currency can still be seen as a sort of IOU: the money shows that you are owed a certain quantity of the economy's products, which you claim when you spend it. It is the confidence that others will honour that IOU and hand over goods in exchange, that gives money its value. To maintain that confidence, governments have to control the quantity of money and act to prevent forgery. If governments start to finance themselves by printing large numbers of extra banknotes, there will clearly be inflation: prices will rise because a larger amount of money is chasing the same amount of goods. Even with gold or silver, the same thing would happen if the metals suddenly became much easier obtain. Thus the value of money depends on the amount in circulation compared to the amount of goods produced and traded. To explore that a little more, it is said that money has three properties or functions, being a:

- Means of exchange – it facilitates trade.

- Unit of measurement – it allows you to compare the value of different products and services.

- Store of value – it acts as a store of value for the individual.

However, the last of these properties needs to be treated with care, because money doesn't really store value at all, it only stores promises. An example of a real store of value is a stash of nuts that you collected in the autumn and that are still good to eat the following spring – ask any squirrel. That's quite unlike banknotes you store in the autumn, which only have any value in the spring because there are other humans in the world who are willing to redeem them in exchange for actual food or other goods that they possess. Money does not and cannot transmit wealth from one whole generation of humanity to the next, only real wealth does so – things like infrastructure, farms, nature, knowledge and art. Money is a zero-sum game when passed on from one generation to the next: if one fund is made bigger then another has been made smaller by the same amount, so what is passed down is the distribution of stuff among humans, not the total amount of stuff in the world – the amount of actual stuff such as land and other assets passed on stays the same, money just affects who owns it.

Understanding that money is only an IOU or promise, helps us to understand why the value of money in circulation is related to the quantity of goods the economy produces. Suppose that in the eight-person economy shown in figure 5.6, the community decides to make everybody rich, by issuing everyone with banknotes with a total face-value of a million silver coins. The next day no-one goes to work because as millionaires they can just buy everything they need ... except that they can't because nobody is producing anything! So they then agree to continue to work, trading at the original produce prices. However, given that everybody now has lots of cash, someone is bound to buy more than they usually do, leaving less or nothing for other people to buy. But since everyone else also has spare cash, they all soon start offering to pay more so as not to go home empty-handed, and they also put up their own prices. Eventually prices and the incomes of sellers, will have to settle at a new higher level appropriate to the amount of money in circulation.

To put that in a more general way: If you have Money-IOUs that will buy you far more goods than would be your fair share of production, you are naturally going to be tempted to redeem them, rather than try to limit yourself to what you guess would be your proper share. Therefore, across society as a whole, the value of money in terms of the goods it will buy, has to adjust (and will via market forces) until the rate at which the population are inclined to redeem 'Money-IOUs' (banknotes), is the same as the rate at which they are earned.

From the above reasoning we can see why the value of money is not arbitrary but depends on the relationship between the amount of money and the amount of production – so changes in either can result in changes in prices. If for example a government attempts to finance itself by printing money, it will result in inflation – prices of goods generally will rise.

In terms of production there are many changes that could affect prices. Some examples based on the illustrative eight-person economy of artisans and resource owners shown in figure 5.6, are:

1. A business becomes more productive. Typically this happens

because of technological advances. For example the baker buys a kneading machine which doubles the number of loaves that can be produced a day, so the price of a loaf should fall since less work goes into each one.

2. A business becomes less productive. Perhaps the best ores at the mine are exhausted and it now takes more work to produce the same amount of iron, so the price of iron rises.

3. A resource becomes scarce. If there are almost no trees left in the forest, the price of wood is bid up, even though the amount of work to fell a tree is unchanged.

4. Monopoly pricing. If there are resource owners who have a monopoly, they are able to charge more than what would be their due on the basis of labour-hours to make the product. So in our example, if there is only one arable farm, then the farmer could demand two-days-work worth of shoes for only one-days-work worth of grain. Traditional economics analyses how much monopolists can charge to get the optimum benefit: it's not unlimited because if they ask for too much they'll get few or no sales (and may provoke government intervention or a movement to seize their business!).

5. Variations in the status or skill associated with different jobs, changes relative pay. In practice a day's work is not paid equally whatever the job. The blacksmith in our economy could insist that his job is more highly skilled and difficult than that of the baker, so for a day of his work he wants more that one-days-worth of bread. Perhaps the village will accept and pay his higher price, especially if there are few volunteers to train up to give him any competition.

Of the above, the most striking development in terms of price changes is point (1). Technology has produced an explosion in productivity; many manufactured and agricultural products have become far cheaper in real terms after correcting for inflation, with some even being cheaper without any correction. For example early

PCs in the 1980s could cost a few thousand Pounds, while a far more powerful modern PC can be bought for a few hundred of today's much less valuable Pounds. Over those forty or so years, prices would have fallen on a wider range of products in money terms as well as real terms, were it not for the fact that as productivity has increased, governments have put more money into circulation, causing an inflation that offsets the falls. The effect of mass-produced 'stuff' having become so much cheaper is to make things where the labour involved has not changed, relatively more expensive, e.g. employing servants, or paying for a builder. The cost of repairing things, being labour-intensive, has become a much greater fraction of the cost of buying a new replacement, thus encouraging a throw-away culture.

We will return to the subject of prices when we take a look at inflation and the money supply in Chapter 23.

5.6   Optimum Swapping

Free markets regulate themselves and are said by economists to provide the 'optimum' distribution of goods and services. The self-regulation is certainly a great benefit as it allows decentralisation and initiative by individual businesses to fill gaps or offer new products. The 'optimum distribution' occurs if we assume that all actors in the market are 'perfectly informed'; in our swap model that means that everyone knows what swaps are possible and all that are mutually desired are made. However it is a funny sort of 'optimum'! If some of the actors in the market are extremely rich and others are dirt poor, then the rich have reshuffled their enormous quantity of goods and services to the most preferred arrangement and the dirt poor will emerge with perhaps a slightly different meagre set of goods to that they started with. It may be an 'optimum' outcome, but that's not the same as a 'good' outcome – such as the dirt poor ending up instead with a decent livelihood.

5.7 Summary

The market is not an amorphous blob where you can sell anything for money provided the price is low enough, and buy anything if you pay enough. What really goes in a free market is the exchange of goods and services between people or businesses, via a series of complicated swaps, in each of which both parties want to make the trade. Money facilitates this, allows short-term imbalances (you don't need to sell and buy at the same moment) and hides the complex chains of swaps involved.

Viewing the economy as a set of swaps helps us to understand how a change in what one person or business wants (a change in demand), can have a knock on effect on the rest of the economy that is much greater than the initial change – the effect economists call 'the multiplier' – and that the same is true for a change in resource availability. We can also see that there isn't some specific natural level that the economy works at. The level of production depends on what the various actors in the economy want, and importantly, may be limited by the wants of one or a few of them being fully met, while production is still at a lower level than needed to meet the wants of others. What that means in practical terms is that in a very unequal world, production will be at a level at which the wealthy have what they want and can't think of anything more to buy, even though that may be a long way below the level required to meet the basic needs of the rest of the world's population.

Introducing the use of money instead of barter, does not, in the long term, allow us to escape the consequences of the economy being a set of swaps and production being therefore limited to the result of those swaps that are mutually desired.

Having explored how markets operate, we'll next consider what it's like to live in one.

Chapter 6

Life in the Market Economy

This chapter will look at how an individual interacts with a modern free-market economy, within the rules that typically apply. What roles do we play? How can we do what every animal needs to do: earn a living?

6.1 Horse, Gentleman and Citizen!

In modern societies, most of us play three quite different roles in the economy. Firstly for much of our lives we are **workers** who produce goods and services, and by doing so earn money. Secondly we are **consumers**: we spend money buying in the market the things we want. Thirdly we are **citizens** who can influence society and the economy in other ways apart from shopping and working – by for example, voting, joining a trade union or political party, supporting a charity, or having a cultural or intellectual influence.

The *worker* is like one of the *horses* that pulled heavy carts before the advent of motor vehicles. For as long as a horse is useful to his or her owner, it is kept fed and stabled, but when it ceases to earn its keep it is sent to the knacker's yard to be turned into pet food and glue; only the luckiest animals are put out to graze for a dignified retirement. Similarly, when we go out to work, we are of no interest to the giant corporations who employ us except in so much as we are useful. The executives who decide whether to maintain or close the factory or office where we are employed, probably have no knowledge of us except as a collection of 'human resources': they may well live in a distant country, speak a different language, and be complete strangers to the places their decisions affect. When we cease to be useful, there is no sentiment in sacking us or if there is, it is suppressed: your boss may shed a genuine tear but will do 'what the business requires' . Happily, since we are of the same species and thus more capable of defending ourselves than the horses are against their human owners, the knacker's yard is not normally an option, though unemployment may still lead to destitution.

Figure 6.1: As WORKERS we work for others, like this horse. [WMC]

The **consumer** is like an eighteenth century *lady or gentleman*, waited on by a variety of servants. The eighteenth century gentlemen sought out the cheapest workforces, often slaves, and benefited from the labour of oppressed labourers working on far away sugar, cotton and tea plantations. When we go out to shop, we become today's version of that gentlemen or lady consumer. We seek products made by the most exploited workers: those working the longest hours for the least pay, often in countries where trade unions are weak or suppressed, and sometimes involving child labour. We give little or no importance to employing workers in our own town or country, preferring the cheapest available globally. Of course, we don't think of ourselves as behaving in such an uncaring way; what we have in mind is 'getting good value' or 'finding a bargain'. We also may be short of money ourselves and under pressure to make it go as far as possible.

Mr and Mrs Andrews by Thomas Gainsborough.
[WMC]

Figure 6.2: As CONSUMERS we are served by others.

As well as being workers and consumers, we are also *citizens*.
As a citizen we have the potential to engage in a variety of social and
political activities to try to influence the economic rules we have to
live under as workers and consumers. This might well have caused
us to be seen as a threat by eighteenth century polite society, or
indeed by many governments and authorities today. They could be
concerned that we may undertake political activity which threatens
the interests of the ruling elite, whether that is the governing party
in a democracy, or a totalitarian hierarchy or dictatorship. Or that
we may proselytise for a religion frowned upon by the authorities.
Or that we may seek to form trade unions or become more militant
in some other way. Or that, if disaffected, we may turn to crime or
engage in mob riots, posing a direct threat to the possessions of the
wealthy and to civil order. But that is to focus only on the more
rebellious citizens – there will of course be others, particularly the
more privileged, who engage in politics and civic society in order
to maintain or reinforce the status quo, not to change it. Typically
however, a large part of the population for most of the time, exercise
their roles as citizens only a little or not at all. They are either too
busy with their own lives and earning a living, or in some countries
fearful of repression, or they feel powerless (that nothing they do
would make a difference), or are simply not interested.

Since the interests of worker and consumer are opposed (one
wants high pay, the other wants low prices), and the majority of

Martin Luther King, Civil Rights March on Washington D.C. [WMC]

Figure 6.3: As CITIZENS we can influence governance.

us have both roles, we can be drawn to opposing points of view: **on Friday** after a hard-day's work we're fed up with being paid 'peanuts' – *"the government should make people pay more for the service we provide"*; **on Saturday** our well-deserved holiday is ruined because airport workers have gone on strike – *"there should be laws to stop them doing that"*. Thus ordinary citizens can be drawn to support quite different political parties, depending on whether their individual circumstances and the influences upon them, cause them to side more with workers or with consumers.

Because we have these multiple roles, we have conflicting interests. As <u>workers</u> we want *high wages and short working hours*. As <u>consumers</u> we want the opposite: *low prices* which creates pressure for *lower wages and longer hours*.

Owners

While most of us are restricted to the three different roles of worker, consumer and citizen, a minority have an additional role as *owners*. This minority own such substantial wealth that most or all of their income is generated from that wealth (via rents, profits, interest, etc.) and therefore they do not need to work, only consume. Being in this situation potentially gives them more opportunity to act as *citizens*, since they have greater leisure to do so and have the money to buy influence.

6.2 Earning a Living – a game with rules

A market economy may be thought of as a sort of game in which we are the players. We are free to make our own economic choices provided that we keep to the rules of the game. These rules encompass such things as the recognition of property, acceptance of money, taxation, conditions of employment, how companies may be organised, and more. The rules are accepted by most people, not only because we are obliged to do so since they are enforced by the state, but also because we see many of the rules as natural and just. Some of the rules may actually be natural in the sense that they accord with basic human drives, but whether they are natural or not, humans are wonderfully adaptable creatures and what we were taught as children and grew up with, tends to seem to us the proper state of affairs.

6.3 Go Forth and Sell Yourself

The economics game starts for each of us, when we first go forth to earn our living in the world. Our task is to find something that we own and others want, that we can exchange for the things that they own and we want. In terms of possessions, most people in the world start out as young adults possessing almost nothing except for their own bodies and minds. Swapping your worn-out childhood toys won't earn you much. And while some desperate people do actually sell bits of their bodies (blood or a kidney for example), most of us expect to '**work**'. Working involves either renting out our physical and/or mental abilities to someone else as an employee, or finding something we can do or make that we can sell directly to customers.

To survive in the game, we need others to be willing to offer us enough to live on in exchange for our work. Of course, the better the qualities and capabilities we are offering (in terms of strength, intelligence, education, training, attractiveness, health, etc.), the more chance we have. But ultimately, if people don't want what we have to offer or can get it cheaper elsewhere, we are out of the game and will have to look for support from the state, family or friends, or if that's not possible turn to begging or theft.

6.4 Playing the Game to Get Rich

When you are consuming goods and services, you are 'consuming' the labour of the people who made them – it's as if they work for you for the time it took them to produce those things. Of course it is the other way when you are working: then others who consume what you produce are 'consuming' your labour.

Now the amount of labour available cannot be more than the world population, so the world average amount of labour 'consumed' per person cannot be more than one person's labour. In fact it will be considerably less than that since many people do not work, e.g. children and the elderly. But of course we don't all receive the average, and how much labour each person 'consumes' is a 'zero-sum game'. In other words, if one person gets more, another must get less. Only technical progress that increases the productivity of labour, can make the world as a whole wealthier.

What this means is that we should not expect to get much richer than our neighbours by working in fairly 'ordinary jobs' – ones which many other people can equally well learn to do. The reason is that if we were demanding in exchange for what we produce in a day, more than the ordinary amount of goods and services that others produce in a day, then we are asking them in essence to do more than a days work to get a days work. Why should they? They could just learn our job and do it themselves.

There are however ways to trade in the market and get more than average earnings, potentially very much more. Two ways in particular:

1. **Your body and/or mind has some rare and valued**

quality that people will give you more for. Examples are brilliant scientists, top footballers, great singers. Others cannot easily emulate your qualities so they cannot switch to your job and compete with you. Apart from such special individuals, many other people do earn significantly more than the average because their jobs are not easy for others to switch into. For example a high level of ability and training may be required or there may be cultural reasons that restrict entry to the profession – you might fancy yourself as king or queen but countries with monarchies restrict the applicants to just one!

Albert Einstein [WMC]

Figure 6.4: A rare and valued quality.

2. **You <u>own</u> something substantial** apart from your body and mind, which you can exchange for other goods. You might have this by inheritance or by slowly saving up for it.

Let's look at the second case in more detail. It could be that you have something valuable that you simply sell off bit by bit – some land or shares or gold, perhaps. Eventually it will all be gone, but if that takes longer than your lifetime, you may not care. However, there are other possessions which have the interesting property that you can exchange them (or what they produce) for things that you want, and they don't get used up in the process. Examples of these are factories, farms, houses and other property that can be rented out. With these possessions, you can allow others to use them for a period in exchange for goods that you want, and at the end of the period you still have them and can do it again. In fact our own capacity to work also has the same property – we rent it out one day, and it is still available the next morning to rent out all over again. If you own an office, factory or farm and don't do the work yourself, then it is also a sort of rental: you allow other people to use it in some way such as managing it or working it, in return for a share of what is produced.

Since there is no limit to how much one person can own, it is possible to live entirely off rental income without having to work at all. Some are born inheriting such wealth, while some others are able to reach that point by accumulating rental possessions during part of their working life. However, clearly everybody cannot live off rental income unless – we totally automate all work. The majority of us live by our labour, although the better off among us may acquire some rental income as well, such as the earnings from savings invested in the stock market or simply by renting out a spare room.

6.5 Game Outcomes

In the board game Monopoly, players move their token around a board by the number squares given by a throw of dice. The squares represent properties which players landing on them can purchase if they are as yet unsold, and thereafter charge 'rent' to other players unlucky enough to land on them. If by a combination of luck and judgement, one player manages to acquire more properties than the others, then that player will probably continue to grow richer at the expense of the others as they are more likely to land on her properties than the other way around. Engineers call self reinforcing trends like this 'positive feedback'. The game ends when all the players except one go bankrupt, so a player who has gained a significant advantage, benefiting also from the effect of positive feedback, is likely to continue to get richer and to win.

Games with rules have probable outcomes dependent on those

Figure 6.5: The rules of a game affect the outcomes. [WMC]

rules. Those that we play for amusement are usually intended to have winners and losers. So in Monopoly for example, it's intended that someone ends up rich and the others end up with nothing. However, rules can be changed: if Monopoly had rules that incorporated a system of income tax that was used to finance hard up players, then perhaps no-one would go broke. Such rules would make Monopoly boring, but are widely considered desirable in the real economy.

A free-market economy has a similar positive feedback mechanism to Monopoly. If the only thing you have to offer the market is your labour, most of your pay is likely to get spent just on day to day consumption. If however, you have inherited or managed to acquire sufficient 'capital' (cash that you can loan or property that you can rent out like houses, factories, farms), then you can potentially receive many times what you need for your own consumption, and the excess can go into acquiring yet more capital – allowing you to grow ever richer.

Thus it is that under free-market capitalism there are clear winners and losers, with all-too-often inadequate protection for the losers. In most wealthy countries today, there is some sort of social security system intended to assist the worst off, but in the past and still in many parts of the world, losers may be worked or starved to an early death. This is not to condemn the free-market economy in its entirety, but if we accept that it tends to concentrate wealth, we may wish to have rules that limit inequality and protect the poorest. Many governments do so to some degree, especially those with strong social democratic traditions; the extent to which they do so is usually a major part of the political debate between left and right.

6.6 Summary

Most of us have three roles in a free-market economy: as **workers**, as **consumers** and as **citizens**. Our double lives as both workers and consumers mean that our political interests as citizens can be contradictory.

Earning a living as workers in a free-market economy is like playing a game with rules. Most of us bring to this game only our own capacity to work, which we hope to exchange for the things we need. A few privileged players bring **ownership** of the places where goods and services are made. In return for our work in these places, they give us a proportion of what gets made and retain the remainder for themselves.

The likely outcomes of a game depend on the choice of rules. The rules of a free-market economy mean that wealth tends to concentrate in a few hands while others may be left with nothing. If we don't want that outcome and want a fairer society, we need to add rules that regulate the operation of the market.

In this chapter we looked at how we participate in the economy as individuals. Next we look at the dynamics of the free-market economy as a whole system.

Chapter 7

Dynamics of the Economy: The Labour Market

7.1 The Economy as a System

All of us are familiar with our own roles in the economy in so much as we know how we earn our living and how we spend what we earn. This and the following four chapters are about the *dynamics of the market economy*, or how the whole economy functions as a system: what economists call "macroeconomics" (as opposed to "microeconomics" which refers to players within the system: businesses and individuals). We will look at:

1. **Will there always be sufficient employment?** The current chapter shows that there is no guarantee of full employment, and Chapter 8 dissects the classical Supply-Demand diagram as applied to the labour market.

2. **Increasing the demand for labour.** Chapter 9 explains why automation hasn't caused far higher unemployment than we actually have?

3. **Long term changes in how much can be produced.** Chapter 10 describes the sources of economic growth.

4. **Short term fluctuations.** Chapter 11 explains why the economy oscillates between booms when things are supposedly going well and slumps when times are harder.

It is important that we as citizens gain a broad understanding of the economy as a whole, because otherwise politicians can too easily sell us policies based on what may sound like common sense, but when applied to the whole economy make no sense at all. Given how often this happens, it seems likely that there is a deliberate intention to fool us into accepting what is not in our interest.

In this chapter we look at the labour market and in particular, examine these two widely heard claims:

- *"Everyone can find work if they try hard enough"* This could only be true if there were definitely enough jobs for everyone, and it's pretty clear that there are not. It really amounts to telling people in a race that everyone can win if they try hard enough, but if there are one hundred runners and only the first three get prizes, then it doesn't matter how hard everyone tries, only three people out of the hundred can be winners. It is a tempting slogan because of course if you are looking for work, or in a race, then trying hard **is** a good strategy for you as an individual since it makes you more likely to be one of the lucky ones.

- *"Everyone can have a job if they accept low-enough pay"*. Again, this sounds reasonable until you think what would happen if everyone's wages were substantially reduced or even made zero. The result would be a catastrophic drop in demand for goods and services, so employers would need far fewer workers to meet the demand and unemployment would soar.

7.2 Will there be Enough Jobs?

Will there be enough work for everyone who wants it? Many economists claim that the market will always provide jobs for all

Figure 7.1: High demand for horses. [WMC]

provided that it is free to operate. By that they mean: no trades unions, no government regulation setting minimum wages and no unemployment pay. Under these conditions they claim that the price of labour will adjust until the market clears, i.e. wages will fall until everyone gets a job. Sadly this claim is simply a lie, however much it is dressed up in economics mumbo jumbo.

The harsh truth is that there is no guarantee that a market economy will offer jobs to all. Until the 20th century there were thousands of horses in our cities. These animal workers were wanted for their strength to pull carts and carriages and their intelligence that enabled them to learn to do the work and respond to commands. In exchange, they received their food, stabling and grooming. The development of the internal combustion engine and motor vehicles took away almost all of their work. You would have seen thousands of unemployed horses standing around on street corners if it were not for the fact that humans control the reproduction of horses and don't breed them if there is no demand for them.

Human workers, like the horses, have frequently been displaced by technical development. Until the industrial age, most jobs required physical strength and stamina; nowadays, much work is mental. The manual work that remains is typically a combination of dexterity and intelligence such as building products on an assembly line. And slowly these jobs too are being replaced by robots. But unlike horses, human workers are not bred only when there is a demand for us. We are able to choose for ourselves to have children; there are a multitude of factors affecting how many children we have, and it's probably safe to say that a careful and accurate assessment of whether our babies will have jobs to go to when they grow up, is not usually one of them. Accordingly, there is no guarantee whatsoever that the number of jobs available will match the number of people seeking work.

Figure 7.2: Robots packing bread. [WMC]

"Aha", say our free-market economists, "people will always find work if they accept 'realistic' (i.e. low enough) wages". But while this claim may sound reasonable, given a moment's thought it is plainly false: even if the price of something falls to zero, we do not want any amount of it. I pay the water company to pipe water to my home; but if water became free I would not then appreciate an entire reservoir being dumped on my house and garden – I'd call that a flood and pay to have it pumped away.

An excess of anything ceases to be a benefit and becomes a nuisance. So it is with humans. Expatriates working in poor countries who receive European or US level salaries, often employ two or three local people to help with housework or childcare. In those countries local salaries for such workers can be as low as $50 a month, so expatriates could easily hire not just two or three servants, but fifty or more. Why don't they? The reason is simple, there is not enough work for them - and you positively don't want dozens of strangers hanging around your house eyeing up your possessions and watching your every move. If they offered to work for free you still wouldn't want them; if they still insisted on hanging around, you'd pay a guard or policeman to keep them off your property.

The belief that the labour market should always clear, provided that it is left alone, leads its adherents to propose the elimination of all restrictions on the labour market such as minimum wage schemes, unemployment pay and other worker rights and benefits, as the way to reduce unemployment. Their theories are used to justify policies that minimise workers rights. The resulting poverty and continuing unemployment tends to be blamed on any remaining rights that the workers have managed to keep and on any actions workers take to defend themselves such as organising trades unions.

Even critics of the market clearing theory often appear to say that it would work in an ideal world, and doesn't work in practice only because the assumption of perfect competition is not fully met in the real world. Given the political influence of the theory, that is not good enough; we shall demonstrate that the theory is not just imperfect, but wrong.

7.3 No Guarantee of Labour Market Clearing

So far in this chapter we have discussed in a general way why there is no guarantee that a labour market will clear. To conclude the chapter we will lay out those reasons as clearly as possible; there are three:

- It's not true that buyers will buy any amount of a product – in this case labour – if you make it cheap enough.

- Workers will also not sell their labour below a certain price because a point will be reached at which the wage doesn't even cover the costs of working.

- The production of labour, i.e. human reproduction and education, is not carried out in response to market demand.

These three points are discussed at greater length below.

FIRSTLY: Buyers won't buy more than a certain amount, however low you make the price

It is not true that any amount of any product can be sold if the price is low enough. If the price of tomatoes drops you might buy more but if it dropped to one dollar a ton you would not buy several tons of them to pile up in your kitchen. Beyond a certain quantity, a product ceases to be desirable and becomes instead a problem, and this is equally true of labour. A wealthy person in a poor country may be able to employ hundreds of servants at a wage of a couple of dollars a day. But hundreds of people in your home are even more unwelcome than a ton of tomatoes: they might break furniture, steal, or even take over the house. So in practice a rich person will only employ as many people as he or she has useful work for and can manage. Incidentally, a wealthy person may well choose to pay the servants that he or she does employ, a higher wage than the absolute minimum necessary, because it is worth doing so in order to elicit loyalty and reduce the need or desire to steal.

Figure 7.3: Dumped tomatoes. [geograph]

SECONDLY: Sellers will not sell below the price at which they cover their marginal costs, i.e. the extra cost of selling their product as opposed to not selling it

Sellers will not sell at any price however low because there are usually some costs involved in selling (e.g. transport to market). There is no point in selling at a price that is below these costs since the outcome will be a net loss. In the same way, workers will not accept less than some minimum wage because they need to cover the additional (marginal) costs of working such as travel to work, wear and tear on clothes, extra food needed, and to make it worth their while to work rather than just beg or look through garbage for something to eat.

THIRDLY: While manufacturers will stop making products that don't sell, we 'manufacture' people without any thought or knowledge about whether they will 'sell'

The reason that the markets in most products generally do clear is that if they don't, the producers stop making them. When the supply of cars exceeds demand, prices drop. When prices drop below the cost of production of some of the producers, then those producers reduce production or go out of business. Either way cars are not produced if they cannot be sold at more than the cost of production. It could be argued that this is a bad analogy because workers are not 'sold' but rent out their time to employers for wages. However, this makes little difference: the same thing would happen even if all cars manufactured were rented to consumers instead of being sold - if you couldn't rent them you would cut production. The end result would still be the same regardless of whether the cars were rented by the manufacturer or a separate car rental company. You certainly wouldn't say that the cars that couldn't be rented were no longer producing car-hours and thus hey presto the car market has cleared because only the car-hours that actually were sold are counted as having been produced.

Now let's look at how this applies to the labour market. Some economists attempt to defend the market-clearing theory by saying that instead of the workers themselves being sold (rented out), the workers produce a product called 'labour-hours' which they sell on the labour market; if they cannot sell their labour-hours at a price that is acceptable to them, they withdraw from the market and cease to produce labour-hours. But this argument twists reality. In fact the product is not labour hours but the workers themselves, though since slavery was abolished they may only be rented by the hour to employers, not sold to them. A worker cannot cut his or her contribution to the total number of workers that would like to sell their labour, because he or she has already been 'produced'. Workers also incur fixed 'maintenance' costs (food, housing, clothes, etc.) regardless of whether they sell their labour or not.

If for some reason too much of a product is produced, the lowest price that the producer will sell at is the extra cost of selling it as opposed to just disposing of it. For example, from time to time farmers do produce surpluses that cannot be sold at a price that makes it worthwhile taking them to market. They then may choose to dump the products without ever having offered them for sale. Likewise, workers who can see no prospect of a job, may 'dump' their surplus labour-hours by not actively offering themselves for work. No one would argue that since surplus tomatoes had never been offered for sale, they had actually not been produced. In the same way, it should not be argued that those workers who do not try to sell their labour, are not really workers.

To turn the workers themselves into commodities, produced according to the quantity demanded by the market, we would have to treat them (i.e. treat ourselves) like we do farm animals. Over the last century the demand for horses declined as they were replaced by trains, tractors and cars – yet there is no over supply of horses because they are 'produced' (bred) to meet market demand. If an oversupply occurs, fewer are bred and some may also be slaughtered to correct it.

Humans however are not farmed. Instead, we make personal choices about how many children to have, influenced by many factors (including of course the availability of birth control). Parents decide (if the pregnancy was planned at all!) to 'produce' new workers without first calculating their expected saleability on the labour market between 18 and 65 years in the future. Thus the supply of workers cannot be expected to adjust itself to make the labour market clear: there is likely to be a surplus or shortage.

Summary of the labour-hours argument. The labour-hours argument is the most obscure of the attempts to justify market clearing. The key point is that some economists[1] see individual workers as *autonomous manufacturers of the* labour-hours *'product', who, if they are unable to sell their product, should jolly well cease to produce it,* just as a manufacturer of widgets would in the same circumstances, and then find something else to sell. But **workers themselves <u>are</u> the 'product'** that is being sold on the labour market – sold by rental per hour, or 'wage'. **They have already been 'produced'** and typically they don't have anything else to sell. At most, they have some minimal personal possessions which once sold would leave them with nowhere to live and no clothes. The idea of workers as 'producers of labour-hours' appears to be little more than desperate mental gymnastics to try to justify existing economic theory.

It is interesting to note that in the capitalist world people are increasingly referred to as commodities. The 'personnel departments' of the 20th century have changed their name to 'human resources' and project planners refer to 'how much *resource*' they need instead of 'how many *people*'. While it may not be much good at solving unemployment, economic theory has quite successfully influenced the way we think.

7.4 Summary

There is no reason to suppose that the labour market will clear because at any given time the supply of labour is relatively fixed and unrelated to demand: it is the population of working age who

---

[1]Those of the 'New Classical Economics' school of thought, I believe.

need to work in order to live. Therefore, if labour demand exceeds supply, wages are good. If demand is less than supply, and remains so even if workers accept the lowest wage at which they could just cover their costs of working, then there will be unemployment.

Reflecting on the millions of people under-employed or unemployed around the world, it is easy to see that currently at the beginning of the 21st century, labour supply exceeds demand (with some local or special exceptions). This conclusion is perfectly in keeping with our *wants, resources, work-effort* model: there will be a surplus of unused work-effort if one of the other ingredients runs out first.

Because of the importance of this topic in setting government policies, we continue with it in Chapter 8 where we examine the classical Supply-Demand diagram used by some economists to argue that left to itself, the labour market will provide full employment and the best outcome for both labour and businesses. Following that in Chapter 9 we will consider why demand for labour is maintained to the degree that it is.

Chapter 8

The Classical Labour Supply and Demand Diagram

The view of classical and monetarist economists is that the 'laws of supply and demand' work in all markets, including that for labour. In standard economics texts you will see supply and demand diagrams like the one in Figure 8.1. The diagram is often used to claim that an unfettered free market eliminates the problem of unemployment because wages will adjust to a level where the amount of work the population are willing to do is equal to the amount of employment businesses are willing to offer. This chapter challenges that claim head on and asserts that the diagram is not applicable to the whole economy. Some of the reasons why have already been covered in Chapter 7, but the diagram is presented in so many economics text books that it merits a chapter of its own to explain why it doesn't match reality, and to suggest what realistic whole-economy supply and demand curves might look like.

However before we go any further, a digression: If you are used to looking at graphs then you would probably expect the axes in Figure 8.1 to be the opposite way around because usual practice with graphs is to put the 'independent variable' on the x-axis (horizontal line) of the graph and the 'dependent variable' on the y-axis (vertical line). 'Wages' are the independent variable here: the graph is saying that if we increase them we can attract more workers. So the x-axis should really be Wages, and the y-axis Employment.

To do otherwise makes it look like we're saying cause and effect are the other way around, i.e. if extra people turn up asking for work, businesses will employ all of them and increase everyone's pay as well! It appears that economics texts have maintained a curious tradition of putting the axes the opposite way around to that followed by most other disciplines since the British economist Alfred Marshall presented his graphs that way in his book Principles of Economics published in 1890. For those of us accustomed to the more usual (non-economist) way of presenting graphs, the graph in Figure 8.1 is shown redrawn in Figure 8.2 with the axes swapped to be the standard way around. Graphs in the remainder of the chapter will also follow this standard; to do otherwise would make them unnecessarily obscure.

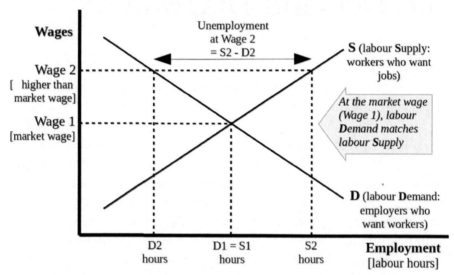

Note: wages on the y-axis as is traditional in economics texts.

Figure 8.1: The classical labour supply and demand diagram, with wages on y-axis.

Whichever version of the graph you prefer to look at, the explanation is the same. Two lines are shown on the graph:

1. The labour Supply curve 'S'. It slopes up because it is assumed that as wages are increased then workers are willing to work more hours (new workers come forward, or the same workers work more hours, or a combination).

90

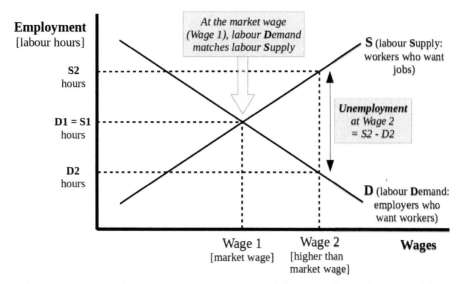

Note: wages on the x-axis as is conventional for an independent variable.

Figure 8.2: The labour supply and demand diagram, redrawn to put wages on the x-axis.

2. The labour Demand curve 'D'. It slopes down because it is assumed that as wages are increased then employers are less willing to pay for labour hours (they employ fewer people, or reduce the hours of the existing workers, or a combination).

If the labour market is left free to operate, then classical economists believe that the market will 'clear' at the equilibrium wage rate where the two lines cross, 'Wage1'; here the supply and demand for labour (S1 and D1) are equal, so unemployment is zero (all labour hours offered by workers are taken up by employers).

However, if the wage rate is forced up by say the government setting a minimum wage or by trade union action, to a higher level, shown on the diagram as Wage2, then the supply of labour increases to S2 while the demand for labour falls to D2. Now there is more supply than demand and the difference between the two is unemployment.

It's a wonderful theory at least for the business owners since it allows them to say "let us pay whatever we like because that gives the perfect outcome" ... and if it turns out that there is unemployment, then "blame the workers for asking for too high wages, not us or the economic system." This matters because classical economists and politicians apply the theory to the whole economy and do use it to argue that unemployment is caused by trade unions or government minimum wage laws, pushing wages up above the market rate. But does the theory stand up?

Why in fact should the real supply and demand curves even remotely resemble the two straight slopes shown in the classic diagram, if the diagram is claimed to describe the whole economy, not just a single company? The next two sections examine this in more detail and suggest what the two curves might really be for the economy as a whole.

8.1   The Labour Supply Curve

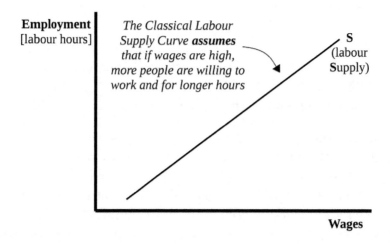

Figure 8.3: Classical labour supply curve, *but with wages on x-axis*.

The labour supply curve is assumed to slope upwards in the classical diagram, meaning that the more you pay, the more workers are willing to work – as shown in Figure 8.3. This likely to be true when applied to a single business because if it begins to pay more, it may attract workers from other businesses, and conversely if it cuts workers' pay, some workers may leave if they can get better jobs elsewhere.

But the assumption is flawed when applied to the whole economy,[1] the reason being because workers have to work to stay alive. In fact the opposite is true: if wages are lowered, workers are likely to try to work longer hours to compensate for the lost earnings. In the years of full employment in the USA and UK in the 1950s and 1960s, many families could live comfortably and buy a home with just one parent working. In more recent decades however, some groups of workers have suffered drops in their real-term wages (wages, after adjustment for inflation) with the result that they struggle to maintain a reasonable standard of living or buy a home, even with both parents going out to work. Table 8.1 shows a more realistic response of labour supply to wage level, taking into account people's need to earn a living.

A more realistic labour supply curve

Now let's make a guess at what a more realistic labour supply curve should look like, based on Table 8.1. We would expect something like the graph shown in Figure 8.4. On the graph, it is assumed that the minimum level of employment is zero when pay is so miniscule that it's less than the cost of going to work. Then the curve rises as pay rises to a maximum at which point the whole workforce is working as hard as it can to earn a basic standard of living. We know that the labour supply must at the very least flatten after this point because with everyone working all hours that God sends, they have no more to give however much you pay them. In practice as pay continues to increase, the hours worked slowly drop off because workers can afford to take some leisure time. Remember that this is a curve for the **whole economy**, and that for a single business we would expect something more like the classical line since as wages are increased by a business, workers will be attracted to switch from other lower paying businesses, with no real maximum unless one business manages to employ the entire working population.

---

[1] And to a single business if workers have no alternative employment.

Wage Level	Labour Supply
Zero.	No-one will work. Either get support from family, state or charity, or beg, borrow, steal or starve.
Less than cost of working (e.g. less than the bus fare to work).	No-one will work. Either get support from family, state or charity, or beg, borrow, steal or starve.
Starvation wages (barely above the costs of going to work).	Some people will work. Others get support or beg, etc.
Barely enough wages (enough to just about survive).	Almost everyone who needs work will work, and for as many hours as they can in order to earn enough.
Good, enough to live comfortably, and without working excessively long hours.	Almost everyone who needs work will work, usually for normal hours.

Table 8.1: A more realistic response of labour supply to wage level.

Assumptions

Two assumptions are implicit in the table and the resulting labour supply curve. The first is that the workforce are all offered the same wage level, and the second is that little or no support is available for the unemployed. In practice wage levels vary substantially across the workforce and many countries do have schemes to support the unemployed and the destitute. Therefore we cannot know from economic statistics what this theoretical demand curve should be. To find out we'd have to offer all workers the opportunity to work for the same wage, slowly increasing the offered wage from zero

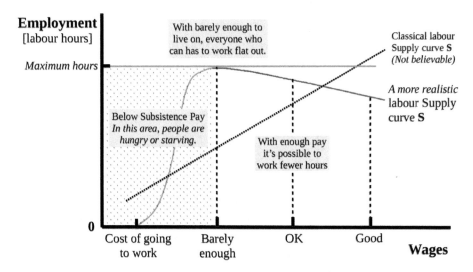

This graph's 'more realistic' labour-supply curve is based on Table 8.1 above. The classical line is shown as well for comparison.

Figure 8.4: A more realistic labour supply curve for the whole economy.

upwards and seeing how many chose to work at each level. No-one is going to conduct that experiment, which in any case would be largely pointless since it wouldn't match real conditions.

However, we can assume that most economies and most workers within them operate at or above the 'barely enough wages' level because if wages across the whole working population were below that level (in the shaded area on the graph), people would be in such a wretched state – both those in employment receiving their miserable less-than-subsistence wages, and those who are trying to survive via other desperate means – that society would collapse with either a revolt or a catastrophic loss of population from famine. Remember that here we are talking of a true and harsh 'barely enough wages' level, which is only just sufficient for survival. Perceptions today in one of the world's better-off countries of what constitutes a barely enough level, might include electricity, running water a fridge, schools, healthcare and the occasional cheap foreign holiday. In 18th and 19th century Britain, coal miners had of course none of those things. They worked 12-hour shifts and pay was so poor that not just the men but their wives and children also worked down the pit. That is what a 'barely enough' level looks like. Had the men been better paid, it is likely that the family as a whole would have chosen to work less.

A girl pulling a coal tub – from official report of the parliamentary commission.

Figure 8.5: What 'barely enough' wages looks like. [WMC]

Thus assuming that most employed workers earn above the 'barely enough wages' level, then for them, the relevant part of the labour supply curve actually slopes in the **opposite** direction to that claimed in the classical labour supply-demand diagram. People work **more** if their pay goes down, not less: they have to do so to make ends meet.

Note that people may be willing to do some work for less that subsistence wages if they have another source of income outside the wage economy. For example in an economy that still has widespread peasant subsistence farming it would make sense in agricultural slack periods to do some waged work, even at rates of pay that would not be viable as the only source of income.

In a modern economy and especially in one of the world's middle-income and richer countries, most workers will earn significantly above the 'barely enough wages' level. Individuals are not under the same extreme pressure to work because they are able to get economic support from state-provided social security or by living with better-paid family members. So the choices of an individual whether to work and for how many hours, do not follow the theoretical all-workers-paid equally curve. For such an individual the curve is likely to be further to the right with fewer people working for less than barely-enough wages, and the peak employment point at a higher wage level than the 'barely-enough' level. There will not be a single curve, but many, varying not only by place and time but also differing from worker to worker depending on the pay level they can command (related to the demand for their skills) and also personal preferences.

People work more if pay goes down

As stated earlier, the graph in Figure 8.4 is a guess of what a real labour supply curve might look like based on the reasoning given in Table 8.1. So is there any evidence that supports this reasoning – for example that people work **more** if their pay goes down (and **less** if it goes up)? It appears that there is.

Country	Annual working hours [*]	GDP per capita [*]
Mexico	2255	$17,888
Bangladesh	2232	$4,818
China	2174	$16,411
India	2117	$6,118
USA	1757	$60,236
Japan	1738	$41,380
UK	1670	$41,627
Germany	1354	$50,922

* Average annual working hours per worker are from 2017, GDP data is mainly from 2020 in constant 2017 international dollars. Data sources: [14].

Table 8.2: Poorer countries tend to work more hours than rich ones.

Data is available for the average annual working hours per worker for various countries and over more than a century. The data shows that as the world's more industrialised countries grew richer over the last 120 years, working hours generally fell. Furthermore, when we look at the recent data for different countries, we see that the poorer countries have longer working hours than the richer ones – as shown in Table 8.2 and as a graph in Figure 8.6.[14]

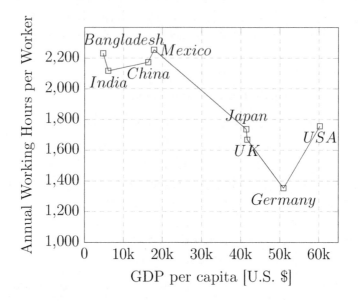

Figure 8.6: Working hours by country.

We can also look at statistics that record how much workers get paid and their working hours. In the UK, one such data set – the Annual Survey of Hours and Earnings (ASHE) – estimates the average and median hourly rates of pay and weekly working hours for over 500 job categories.[15] The graph in Figure 8.7 has been generated from this data and shows how as pay rates increase beyond a certain point, people tend to work fewer hours per week.[2] Note that the more highly paid employees who the graph shows tend

---

[2]The data used is a 2022 estimate for all UK employee jobs; it does not cover the self-employed. To generate the graph the data has been put in ascending order of median hourly pay. The median hours worked per week curve has been smoothed by a moving average to show the trend (there is of course a considerable scatter in the unsmoothed data).

to work fewer hours, are mostly in high-status professional jobs – jobs that are usually considered attractive. The graph cannot tell us how the rest of the workforce would respond to higher pay, but it seems likely that they would also opt to work fewer hours, especially those in work that offers little in the way of job satisfaction.

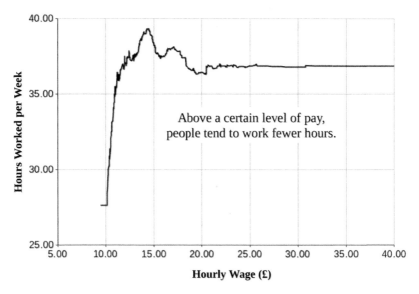

Data has been smoothed to show trend. Data source: [15].

Figure 8.7: Hours versus wages for UK employees.

8.1.1   How lower wages make people offer to work longer hours

To visualise the effect of lower wages on working hours, imagine[3] how a maid on a low income might respond to a pay cut:

> *Maria is from Mexico and now works as a maid in the USA. She earns the US average annual salary for a non-live in maid, of $24,630 per year, and gets the US average hourly rate of $11.84, working a total of 2080 hours*

---

[3]While this is an invented example, the earnings figures for a non-live-in maid are real data for 2017 from the U.S. Bureau of Labor Statistics.

a year. That corresponds to about forty hours a week, with no vacations or sick leave. Maria's employer has told her that he's found another maid willing to work for $1 an hour less, so reluctantly Maria accepts a pay cut of the same amount to keep her job. But now she is struggling to pay her rent and feed her two children. Sunday is her day off, but she's found another employer who'd like her to do four hours work on Sunday mornings, which would approximately make up the lost pay. Maria's oldest is fifteen and quite responsible. Reluctantly Maria decides to leave her oldest child in charge on Sunday mornings and do the extra four hours, rather than let her children go hungry.

While Maria's story is invented, I have little doubt that there are plenty of very similar real-world examples in the gig economy. A documented actual case of falling wages associated with longer hours is that of US truck drivers over the last four decades, whose hours have increased as their real pay has decreased:

Truck drivers in the USA are working longer hours in 2020 than they did forty years earlier. Adjusted for inflation, median wages in 1980 were about $110,000 a year; in 2020 they were $47,130 a year – less than half. Despite this drop in real wages, the number of truck drivers has increased – up from about 1.57 million in 2000 to almost 2 million in 2020. Most truck drivers work 60 to 70 hours a week – working harder, longer hours, and with less job security. – *based on reports in The Guardian[16] and Money[17]*

8.1.2   What about products?

The supply-demand curve makes much more sense when applied to products (as opposed to people, i.e. labour) because unlike people, products are manufactured to meet a demand, so if there is no demand, manufacturers cease to make them and the market clears.

Ideally the manufacturer finds something else to make instead for which there is a demand.

However, some people may find themselves in a situation in which it is very difficult to switch to a different product. Imagine that you are a coffee farmer in a small and mainly agricultural country. It may not be easy to find a crop with better export prices, let alone switch to it and set up the supply chain into export markets. Abandoning farming altogether and producing a high technology manufactured product is almost certainly near impossible. So faced with lower prices, you might easily try to compensate by producing more, rather than less, in order to maintain your income. It is a situation similar to that of the maid and the truckers described above.

Coffee production and earnings

The charts in Figure 8.8 show world coffee annual production and price (adjusted to 2020 dollars). They show a fairly steady growth in production, while the real price has been extremely volatile and was lower in real terms in 2020 than it was thirty years earlier.

To better understand what is happening, we'd want to know how the wages of the coffee farmers have changed over that 30-year period along with the size of the workforce and the hours worked per person. That's beyond the scope of this book, however it does appear to be the case that coffee farmers do indeed live at subsistence level.

"Around 80 percent of the world's coffee is produced by 17.7 million small-scale coffee farmers." – *from 'Assessment of Fairtrade Coffee Farmers' income'.[18]*

Smallholders make up 96 percent of the families who tend the world's 12.5 million coffee farms. Over the last 30 years, coffee farms have become smaller because the rural population has grown and successive generations have subdivided agricultural land; in Uganda the average farm size has gone from four hectares in 1965 to a single hectare by 2019. As farms shrunk, farmers earned less, and they found themselves trapped in a cycle of poverty. 80 percent of the women and men tending the world's coffee farms live on less than $2 per day. *– from article 'The Coffee Price Crisis' in Business Fights Poverty.[19]*

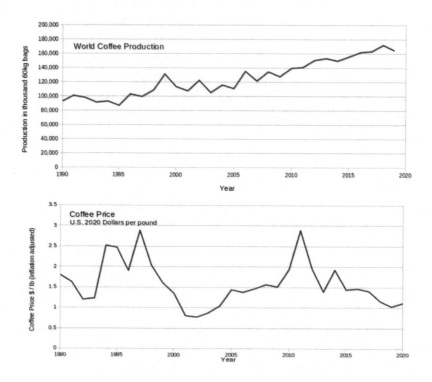

Coffee production has steadily grown while real returns for farmers have not. Data sources: [20].

Figure 8.8: Coffee price and production.

Coffee farmers like any worker, have to work: they cannot withdraw their labour from the market because they don't fancy low wages. Since it is difficult for them to work in anything other than growing coffee on their smallholdings, the 'supply' of coffee has not fallen because of low wages but has actually grown – once again contradicting the assumption made in the classical labour supply-demand diagram.

8.2 The Labour Demand Curve

We've examined the classical labour supply curve, and found that it doesn't match reality when applied to the whole economy. Now we turn to the other half of the labour supply-demand diagram: labour demand. In traditional economic theory it is said that a firm will employ more labour if wages are lower. So a labour demand curve (a graph of Wage Rate against Labour Hours, like the one in Figure 8.9) will be downward sloping.

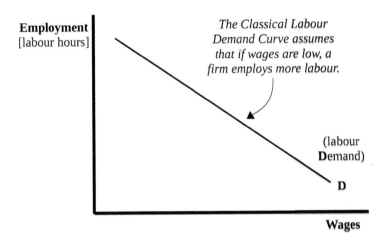

Figure 8.9: Classical labour demand curve.

Classical economics claims that if this true for a firm it must also be true for the whole economy. Typically, they assert something like: 'aggregating all firms to obtain the market demand for labour, we also have a downward sloping curve', which sounds vaguely reasonable. Unfortunately however, reasonable-sounding generalisations are often flawed. By way of illustration, here is a more obviously false generalisation:

> "A group of people are eating from a single bowl of soup. If one eats faster, he or she will get more soup. Therefore the whole group can get more soup if everyone eats faster."

In a similar way, the assumption that the labour demand curve is downward sloping, is flawed when applied to the whole economy. This is because if all companies in the economy give lower wages to their workers, then the workers will not be able to buy as much, so there will be unsold goods, and as a result companies will require less labour not more. Let's therefore explore what the actual relationship should be between wages and employment in the economy as a whole. To understand this, we shall simplify the world into two groups:

1. The owners of all businesses;

2. All workers (who have to sell their labour to live).

Imagine first of all that the workers are willing and able to work for nothing. If that were so, the businesses wouldn't need to produce anything for the workers consumption, only what the owners required; businesses would only need to employ enough workers to produce what the owners themselves consumed. If we now imagine increasing wages progressively from zero, businesses then have to manufacture what the workers consume (paid for by their wages) in addition to what the owners require. Figure 8.10 illustrates how as wages become an increasing proportion of what workers produce, then more and more labour is needed, not less.

An example: a country estate

To make this more real, consider a country estate in a pre-industrial epoch, that has enough farmland and artisan workshops to allow it to be completely self-sufficient. The Lord and Lady who own the estate, who we'll refer to mostly in what follows as the 'owners', want to consume a daily amount of goods which we'll call *OwnersWants*. What a single worker can produce in a day we will call *WorkerOutput*. So the number of workers 'N' needed to produce *OwnersWants* for the Lord & Lady will be:

$$N = \frac{OwnersWants}{WorkerOutput} \qquad (8.1)$$

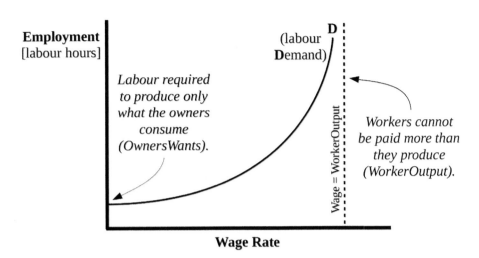

Figure 8.10: A more realistic labour demand curve for the whole economy.

As an example, let's assume that the Lord & Lady want to consume an amount equal to the full-time labour of 50 workers, so: $OwnersWants = 50 \times WorkerOutput$ and N is 50. However the Lord & Lady know that their workers cannot live off nothing, so they decide they will pay each worker a $Wage$ of half of the goods he or she produces every day, and take the other half for themselves. As a result, the Lord & Lady have to employ more workers since the amount they get from each one is less. Therefore the formula in equation (8.1) for how many workers they need has to be modified and becomes:

$$N = \frac{OwnersWants}{WorkerOutput - Wage} \qquad (8.2)$$

If the fraction of what the workers produce that the Lord & Lady owners keep, is called $OwnersFraction$, then we can also write equation (8.2) above as:

$$N = \frac{OwnersWants}{OwnersFraction \times WorkerOutput} \qquad (8.3)$$

So if the owners are keeping half of what the workers produce, the $OwnersFraction$ is 0.5, and putting our values into equation (8.3) we can calculate how many workers are needed as:

$$N = \frac{50 \times WorkerOutput}{0.5 \times WorkerOutput}$$

$$= 100$$

So our owners need 100 workers, producing a total of $100 \times WorkerOutput$ which they then split as follows:

They keep for themselves $50 \times WorkerOutput$ (the amount which they wanted);

They use the other $50 \times WorkerOutput$ to pay the workers (because each of the 100 workers gets half of what they produce).

Figure 8.11 illustrates the operation of the estate with the above split.

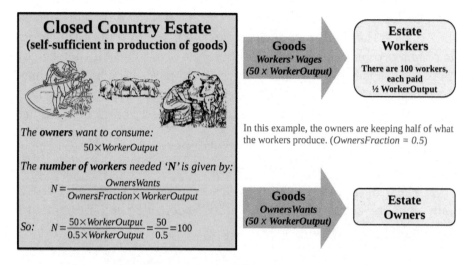

Figure 8.11: Employment on a self-sufficient estate.

Now let's see what happens if the owners decide that instead of keeping half (0.5) of what the workers produce, they keep a different fraction. That fraction has to be somewhere between 0 and 1, where 0 means that the owners pay the workers everything and keep nothing for themselves, and 1 means that the owners take everything that the workers produce and the workers get nothing. So for example, if instead of a half, the Lord & Lady keep only a tenth of what each worker produces ($OwnersFraction = 0.1$), then instead of being one-hundred, the total number of workers they need will be five-hundred:

$$N = \frac{50 \times WorkerOutput}{0.1 \times WorkerOutput} = 500$$

$OwnersFraction$ (the share of a worker's production kept by the Lord & Lady)	$WorkersFraction$ (the share of production kept by estate workers)	N_{TOTAL} (the resulting number of workers needed on the estate)
90%	10%	56
75%	25%	67
50%	50%	100
25%	75%	200
10%	90%	500
5%	95%	1000

The total workers needed to provide an amount of goods to the owners of our country estate equivalent to the output of 50 workers, varies with how output is shared between the owners and workers. A higher workers' share increases the number of workers required.

Table 8.3: Employment on a self-sufficient estate varies with the share taken by the owners.

Table 8.3 gives some values for the number of workers the Lord & Lady will need on their country estate for different values of

OwnersFraction, assuming that in all cases they continue to want a surplus for their own consumption *OwnersWants* that requires the full-time work of fifty workers. Note how when the share kept by the owners is small, the number of workers becomes very large; it is this that gives the graph in Figure 8.10 its upwardly curved shape.

Increasing employment on the estate

From this analysis we can observe that in a simple 'Owners and Workers' economy like the country estate described, it is possible to increase total employment by any of the following ways:

(a) Reducing *OwnersFraction* (as illustrated in Table 8.3).

(b) Increasing the total amount that the owners consume *OwnersWants*, assuming that they get the extra goods by hiring extra workers, and not by cutting wages. E.g. if *OwnersWants* instead of being $50 \times WorkerOutput$ as we assumed in the example, was $100 \times WorkerOutput$, then the number of workers needed is doubled.

(c) Decreasing *WorkerOutput*, the amount produced per worker. We assume that the owners really want a fixed quantity of goods, not just $50 \times WorkerOutput$ whatever that happens to be. So if workers for some reason start producing less per person and *WorkerOutput* fell to only half of its former value, then the owners would want not 50 but 100 times *WorkerOutput*; in other words, they'd need to hire more workers to produce the same amount of goods. On top of that, if *WorkerOutput* decreases, it is likely that the *OwnersFraction* will also have to be smaller, which will further increase the number of workers needed; this is because owners cannot reduce the amount they pay workers below a certain minimum subsistence level if they want their workforce to stay alive. In practice of course, the amount a worker can produce has grown astonishingly since the onset of the industrial revolution and continues to do so. As a result, while before the industrial revolution a small aristocracy required a huge mass of manual workers to support their luxurious lifestyle, by contrast, today's workers can support a large section of the population who are not engaged in production.

Deriving a whole-economy labour demand curve

Using the formula developed above for the total number of workers required N, we can draw a labour demand curve for any specified level of owners' consumption $OwnersWants$. Figure 8.12 shows two example curves. The quantity of stuff the business owners want to consume $OwnersWants$, is expressed as the fraction of the economy's workforce that are needed to produce it (or in other words as a fraction of the maximum the economy could produce with full employment). Each curve shows how the amount of employment increases if wages are increased to give workers a larger share of what they produce.

Suppose the business owners want to consume an amount of stuff that needs a quarter of the economy's workforce to make it: that's shown by the lower curve in the figure. So if the owners could pay the workers absolutely nothing then by definition they only need employ a quarter of the workforce – accordingly the curve starts at $1/4$ of the workforce employed. But people don't work for nothing, so if instead the workers are paid half of what they produce (Wages $= 1/2$), then the curve shows that $1/2$ of the economy's workforce are needed: a quarter to make the stuff for the business owners and a quarter to make the stuff that the workers get as pay. If wages are increased again so that a worker gets $3/4$ of what they produce, we reach full employment and therefore also maximum production. After that wages cannot be increased further except by cutting down the amount the owners consume (making it less than a quarter of maximum total output) which would move the whole curve to the right.

The other example in Figure 8.12 (the upper curve) shows what happens if business owners want to consume half of the maximum that the economy could produce, instead of a quarter. Both examples in the figure are smooth lines because we implicitly assume that all workers are equally capable and willing. So if you go from the beginning of the upper curve where half the workforce are employed, to the end, where all of them are employed, total production has doubled: the second half of the workforce turn out to be just as productive as the first half! Perhaps in real economies that wouldn't be the case: at low levels of employment you might pick and choose the better workers and as employment increases the additional workers might not be as capable or motivated. However, if that were the case, the curves would slope upwards even more steeply.

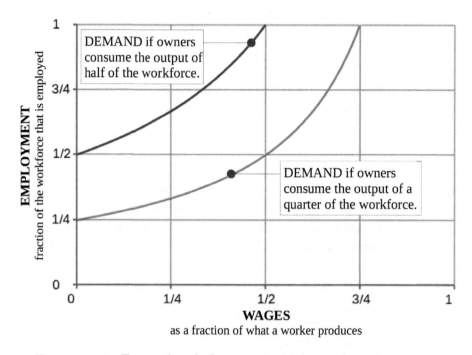

Figure 8.12: Example whole-economy labour demand curves.

Evidence for upward-sloping whole-economy labour demand curve

We have shown that for an entire economy, labour demand curves can be expected to slope not down but <u>upwards</u>, as illustrated in

Figures 8.10 and 8.12. Once again we have a result that is the **opposite** to that claimed in the classical labour supply-demand diagram. So if business owners are obliged to share more of the world's production with workers (i.e. pay workers higher wages), then in order to get what they want for themselves, the business owners will have to employ **more** people not fewer. Is there evidence to back up this finding?

In looking for examples, we have to remember that the analysis applies to a closed economy (either the whole world, or a closed economy within it); increasing wages in a single firm or in a regional economy subject to external competition is <u>not</u> a sure-fire way to increase the demand for workers because competitors who don't increase wages will be able to undercut the prices of businesses who do, thus reducing their sales and causing them to employ fewer workers not more. Accordingly, finding adequate data and examples showing the opposite slope of the labour demand curve may be hard. A possible example could be the growth experienced following the Second World War (WW2).

In the three decades immediately following WW2, the industrialised economies were far less globalised than they are today, and thus had to rely more on their own better paid workforces than those of distant poorer countries. World Trade was a smaller proportion of World GDP and national economies were less connected. This is demonstrated by the figures in Table 8.4 for exports as a percent of GDP for 'global merchandise exports' (i.e. goods) and for goods & services combined; in both cases they were a lower share of GDP prior to the 1970s.

In Western Europe and the USA, those same decades were considered the 'golden years' of rising wages and a strong demand for labour – so strong that the UK invited people from its colonies in the Caribbean and elsewhere to work in the UK in order to fill the labour gap.

During those golden decades the share taken by labour was historically high and rising, and in the same period unemployment was low. Subsequently, from about 1980, the share of GDP taken by labour fell in both the USA and UK, and unemployment rose –

Value of exported goods as share of GDP	
From 1946 to 1972	Between 5% and 10%
From 2003	Over 20%

Exports of goods and services as share of GDP	
1970	12.5%
2008	31.0%
2020	26.1%

Data sources: [21, 22].

Table 8.4: World trade was a smaller proportion of world GDP.

the labour income share for nine major economies (including UK & USA), falling from about 72% in 1978 to 63% in 2011.[23]

8.3 A Realistic Labour Supply-Demand Curve

Combining the revised supply and demand curves explored in the previous sections, we can put them together to get a new 'whole-economy' supply and demand diagram, which is shown in Figure 8.13. The purpose of the diagram is to convey the general shape of the curves – the magnitudes shown are only illustrative. For example, the demand curve has been drawn on the assumption that business owners want to consume an amount equivalent to what 40% of the total workforce could produce: no claim is made that this is accurate, it is chosen only as a reasonable ball-park figure, given that estimates for labour share appear to be in the range 50% to 70% (corresponding to capital shares of 50% to 30%) and that labour's share is said to have been declining in recent years.[23, 24]

It is assumed that under normal circumstances an economy cannot operate with wages of the whole workforce below a minimum subsistence level (the shaded area on the figure). So the relevant

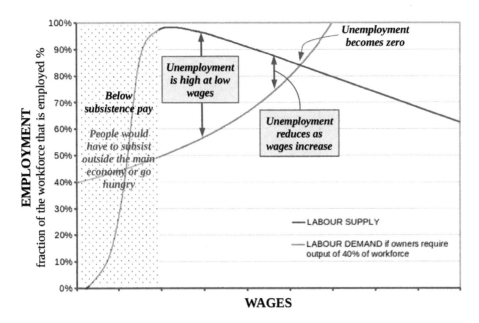

Figure 8.13: Revised whole-economy supply and demand curves: increasing wages cuts unemployment.

part of the labour supply curve slopes down as wages increase and workers are not forced to work extreme hours. Meanwhile, the labour demand curve slopes up, since rising wages increase overall demand for goods and therefore demand for labour.

No magical full-employment balance point

The classical labour supply demand diagram is often used to claim that left unfettered, the market will find an ideal 'balance point' where the two lines cross and supply matches demand, thus achieving full employment. By contrast in Figure 8.13, there is no magical 'balance point'. If labour supply exceeds demand, there will be pressure on businesses in a competitive market to push wages down towards a basic minimum, motivated both by maximising profits and by simply remaining competitive. It is in the interest of workers to push in the opposite direction and press for higher wages throughout the economy, both to increase their earnings and to decrease unemployment. Accordingly, actual employment might be anywhere along the curves highlighted by the thick grey line in Figure 8.14. As wages increase we move up the labour demand curve until it meets labour supply. If wages continue to increase then we move down the labour supply curve as workers opt for greater leisure, and consumption by labour eats into the business owners' consumption which will cease to be the 40% of maximum workforce output that they wanted, and head downwards eventually crossing an additional line in the diagram showing labour demand if business owners' consumption is 20% of maximum workforce output instead of 40%.

That additional line has been included also with the purpose of showing that if business owners are satisfied with a lower consumption level, then the potential for unemployment is greater. This represents a problem for workers should owners undergo an unexpected bout of frugality, or if automation allows owners to produce all they want with ever fewer employees.

It must be emphasised that these curves are for a **whole economy**: they are **not** a recipe for increasing employment in only one part of an economy. If you increase wages only in a single firm or a local economy, then outside competitors may undercut you and take business, resulting in a local loss of jobs, not an increase. So a policy of increasing wages to cut unemployment needs to create a level playing field by means of rules that all competing businesses have to comply with, such as for example minimum wage legislation. Where this is done in one country or group of countries but not universally, then trade barriers will be required to prevent undercutting by other countries where labour is cheaper.

The labour supply and demand curves presented here are of course not accurate graphs but gross generalisations – but then so are the classical diagrams. In reality there is no single curve for either demand or supply, as they will vary not only by place and time but also differ from business to business, from job to job and from worker to worker depending on the pay level they can command, the demand for their skills and personal preferences. But we can say that the curves for the economy as a whole are quite different to those for a single business.

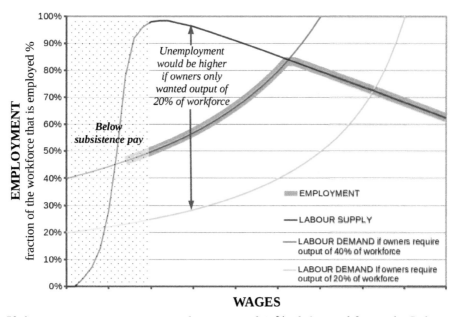

If the owners want to consume the output of 40% of the workforce, the Labour Demand curve starts at 40% and rises as wages are increased from zero because additional workers are needed to make the goods that constitute those wages. Employment follows the grey-highlighted part of the Demand curve up to the point where it meets the Labour Supply curve. If wages increase further, then employment follows the grey-highlighted part of the Supply curve, and owners' consumption will fall below 40%.

Figure 8.14: Revised whole-economy supply and demand: employment level as wages increase.

8.4 Summary

The classical supply-demand diagram does not apply to the labour market as a whole. Workers have to work in order to live, so reducing their wages towards the minimum subsistence level does not reduce 'supply' (their need to work), but increases it since they will have to work longer hours to make ends meet. Reducing wages further so that they are below the minimum subsistence level, is unsustainable as well as unethical as it means that you are imposing mass hunger or worse, and inviting social breakdown.

Conversely, increasing wages above the minimum subsistence level, allows workers to reduce their working hours and reduces the need for every adult in the family to have paid work. Real world data bears this out with the shortest working hours seen in countries with high GDPs per capita.

It seems likely that the same logic will apply not just to labour, but to manufactures or crops where the producer has few options to switch to producing a different product or working elsewhere. Therefore, in order to survive, they have to continue producing even if the price they get falls to barely more than subsistence level.

The assumption that the labour demand curve is downward sloping is also flawed when applied to the whole economy, since if all companies in the economy pay less, then fewer goods need to be manufactured for the workers' consumption, and thus fewer workers are needed.

A revised labour supply-demand diagram illustrates that there is no ideal balance point but a range of outcomes that depend on the balance between the market pressure on businesses to push down wage costs to a minimum, and the ability of the workforce to press for generally higher wages that will increase their earnings and decrease unemployment.

In the next section we will consider why demand for labour is maintained to the degree that it is, and what factors determine the level of unemployment. Why hasn't automation caused far higher unemployment?

Chapter 9

Dynamics of the Economy: How Labour Demand is Increased

The last two chapters 7 & 8 described how there is no guarantee that a market economy will provide employment for all who need it. Yet despite extensive automation of farm and factory work, most people continue to find jobs in highly industrialised countries. In this chapter we ask why that is so and see how demand for labour has been maintained to the surprising degree that it has.

The supply of labour can be altered to some extent by increasing or decreasing the numbers in employment or hours worked by each employee, or by migration in or out of the country. However, labour supply is otherwise fairly inflexible because the total number of workers will change only slowly. It is not possible to create new workers swiftly when more are needed because producing new workers means having children and bringing them up – a slow affair requiring about twenty years – and in any case we don't expect parents' decisions to have babies to take much if any account of the future demand for labour. Similarly, there is no mechanism to reduce a surplus of labour by removing unwanted workers, since fortunately it is not politically acceptable to cull human beings.

So the question then arises, "Why are employment rates in Europe and North America as stable as they are?" Would we not expect the automation of much of agriculture, industry and now office work, to leave most of the population unemployed? In fact there is a corrective mechanism: modern capitalism has created a huge number of new products and services, and has persuaded us to want them. The production and sale of these new products soaks up at least some of the workers displaced from earlier industries by automation.

We said earlier in Chapter 2, that for production to take place there must be:

Want – the need or desire for something;

Resources – the required materials and energy;

Work effort – available labour to do the work.

In a free-market economy, *want* is expressed by people with money being willing to spend it – 'demand' in economists terms. But as we have seen, the operation of the market tends to concentrate wealth. Wealthy people, whether the very rich or just the relatively well off, can live comfortably without spending all their income, or in other words, run out of wants. If they do, then society as whole will run out of wants before all work effort has being used, and as a consequence there will be unemployment. However, market economies also contain a corrective mechanism that tends to create employment, which is that they incentivise the creation of more and more wants.

9.1   The Creation of Wants

In order to survive, humans in a market economy must produce something that we can exchange with others. The need to survive and the desire to increase our share of wealth gives us an incentive to produce products or services that others want. As a player in this market game, your aim is to:

- Maximise the desire for existing products;

- Persuade customers to desire your version of a product in preference to a competitor's as this will allow you to sell more and charge more;

- Create desire in the heads of potential customers for new products that you dream up.

A lot of money is spent promoting existing products by advertising – think of all those washing powder adverts. But an even more powerful way to expand long term demand is to generate a continuous stream of new products and services for people to want. With only two or three products in your shop there is a limit to how far you can expand demand for them: the novelty will wear off and customers will only buy to replace what they have used up. But with an ever-growing range of new products to buy, demand can grow indefinitely. The originator of a new product may also enjoy monopoly profits by being first to market and possibly by having patent protection.

Figure 9.1: Technology creates new things to want. [WMC]

Thus creating something new that people want is one of the most effective ways for an individual or a corporation to become wealthier: as demonstrated by the spectacular growth of computer companies and latterly mobile phone companies. New wants don't have to be technically sophisticated: people have made money by selling socks from kiosks at railway stations, by delivering pizzas, or even by delivering telegrams while dressed as a gorilla ('gorilla-grams'). Nevertheless, many new wants are high-tech because the same technical progress that makes automation possible (thus cutting jobs), also makes an abundance of new technological products possible and with them new job opportunities. Many thousands of people across the world are actively trying to think up new wants, and many millions are employed because of what is dreamt up. It only takes one person to come up with an idea like a singing telegram or portable sound system or smartphone, to create employment for many in the design, manufacture and delivery of such new products.

What sort of wants must be created? It's of limited use creating more desires among the very poor because they have little or nothing to give you in exchange. So instead you need to concentrate on creating desires amongst those people who have a surplus of the goods that you want in exchange, i.e. those with money to spend. Our economy now depends on dreaming up enough 'wants' to ensure that the richer part of society spends its money and so keeps the rest of us employed.

Figure 9.2: 'Wants' for the rich: watches costing € thousands.

It is in this way that the market economy advances, as individuals or businesses attempt to obtain a larger share of the world's wealth by inventing new goods or increasing production of existing ones, that they can exchange in the market. If they fail to do so, then their share in the increasing volume and variety of the total goods available, will fall – and their relative wealth to other people will be correspondingly less.

Our economy is dedicated to finding more and more things for people to want, which produces growth in demand for goods and services and thus compensates partially for the decline in demand for labour due to automation. Because it is based on people wanting ever more stuff, we can call it **'an economy of want'** *where 'want' has the meaning of 'desire'.*

Despite this corrective mechanism, many across the world find themselves unemployed or underemployed.

> **'Unemployed'** – someone of working age who has no paid or productive work at all; he or she must survive on state welfare if available, or by begging, stealing, etc.

> **'Underemployed'** – someone of working age who has only occasional work and whose work is so poorly regarded and poorly paid that no-one would do it unless desperate.

People desperate to survive will search for any way to earn a living. Some economists may regard the 'job' of cleaning car windows at traffic lights as an example of the market successfully providing employment. Alternatively, we may view the fact that so many in the world can survive only via such marginal jobs as 'underemployment' and as a failure of the economy to offer real work and an adequate standard of living.

Given that there is so much emphasis on encouraging consumption across the globe, and so much unemployment or underemployment, we can conclude that what limits the world economy is for the most part, people with money not wanting to consume more, i.e. 'running out of *wants*' in the three-ingredient model. But that conclusion is very definitely **not** a policy recommendation to further increase consumption, because doing so would cause even greater damage to our already fragile planet; we shall need to find other ways to provide employment and livelihoods.

Figure 9.3: Cleaning windscreens at a traffic light: a 'real job' or 'underemployment'?

9.2 Running out of Resources or Work Effort

The evidence indicates that the world economy today is mainly limited by 'running out of *wants*'. But let's digress for a moment to consider how economies at different times in history and in different places may have been constrained by one of the other three-ingredient model limits – '*resources*' or '*work effort*' – and how such societies might respond.

If '*resources*' are the limitation, but the desire for more goods exists as does more than enough work effort, then workers will be in a weak position and some left unemployed, much as when it is a lack of 'wants' that is setting the limit. There would be an incentive to create new 'wants' that require little or no resources, and to minimise the resources used in manufacturing the goods that meet the existing wants.

If '*work effort*' is the limitation, and the desire for more goods exists, then workers should be in a good position to negotiate higher wages and there should be little unemployment, as appears to have occurred in the USA and UK in the two decades following WW2. However, very different outcomes also appear possible. For example the European colonialists in the southern USA and the Caribbean found themselves in large fertile lands but with little available labour – the indigenous populations having been decimated by disease – and their solution was slavery. In medieval Europe, labour shortages meant that serfdom was common: landlords of great estates legally obliged the peasants on their estates to remain with them and work for them.

9.3 Summary

As automation eats away at the jobs that provided basic needs, unemployment has grown less than we might expect because of a huge increase in the quantity and variety of goods and services that can be produced.

To get a share of the wealth, the majority of the population – working either individually or for employers – must come up with an ever-growing volume of products or services that they can sell to the relatively rich, from sophisticated electronic gadgets to cleaning car windscreens at traffic lights.

The pressure to sell also means that society is bombarded with adverts, promoting consumerist and throw-away attitudes. We live in an economy that has as its main focus, doing everything possible to make people *want, want more, and want even more.*

Chapter 10

Dynamics of the Economy: Growth

We have described how our economy has a drive to continually grow production and consumption, and how that growth compensates to an extent for rising productivity, by creating new jobs which replace some of those lost to automation.

By **growth** economists mean that people are on average getting richer in terms of how much **stuff** they have – or more formally how many goods and services they produce and consume each year.

Note that while people sometimes think of growth in money terms, it is meaningless to do so unless the figures are adjusted to account for inflation; such adjustments are made by comparing the quantity of goods and services you can buy at different times with the same amount of money, so we are back to measuring in terms of stuff!

Everybody wants the economy to grow:

> **The rich** want growth to get even richer;

> **Ordinary people** want growth to maintain or increase employment;

> **Politicians** want growth because they need votes. *Growth pleases both rich and poor, whereas helping the poor by re-*

*distributing existing wealth encounters fierce opposition from
the rich and influential – owners of newspapers, TV stations,
etc.*

So it is no surprise that one of the main concerns of economics
is what makes the economy grow.

10.1 How Economies Grow

How then can economies grow? Assuming that resources are abundant and not the limiting factor, there are two ways:

1. **Increase the population.** With more workers you can produce more, but while this increases the total output, it doesn't increase the output per person. In terms of land and natural resources, dividing them between more people means the average person becomes poorer, not richer.

2. **Increase the capabilities of workers.** With better education and technology, each worker can produce more.

We'll look briefly at (1), and then concentrate on (2), being the more interesting case and the one that has transformed our world.

10.1.1 Population increase

Growth of a national economy can be achieved by growth in the population – if there are more workers, more things can be produced. But this doesn't necessarily raise the standard of living of ordinary people because the increase in production due to the extra people is consumed by those extra people. Nevertheless, governments and ruling classes can be interested in this sort of growth: a country's power comes from the total number of tanks and planes it has, not the average per person. Similarly, a small aristocracy can increase its own riches if it has a few more millions of peasants labouring for it. But a large population does permit more specialisation and makes possible industries that can only be built or only be competitive at a large scale.

Figure 10.1: A large population increases a country's power but not necessarily its wealth per person. [WMC]

10.1.2 Increased capabilities

In Chapter 2 we saw that the maximum possible output that an animal can produce, if it works as hard as it can and resources are abundant, is determined by the *capabilities* of the animal concerned – qualities like: strength, knowledge, skill, intelligence. For most animals, these capabilities change only slowly with evolution. By contrast, in just a few thousand years, humans have made huge advances in our capabilities not by evolving but by *learning* new knowledge and skills and passing these on to future generations by education and training (informal and formal).

It is this increase in human **capabilities** that makes possible the growth in goods and services produced per person (per capita growth). Neglecting fluctuations due to weather etc., growth per person can only occur via *technical development*, in the wider sense of technique: knowledge and methods as well as machines.

Following a new technical advance, it may take time – perhaps many years – for the application of the new technique to spread across the world. Reasons why people might not adopt a technical advance include: geographical distance, political barriers, level of education, cultural prohibitions, lack of capital (they are so poor that they cannot save up enough to acquire the new technique). So the growth spurred by the technical advance will be spread out over a period, not a step change. However, technical advances may never spread to some people, because in a world where production is limited by insufficient demand ('wants'), there will be pockets of unemployment and under-employment even in rich countries and certainly in poor ones. What may happen over time, is that manufacturing migrates to where labour is cheaper, thus enlarging the pockets of unemployment in the rich countries and creating pockets of high technology in the poor ones.

The amount of capital employed per worker will be governed by the most profitable combination which in turn depends on:

a) The wage of the worker.

b) The cost of the capital per unit output, over its life.

c) The increase of productivity that will be achieved.

The purpose being to minimise cost per unit output. Therefore, for new capital to be employed it must be either cheaper or more productive than the old.

10.2   Limits to the Growth of Capabilities

Can human capabilities increase indefinitely? This is a fascinating question. Some people believe that we may be nearing 'the singularity' – the point in history when computers become cleverer than humans and can therefore design even better computers, leading to a run-away growth in machine intelligence. But would this be an increase in *human* capabilities? ... Perhaps the machines would just take over. We also may be nearing the point when we can augment our human bodies to increase human capabilities, for example by increasing the size of our brain or by interfacing it to computers.

For the moment I will leave such possibilities aside and in the next sections consider whether growth in human capabilities will run out of steam either because:

1. Technology gets too expensive – an idea within Marxism.

2. The sum of human knowledge becomes so vast that we can't grow it further.

10.3 Will Technology Become Too Expensive?

Marx believed that capitalism had a fatal flaw because as technology advanced, more and more capital (machinery) would be employed per worker, which would steadily erode the rate of profit a business could make. This is based on his theory that the value of a product comes only from the human labour that went into it. So if a business has to buy more capital, its costs (which are *capital* + *labour*) increase and the profit (coming only from *labour*) therefore becomes a smaller proportion.

There are three assumptions made here:

1. Industrial capital gets more expensive as technology advances.

2. The labour theory of value – the value of a product comes only from the labour that went into it.

3. Industrial capital is qualitatively different from labour

All of these assumptions can be questioned, but in this chapter I want to focus mainly on the first because if it were true it would seem to put a limit on technological growth: if capital goods (machines, etc.) were to become more expensive as technology advanced, then eventually any further advance would be too expensive. The evidence of industrial history since Marx, is that this is not so. Let's now examine the three assumptions one by one.

Assumption 1. Industrial capital gets more expensive as technology advances

Is it true that as technology advances, more and more capital (machinery) will be employed per worker? Well it may be in terms of sophistication, but it is not true that the capital will be more expensive. In fact the opposite is happening: many and probably most capital items must be getting cheaper. We can deduce this from the fact that industry as a whole needs less labour as technology advances, not more, and that its declining pool of labour is still able to produce both capital and consumer goods. This implies that the capital items are being maintained or replaced by ever fewer workers, because if it were otherwise and the numbers required for maintenance were growing, then they would be a growing proportion of what is a diminishing workforce, and we'd lack workers to do anything else (which is plainly not the case).

Figure 10.2: Capital item: a 1970s mainframe computer. [WMC]

Figure 10.3: A 2020s laptop computer: more powerful and a fraction of the price. [WMC]

Although it is easy to gaze at the quantity of machinery a modern business possesses, and think: "surely there must be more work in making all those machines that just doing the work without them?", it plainly cannot be true because if it were then businesses that didn't employ the 'expensive' capital machinery, would undercut and bankrupt those that do.

Assumption 2. The labour theory of value

The labour theory of value is widely applicable but not universally so because it does not cope with scarcity or monopoly.

It is widely applicable because:

- The value of something in monetary terms is always 'exchange value', i.e. how much stuff someone would swap you for it. We refer to stuff rather than money because the only way we know the value of money is in terms of how much stuff it buys (inflation is measured by how the cost of a typical household's purchases changes over time).

- When we swap (trade) manufactured goods, we do so roughly in proportion to the hours of human work required to make them. For example, it wouldn't make sense to swap a table that takes five hours to make for a chair that takes only one hour to make: you would do better to make the chair yourself. In practice, you don't need to learn to make chairs yourself because in a competitive market, other businesses will move into manufacturing chairs when they see that they can be traded so favourably and drive the price down.

But it is not universally applicable because:

- Some things cannot be manufactured by anyone, so it is not easy for other businesses to move into the market, and those things remain genuinely scarce. For example, a top footballer earns a fortune, because what they can do (score vital goals when playing at world-class level) can only be done by very few people.

- There are things that cannot be manufactured at all. One example would be a piece of prime real estate with a special location, e.g. a palace overlooking the Grand Canal in Venice. Another would be paintings by a famous artist no longer alive: no more Picasso paintings can be made however much labour you expend, and if you want a particular one, there is only one of them. For things like these, the price is what people are willing to pay and depends on the number of rich people, how rich they are, and their tastes.

So we therefore conclude that value does not derive solely from labour.

Assumption 3. Industrial capital is qualitatively different from labour

If a business has to buy expensive long-lasting capital, it is taking a risk on future sales to pay for it which may not materialise. Furthermore, if a large proportion of the sales earnings of a firm has to be used to buy capital then the profit margin could be small. On the other hand the overall gains have been shared with the suppliers of the capital who also made a profit when they sold it.

When a business buys a capital item such as a machine, it is actually paying for the labour of the people who made the machine. The only difference is that the purchase of labour is typically monthly (the worker's salary) and the purchase of a machine is usually less frequent. To illustrate this, imagine a company that does everything for itself: it makes the products, and it makes the machines that make the products – the 'capital'. At any given time it employs a workforce, some of whom are making the products and some of whom are maintaining or replacing the machines. Whatever the proportions, its costs are always just labour. It simply chooses the best combination of machines and manual work that gives it the lowest labour cost per unit of output. Capital is really just labour purchased less regularly.

Conclusion: technology does not become more expensive

Having worked through the above assumptions, the conclusion seems to be that technology does not become ever more expensive. The evidence suggests that with advances in science and automated manufacture, capital goods can become more technologically advanced and capable, without an increase in cost. In any case we can reasonably assume that businesses would not normally replace labour with capital goods if doing so didn't give them an overall cost (and therefore labour) saving, unless there were some other advantage such as a quality improvement.

10.4 Limits to Growth of Knowledge

Humans have been able to make extraordinary increases in our capabilities via **technical development**, and by passing on this growing body of knowledge to the next generation. Can this process continue indefinitely? It's interesting to consider some possible implications and limits. Knowledge has been called 'intellectual capital', and like physical capital, it has maintenance costs.

10.4.1 Passing knowledge to the next generation

For learnt knowledge to be retained by humanity, it has to be passed from one generation to the next. Long before writing was developed, our ancestors gave their children extensive training. Formally or informally, they would have taught them what plants are edible, hunting skills, escaping from predators, finding or building shelter, tool making, and the language and culture of the tribe. Fast-forward and centres of learning emerged, and eventually formal school and university education. Nowadays our children often reach their mid-twenties before they complete their formal education, and undergo on-the-job training after that.

This represents a huge investment undertaken for each generation. Fit young people who in a previous age would have carried out useful tasks since they were small children, and could be doing adult work from early to mid-teens, now spend 15 to 20 years producing nothing except exam results. Could the amount of knowledge to transmit become so great that the task becomes impossible: by the time you've learnt it all you've reached retirement age? One way to reduce how much an individual has to learn is by specialisation, another is to accept that some knowledge becomes obsolete.

Specialisation

Since the dawn of history, the body of human knowledge has probably been too great for any one person to absorb and become proficient in practising; in hunter-gather societies people had varied roles, and early farming communities who built large structures like that at Stonehenge[1] in the UK, certainly contained specialist skills. However, an individual could probably acquire sufficient knowledge to understand a wide range of tools and machines at least up to a few hundred years ago. That possibility has gone now. Many artefacts are so complex that no one human could possibly understand all parts of them. So the only way in which each generation can learn and use our growing body of knowledge is by ever more specialisation. This gives an advantage to countries that have a large population and densely-populated areas and cities, since they can more easily support the numerous communities of specialists that the modern world now requires. Smaller countries need to either focus on a limited number of specialisms, or make sure that their specialists can participate in wider regional or global communities of their peers.

Obsolete knowledge

Fortunately, every single piece of knowledge that humanity has ever acquired, does not need to be taught to each generation. In industrialised countries, we no longer feel the need to teach our children hunting skills, how to make flint tools, use log tables or slide rules[2], or a host of other technologies that have been superseded by more recent technologies. Although hopefully, small numbers of historians will guard this legacy for the interest it provides.

---

[1]Stonehenge is a prehistoric structure in southern England, whose construction commenced about 5,000 years ago.

[2]Tables of logarithms were used for calculation before the development of electronic calculators; a slide rule is a mechanical calculating device based on logarithms. Both were routinely used in schools and universities until about the mid 1970s.

10.4.2 Storing, managing and searching accumulated knowledge

Writing was developed about 5,500 years ago (about 3,400 BC). Before that and later in communities that had not yet adopted it, human knowledge had to reside only in the minds of those currently alive and be passed on by them to the next generation as oral history or by example. That also meant that it had to be passed on personally: you had to be physically with the teacher to learn it. The absence of writing put a significant limit on how much knowledge could be accumulated by humankind over time. Perhaps it is from this distant past that we have a folk memory of wise sages who have to be sought out so that they can pass on their wisdom, as often pictured in fiction and film.

Once we had writing, knowledge could be preserved over multiple generations without each having to fully absorb it, and if copies were made could exist in multiple places. But copying by hand is laborious so few copies were likely to exist and the libraries that possessed them were very special places. The advent of printing, initially in China and later in 15th century Europe when Gutenberg invented his press, transformed the situation, allowing books to be mass-produced and made widely available. However, specialist texts of interest only to small numbers of people working in that field, would still be printed only in small numbers if at all, and those interested in them needed to visit a leading or specialist library or bookshop to access them. Those documents that were never printed and remained handwritten (or later, type written), were probably kept, if at all, only in the filing cabinets of the institution where they were produced.

Indexing and searching

As the body of human knowledge expanded, the problem became finding it. You might need to make a long journey to visit the expert with the knowledge you needed and hope that they would impart it.

In 1811 a Peruvian mining engineer, needing an engine that could drain high-altitude silver mines, travelled to England in order to buy a high-pressure steam engine developed by Cornish engineer Richard Trevithick. The engine did the job, and he later made a second trip, this time persuading Trevithick to come to Peru. Trevithick was away for eleven years in the Americas. It is quite something to contemplate the length of these journeys made by sailing ship and horseback compared to a modern business trip.

Improved means of transport – ships, trains, planes – made it easier to travel to libraries, or to locations where you could meet experts in the field of interest – at a conference, perhaps. Once you got to a library, you had to find the information you required among its collection; until computers came along, you needed to know how to navigate the card indexes libraries maintained for this purpose, or just browse the shelves.

Another common need is to find a business who can supply a particular product or service. Before the internet and search engines, a variety of paper directories were published, listing businesses by the type of product. One of the most famous of these are the 'yellow pages' print directories published in many countries; each provides an alphabetical listing of businesses within a specific geographical area which may be a town or part of a city. To search across a wider area required finding a whole set of them covering that area (perhaps in a local library), and a lot of reading time. If what you want is only manufactured by one company at the opposite end of your country, or even worse, abroad, locating it was a real challenge.

Computers and the internet

In just a couple of decades, computers, the internet, the worldwide web and search engines, have transformed both the storage and dissemination of knowledge.

In terms of storage, even undergraduate theses are routinely typed up and stored electronically, allowing any number of copies to be made, and if placed on the web, worldwide access. By contrast, before the widespread availability of personal computers, you submitted a single paper copy either handwritten or typed on a mechanical typewriter.

In terms of search, you can find books, documents, business details, how-to videos, and so forth, from across the world without moving from your chair. Where once you would have had to find someone to teach you, or purchase a suitable book, it is now possible both to undertake serious research or study, and to acquire more day-to-day skills such as how to do a DIY task, play an instrument or cook something – quite often from information posted by other members of the public, as well as that from recognised institutions and experts.

10.4.3   Knowledge growth in the future

Humanity's ability to manage and disseminate knowledge, has advanced in leaps and bounds, and clearly with technologies like AI will continue to progress. But could there be some limit where the volume of knowledge becomes so colossal and systems so complex, that we can do no more than tread water? It seems unlikely at present, but the growth in education and specialisation will certainly continue.

Increasing specialisation makes it harder for any one individual to get an overview of several fields. That in turn makes it more of a challenge to design systems that combine different technologies. Teams working on complex multidisciplinary projects are likely to become larger and more unwieldy. A nineteenth century railway engineer like Robert Stephenson or Brunel, probably understood most of the technologies used on the railways they built. By contrast what proportion of today's railway technologies would a twenty-first century railway engineer understand in detail, given the multiple specialisms involved in areas like electrical engineering, advanced materials, electronics, computer networks and software?

Figure 10.4: 19th century engineer Isambard Kingdom Brunel. [WMC]

However, even if humanity's ability to manage and disseminate knowledge did become a limitation to continual technical advance, that limit might still be overcome if we succeed in building computers cleverer than we are, as they could continue to progress – although by leaving us their human creators behind.

10.5   Bad Growth

Growth figures quoted by politicians or economists will normally refer to Gross Domestic Product (GDP) which is a measure of how many goods and services a country produces, expressed in money terms and usually adjusted for inflation (when adjusted it is called 'real GDP'; 'nominal GDP' is unadjusted).

The problem is that GDP includes all goods and services, even those which we would really prefer weren't needed. So for example not only is cigarette production included, so is all of the cancer treatment that occurs as a result of smoking. If you crash your car, GDP goes up because of the cost of repairs and hospital treatment. If the air is polluted, sales of masks, air purifiers, asthma inhalers, etc. all add to GDP. Weapons manufacture is included of course. Crime boosts GDP by generating spending on locks, alarms, policing, courts and prisons. A nuclear disaster adds to GDP for many centuries, obliging future generations to fund the clean-up. If we wreck our planet by climate change, the costs of trying to cope with it, whether through air conditioning, sea walls and flood defences, fences to keep climate migrants from crossing frontiers, or de-salinisation and irrigation where natural fresh water resources have disappeared, all add to GDP.

Some bad GDP is less obvious: perhaps you need a car because the local shop, hospital or school has been closed, or because you have to travel further to work; that car and its fuel add to GDP, and the longer the commute the more it adds! Similarly, if your house or flat is badly built and needs lots of fuel to heat, the gas, oil, or electricity you buy, adds to GDP.

Unsurprisingly some alternatives to GDP are proposed, such as a Genuine Progress Indicator (GPI) or Human Development Index (HDI). However, in terms of our economy's need to continually grow production and consumption in order to keep unemployment down, the GDP measure works fine because bad growth works just as well as good in terms of generating employment. Politicians will happily tell us that they've done a great job providing jobs and GDP growth, even if half of us are employed clearing up pollution or building nuclear waste dumps.

10.6   Summary

The main source of the spectacular growth in what humans are able to produce is the growth in human capabilities achieved by learning – especially about technology and science – and passing this learnt knowledge on to the next generation. This has driven a huge expansion in education, and in infrastructure for the maintenance and distribution of knowledge.

History has not borne out Marx's belief that capital would become ever more expensive. New capital technology applied to production normally results in lower costs per unit produced – if it were not so, businesses would not invest in it.

Large populations don't necessarily produce greater output per head, but can make a country more powerful – especially in the past when warfare required large armies. Large populations can also support a larger educated class, make it possible to have specialists trained in a greater number of fields, and allow larger-scale industries and businesses.

Growth in terms of increasing quantities of goods and services as measured by GDP, is not wholly positive. The reason being that some of the goods and services produced are either in themselves harmful, or they are only needed in order to deal with the harmful consequences of other products or economic activities (such as cigarettes, or pollution by industry), or with the ills of a troubled society.

Chapter 11

Dynamics of the Economy: Booms and Slumps

Most of this book is about the long term trends: what sets the average level of economic activity, rather than what makes in fluctuate from year to year. In this chapter however, we shall take time out to look at the 'waves' or economic cycles – the booms and slumps – and explain why they occur. We shall see that the cyclical nature of the economy is not difficult to understand, although that doesn't mean that the timing of the cycles can easily be predicted.

11.1 Recession and Instability

Free-market economies are naturally unstable and go through cycles of boom and slump. Because we are a short-lived creature, we tend to focus on these ups and downs of the economy more than on its long-term problems, with the short term fluctuations being endlessly discussed by politicians and the news media. By way of analogy, imagine a lake big enough to have waves. If you are out on the lake in a small boat, you will naturally focus mostly on the effect of the waves in making your boat rise or fall. But over a much longer period of time the total amount of water in the lake can matter more: a drought might leave your boat grounded on the lake bed.

This focus on short term cycles means that politicians and the media identify the booms as the 'good times', lauding them as an example of when the economy is performing well. But such booms are not good times for everybody: often a substantial part of the population continue to suffer high levels of deprivation and unemployment. Those peaks in the economic cycle tell us that the economy can perform at least up to that level, but they don't tell us what the best level achievable would be: its maximum. The peaks could be quite a long way below the maximum, as illustrated in Figure 11.1 – we just don't know. So it is quite possible that the economic cycles are just between peaks that are bad and troughs that are even worse; at the very least that appears to be the lived experience for part of the population.

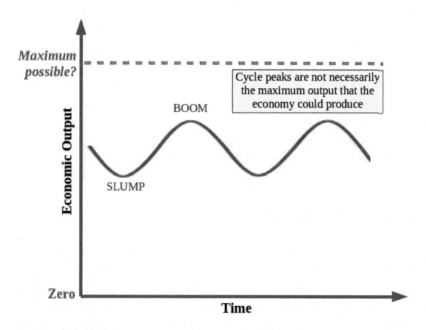

Figure 11.1: Economic cycle production peaks are not necessarily the maximum possible.

The boom-slump oscillations are around a level of employment and output set by how much business owners want to consume and how many workers they need to produce it, as we described in

Chapter 8. Note that the explanation of the business cycle given in conventional economics textbooks is likely to be very different: that there is a natural full-employment level of output, and the business cycles are oscillating around that level.

11.2 Economic Cycles and Positive Feedback

In a free-market economy, changes in the level of activity are amplified by what is called 'positive feedback', resulting in booms and slumps. Positive feedback is a well known engineering term. Positive feedback is occurring if when something starts going in a certain direction, then that very movement causes an increase in speed in that same direction. An example would be a ball rolling down a hill that is getting steadily steeper (or a ball-bearing balanced on top of a beach ball beginning to roll to one side). In the real world a limit will be reached that stops the positive feedback. In our example of the ball rolling down hill, a hill cannot get steadily steeper for ever since once it becomes a vertical drop, nothing steeper is possible; and eventually the very movement in that direction comes to an end since all hills have a bottom.

Figure 11.2: Pushing a swing: a positive feedback example.

An example of an oscillation that occurs due to positive feedback is when you push a child on a swing. You stand at one end of the swing's arc, and when the swing is moving away from you, then you push. This is positive feedback: the swing moving away is your queue to push and make it move away faster. Were you to decide to do the opposite and push the swing when it was coming towards you, thus slowing it down, that would be 'negative feedback' – again a well known engineering term, and a technique widely used in electronics. Note that 'positive' and 'negative' do not imply good or bad; positive just means that the feedback is adding to the movement and negative that it is slowing it.

Systems with feedback can be tricky to control. Suppose you build a robot that is intended to slow down the swing by applying negative feedback. You have a sensor that detects when the swing is coming towards the robot, the robot's computer 'brain' processes that sensor information and energises an actuator arm to push against the swing to slow it. That sounds like it should work, but suppose there is a lag in the system: maybe the 'brain' thinks for too long or the actuator is slow to start moving? If the lag is long enough, the swing may have completed its arc towards the robot and have begun to move away by the time that the robot actually pushes. Disaster! The robot is now applying positive feedback, accelerating the swing, rather than slowing it down. Economies are full of situations in which there are lags between a measurement, implementing a policy as a result of the measurement, and the policy having an effect.

In the economy, positive feedback occurs because when demand is growing in the economy, money is spent on new factories, etc. to meet that demand and this spending increases demand further. The positive feedback works in the opposite direction too: if demand falls, plans for new factories are shelved and workers in existing factories may be laid off, and this drop in spending decreases demand further. Notice that is still 'positive' feedback because it is increasing the tendency to move in that direction (declining spending), rather than slowing it.

It seems likely that new widely-desired products, start or at least fuel booms. If a new thing that people want is invented – say mobile phones – investors see an opportunity to make money ... but first they must spend money to build factories to produce the

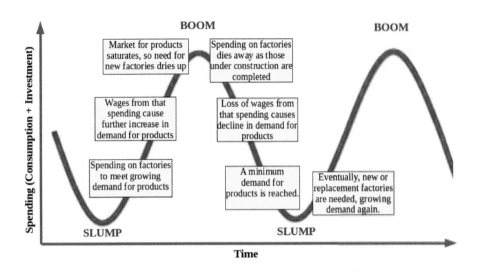

Figure 11.3: Booms and slumps.

phones. That creates extra employment, so there are more workers with money to spend and demand for other goods also increases. There is a knock-on effect because the manufacturers of those other goods may then also invest in new factories to meet the demand.

At some point demand for the new product will stop growing and there will be no need for investment in additional factories. The wave of investment ends and after a lag (while investments already underway are completed, e.g. half built factories are finished), spending on new plant falls; the boom has reached its peak and the economy begins to head down into recession.

However, you don't have to have a new product to start a swing in the economy. In a system with positive feedback, only a tiny movement in one direction is amplified by the feedback, so economic cycles could occur even in a technologically static economy in which there are no innovations or new products.

Since booms reach a peak and recessions bottom out, there must be something that reduces or opposes the positive feedback as the economy approaches a peak or trough, otherwise the movement would not be cyclical but once started in one direction, continue. Peaks could be limited because demand falls off or because of resource or labour shortages. Troughs are limited by the minimum spending people and businesses have to make simply to live or operate, and by increased government spending or speculative private investment. Figure 11.3 illustrates how the swings are amplified by positive feedback, and what limits them.

Standard economics texts describe how business investment to meet growing demand, adds to that demand, but the ones I've looked at do not describe it as 'positive feedback' or even mention the concept. Keynes described what he called the 'multiplier effect': if there is an increase in spending on machinery of say a £1 million, then that increases the earnings of the machine manufacturers and their employees, who in turn may increase their spending, and their extra spending may in turn increase the spending of other businesses and their employees, and so on. Thus the total extra spending in the economy is higher that the original £1 million. This is effectively a description of positive feedback.

Keynes advocated government spending to reduce the depth of slumps. Many governments choose to do this, particularly if the spending is on long-term infrastructure such as roads or railways. Governments are in any case likely to be forced to spend more during slumps, on items such as welfare payments to the unemployed, retraining programmes, and perhaps law and order.

11.3   Credit

Widely available credit will prolong booms and deepen the subsequent slumps. During a boom it is easier for workers to borrow as more of them have jobs and earnings are rising; businesses are also more likely to borrow to fund expansion or new ventures. When the borrowed money is spent it adds to the already increased spending that is fuelling the boom (an increase in the positive feedback). But when the boom ends and a recession starts, workers and businesses are less likely and less able to borrow. Workers are less likely to borrow because they are less confident in their ability to repay; though an exception may be those who are so desperate to cover a current shortfall that they borrow regardless of whether they can realistically repay in the future. Businesses have less reason to borrow because they are unlikely to be expanding. Lenders are less willing to offer loans to either workers or businesses as their prospects of future earnings are poorer. When workers and businesses cease to borrow, they will have to reduce their spending not only to the level of their actual income but to even less, because they must now pay part of that income as interest and repayments on previous loans. The slump is accordingly deeper.

Thus it is, that bank lending to NFCs (Non-Financial Corporations, i.e. normal manufacturing and service businesses excluding the financial sector) tends to track GDP changes, lagging slightly. Lending increases when GDP is growing more strongly (a boom) and falls when GDP growth is weaker (a slump).

11.4 Economic Cycles and Maximum Output

Remember how earlier we said that while peaks in the economic cycle tell us that the economy can perform at least to that level, they don't tell us what the best level achievable would be (the maximum). Perhaps the typical peaks fall far short of the maximum the economy can achieve, as pictured in Figure 11.1. As evidence that this may be the case, we will look at GDP growth and unemployment levels in the UK over a period of 70 years. If unemployment remains high during booms, that suggest that the economy was not operating at its maximum, since if it were, you would expect full employment.

The graph of GDP Growth Rate in Figure 11.4 shows the various booms that have occurred in the UK since 1950 – the periods of high GDP growth. Below that is a graph of unemployment for the same period. Note how unemployment remains high during the recent 'booms', and this despite changes made by governments that cease to count certain categories of people as unemployed; the growth of the gig economy also means that many who are nominally employed have precarious and partial employment. Given the persistent high unemployment, there is no reason to suppose that economic output (GDP) during the recent 'booms' show what the economy could really produce if it were to be firing on all cylinders.

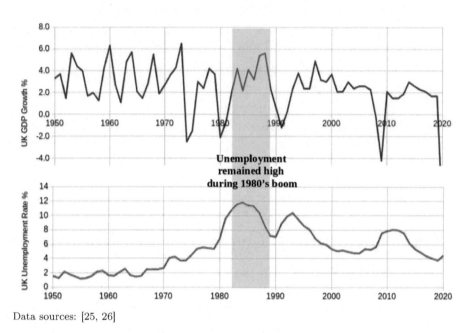

Data sources: [25, 26]

Figure 11.4: During the 1980s boom and later booms, unemployment remained high.

To conclude this chapter, our final graph (in Figure 11.5) shows the UK unemployment rate for the 20th century. There are just two periods when the rate falls to almost zero – the years of the two world wars. Rates also remained low in the years immediately after World War Two, during the decades of high spending on post-war re-construction, Cold War arms spending and the development of new technologies that had emerged in the war.

When employment fell to almost zero during WW1 and WW2, production soared above the pre-war levels. Perhaps then these wartime peak GDPs are a better guide to the true maximum output the economy can produce than any routine peacetime boom? I can almost hear critics say "No, you cannot produce at wartime levels, these are times of supreme effort and are no guide to what is possible

148

in peacetime". Well may be so, but consider that during WW2 the UK's commerce with most of Europe was cut, its shipping routes disrupted by submarines, its cities and factories bombed, and up to about 4.5 million of its fittest and most able were serving in the military. Even under these conditions and with a civilian workforce that had incorporated large numbers of people without previous factory experience, production grew! Imagine then what might be possible if governments were similarly focussed in peacetime. It's not even necessary to imagine, as there are plenty of examples of countries that have demonstrated extraordinary rapid growth, such as the Asian 'tigers', and in recent decades, China. Admittedly these examples of rapid industrialisation may have involved a degree of coercion, hard working-conditions and a lack of freedom. But then are there many examples of industrialisation being achieved in a more attractive way? Certainly not the UK whose 19th century factories are referred to in the hymn *Jerusalem*, as *'dark satanic mills'* and where the working classes of the time had no vote.

Lastly let us spare a thought for the 'unemployable': the people that Marx called the 'lumpenproletariat' – a term typically used to refer to the chronically unemployed, the homeless, and career criminals, who make no positive contribution to an economy. So is unemployment not really a problem with the economy but instead a social problem of too many people in this category? Certainly it is easy to find comments bemoaning the unemployable: one article in the British press quotes a Conservative MP as saying that he recommends vasectomies and that Britain would be *"drowning in a vast sea of unemployed wasters"* unless those out of work limited the number of children they produce; in another article, a teaching official is quoted as saying that we have a significant proportion of *"uber-chavs"* who are unteachable and unemployable.[27, 28]

Well I do not know whether there is anything about the UK's 21st century unemployed that makes them less employable than those out of work in the 1930s, as some seem keen to assert, but I doubt it. I doubt it because what is very striking about the graph in Figure 11.5 is that the UK's huge numbers of unemployed during the interwar years (10% to 20% of the workforce), all of a sudden at the outbreak of WW2, ceased to be unemployed and either became members of the wartime workforce achieving record output levels, or became valued members of the armed forces. Furthermore, they continued to be productively employed for decades afterwards as very low levels of unemployment were maintained postwar until the 1970s (and that includes the demobbed soldiers who re-joined the workforce). The message of the graph in Figure 11.5 is clear: **blame the economy for unemployment, not the unemployed**.

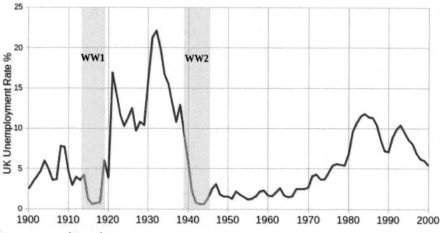

Data sources: [25, 26]

Almost everyone became 'employable' during the two world wars.

Figure 11.5: UK unemployment in the 20th century

11.5 Summary

Market economies are naturally unstable, oscillating between boom and slump. The cause is a phenomenon called 'positive feedback': when the economy grows, increased employment and higher wages increase demand which causes businesses to invest, creating yet more spending, employment and wage growth. Borrowing to invest, adds to the boom. At some point the boom runs out of steam – for example because the market for the latest new product saturates and investment in further factories to manufacture it dries up.

As the decline begins, positive feedback operates in that direction too: declining markets discourage spending by both business and consumers, causing further decline until some minimum is reached.

The maximum output an economy is capable of is not necessarily that achieved at the peaks of the booms. Unemployment often remains high even during booms, which suggests that a higher level of output should be possible if they could be put to work.

Some politicians blame the unemployed themselves for their plight, accusing them of being 'unemployable'. The UK's wartime experience refutes that claim, since the very high unemployment of the 1930s fell to almost zero during WW2, and output increased: the unemployed workers of the 1930s became usefully employed, and remained so after the war as unemployment continued to be low well into the 1960s.

Chapter 12

Connecting Economies

There is not one single world economy but multiple local economies for each product or service, which are of various sizes and interconnected to various degrees. Non-perishable goods can be traded widely, while perishable goods may be harder or at least more expensive to transport long distances. Labour markets are more local given the obstacles and cost of migration or long-distance commuting. Over time these economies or markets have become more interconnected – especially in recent decades. This chapter is about what happens when previously separate economies are joined. It's a very topical subject because 'globalisation' and its effects are a major concern. We shall to try to understand what happens when economies become more connected, using simple examples to illustrate the process.

Not so very long ago there were no telephones or internet or electrical equipment of any sort, the fastest means of transport was a horse and most people got around by walking. It was slow and expensive to transport goods very far, so a higher proportion of goods were sold close to where they were made, often in an actual physical marketplace in the nearest village or town. For the same reasons, international trade was smaller than it is today: goods had to travel by horse and cart overland, and cross seas in the holds of wooden sailing ships that might take months to reach their destination. As a result, much economic activity was by necessity very local, and we should see the world as many local economies of various sizes and interconnected in limited ways, or sometimes not at all as the Americas and Europe were not before Columbus. Individual villages were patrons of their own farmers and artisans: you were likely to eat food grown by local farmers, wear clothes made by a local tailor, and drink beer from a local brewery.

Today, technology has made it possible to trade many more goods over long distances. That technical advance, backed by a free-market ideology that favours eliminating barriers to trade, has caused and is causing markets that were once quite separate and different to become progressively more connected. It is a process that has gone on for centuries – the Roman Empire traded some wares over long distances – but it has accelerated in recent years thanks to rapid advances in transport and telecommunications, and now enjoys the title of 'globalisation'. For all that, we continue to live in multiple markets interconnected in varying degrees depending on geography, political boundaries and how readily a good or service can be transported or offered at a distance. Few of us would travel more than a mile or two to get a haircut, let alone to another country.

12.1   Joining Unequal Economies

Politicians frequently propose better transport links as a way to improve the economy and economists also usually recommend the removal of barriers to trade. But what happens when unequal economies are joined? Breaking down barriers to trade also breaks down the defences of weaker businesses – and 'weaker' may simply mean that they have lower profit margins because they pay their workers better. Cheap transport exposes firms to wider competition and a race to the bottom in terms of workers' pay and conditions. It also obliges firms to expand the area across which they market, meaning that they have to transport goods over longer distances, and resulting in increased costs and negative environmental impacts. The story below illustrates what might happen when an isolated village is connected to a town:

Chang's Cheese Shop

Imagine a remote mountain village where a Mr Chang runs an excellent cheese shop. Buying milk from local farmers Mr Chang makes the cheese himself. Almost all the villagers buy from Mr Chang as it is too far to go by mountain track to get cheese from elsewhere. Similarly, Mr Chang only sells locally as it would be too difficult to transport the cheese to other towns. Mr Chang spends most of what he earns locally too, e.g. hiring domestic help, paying for repairs or improvements to his house. Now developers arrive to sell the benefits of a new road. They explain to Mr Chang that the fine new road will make it possible for him to buy a van and sell his cheeses far and wide. Soon Mr Chang has a vision of a whole fleet of vans taking Chang's Cheeses to the world and making him rich. What actually happens when the road is completed is something quite different. Vans from the nearest large town begin visiting the village and steal away much of Mr Chang's market as well as that of other local artisans. The factory-made cheese of the town is cheaper. Mr Chang is obliged to spend money on a van and fuel, and visit various neighbouring towns to try to sell his 'craft cheeses' elsewhere.

While the above story is fictional, countless villages across the globe have experienced these sorts of changes when modern transport connected them more closely to towns and cities. Within living memory, tailors, shoemakers, carpenters, bakers, and more have disappeared from villages and small towns – the products now being supplied from distant factories, often thousands of miles away.

To understand why and how these changes occur, we will explore the effect on village artisans of improved transport links to nearby towns, by putting some numbers to a simple example. We'll imagine a village and a town which initially are isolated from one another and subsequently become connected. We will assume outputs per worker for artisans and factory workers which keep the maths simple and are not intended to bear any relationship to the real output of such producers except for the key assumption that factory workers produce more per day than artisans.

At first the two economies are unconnected

The table in Figure 12.1 shows the two isolated economies, village and town: there is no trade between them.

In the village economy, the three artisan manufacturers – tailor, shoemaker and hatter – produce one item a day using mainly hand tools. Those items can be swapped for any other item or service that takes the same amount of work, thus one pair of shoes swaps for one hat or one shirt or 10 haircuts.

In the town economy, factories have replaced artisan manufacturers and each worker in them can produce in a day ten times what the village artisans produce, as the table shows. However, hairdressers in the town work in much the same way as in the village, so their daily output per person is the same as that of the village hairdresser. We can see that if people swap based on the amount of work, then in the town the swap rate is different: everyone produces 10 things a day, so you can swap 10 of anything for 10 of any other thing, which is the same as being able to swap 1 for 1. So a pair of shoes still swaps for one hat or one shirt as they did in the village, but is also worth only one haircut, not 10 as in the village.

Producer	Output per Day per Worker
Tailor	1 shirt
Shoemaker	1 pair of shoes
Hatter	1 hat
Hairdresser	10 haircuts

Village Economy

Producer	Output per Day per Worker
Shirt Factory	10 shirts
Shoe Factory	10 pair of shoes
Hat Factory	10 hat
Hairdresser	10 haircuts

Town Economy

Table 12.1: Village and town economies are unconnected.

What has happened here? We can understand that the workers in the factories have become 10 times more productive than the village artisans and – assuming that they own the business as a cooperative or something and get the whole benefit – can pay themselves 10 times as much, i.e. 1 days work in the shirt factory is worth 10 shirts. More surprisingly however, the town hairdressers are no more productive than the village one and yet are paid ten times more in terms of the shirts, shoes or hats they can get for a day's work.

What this illustrates is that as manufactured goods get cheaper due to automation and mass production, then services and anything else that hasn't been automated, appear to get correspondingly more expensive. That is why the 21st century British middle classes possess far more manufactured stuff than their Victorian counterparts but can't afford as many servants.

Then we connect the two economies

Suppose now that the town and village are connected and a few tourists from the town visit the village. Among them is a worker from the shirt factory who discovers that with her pay (equivalent to 10 shirts per day) she can buy (exchange a shirt for) the same number of shoes or hats as in the town (assuming the factory and artisan products are seen to be equally good), but haircuts in the village hairdresser are ten times cheaper – at least until the hairdresser realises that the visitors are accustomed to paying more and ups the prices by a bit. Although note that the village hairdresser cannot increase his prices all the way up to the same level charged in the town because most of his customers are still the local artisans who would not be willing to swap an entire day's work for a haircut – they'd be better off learning to cut their own or each others. Nevertheless, the artisans are a bit worse off in terms of haircuts if the hairdresser has at least somewhat increased prices. Anyone from the rich industrialised world who has visited a poorer country with lower levels of productivity will be familiar with the scenario described: services are far cheaper and hand-made goods that take several days to make can be purchased with what you are paid back home for just a fraction of one day.

Worse is to come

After the tourists put the village on the map, a better road is opened up and goods can readily be traded with negligible transport costs, though the journey remains too long for anyone to commute. In our example this might not change things too much because the artisans are all equally less productive than the town factories (by ten times) and you can't send haircuts in a truck. But suppose there is another local producer in the village – a potato farmer – and that there are also potato farmers near the town.

Producer	Output per Day per Worker
Potato Farmer	1 sack potatoes

Village Economy

Producer	Output per Day per Worker
Potato Farmer	2 sacks potatoes

Town Economy

Table 12.2: A potato farmer near the town is assumed to be more productive than a village one, for our example.

Having little machinery, the village farmer is less productive than the farmers near the town, but only by two-fold as shown in the table in Figure 12.2. This is a much smaller productivity difference that the ten-fold dfference between the village and town artisans. Accordingly, when the two economies used to be isolated from each other, the swap rates were:

- **In the village**, one sack of potatoes swapped for a day's work which is one pair of shoes, or one hat or one shirt or 10 haircuts.

- **In the town**, one sack of potatoes swapped for half a day's work, which is 5 pairs of shoes, or 5 hats or 5 shirts or 5 haircuts.

However, now that the economies are connected, our village farmer is no longer obliged to sell locally but can sell to the town. At the swap rate in the town he can get 5 times the goods (shoes, shirts or hats) in return for his potatoes than he could get in the village. The effect on the village artisans is devastating: not only are they having to pay a bit more for haircuts because of the tourists, but now potato prices have gone up fivefold (since the farmer won't sell to them for less than he can get in the town). Other farm products may well follow suit. Slowly the artisans are driven out of business and their sons and daughters, finding no work in the village, migrate to the town where they can earn more in the modern factories than they could by continuing the traditional family trade.

Note also that as economies are connected via cheaper, easier trade, we can expect booms and slumps to tend to synchronise across the whole market, rather than occurring independently.

Wages in the town

In the example above, we assumed that workers in the factories in the town, own the businesses and get all the benefit of the increased productivity. However, in the real economy, the factories are more likely to have private owners who pay the workers they hire the minimum necessary. Much of what the workers consume will be goods or food from factories and farms that are increasingly productive thanks to technology. Because of the higher productivity, less labour is required to produce the minimum necessary for a person to survive. Thus there is more scope for owners to pay workers a smaller share of the growing daily output of the business. To what extent they do so depends on the labour market: if what is limiting production is a shortage of work effort, then workers should be able to get a favourable share, but if it is wants or resources that are limiting production, then workers are in a weaker position.

Let's revisit our two economies before and after they join. We will start assuming that the factories in the town do have owners (i.e. they are not workers cooperatives) but nevertheless pay the workers most of what they produce because there is full employment and a labour shortage – we'll assume their wages are 90% of what they produce. The table in Figure 12.3 shows the wages producers receive in village and the town; note that as the artisans and farmers are self-employed, they continue to get 100% (although of course they may have some business costs to cover). Wages are maintained at this level because there are multiple factories in competition for

159

labour and if one of them under pays, then workers will move to another employer.

Producer	Output per Day per Worker	Wages per Day
Tailor	1 shirt	1 shirt
Shoemaker	1 pair of shoes	1 pair of shoes
Hatter	1 hat	1 hat
Hairdresser	10 haircuts	10 haircuts
Potato Farmer	1 sack potatoes	1 sack potatoes

Village Economy

Producer	Output per Day per Worker	Wages per Day
Shirt Factory	10 shirts	9 shirts
Shoe Factory	10 pair of shoes	9 pair of shoes
Hat Factory	10 hats	9 hats
Hairdresser	10 haircuts	10 haircuts
Potato Farmer	2 sacks potatoes	2 sacks potatoes

Town Economy

Table 12.3: Wages when village and town economies are unconnected.

Wages when we connect the villages to the town

What happens a new network of roads is built connecting the town to not just one but various villages? As discussed before, village farmers can now sell to the towns and get more goods (shoes, shirts or hats) in return. The village artisans will tend to go out of business and migrate to the town. Suddenly there isn't a labour shortage any more with the arrival of these migrants from the countryside. Since the factories are so much more productive than the artisans were, they don't need to employ that many more workers to supply the villages with goods to cover the lost artisan production. Even better, just look at the wages those ex-artisans are used to – just 1 shirt or 1 pair-of-shoes or 1 hat per day! Surely they'll be very happy if the owners pay them not 90% of what they produce in the factories but 50% (in other words, 5 shirts/pairs-of-shoes/hats, instead of the 9 that the current workers get).

No doubt over time, the wages of the existing workers will get adjusted downwards too. The town hairdresser probably has to trade his 10 haircuts a day for no more than the 5 shirts (or shoes, etc.) that the factory workers get paid, as if it were more, factory workers would give up their jobs and set up as competing hairdressers. The potato farmer near the town might be luckier if there isn't much spare land available for others to set up as farmers – let's assume a bit of competition so his 2 sacks of potatoes trade for 8 shirts instead of 10, and therefore the village farmer's one sack for 4 shirts. The village hairdresser now works mainly for local farmers and so accepts the same wage rate.

What choice do workers have, other than accept the lower wages? Not much given that there is now a labour surplus. They could move back to the village, but there are fewer jobs there now. Even if the potato farmer wanted to hire labour he'd struggle to do so because his village farm is less productive than the larger more mechanised ones nearer the town. His day's production is equivalent to only 5 shirts/pairs-of-shoes/hats from the town factories, so he couldn't pay more than the factories offer; he may even want to mechanise his farm and shed labour. We up with a situation something like that shown in the table in Figure 12.4.

Producer	Output per Day per Worker	Wages per Day
Tailor	Moved to town	Factory wage
Shoemaker	Moved to town	Factory wage
Hatter	Moved to town	Factory wage
Hairdresser	10 haircuts	10 haircuts (= 4 shirts)
Potato Farmer	1 sack potatoes	1 sack potatoes (= 4 shirts)

Village Economy

Producer	Output per Day per Worker	Wages per Day
Shirt Factory	10 shirts	5 shirts
Shoe Factory	10 pair of shoes	5 pair of shoes
Hat Factory	10 hats	5 hats
Hairdresser	10 haircuts	10 haircuts (= 5 shirts)
Potato Farmer	2 sacks potatoes	2 sacks potatoes (= 8 shirts)

Town Economy

Table 12.4: Wages when village and town economies become connected.

Global wage differences

We can see from the analysis above that a country where modern industrial towns have access to a vast rural hinterland in which artisans and small farmers have low levels of productivity, can keep wages quite low, even in modern productive factories, because of the large surplus of labour accustomed to low wages and with little alternative employment. This enables us to understand the considerable differences in salaries available to highly skilled workers, depending on where they live in the world. Thus it is, that a search on the web suggests that in the high-tech city of Bangalore in India, the average salary for Software Engineer is about $11,250 per year (in February 2022, converted into US dollars at current exchange rates), while a similar search for the USA gives average salaries in the range $90,000 to $120,000 per year – something like ten times more.

Figure 12.1: Rural India. [WMC]

Indian engineers can get a big increase in salary by migrating to the USA or Europe; some do, but not everyone wants to leave their country, family and friends, and moreover there are barriers to migration. One of the common barriers is that a job offer is required to get a work visa. While it may suit some employers to arrange a visa, others see an attractive alternative: set up an office in India and employ the Indian engineers there, where they can be paid a fraction of a US or European salary. That brings us nicely to the subject of de-industrialisation.

Figure 12.2: High-tech Bangalore. [WMC]

12.2 De-Industrialisation

Since the 1980s there has been an extraordinary migration of manufacturing industry out of Western Europe and the USA – countries which were once workshops of the world. To the casual observer this seems remarkable – why would countries turn their back on the industries that brought them so much power and wealth? The answer lies in the operation of the market as economies in different parts of the world have become more connected. Let's see how it happened, taking the UK as an example.

The UK was one of the first countries to industrialise. As the industrial towns developed and transport improved, the local economies of town and village were connected as described in the hypothetical example earlier. At first the industrial towns had a rural hinterland: workers migrated into the towns, artisan-made goods were replaced by factory-manufactured goods, mechanisation began to be applied to agriculture. The whole process took a long time and of course has never really stopped: the workforce on UK farms fell from 890 thousand in 1923 to 400 thousand in 1970 and to 180 thousand in 2018.[29] Thus the rural hinterland of low productivity largely disappeared over time and wages came to be dominated by what industry would pay – you could say that the whole country now had the 'industrial town economy' in terms of the simple model used earlier.

CHAPTER 12. CONNECTING ECONOMIES

For two or three decades following the Second World War, industrial economies like that of the UK were far less connected to large less-developed economies. They were the years of the 'Cold War' so the communist block countries of Russia, Eastern Europe and China were mostly closed to western business. In any case, transport and communications were primitive by today's standards: it was still normal to cross the Atlantic or travel to Australia by ship rather than plane, the internet didn't exist, telephony was electromechanical and expensive. With few options for employers to access cheaper labour elsewhere, they were good years for workers in countries like the UK or USA in terms of wages and employment.

Today the situation is transformed. The 'industrial town' economy of the USA and Western Europe has been connected to the huge labour market of Asia whose industrial towns still have an enormous rural hinterland, keeping wages far lower than in the old industrialised countries. Modern communications make it easy for factories in those places to supply global markets. The operation of the free market puts pressure on business to re-locate to these areas of low-cost labour or use suppliers from there, because otherwise they will be undercut by competitors who do so.

Governments in the de-industrialising countries have largely accepted the process because they are believers in the ideology of free markets and also probably attracted by the high profits and low prices possible when using labour that is so much cheaper. The standard answer to the problems of globalisation is that trade leads to overall growth even if certain areas initially suffer, and that those areas that lose out need to find alternative work where they have a comparative advantage. Therefore, workers in the old manufacturing towns of the USA or UK should appreciate that we all benefit from being able to buy cheaper imported versions of what they formerly made, and they should seek to retrain in something else. Yet it's hard not to ask "Retrain in what else?". Since most manufactured goods can now be made in the factories of China (the new 'workshop of the world'), that leaves the choice as being predominantly services, construction and agriculture, plus very high-tech emerging industries that China doesn't yet dominate.

To some extent economies have adjusted. Long-industrialised countries like the UK and USA have extensive education and research capabilities giving them the possibility of developing advanced new technologies. But in those same countries, old 'rust belt' areas are often left behind since the best high-wage and high-technology jobs tend to congregate. High-tech employers tend to choose places with good infrastructure, attractive cities, world-leading universities and large educated populations from which to draw workers. Thus, in the UK, many of the famous industrial towns have not only lost much of their old industry, but also struggle to attract such high-tech new jobs as exist, which tend to concentrate in a few leading university cities and especially in London. Curiously one government strategy that is supposed to address this issue is the construction of an expensive high-speed railway from London to a number of northern cities so that they are 'easier to get to'. However, as we have seen, connecting richer more productive areas to poorer ones doesn't always work in the latter's favour – the result may be that it is only London that reaps the benefits, becoming even more attractive and easier to get to.

12.3 Everything Everywhere and the Environment

Connecting markets obliges producers to be present in as many markets as possible. To illustrate this we'll continue the story of Chang's Cheese Shop described earlier in this chapter. Recall that when his village was isolated, Chang used to be able to sell all his cheese locally. But once a new road to the town was built, several other competitors' cheeses appeared on the shop shelves both in his home village and in others nearby. Customers tend to spread their purchases reasonably evenly across the cheeses available, so as a result Chang now only gets a modest percentage of the sales from any one shop. To maintain his total sales volume he's been forced to spend money on a van and fuel, and supply multiple shops over a wider area.

CHAPTER 12. CONNECTING ECONOMIES

You can see this phenomenon on the shelves of any large supermarket. In Britain for example, I can expect to find yoghurts from half a dozen other European countries jostling side by side with British yoghurts for my attention. At the channel ports, trucks bringing those imported yoghurts pass other trucks travelling in the opposite direction carrying British yoghurts to sell in the other countries. The same goes for scores of other products. Of course choice can be nice, but this level of duplication is only possible because of cheap transport based on the burning of fossil fuels. There is an environmental cost in pollution, climate change and more of our countryside concreted-over for roads.

Small producers may struggle with the need to be present in as many markets as possible in our highly connected, 'globalised', world. Large multinationals will clearly have the advantage over them in managing the supply of products to many shops in many countries, and dealing with the administration and different legislative environments that doing so requires.

Market competition also imposes a different sort of duplication. Assuming again that customers spread their purchases fairly evenly across the products available, producers can get a bigger share of the market by producing multiple similar products. So for example, if you manufacture one type of laundry powder, and it sits on a shelf beside five similar products from competitors, the chances are you may get only one sixth of the total sales. However, produce five varieties of your product so that on the shelf the customer now sees a choice of ten different types (five from you and the five from competitors) and you can hope for half of the sales. Laundry powders are a well known example of this phenomenon, and the many different laundry powder products you see in a supermarket are typically manufactured by a far smaller number of companies. It's not a direct result of globalisation, but no doubt amplified by it, given the greater number of possible competitors.

12.4 Summary

Wages in rural areas with little or no industry are of necessity low since productivity is low. In areas that have industrialised and therefore have higher productivity, wages can rise; by how much, depends on the local labour market. If labour is in short supply, workers have a better chance of securing a large share of what they produce. As industrial towns developed, the economies of the villages connected to them had to compete with factory manufactures which over time displaced village artisan-made goods.

In the older industrialised countries such as the USA and UK, agriculture eventually became highly mechanised and the proportion of the workforce engaged in agriculture quite small. In the early years after the Second World War these industrialised countries had labour shortages that led to improved conditions and pay for workers. Their economies remained relatively separate from the world's poorer countries because of geography and political differences with the communist block countries.

In recent decades, with radically improved transport and telecommunications and with the opening up of the former communist block, western businesses have been able to relocate manufacturing to countries in Asia and elsewhere where wages are lower. Wages remain comparatively low in these poorer countries because their labour markets are affected by a large rural hinterland of low labour productivity.

Interconnected markets may oblige businesses to be present in multiple markets, increasing the transport of goods about the world and resulting in a corresponding increase in environmental damage.

Chapter 13

Environmental Impact of the Market Economy

All animals have an effect on the environment, but humans are having such a dramatic and catastrophic impact that scientists have suggested that we are in a new geological epoch: the 'Anthropocene'.[30] This impact is a result of our growing capabilities due to advances in technology, which affects the planet in two ways:

1. **Population – There are a lot of us**. Technical advances have enabled the human population to rocket: so much so that we are now easily the most numerous of large mammals (those as big or bigger than a cat or dog). In terms of weight humans are over a third of the biomass of all mammals, with most of the rest (about 60%) being our domesticated animals (cows, pigs, sheep, etc.); wild mammals are only 4 percent.[31]

2. **Consumption – We consume voraciously**. Other animals don't do much more than fill their stomachs and perhaps dig out a bit of a hole in the ground to live in. Not so us! Technology has allowed us to produce a great deal more than just food. So now we need concrete houses, shopping malls, motorways, cars, ships, aeroplanes, TVs and much much more, all of it washed down by burning millions of year's worth of

fossil fuels to keep the whole lot running.

Multiplying the number of people by the average amount each of us consumes, gives our impact on the Earth:

IMPACT = Population × Consumption

More people consuming more stuff means more pressure on the Earth's resources and less space left for wild animals and plants.

People on Earth
1900: 1.6bn; *1950*: 2.5bn; *2000*: 6.1bn; *2024*: 8.0bn

Figure 13.1: Once we were fewer than one million worldwide with very little 'stuff'; now we are over eight thousand million. [WMC]

13.1 Why Do We Do It?

Population growth

It's not surprising that we would increase our numbers. It's normal biology that an organism tries to grow its numbers; those that evolve not to reproduce are unlikely to be around for long. Throughout most of human history it was common for children to die before reaching adulthood, so it was advisable to have several children to guarantee that some would survive.[32] In any case in the past people had little choice, since it is only recently that we have had effective contraception allowing us to limit births.

In wealthy and stable countries where women have education, career opportunities and access to contraception, significant falls in birthrates have been observed; a woman's confidence in stable countries, that the children she does have will survive, is also believed to be a factor. Unfortunately in many parts of the world these conditions don't exist. But what has changed across almost all of the world, is that technology has greatly reduced child mortality: health measures like vaccination are cheap and modern communications and transport allow food to be moved to where it's needed if famine strikes. Thus, in places where birthrates have remained high while child mortality has fallen, there is rapid population growth.

Proposing that humans limit their numbers has become a political hot potato. China made the most famous and successful attempt to control population with its one-child policy that was in force from 1980 to 2015. From 1980 to 2021 China's population went from 1bn to 1.4bn. Over the same period India's population has doubled from 0.7bn to 1.4bn and has now overtaken China as the world's most populous nation.

Suggesting that population growth is a problem, especially when referring to poorer less-industrialised countries, is often said to be a new sort of imperialism: the rich blaming the poor for environmental degradation and pressure on resources. Instead, it is argued, we should focus on the enormous consumption per capita of the rich countries. The drawback with this view is that, unsurprisingly, most of the world aspires to the standard of living they see in rich countries. When overpopulation began to be discussed in the 1960s and 70s, the cities of Asia and Africa were full of bicycles. Today they are far larger and their streets are jammed with the cars of the rising middle classes. A plan based on the idea that populations in poorer countries can continue to grow because they will be willing to stay poor, simply isn't viable.

We cannot escape **IMPACT = Population × Consumption**, and we cannot ask other nations to live sustainably if we won't. We need to work out the consumption level that would be sustainable if the whole world adopted it, and where we are currently consuming more, be prepared to cut back. Countries that cannot support their populations without importing vast quantities of food and materials from the rest of the world should at least be asking themselves whether they are overpopulated; my own country the UK is among those in that category.

Beijing: bicycles then, cars now. [WMC]

Figure 13.2: People in industrialising countries naturally enough, aspire to the consumption habits of the richest countries.

Consumption

It's not at all surprising that we want the comforts and luxuries that our technology offers us. My cat likes a comfortable armchair and a warm radiator as much as any human does; the difference being that cats cannot manufacture armchairs and radiators, while we have learnt how.

But there is a far stronger pressure for increased consumption than our natural desire for creature comforts. The free-market economy by its nature, drives consumption growth. Only by continually persuading people to want a bigger variety of things and more of them, can we increase the demand for products and thus sustain a reasonable level of employment, which would otherwise decline as jobs are eliminated by automation. The free market provides all the incentives needed for the invention and marketing of those new wants: businesses, the rich, and ordinary workers, are all united in seeking growth. Businesses cannot stand still but must continually innovate and cut costs because if they don't their competitors will. The rich want to maintain and grow their wealth and guarantee their financial security. Ordinary workers want a booming economy to guarantee employment and increase wages.

13.2   The Earth is Used for Free

Any human activity can result in damage to the environment, whatever the economic system. In antiquity, crop cultivation and livestock grazing changed the landscape, the smelting of metals generated pollution, forests were cut down for construction and fuel. The Earth charges **nothing** for the resources we take from it or the damage we do to it – *if you are charged for a resource it is by another human who has already laid claim to it, not by our planet.* Since we are charged nothing for what we do to the Earth, we humans find it fairly easy to accept damage to the environment:

- We simply don't notice it, or see it as of no consequence;

- We perceive it as desirable, e.g. replacing impenetrable and 'scary' jungle with orderly fields;

- We consider it an inevitable consequence of the activity, there's no way to avoid it;

- We've been told that it's uneconomic to avoid it – the measures would be too costly and affect profitability.

Perhaps the most important of these points is the last. The logic of the free market demands "thou shall cut costs to the minimum necessary to maximise profits and avoid the risk of being undercut by a competitor". The Earth doesn't charge for the damage inflicted, so paying to protect it is pointless charity. There are two sorts of natural resources that businesses can exploit: **resources**

Figure 13.3: Derelict opencast mine. [WMC]

they own and resources that are part of the **global commons** (like air and the oceans).

To own a resource, typically the business owns the land where it is located, examples are a mine or a farm. When the resource is owned, then there may be an incentive to protect it to some degree. If the resource is a farm there is an economic incentive to look after its soils so it continues to produce in the long term (although there is also an incentive to grub up all the hedgerows, slap on herbicides and pesticides, and maximise profit for the owners/investors in the short to medium term). If the resource is a mine, there is no incentive to maintain the condition of the land or restore it after mining ceases, unless the owner perceives some profitable use for it post mining.

Apart from resources that can be privately owned, there are also resources that are part of the *global commons* – that is, they are owned by no-one ... or in a sense everyone. Chief among these are the atmosphere and the seas. Some rivers, lakes, and areas of land also have the status of commons. Economists speak of the *'tragedy of the commons'*, because nobody has an economic incentive to protect them. The concept is simple enough to understand. If you own pond, it is not in your interest to catch all the fish because you want some to remain for the future, and since they belong to you, it is your decision – no-one else is going to take them. But on the global commons of the open seas there is no incentive not to catch and sell the very last fish, since if you don't, it's likely that another fishing fleet will.

Figure 13.4: The seas and wild fish: part of the 'global commons'.
[WMC]

The same logic applies to damaging the global commons. Why should your factory install expensive pollution filters to clean your waste water, cutting your profit margin, if other factories don't have to? Why should you manufacture cars that emit less climate-changing CO_2 into the atmosphere if other manufacturers are not obliged to? We shall talk more about the tragedy of the commons concept in Chapter 17.

13.3 Internal and External Costs

Costs imposed on society by business activity, like damage to the environment, are referred to by economists as **external costs**.

The production and consumption of all economic goods and services have both internal and external costs. The price a consumer pays for a car reflects the costs of the factory, raw materials, labour, marketing, shipping as well as mark up to allow a car company and its dealers to make a profit. After the car is purchased the buyer must pay for petrol, maintenance, and repair.

Direct costs that are paid by the seller and the buyer of an economic good like a car, are called internal costs. But production, distribution and consumption also involve 'external costs', sometimes known as social costs or the losses that are not included in the market price. Examples of these external costs or 'externalities', imposed on society during the manufacture of a car, include: depletion of natural resources and energy, hazardous wastes, spoilt land, air and water pollution, greenhouse gas emissions causing global warming, and reduced biodiversity.

As customers, we are complicit in this environmental damage because these harmful costs are not included in the market price of the goods that we buy. When you buy a car, neither you nor the maker pays for the damage caused by the CO_2 emissions generated during its manufacture; those costs fall on society as a whole and more on some than others. When you drive a car you don't have to pay the residents of streets you pass through, compensation for the contaminated air, tyre dust, or noise pollution, that you impose on them – nor recompense the citizens of island nations whose homes are disappearing as sea levels rise due to climate change caused by carbon emissions. But ultimately all of us will pay the price of a degraded environment, including car drivers and their descendants.

13.4 Can a Service Economy Save the Environment?

Could we get around the 'growth damages the environment' problem by not producing more material products and instead focussing all growth on services? For example, entertainment distributed over the internet is a service without any physical product. If services or knowledge become a 'product' why can't production and consumption continue to grow but in terms of non-material goods? There are several reasons why this appears highly unlikely unless the current structure of society is radically changed:

- There is a surplus of labour (work effort) worldwide, which means that businesses have no incentive to pay more than they can get away with. What they can get away with will be something approaching subsistence, the minimum needed to cover food, housing, clothing, and so forth, plus perhaps a few cheap luxuries such as an electronic gadget or two. This is shown by the size of the worldwide median annual household income of $2,920 per-capita.[33] That businesses will pay the minimum they can was recognised by Adam Smith in The Wealth of Nations.[1]

- Most services are not subsistence necessities. Subsistence requires mainly material products: the needs of a human are mainly material and do not change with time. Accordingly, services are unlikely to form a large part of workers consumption if wages are near the subsistence minimum.

- Income and wealth are so unevenly distributed that worldwide, only a few are classed as 'rich' and the rest of us are classed as middle income, low income or poor.[34, 35] This means that the number of people with a lot of spare cash to spend on non-essential nice-to-have or luxury services, is limited to the wealthy.

- Although the wealthy do provide a market for services, there is a limit to how many domestic servants, musicians, lawyers, accountants, personal assistants, fitness trainers, etc. that any rich person can be persuaded to hire. Nobody wants more than a certain number of people around them.

Even the extremely rich (like the world's twenty-six richest people who own as much as poorest half of the world [36]) are not going to employ more than a certain number of people providing services. However, what they <u>can</u> do is consume prodigious amounts of goods whose manufacture generates employment, and there is a world of businesses trying to come up with such goods in order to tempt the

---

[1]"But though, in disputes with their workmen, masters must generally have the advantage, there is, however, a certain rate, below which it seems impossible to reduce, for any considerable time, the ordinary wages even of the lowest species of labour. A man must always live by his work, and his wages must at least be sufficient to maintain him." – Wealth of Nations, Book 1, Chapter 8.[12]

very rich to spend. Think of billionaires who have their own space programme, think luxury yachts, villas, private jets, race horses, private zoos, and insanely expensive cars, clothes and watches. Those who want influence can also spend on businesses that may run at a loss but serve for self-promotion, such as newspapers, TV stations, sports clubs and the like. In this manner the extremely rich do create some employment, but at the expense of the production of large quantities of unnecessary stuff with its accompanying resource use and environmental damage.

For an economy based on service industries to work, we would need to radically reshape the economy in a way that provided people with an income that allowed the purchase of a large variety of services, but limited the purchase of material goods both in quantity and to products that are not unduly damaging. Our existing market economy will not do that. By its nature it tends to give the workforce only the minimum materially necessary; it has no incentive to pay workers extra to be spent on services not essential for their subsistence.

13.5   Can Consumers Protect the Environment?

One approach to tackling the problem of business that damage the environment, is to mount consumer campaigns to buy from 'responsible' companies and boycott the bad ones. This may be worth doing in order to demonstrate alternatives. For example, environmentally aware consumers may be able to kick-start an alternative, driving its price down and making it become available more widely. Organic foods are an example: once they were available only in specialist health food shops, whereas now most large supermarkets stock an organic range.

However, while there is no harm and hopefully some good in encouraging people to be responsible consumers, it seems very unlikely that trying to persuade all consumers to be 'good' consumers could ever solve the problems created by the uncontrolled operation of the market economy, for these reasons:

a) There are too many manufacturers and products to campaign about. For example, rainforests are being cut down to make way for palm oil plantations, but palm oil is in hundreds of products – foods, cosmetics, soaps, etc. – we would need consumers to verify that every such product they brought had been sourced sustainably.

b) Products from responsible companies are likely to be more expensive because of the extra precautions they have to take. Needy, uninformed or selfish buyers won't pay that extra. Even concerned shoppers may be reluctant to pay the extra for the responsible company's product if they doubt that enough other people will do so to make a difference.

c) The best way to be a good consumer would be to consume <u>less</u>. But if everyone did that and saved much of their salary instead of spending it, then the economy would slow down – throwing many out of work and the government that promoted the policy out of office.

d) It's difficult to persuade the majority of the population to take even simple voluntary actions. UK campaigns asking shoppers not to use the disposable plastic carrier bags provided free by supermarkets, had little effect; but when a 5p charge was introduced in 2015, use of the bags plummeted by 95%. Laws and incentives work better than exhortation.

The evidence is there to see. 'Green' consumers have some successes, but the market has done what it does best: find **more** stuff to sell, whatever the market sector. So the environmentally conscious consumer has to some extent become just a target market for more unnecessary stuff that can however somehow be branded as 'green'.

Consumer choice is also ineffective in cases where you cannot choose an alternative unless almost everyone does. An example is the private car. Not so very long ago, all roads were the preserve of pedestrians, cyclists and the occasional horse and cart. Children played in them, and the only pollution was horse-manure. When cars appeared, if you chose to buy one you gained a significant benefit in your personal mobility but made only a small difference to the total number of cars on the streets. Suppose you as a consumer, would like to return to those peaceful unpolluted streets of the past? You could scrap your car, but in return for giving up its convenience, the benefit you get is infinitesimally small: there will only be one less car on the streets. It is essentially the same scenario described as the 'tragedy of the commons' earlier in this chapter: roads are not part of the global commons like the oceans, but they are a shared space. Therefore, achieving quieter healthier streets requires civic action and government-imposed rules – and the same is true for many other public goods and benefits. We shall return to the tragedy of the commons concept and the example of motor traffic, in Chapter 17.

13.6 The State and the Citizen

If not the consumer, who then can prevent businesses from damaging the environment? The obvious candidate is government, which can regulate to prevent or limit processes that damage the environment. The state sets the rules under which businesses operate, and the state can set aside areas of land or sea to be protected. It is not necessarily a problem for a business to incur extra costs provided that their competitors also have to obey the same rules. State regulation provides the most effective environmental controls that we have so far managed to secure, even though they fall far short of what is needed.

Regulation is nevertheless fraught with difficulty. For one thing, the scale of the problem is continually growing because of the sheer number of products and processes technology makes possible. For another, regulation has to be applied in most or all countries; if it is not, unregulated countries can sell products more cheaply and undercut the responsible ones. Reaching international agreement on regulation is slow and difficult with business groups in each country often lobbying fiercely against, for fear that they will lose out.

As individuals our best chance of tackling the environmental crisis is as citizens, not as consumers. We can press for action at all levels of government as well as in other institutions where we have the opportunity. However, business interests also lobby government; government is not automatically the environment's friend.

13.7 Summary

Humans are having a dramatic and catastrophic impact on the environment as a result of rapid population growth and soaring human consumption per person. The ability to grow our numbers and to produce more per capita are the result of our growing capabilities due to advances in technology. The market economy requires and incentivises growth as being necessary for the rich to get richer, the poor to keep their jobs and businesses to survive and grow. Businesses are under market pressure not to take on costs that their competitors don't have to, such as environmental protection; government regulation is therefore required, thus maintaining a 'level playing field' between businesses.

A shift to a mainly service-based economy that doesn't damage the environment because few material resources are used, is not possible for a free-market economy without government regulation – the reason being that businesses won't pay workers much more than the minimum required for subsistence material goods, and services are for the most part inessential. Business owners and the wealthy are too few in number to consume so many services that the economy becomes service-based due to their consumption alone.

'Ethical consumers' may make some difference but cannot 'save the environment' via their shopping habits because there are too few of them and because the variety of products is too great for an ethical choice to be made or even be available in every case.

Effective measures require collective action. Action as citizens and by government are the best tools we have to increase environmental protection, though since governments are also lobbied by the polluters, there is no guarantee of success.

Chapter 14

How the Economy Shapes Society

Most of us play multiple roles in the economy. As described in Chapter 6, we are *workers* who must sell our labour to earn a living, we are lady or gentlemen *consumers* who employ people to work for us through the goods and services we pay for, and we are *citizens* who have the potential to change society's rules.

The economy shapes our experiences in these roles in different ways. As workers, we may have long, tough and stressful working days. But when we leave work and become consumers, the boot is suddenly on the other foot: we can shout at the waiter or other service staff; we can shop for the cheapest 'best-value' products – thus employing the industrial and agricultural workers who make them for long hours at low pay. Whether or not we play full roles as citizens depends on whether the economy allows us the time and space to form stable communities within which our voices can be heard, and access to the economic levers of power.

Free-market economists promote the idea that if each individual pursues his or her self-interest, he or she will indirectly promote the good of society. Society's highest and overriding goal should therefore be promoting self-interested competition in a free market. However, while the market does provide an incentive to produce attractive products at reasonable prices, that is far from enough to ensure the good of society, because:

1. The market has no incentive to provide decent satisfying jobs. Quite the reverse: the incentive is to minimise labour and pay.

2. As products become more complex and diverse, it grows increasingly difficult for buyers to verify their true quality, rather than just their attractiveness. Some products directly harm the purchaser, such as alcohol, tobacco and junk food. Many others damage the environment and impose heavy costs on society that are not reflected in their price; with continual growth, ever more powerful technologies and soaring populations, the extent of such damage is increasing.

3. The concentration of wealth in the hands of a very few private individuals, corrupts the democratic process as they are able to oppose any control over market ills, through their ownership and control of the media and lobby groups.

14.1   How the Economy Affects Our Lives as Workers

Pressure to find employment and fear of losing it

Most adults of working age need to find a job in order to earn a living. Once independent of their parents they acquire financial responsibilities that require a regular wage to cover them: supporting a family, rent or a mortgage, utility bills, hire-purchase payments for expensive items, and so forth. If the regular wage ceases, the life they have built up can quickly unfold. However, after the Second World War, there was a period in the UK and many other western nations during which a shortage of workers plus strong trades unions, combined to provide long-term job security to many workers.

But today that security is missing because it is the level of 'wants' that now limits the economy, there is unused work effort and the bargaining position of workers is weakened. As a result, increasing numbers are employed in the gig economy where there is no certainty of employment from day to day. Even if you do have a 'permanent' job, the modern economy is changing so rapidly that there is little likelihood of it being a job for life. Working lives are characterised by constant impermanence and insecurity, which make it harder to settle in a location or to take on responsibilities or hobbies that require continuity. The frequent need to move to a new job may mean uprooting the whole family, affecting their sense of place and belonging. Poor quality jobs are usually also poorly paid, meaning that even if employed, the worker may live in poverty or scraping by at what UK politicians have taken to referring to as the 'just about managing level'.[1]

Conditions of employment

The market economy's inbuilt drive to reduce labour costs, puts businesses under pressure to pay the least they can and extract long working hours in return. Keeping costs low also means minimising spending on health and safety at work. Workplaces have not historically been especially safe places – jobs were often physically wearing with long hours, unhealthy conditions and danger of injury; some still are. To these we can add the more modern risks of unhealthy shift patterns, long periods sitting or standing, and lack of exercise.

As well as physical effects, there are psychological effects. Computers have provided employers with the ability to micro-manage their workers and monitor their every movement: a level of control that makes bullying and coercion easy, and removes the worker's freedom to choose how to carry out a task. Mobile phones and email mean that employers can contact employees at any time of the day or night, and during weekends and holidays.

Minimising labour costs entails breaking down tasks into simple ones that can be carried out by unskilled staff with a minimum of training. This also makes it easier to monitor the workforce

---

[1]A 'just managing' family has been defined as one that is in the lower half of the income distribution.

and measure their output. The downside for the worker is dull, repetitive work and a weak negotiating position – you are easily replaced. With no shortage of workers to choose from, employers are reluctant to train, limiting opportunities for individuals to upskill.

Another way to keep labour costs down is to hire on a short term basis, paying just for the hours worked. This was common practice in the past for many manual jobs: dockers used to queue at the dock gates each morning and the companies took only the men they needed that day. Trade unions fought against the practice and for legislation to enforce employment contracts providing benefits such as holiday and sick pay. However, in recent years, business has sidestepped such laws by outsourcing: they pay an external company to provide them with casual workers instead of paying the workers themselves. The external company can be an agency that provides no guarantee of employment and only casual work to people on their books – the so called 'gig economy'.

Is exploitation the fault of business?

Businesses should not necessarily be condemned for seeking to maximise output per worker and minimise costs, because in a market economy they have little choice: it's that or risk being undercut by competitors in which case they would go out of business and their employees would all lose their jobs. Nor does getting the best out of the workforce always involve poor working conditions. Good working conditions and adequate pay may result in higher productivity that more than compensates for the extra costs, especially when the task is complex and highly skilled, and in areas where it is hard to measure the quality of the work in a simple objective manner meaning that employers have to rely on the judgement and professionalism of their staff. By contrast, low-skilled jobs and jobs where the output is easily measured, are more vulnerable.

To flesh this out, here are two examples of jobs, the first being one in which it's in the employer's interest to treat the employee well, and the second where the employer has little incentive to do so:

1. The employer's interest is to treat the employee well: *A bank employs a software engineer to write programs that will handle financial transactions. If the engineer is employed on a temporary contract, treated poorly, pressed to complete the task in the minimum time and over-stressed, then while they might deliver software that nominally works, they have little incentive to worry about quality aspects such as ensuring that: the software is secure (resistant to hacking attacks), is reliable and robust (will perform well under various scenarios, and not crash if the load increases), is written in a way that allows it to be maintained and extended in the future. These quality aspects are hard to understand and measure even by experts, so the bank needs well-motivated, loyal staff to write and check such software.*

2. The employer has little incentive to treat the employee well: *A self-employed delivery driver required to provide their own vehicle. From the employer's point of view, the output and quality of work is easily measured: modern software combined with GPS equipped smartphones, allow the driver's every movement to be tracked and proof of delivery obtained, with the possibility of a fine if targets are not met.*[2]

Meaning of employment

Throughout history up to the outset of the industrial revolution some 200 years ago, most work was related to production of goods and services that can be seen as the necessities of life: food, clothing, housing, and so forth. Added to that would be whatever was required by the church, monarch and armed forces. Most people had professions which would be familiar to their peers. Here are the kinds of jobs you would find in a town in 15th century Europe:

Medieval Jobs: Butcher, Baker, Stonemason, Weaver, Winemaker, Mason, Farmer, Watchman, Shoemaker or Cobbler, Wheelwright,

---

[2]The 2019 film 'Sorry We Missed You' directed by Ken Loach, is based on the conditions of employment of such drivers.

Roofer, Locksmith, Tanner, Tax Collector, Belt maker, Grocer, Merchant, Armourer, Carpenter, Cook, Blacksmith.[37]

Even today, most people continue to recognise those trades and understand their purpose. Contrast those jobs from the Middle Ages with the extraordinary number of esoteric professions encountered today. Many of us have job titles that are meaningless to most of our compatriots. Even if the job title is one you've heard of or gives a clue to the sector, what that person actually does is still often obscure to anyone except those who work in the field. Here are a few modern job titles – do try your hand at imagining how they spend a typical working day:

21st Century Jobs: Project Owner – Retail, Senior Procurement Category Manager, Duty Engineer – Terminals, Chemical Engineer, Compliance Monitoring Officer, Binder Broker, Financial Crime Associate, Python Software Engineer, Mulesoft Developer, Medical Affairs Manager – Rare Oncology, Microblading Tutor, Fragrance and Beauty Sales Consultant, Emergency Planning and Business Continuity Officer, Embedded Software Engineer, Simulink Code Generation Engineer, Algorithms Engineer, Arable Operator, Assistant Growing Manager, Digital Marketing and SEO Specialist, ASIC Design Engineer, Customer Experience Specialist, Scrum Master, Cyber Operations Specialist, Geospatial Engineer, Horizontal Construction Engineer, Diagnostic Medical Sonographer, Web Developer.

Technological development inevitably grows the number of specialist professions, whatever the economic system. It is to be expected that you may find yourself in a job that is obscure to others, hard to explain even to your family and definitely not a subject for small talk at parties. Technology allows the creation of bigger and more complex systems in which many jobs represent just a small part of the process, making it harder to feel part of an overall objective rather than just a cog in the machine.

However, our modern want-driven economy can make such feelings of alienation worse if the objective of a job feels pointless because the product is one of the unnecessary and wasteful products or services generated by the pressure to create more and more 'wants'. In cases where the product is harmful to society or the environment, employees may have to struggle with their consciences if are aware of the harm caused yet need the job too much to leave it. Workers, their trade unions and local politicians, can end up defending damaging industries because they provide jobs; examples are the fossil-fuel industries, nuclear power, weapons of mass destruction, junk food, tobacco, gambling.

14.2 How the Economy Affects Our Lives as Consumers

The free-market economy has an in-built drive to continually persuade people to want a bigger variety of things and more of them. The resulting steady increase in the demand for products has sustained a level of employment that would otherwise have fallen due to automation. In recent years, the level of production does not appear to be much limited by resource shortages (despite how rapidly some are being used up), or work-effort, but by a 'want' shortage – there are not enough things for the rich to desire sufficiently to get them to spend their money. Accordingly, much of current economic activity is devoted to inflating society's desires: dreaming up new things to want and intensively marketing what already exists.

What gets made affects the nature of society. In the past when human productivity was far lower, what got made could be more reasonably seen as the result of consumer choice because most consumption would be for the basic human needs – food, clothing, shelter. But many products in today's economy are dreamt up by corporations whose only motivation is to generate more and more 'wants'. To what extent are consumers really making independent choices, as opposed to finding themselves more akin to putty in the hands of the corporations?

14.2.1   Driving us crazy with desire

An economy devoted to inflating society's desires - "driving us crazy with desire" - might sound rather exciting, until you realise that the desires promoted are for one brand of washing powder instead of another, for a sugary fizzy drink or a plastic sports shoe.

To extract the most profit from the market, companies want to mark up the price of a product as much as possible (i.e. sell it for much more than it cost to make) and sell it in large numbers. There is a trade-off between the two: for example if you try to sell too many, the price you can charge may fall, and you could actually end up earning less. Thus, the advertising industry is dedicated to making you desire a product so much:

- that you will buy more of it, even if you hardly have a use for it or don't need it at all;

- that you will pay more for it;

- that you will choose it even in preference to other cheaper products of equal quality.

Businesses seek out all possible opportunities to encourage the consumer to spend. They build huge shiny shopping malls. They use every means invented to get at the consumer day and night, subjecting us to a barrage of propaganda: paper mailings, billboards, illuminated digital billboards, adverts on the sides of buses, on stations, in the metro, in sports stadiums, on sports and celebrity clothing, radio adverts, TV adverts, cinema adverts, adverts in smartphone apps, on websites, via social media and email, in newspapers and magazines. They target the vulnerable: films for kids with associated branded merchandise; junk food with excess salt, sugar and fat, in packaging decorated with characters from TV and film; supermarket shelves full of these tempting products placed at head height of the targeted kids.

But it's not just the advertising industry trying to drive us crazy; it's a very large part of the global economy which produces less than it could because our society doesn't 'want' any more: it has run out of wants/desires. Of course there are lots of people who do desperately want things out of genuine need and may even be going hungry, but they don't count since they produce no 'demand' in the economy if they haven't got money. The people who could produce demand are the more wealthy who have money piled up in their bank accounts and can't think of anything that they want to spend it on. Accordingly, companies are motivated to dream up more and more products in order to tempt the wealthy to part with their cash. The result is an avalanche of products and services, some of which are genuinely useful, interesting or fun, while others reach levels of ludicrousness or pointlessness that can be hard to believe. Among the latter are wristwatches that cost thousands or even millions of dollars. A quick search in-line found one such for $38,000 which offers "Day, Date and Moon Phase", all of which I found to be available on a $45 watch and in smartphone apps that are free.

While the rich have the most to spend, the poorer part of society is not completely ignored, with shops full of countless cheap knick-knacks (small worthless objects) which might tempt those with only a few dollars to spare. Betting shops and slot machines are common even in run-down suburbs.

Unless constrained by law, advertisers and the creators of new products dedicate themselves to exploring and probing every human weakness in order to tempt consumers to buy, without any regard to the damage that may be caused to the customer, society, or the environment.

Human weaknesses

Plants and animals have evolved to explore and take advantage of every nook and cranny of our planet. In the same way, businesses in the market seek out every way that we can be tempted to buy. There are markets of the most rarefied sort for products that appeal only to small subsets of society. For mass markets however, we need to appeal to the desires most of us share. What are these desires shared by most humans? They are not so very different from those of other higher animals. A chimpanzee's interests probably include something like:

- Food (and getting the best bit)

- Being top chimpanzee

- Mating

- Keeping in with the top chimp

- Not getting eaten by lions

Since humans are chimpanzees' closest relatives, we unsurprisingly have some rather similar interests, as shown in Figure 14.1.

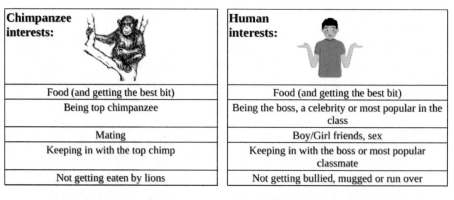

Chimpanzee interests:	Human interests:
Food (and getting the best bit)	Food (and getting the best bit)
Being top chimpanzee	Being the boss, a celebrity or most popular in the class
Mating	Boy/Girl friends, sex
Keeping in with the top chimp	Keeping in with the boss or most popular classmate
Not getting eaten by lions	Not getting bullied, mugged or run over

Table 14.1: Some interests are basic to many animals.

If comparing us to chimps isn't to your taste, you could refer to the five-tier model of human needs known after its originator as Maslow's hierarchy of needs, typically set out as shown in Figure 14.1.[3] Although phrased differently, the overall picture isn't that different.

---

[3]Originally described by American psychologist Abraham Maslow in a 1943 paper.

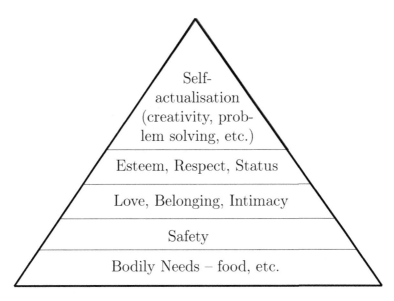

Figure 14.1: Humans have a hierarchy of needs.

To sell products, the market explores all of the human needs that it can, stimulates them to the maximum and exploits them to the full. All profitable segments of the market get attention, so minority interests are catered for including 'refined' tastes in the high arts. But mass marketing goes for the guts, the basic drives we all share – everybody has a stomach!

Humans evolved to like sweet things – fruit is sweet when it is ripe and best to eat. Before we became Homo sapiens and throughout most of human history, we didn't have the means to extract refined sugar from cane or beet. Therefore, evolution did not weed out the desire to consume huge quantities of sugar because it didn't need to, since nobody could. There is a lot of money made out of that sweet tooth. The purveyor of a famous fizzy sugary drink uses phrases like these in their advertising:

Delicious and refreshing, revives and sustains, life tastes good, make it real, love it light, open happiness, twist the cap to refreshment, life begins here.

The UK's National Health Service budget in 2011 for 'targeting improvements to the lives of young people' was £4 million (about $6.4 million), and had to cover a whole range of health issues, not just sugar-loaded drinks. That year the famous fizzy drink manufacturer had an advertising budget that has been estimated at about $3.25 billion.[38] Here are some rather more informative phrases about sugary drinks – but you are unlikely to see these in any advert, as there isn't any money to be made advising people NOT to consume something:

Sugar causes tooth decay. Foods with added sugars contain lots of calories, but often have few other nutrients. Eating these foods often, can contribute to you becoming overweight. Being overweight can increase your risk of health conditions such as heart disease and type 2 diabetes.

Evolution has given us no resistance to the totally new

While we have evolved to be aware of obvious physical threats (by natural selection favouring those who handled them more effectively), evolution takes place over very long time periods. So it is not just refined sugar that is too recent a thing for us to have evolved to use judiciously, but a host of products and practices.

Our hunter-gatherer ancestors were obliged to exercise if they wanted to eat, or go anywhere; in fact, until the 20th century, most humans continued to travel only or mainly by walking. So there was no need to evolve a desire to exercise just for the sake of it. But now, cars and supermarkets allow modern humans to be almost entirely sedentary. Similarly, we evolved psychologically to have a sophisticated social ability – but it evolved to deal with the few people in sight or earshot of us, not with continual communication from potentially hundreds of people via social media.

Traditional wisdom

Traditional teachings show a long-standing awareness of human weaknesses and the wisdom of moderation in one's wants. Of the human weaknesses available to exploit, just consider the 'seven deadly sins' described in Christian teachings: pride, greed, lust, envy, gluttony, wrath and sloth. It's pretty easy to see how you could sell a product that appealed to one or more of those 'sins'. So what about marketing things that appeal to our virtues? Four 'cardinal virtues' were recognised in classical antiquity and in Christian teaching: Prudence, Courage, Temperance, Justice. No doubt there are products sold that support those virtues, but you can see it might harder: 'Temperance' is the practice of restraint, self-control, abstention and moderation ... scarcely qualities you want in your customers, they might never buy a thing.

The Seven Deadly Sins	The Four Cardinal Virtues
Pride	Prudence
Greed	Courage
Lust	Temperance
Envy	(restraint, self-control, abstention, moderation)
Gluttony	Justice
Wrath	
Sloth	

Table 14.2: Sin offers more sales opportunities than virtue.

What it boils down to is that while philosophers and religions throughout the ages have concluded that wisdom and moderation are the keys to a good life, it is unfortunately the case that these qualities are quite the opposite of what you want to promote if you want to sell shedloads of stuff. An amusing summary of the good life is given at the end of the Monty Python comic film The Meaning of Life: "Try to be nice to people, avoid eating fat, read a good book every now and then, get some walking in, and try and live together in peace and harmony with people of all creeds and nations" Certainly not a great sales opportunity is it: a few books and a pair of walking boots!

A book that examined the marketing machine and became a classic of its time, is 'The Hidden Persuaders' by Vance Packard(1957).[39]

14.2.2 Removing barriers to consumption: shop all the time and everywhere

In making us want more, the market is unwilling to leave any stone unturned. Medieval society placed many restraints on commerce: through religion, deference to authority and custom. These have been slowly eaten away because modern capitalism tries to remove any obstacles to making money.

When I was a child there were strict Sunday trading laws in the UK which required most shops to stay closed on Sundays, allowing only newsagents to open, and then only for the sale of Sunday papers and a limited range of goods. I once tried to buy a battery for a toy and was turned away because a battery is non-perishable and could have been bought on a weekday. Shop hours were usually 9am to 5.30pm, sometimes closing for an hour at lunchtime. Wednesday or Thursday, depending on the town, was 'early closing day' when the shops closed in the afternoon to give the shopkeepers a half-day rest mid-week. Working on a Sunday was frowned on as sinful. Pubs had limited opening hours and in Wales were closed entirely on Sunday. After midnight in most towns and cities, nothing remained open. Most of these restrictions would astonish a young Briton today. Nowadays, people are proud of 'cities that never sleep'.

My impression is that most of these changes have come about by businesses pressing for more opportunities to sell, although I accept that among a public educated over many years in consumerism, many of these measures are popular – and like everyone else, I've become accustomed to the shops being open seven days a week. But why did our ancestors evolve the rule of not working on Sundays? Was it just religious observance, or was there wisdom, channelled via that religious stricture: that it is good for workers to be guaranteed a day of rest and for society to have a day of relative peace and quiet? If that was the motive of the 'Sundays Closed' rule, the fact that some of us can be tempted to shop on a Sunday or even like it, doesn't necessarily negate the wisdom of the former practice. After all, the whole point of wise advice is that it works out better in the long run than following your immediate inclination would do.

The continual and accelerating change that is characteristic of our modern economy is very eloquently described by Marx and Engels in a passage I shall quote below. They were however, very focussed on the owners of industry or 'capitalist class' which they refer to as the 'bourgeoisie', and unfortunately that leaves the reader with the impression that the whole system has been dreamt up and is managed by these 'bourgeois' schemers. I believe that we are better off understanding the creation of free-market capitalism in terms of social evolution: capitalism was not the result of a plot by a few people or a class, but the outcome of the actions of numerous people who were merely following their own interests. In the process some people ended up as capitalist owners (or 'bourgeois') and some as workers. Lions and zebras have a shared mammalian ancestor, but there was no lion ancestor who planned a future in which his or her descendents would eat zebras; evolution brought that about, without planning by any lion ... or for that matter by any zebra. In fact Marx argued that the technology that a society is based on determines the type of social structure that it has, i.e. the 'bourgeoisie' are the creation of the economic system rather than the other way around. Accordingly, I have slightly edited the passage quoted below to replace references to the 'bourgeoisie' (retained in parentheses) with references to the free-market or business (in bold), which makes it into a very effective description of today's economy:

> "The **unconstrained free-market** (bourgeoisie) cannot exist without constantly revolutionising the instruments of production, and thereby the relations of production, and with them the whole relations of society. Conservation of the old modes of production in unaltered form, was, on the contrary, the first condition of existence for all earlier industrial classes. Constant revolutionising of production, uninterrupted disturbance of all social conditions, everlast-

ing uncertainty and agitation distinguish the **free-market** (bourgeois) epoch from all earlier ones. All fixed, fast-frozen relations, with their train of ancient and venerable prejudices and opinions, are swept away, all new-formed ones become antiquated before they can ossify. All that is solid melts into air, all that is holy is profaned, and man is at last compelled to face with sober senses his real conditions of life, and his relations with his kind."

"The need of a constantly expanding market for its products chases **business** (the bourgeoisie) over the entire surface of the globe. It must nestle everywhere, settle everywhere, establish connexions everywhere." – *The Communist Manifesto, with author's aforementioned edits.*

14.3 How the Economy Affects Our Lives as Citizens

14.3.1 Participation in community life and democratic institutions

Our working lives in the modern economy suffer from impermanence – frequent changes of job and the need to move or migrate in search of work. That impermanence, combined with the intrusion of work via long hours and continuous communication interrupting what was formerly free time, make it difficult to participate in community life – involvement in things like churches, social groups, sport, pastimes & hobbies, political parties and unions. Job changes make it harder to live close to family and friends, and affect the whole family if a spouse and children are also obliged to move.

14.3.2 Pernicious influence

The very rich are inevitably tempted to run the world in their own interests. Wealth, like power, corrupts: if you are fabulously wealthy then it's very easy and convenient to believe that it is because you are special and therefore deserve privilege and political influence. The public are fascinated by those who build large fortunes thorough 'clever' investing or a successful business idea, often seeing them as sages or gurus, and pouring over their biographies for clues to their success. But are people who build up large fortunes, cleverer or wiser than the rest of us? We should beware of assuming so because:

1. **They may have just got lucky**

   A key element to their business success will often be simply that they tried; entrepreneurs are after all often referred to as 'risk-takers'. But the problem with trying to emulate successful risk-takers is that we are forgetting how many took similar risks and failed. I recall reading about a brave soldier who won a medal by running across a battlefield under fire to capture an enemy dug out. I imagine that such a man is well aware of his luck and conscious that other soldiers have taken similar risks and been killed. Many risk-taking entrepreneurs simply lose their money (or someone else's). The successful ones are not necessarily sages – they may just have got lucky.

2. **Money and enrichment may be their main or sole focus**

   One reason that people get rich is that they have devoted themselves to making money. Most of us want to have enough, but beyond that other interests take over, such as family life. And those of us who do devote a great part of their life to work, are often not motivated primarily by money, but have a vocation; they are passionate about something, be it art, theatre, teaching children, caring for the sick, scientific research, protecting wildlife, or something else. Such vocations may earn you an adequate living (though sometimes not even that), but don't usually make you into a billionaire. So we have to ask ourselves, would we rather have an ex-teacher who isn't rich but understands schools, as minister of education, ...

or someone who got lucky in business or spent their career in banking extracting as many millions in bonuses as they can?

Organised pressure and lobbying comes from those with the money to do it, which means from the very rich and from corporations (often of course these overlap as those owning or running corporations are likely to be among the very rich). They are able to directly fund and lobby politicians and also build public support via the newspapers, websites, TV & radio stations that they own. This means that the corporations and the wealthy, are not only able to dominate any debate – they can also largely set the agenda of what gets debated in the first place. Causes that are of no interest to the wealthy or to corporate interests, must rely on forming campaigning organisations or political parties and then raising what they can from non-wealthy individuals who by definition have less to give, or from the occasional rich benefactor who sympathises.

Data on the funding of newspapers, websites, TV & radio stations, lobbyists and political parties, readily show how many are owned or financed by billionaires. Many of those media outlets maintain a continuous campaign of vilification against social organisations they see as a threat to the business interests of their backers; their targets include public-service broadcasters (like the UK's BBC), trades unions, opposition parties, and the green movement. In some parts of the world this extends beyond vilification, to murder: twenty-seven land and environmental activists were murdered in 2020 – the highest number ever recorded for a second consecutive year.[40]

14.3.3   Threat to commons and public provision

The drive to seek out more areas where the market can operate and make a profit, puts public property and the world's commons, under threat.

Funding for the public sector is dependent on the economy. So a global 'race to the bottom' via unfettered competition makes it a struggle to develop and maintain schools, hospitals, libraries, parks, etc.

The world's commons and public spaces – the air, the oceans, the Antarctic, outer space – are all eyed up as the next exploitable resource. The public will be seduced with promises of jobs and wealth but will end up with a degraded planet and empty pockets.

14.3.4　Sense of purpose: the direction of society

Should societies and governments have a purpose, in the sense of a goal that they strive for? Have they done so in the past? For example, motivating themselves in the cause of:

- Glory – of king or country or empire;

- Ideology – communism, capitalist democracy, fascism;

- Religion;

- Sociopolitical ends – welfare state, education and well-being of population, wealth, happiness.

Some consider that modern free-market societies do not need and should not have any collective overall sense of direction. Instead, the individual should be sacrosanct and the only purpose of government is to create the conditions in which individuals can find their own fulfilment. But individual citizens are too disparate and isolated to be able to influence policy on a day-to-day basis. Such influence as they have, and then only in democracies, is limited to the rather blunt instrument of being allowed a vote every few years to choose between a small number of political-party slates, that are marketed to them in an election.

It can be argued that citizens get to choose the direction of the economy by their purchases, but they can only do that as individuals or to a limited extent via clubs, societies and charities that they support. They don't participate in decisions about where the serious money goes. That is decided by national government, corporations and the very rich.

Humanity's goal is now just 'Sell More Stuff'

So what does set the direction of society? Corporations and the very rich are forever on the lookout for new things to market. As technological development throws up new possibilities, they seize on every new product opportunity regardless of any consideration of its effect on society, the sole consideration being whether they can sell it at a profit. They and their owners lobby government to remove controls and regulations that limit what they can sell. Where controls continue or are strengthened, it is often only because of overwhelming evidence and a tooth-and-nail fight against corporate interests, such as in the case of tobacco.

So for example fizzy & energy drinks, junk food, alcopops, addictive or violent video games, and addictive social media platforms that allow on-line abuse, all exist not because after careful consideration society thought we could benefit from them, but simply because there's money to be made and no law against them. Only when the damage is done and the negative effects appear does society struggle to catch up and consider some sort of regulation or limit, but then lawmakers have not only to face down the suppliers of the product, but also deal with the generation of addicts that has been created.

Where are the risk assessments? In the UK as no doubt in many other countries, 'risk assessments' are often requested for activities that are fairly innocuous – taking children on certain types of school trip for example. Some may regard this as 'health and safety gone mad' and others as a sensible precaution. But what is really astonishing is that while a risk assessment may be considered necessary for a school outing, no such risk assessment was required for introducing into the bedrooms of the nation's children, equipment that gives them access to extreme violence and pornography, and bombards them with advertising, misinformation and conspiracy theories. While any adults helping in a school or on a school trip who may be alone with children, will be required to have a criminal record check,[4] the tech companies have provided unsupervised access to our children by random and often anonymous adults from anywhere in the world, without any checks on their identity whatsoever, let alone a criminal record check.

For more about the effects of the smartphone and internet access on children's mental health, see the work of US social psychologist Jonathan Haidt who has a book on the subject: The Anxious Generation.[41] Smartphones however, are merely one example. There are a host of products that are marketed at children and adults that are a major threat to physical and mental health, and that have never had to go through the risk assessments that are imposed on bodies like schools – which are after all far more likely to care for the pupils in their charge than private companies seeking only to make a profit from them. The avalanche of new products constitutes a vast experiment with the mental and physical well-being of the population, which we are carrying out blindly.

An Alternative?   Surprisingly few societies have seriously proposed a goal other than maximising the amount of cash we make out of each other. However, Bhutan – a small, landlocked country in South Asia – has adopted a philosophy of promoting Gross National Happiness over GDP (Gross Domestic Product).[42] Surely the rest of the world ought to be capable of finding an alternative to the current GDP obsession of most countries with its destructive tendency to maximise the amount of garbage produced?

14.4   Summary

The goal adopted by the modern free-market economy is 'produce and sell more stuff'. This goal overrides responsibilities to provide decent jobs and livelihoods, protect the environment, and promote the happiness, health and fulfilment of the population. An uncontrolled market actually incentivises low levels of employment, low pay, wanton consumerism and damage to the environment. It also

---

[4]In the UK, a DBS check – Disclosure and Barring Service.

leads to gross inequalities and unwarranted interference in public life by the very rich in pursuit of their interests.

Free-market purists will argue that it is no business of the state to promote goals such as decent jobs, the environment, happiness, health and fulfilment, which should all be left to individuals and consumer choice. But isolated individuals subject to a barrage of advertising, are in no position to achieve those goals, which require social action not individual action. As a result it is unfettered corporate interests and the wealthy, who primarily set the direction of society.

Collective action is required to achieve those other goals. There is no reason why society cannot have a collective view as well as an individual one – indeed, multiple collective views, as the state need not and ideally should not be the only actor. The free market can be a valuable tool, but governed and controlled by broader human values.

Chapter 15

Spending Alone or Together – Private or Public

Neoliberal free-market ideology promulgates the idea that taxes are bad and that if individuals were allowed to keep for themselves the money that they currently pay in taxes, they would spend it in a better way than the government does. The US economist Milton Friedman made the case by describing four ways in which he says money is spent. He described them in an interview with Fox News, and they are widely quoted by free-market think tanks.[43, 44] A summary of them is given below, and then we will review their validity.

Friedman's 'Four ways in which money is spent':

1. *You spend your own money on yourself.* When you do that, you pay attention to both the quality of what you are buying and good value (best price).

2. *You spend your own money on somebody else.* For example a gift. In that case you are less concerned about quality since it isn't for you, but still care about getting a good price.

3. *You spend somebody else's money on yourself.* Such as when buying a business lunch with a corporate credit card. Then you aim to get great value but don't care about the cost.

4. *You spend other people's money on other people.* Then you are not much bothered about the quality of what you are buying since it's not for you, and don't care much about the expense either since it's not your money. This, says Friedman, describes how government money is spent.

Friedman's argument is easily understood and sounds commonsensical – but does it really match reality? For example the so called 'second' and 'third' ways are hardly relevant or serious: few of us have so much money that we can hand out a large proportion of it in gifts, or let someone else run amok with our credit cards. He also omits the most common way that we do spend our money on others which is supporting our children and families.

However, his main charge is of course the last point: he believes that government spending is inefficient, resulting in worse quality and higher costs. Let's take this apart bit by bit. First there is simply the phrasing 'other people's money on other people' which ignores the fact that all of us, including politicians and government employees, are taxpayers, and equally that all of us benefit from good national services and infrastructure. Added to which, many countries have developed strong traditions of public service and duty. So it would be perfectly reasonable to use instead the phrase 'spending our money on ourselves'.

Even more questionable is the assumption of worse quality and higher costs. The UK has a public body called The National Institute for Health and Care Excellence, known by the acronym NICE.[45] It provides national guidance and advice to improve health and social care. To do so it brings together experts in numerous fields, and it provides that guidance to the UK's National Health Service (NHS). There are now many thousands of drugs, and medical interventions. No individual patient, or for that matter individual doctor, could hope to evaluate them and make an informed choice. So NICE is an example of how government can bring expertise to bear resulting in far superior estimates of the quality of medical products and services than an individual or single business could possibly make.

So government can marshal greater expertise to ensure quality, what then about cost? Once the most effective drugs have been identified, a state health service has far greater clout and knowledge when it comes to negotiating with drug companies on price. Contrast that with the plethora of branded over-the-counter creams, pills and vitamins on sale to the public, many of which are of doubtful benefit, or even where effective are merely a cheap generic ingredient like paracetamol, spiced up with flavouring and colouring and sold at an inflated price. In this example and many others, there is every reason to suppose that good government can get better value than individuals could.

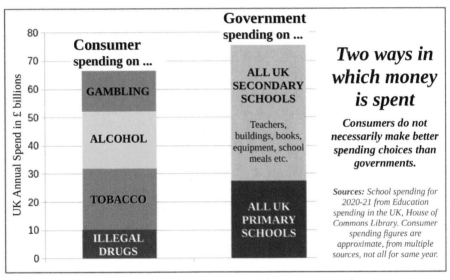

UK private spending on tobacco and illegal drugs is more than government spending on the UK's 20,000 primary schools.[46, 47, 48, 49, 50, 51]

Figure 15.1: What is better value: schools, or tobacco & drugs?

We have seen that government can make better quality judgements and get better value, but there is a further aspect that Friedman's schema ignores: that of what gets bought. Governments can spend on major long term public projects, but individuals cannot. For example, some of the most important health interventions are things like clean water, effective sewers & waste treatment, clean air, and mass vaccination programmes. You don't buy those in a shop. Figure 15.1 shows how UK consumers spend almost as much on gambling, alcohol, tobacco and illegal drugs, as the entire UK government's schools budget. The money citizens have after taxation is for them to spend on themselves, and it's their choice how to spend it. Nor would it be realistic to expect consumers en masse to club together to fund a national education system: that's the job of government. But most of us probably can agree that the UK government, by providing the nation's 20,000 primary schools for less than UK consumers spend on tobacco and illicit drugs, get better value for the money.

Of course Friedman has a point that public spending incurs a risk of poor administration or even corruption. But it is a risk we have to run if we want a country worth living in, because when we the public spend as individuals, we cannot buy a museum, park or subsidised rail network. These things can only be planned and financed collectively through some layer of government; when done well, they hugely enrich society.

Yet what Friedman does highlight, albeit unintentionally, is the limited range of choices we have in terms of how to spend as a community. In a typical western democracy, the public can choose how they spend their own money as individuals but are likely to feel that they have little influence on government or corporate spending decisions, because such influence as they do have is exercised only indirectly in the following two ways:

1. ***Democratically*** – Through the vote they can influence who is in power and thus the spending choices of government, but only once every few years, and many people won't have voted for the winning party. In some voting systems such as the UK's 'first past the post' the ruling party can win a large majority of parliamentary seats with well below 50% of the vote.[1] Even if you did vote for the ruling party it is frequently on a 'least-worst' basis, without supporting many of its policies. It's easy therefore to see why people can feel disconnected

---

[1]No UK government has won 50% or more of the vote since 1935.

from government decisions.

2. *As Consumers* – Through their purchasing decisions they affect the market for products which may in turn affect investment decisions by business, although it is rare that individual customers can point to a change that they feel that they have directly brought about in this way.

The problem is that there is a big gap between the individual and family level of decision-making, and the level at which local and national government decisions are made. Take a moment to consider what communities you are part of that take spending decisions. You may end up with a list of spending levels something like this:

1. **Individual Spending** – what you decide by yourself to spend.

2. **Family Spending** – what you and your family (or the people you live with) decide together to spend.

3. **Social Spending via voluntary societies** – groups you belong and donate to, and whose spending you may have some say over, such as churches, community groups and charities.

4. **Social Spending via local and national government**.

Almost all of our after-tax spending occurs at the individual and family levels 1 and 2. Collective spending via donations to community groups, while very valuable for society, is far smaller – many such groups are charities, so figures for charitable giving may give us an indication of what we may be contributing and spending at level 3 the voluntary level (giving by individuals varies by country, but appears to be typically less than 1% of GDP [52, 53]).

Our tax gets spent at level 4 by local and national government. Most people live in countries whose national governments rule over many tens of millions of people and therefore inevitably feel remote to individual citizens. Even local government can be pretty big –

where I live in the UK there are two local levels, one covering about 350,000 people and the next 9 million.

So the levels close to most of us are 1 and 2, where we can take decisions by ourselves or with our family. There is then a huge jump from the family level to what may be the local government of a whole town or city and the national government, as can be seen in Table 15.1. Little wonder that there is not much feeling of participating in public life.

LEVEL	Size of Group	Proportion of Spending
Individual:	1*	Large: About half or so
Family:	Commonly 2 to 4, rarely above 6**	
Voluntary societies:	10 to a few hundred, or many thousands if a national charity	Small: may be 1% or so
Local government:	Tens of thousands to a few million	Large: About half or so
National government:	Tens of millions to a billion	

* 28% of UK households in 2020 are one-person households (about 12% of the UK population). ** In 2020 the average household size in the UK was 2.4; only 0.6% households in the UK had seven or more people.[54]

Table 15.1: Social levels at which spending decisions are taken.

15.1   The Need for Public Spending

Once our homes are comfortable, there is little extra happiness to be gained by filling them with ever more gadgets and knick-knacks. There is a great deal of felicity however in living in a fine city with beautiful public spaces and facilities, and not in a polluted featureless suburbia with nothing to offer except shopping malls and petrol stations.

Consumers normally purchase goods as individuals or families. However, most of the things in our surroundings that promote well-being, cannot generally be supplied on an individual basis. That goes for decent infrastructure: electric power, water, roads, railways, trams, buses, and metros. It goes for essential services: police, firefighters, defence, schools and universities. It goes for care: universal public health care, old age pensions, and social services. To these basic benefits, we can add many of the pleasures in life: city parks and gardens, national parks and wild areas, the great public museums, art galleries and concert halls, trusted and regulated public service broadcasters that are so essential to balance the output of a media that is otherwise mostly owned and acting in the interest of billionaires.

In cases where such things can be supplied on an exclusive basis it may be that the market will provide a few of them: swimming pools are often now provided by exclusive health clubs, paid for by the subscriptions of members. But where it is difficult or impossible to make a good or service exclusive, it will need to be supplied by government (or occasionally if you're lucky, a philanthropist). This is because only government can oblige everyone to contribute to the cost via taxation. Although in theory individuals could organise a group to supply the good or service, in practice they are likely to be put off by the prospect of incurring all the costs themselves while others partake of the benefits without contributing – known as 'free-riding'.

Government can also supply public goods more efficiently and widely: an annual subscription to a health club in the UK can easily cost as much as the typical local council tax bill for the year, yet for that money the councils supply not only public swimming pools but numerous other services including housing, education, libraries, social services, parks, roads, street-lights, refuse collection, recycling, public transport, and a myriad of others.

15.2 Public Property and Ownership

As much as we need public property, it does appear to be harder to create a sense of ownership in the population. It's common to see public property misused or vandalised, often by people who live in the area and for whose benefit it was built. It seems that people tend to view public property as belonging to no-one. Naturally enough most people's first concern is to look after and protect their own property. But it's also noticeable that people are inclined to respect the <u>personal</u> property of others – it is unusual to see graffiti on cars and private houses even though they are much more accessible targets than trains and public buildings. Presumably this is because public property belongs to organisations that are perceived as remote and impersonal, and that individual citizens don't easily identify with. This attitude extends to the size of businesses: it is common to hear the view that stealing from a large supermarket chain is not as bad as stealing from a family-run corner shop.

Figure 15.2: Public property attracts more graffiti than private.
[WMC]

The lack of a feeling of 'ownership' of public property may partly be due to the huge gap between the level of the individual and family, at which most of us have control over spending, and the remoteness of the next level up of governance – typically the city council. As a result there is a sharp cut-off between private space and public. In your own home you make your own decisions about the things around you: what to buy, what to plant in the garden. But a few yards outside your house, the decisions about what trees get planted beside the road, the speed limit and the type of lamp-post, are most likely made by people several miles away that you have never met. And in the name of economic efficiency the tendency (certainly in the UK) has been to move such decisions ever further away by amalgamating smaller levels of government into larger ones, so that the local council you could once walk to is now some miles away. Similarly, if you have a problem with a colleague at work, there will probably be a manager close by in the same building who knows you both and that you can complain to; but if you have a problem with a neighbour in your street, you will have to go to a distant local government officer who knows nothing of either of you.

To combat alienation and create a greater sense of community, we may need to create some levels of government that are very local (perhaps street, neighbourhood or suburb?) and that allow people to participate more actively in the decisions that affect where they live. City governments could support or part-run a suburb or neighbourhood layer of government. City governments can also look for new ways to engage citizens, and recent experiments with citizens' assemblies have been very successful. These assemblies co-opt a group of members of the public to participate in a lengthy process during which they have access to experts in the areas under discussion and extensive opportunity to ask questions of the experts and to discuss among themselves. This gives a very different result to just asking people to vote or fill in a questionnaire from home, having had no input apart from what they may have seen on the web or in the media, and no discussion or reflection. Another possibility is to try to involve local people in the work carried out in their area. Japanese children are expected to help clean their school. Perhaps local government could support, fund and guide or supervise, residents efforts to remove graffiti and litter, maintain parks, and so forth.

What we cannot do is abandon the public sphere. The far-right hostility to government spending may be led by those who don't care about the conditions ordinary people live in and don't want to pay tax to improve them, but they find support from those who do care but are alienated from government and persuaded to think only of the tax burden and not of the public benefits. Yet almost no-one even on the extreme right, would suggest that an effective way to defend a country would be to hand back all the money currently spent on the military to individual citizens and tell them to defend themselves by clubbing together to buy a tank or an aircraft or two. The same logic applies to other public goods. The world beyond our front doors will only be a safe and pleasant place if we have effective local and national government – and if those layers of government are currently experienced as too remote, then we need to tackle that, not dismantle all government.

15.3   Wealth and Philanthropy

Among the very rich are some who donate large sums to the public good. Should we rely on the rich to fund the public spaces and facilities through philanthropy? When Britain became prosperous in the 18th and 19th centuries, travel was slow, uncomfortable and perilous, so the wealthy were more likely to take their pleasures close to home and take an interest in their local town. Through local taxation, public subscription or individual philanthropy, they backed the construction of local amenities such as libraries, art galleries and parks.

Similarly, when the railways arrived the rich were obliged to use this public form of transport as no fast private transport existed. It is striking that even quite small railway stations built in this period were well staffed, typically with a warm fire in the waiting room, toilets and perhaps a cafe, and larger stations were built to be positively splendid, often with a luxurious hotel attached. In the second half of the 20th century as the rich adopted the private car and air travel as their preferred way of getting around, the railways underwent a decline.

We can observe a general rule, that when the wealthy do not use or need something it will tend to decline. As with the railways,

A railway station building from 1850s   A railway station building from 1980s

Figure 15.3: Fine stations were built when the rich had to travel by rail; less so now. [Photos WMC]

and so with their local town – the wealthy are no longer dependent on local amenities – they can travel in comfort to private pleasures in the likes of Dubai or some island resort. Today's rich can escape locality in a way that the Victorians could not.

15.4 Summary

The public goods that make life beyond the protection of our front door, safe, comfortable and worth living, depend on collective spending by local and national government. Unfortunately the taxation that pays for such collective spending is a tempting target for neoliberal economists and for wealthy citizens who resent contributing. Their arguments, heavily promoted by billionaire-owned news media, gain more of a foothold if the population see government as remote and don't have a sense of ownership of public property.

There is a huge step between participating in spending decisions at a family or household level of no more than a handful of people, and participating at the first level of local government which may well cover tens or hundreds of thousands of people. Creating lower levels closer to the community at which the public can participate might help create a feeling of ownership, as would citizens assemblies and other forms of participation.

Philanthropy by the rich is unlikely to provide the amenities that our public spaces need, since with modern travel the rich can largely cut themselves from the rest of society and don't depend on a single locality.

Chapter 16

Market Impact on Communities and their Responsibilities

We live in a nested set of **governed** communities, where 'governed' means that there is a group of people or leaders whose task is to take decisions concerning the community and ensure the well-being of its citizens. This chapter is about how the control that governing bodies have over the economy in the area they cover, matches up to their economic responsibilities – responsibilities like support for the unemployed. We shall point out that governments are often expected to deal with the consequence of problems when they have little or no control over their causes.

The various levels of political government that humans live under across the globe, typically correspond to the familiar geographical boundaries of villages, towns, counties and nation states. The lowest level of formal government is usually the local council of a village or town. Above that there may be a county or regional council. Eventually there will be a national government and beyond that international governance exercised through treaties and bodies like the EU and the UN, although as yet, we have no world governing authority.

These political entities often have long histories, varying from decades to centuries or more.   In the past, the areas they controlled were likely to be far more autonomous economically than they are today in the sense of producing locally a higher proportion of what they consumed. That has changed because as described in Chapter 12, technical advances in transport and communication have increasingly connected local markets to regional, national and international markets. Connecting markets in this way however, throws up a problem, because community responsibilities have not been globalised to the same extent as economies have. The various levels of government continue to have responsibility for the economic prosperity and social well-being of their citizens, but they lack the economic control necessary to shoulder that responsibility because so many of the decisions that decide economic activity are now taken in distant places outside their jurisdiction.

Community responsibilities have not been globalised to the same extent as economies have.

If you are responsible for governing a community – whether it is a household, a town, or a country – it makes no sense to allow external competition that leaves members of your community unemployed, if as a result you then have to support them financially, pay for police to control them if they protest, and so forth. Yet this is what frequently happens, and furthermore is generally justified by free-market ideology because maximising competition and trade is meant always to lead somehow or other to the best outcomes. This puts governments in a dilemma: should they subject their citizens to the 'bracing winds' (or 'icy blast') of globalised market forces, or instead moderate interactions with the wider world to protect the local community. The latter – dubbed 'protectionism' – is usually frowned upon by economists and politicians, at least in the Anglo-Saxon world. Yet there is one part of society that still resists market forces and usually follows a protectionist route: the family.

It is a curious thing that politicians who back neoliberal economic policies are keen to say how reducing taxes means 'hard-working families' keep more of their money. They never seem to notice that those same hard-working families – and laid-back and bone-idle families too for that matter – are not neoliberal at all, but bastions of planning, protectionism, cross-subsidy and inefficient working practices! So strongly do families hold out against neoliberal economic policies, that most of us take it for granted that free-market ideology has no place in our homes. As an exercise it is valuable to imagine the opposite – a home where the free-marketeers had their way – because it throws light on what has happened at other levels of the economy. Join us briefly on a visit to an imagined 'free-market home':

The Free-Market Home

In our free-market home, the 'chief executives' (formerly known as Mum and Dad) have introduced proper market practices: the children are made to buy their own clothes and toys and pay for accommodation and food. In order that they could do so, their parents initially paid them a salary for washing the dishes and walking the dog. All was well until the daughter of a nearby family offered to carry out the same tasks at a fraction of the pay, and our home's chief executives being good free-marketeers were forced to sack their own children. However, as they have a duty of care to their children, our chief executives could not let them starve or become homeless, so they were then obliged to set up an unemployment benefit scheme and pay the children anyway. They've also had to hire a psychiatrist because their children have been suffering from feelings of rejection now that they are excluded from helping in the house. As a result, the family's overall costs have actually gone up.

The free-market family home just described may seem ridiculous, but if we move from the family level of government to the local town council (which is typically the next level up from families) our imaginary scenario ceases to be a fantasy and becomes all too real. If the council closes its call centre and moves the work to a distant country, some of the redundant workers may well be driven to claim housing benefit and free school meals, paid for by the council. If things go really badly for them and their families, they may need attention from social services, or even the police and the criminal justice system. There is a knock-on effect at the national level, since jobs that migrate abroad mean lost tax revenue, increased spending on unemployment pay and increased spending on dealing with the social ills produced. Outsourcing the call centre reduces the council's salary bill but is likely to make both the council and the national government incur substantial new costs.

The same scenario frequently occurs at the national level. An example of this is what happened when in the 1980s the British government closed most of the state-owned coal mines because they were 'uneconomic'. The reason that they were considered uneconomic was that Britain could buy coal more cheaply from countries like Vietnam whose miners, although actually not as productive as British miners in output per hour worked, were paid far less. However, the real costs to Britain of importing coal instead of producing it, are not at all obvious from a simple price comparison. When British coal is purchased, much of what is spent on it comes straight back to the government in the form of the income tax and national insurance deducted from the miners' wages, so the net cost to the UK is much less than the purchase price. On the other hand we should add to the price of imported coal the cost of support to British miners that are left unemployed as a consequence. On top of that, since the benefits unemployed miners receive will be less than their former wages, they will spend less locally and other businesses may fail causing more unemployment and imposing yet more costs on the government.

There are of course counter-arguments. One such argument is that it is beneficial to close British mines if it obliges the workers to move into newer more profitable industries where they can make more money than they did in mining; the question then is does this actually happen? Another argument made is that even if closing mines is bad for Britain, it is a good thing globally because of the

Coal mine. [WMC]

Figure 16.1: An industry is deemed 'uneconomic' if a competitor though less efficient, pays its workforce far less.

benefits to foreign miners and the countries they live in. Note that with hindsight we know that the world needs to end the use of coal because burning it is causing catastrophic climate change – but that was not the logic or motive at the time and in any case would not justify the cruel way it was done and the failure to plan alternative employment.

16.1   When is it Economic to Work, and When Not?

We have discussed how it may not be economically beneficial for a community to purchase cheaper products from outside that community instead of those made by local workers, if as a result the local workers are made unemployed and have then to be supported by the community. We'll now try to be more precise about how many of its members a community should aim to provide with employment.

If people are not dispensable and everyone is to be supported, then all should work, provided that the additional produce is worth more than the expense of (a) the resources used up when they work, and (b) the extra you have to pay to give them a wage rather than unemployment pay. In other words you want people to work unless they are so unproductive that they consume more by working, than they produce. Note that it doesn't matter how slowly the work is done. If workers hand-built a bus in the course of years, it would be better than doing nothing, provided that the sale of the bus paid for the additional cost incurred above that of just supporting the workers in unemployment. Note also that we consider net wages (i.e. after tax), since that is the real cost to the government and the country (the taxes deducted from gross salaries come straight back to the government). These conditions can be expressed as:

$$ProduceValue > NetWages - UnemploymentPay + InputsCost$$

Where: the symbol '>' means 'is greater than', 'NetWages' is wages after tax, 'UnemploymentPay' is the cost of supporting the workers if they were unemployed instead, 'InputsCost' is the cost of materials required to manufacture the produce.

Analysed in this way, many state industries that are deemed loss-making, may in fact be profitable. This is because although the government after paying the workers, sells the product at a nominal loss, it then gets back almost half of the salaries it paid, in income tax, national insurance and sales taxes. Effectively the government's salary bill is half of what it seems to be. Additionally, the government saves the expense of social security payments that would have been paid to those who would not be able to find other work if the industry closed down. The same logic applies to a nominally loss-making private industry: it may be cheaper for government to maintain it via a subsidy than incur the loss of tax revenue and expense of unemployment pay, should the business close. However in both of these cases, support mechanisms have to be well-thought-out, as there is a risk of losing market discipline (affecting efficiency and cost), and in the case of private industry, of possible manipulation such as the playing off of one country against another in a subsidy bidding war.

Based on this analysis, a country should aim to find ways for all citizens to contribute, just as a well run family does, provided that the costs of doing so are less than the cost of giving them unemployment benefit. Even if the nominal costs are higher, it may still be worth keeping people in employment if there are other benefits, such as social peace, a well-trained workforce, or carrying out work that otherwise wouldn't get financed such as support for the elderly or environmental projects.

This aim may sound simple but still represents a challenge, especially for small countries with a weak or non-existent industrial base. Very low productivity means that even with low wages it is difficult or impossible to meet the above criteria in competition with countries that high volumes of sales, advanced automated factories, and often low wages as well.

16.2   Fair Competition

If industries migrate to wherever wages are lowest, countries have to compete in what is called a 'race to the bottom', as they cut workers' pay and benefits. One approach to tackling this problem would be to try to ensure that international competition was fair. Those countries that have succeeded in building a welfare state that provides benefits such as unemployment pay, sick pay, pensions and a health service, typically pay for them to a large extent via income taxes. These taxes are levied on the pay of workers, so the gross wage companies have to pay is often almost doubled because part will go straight to the government as tax. In countries that provide few if any benefits, income taxes can be correspondingly lower and thus gross wages paid by companies can also be lower. This is unfair competition: 'we can sell for less because we treat our population badly'!

Taxes on labour are pernicious if that labour is in competition with labour in other countries where they don't levy such taxes. Governments that want to protect their welfare states from being undermined could try two approaches:

- Work with other countries and overseas suppliers, to agree minimum standards for worker pay and conditions, and either don't trade with companies that don't comply, or apply a tariff to their goods.

- Reduce or stop the taxing of wages (at least not at the lower end of the salary range) and move to taxing consumption instead via higher sales taxes. The sales taxes would be levied on imported goods as well as those nationally produced, and thus level the playing field. Sales taxes are sometimes considered not as progressive as income taxes because everyone pays them at the same rate. They are however, harder for the rich to escape ... and rich people buy more stuff! It's also possibly to charge higher rates on luxury items, and lower or zero rates on basic necessities – many countries do this to some extent, so in the UK for example, the sales tax VAT is not charged on a number of categories of goods, including most food, some medical supplies, children's clothes, and books.

There is an additional employment benefit to shifting taxation from wages to sales (apart from that of levelling the playing field in the face of external competition) because taxing labour makes it more expensive and so increases the incentive to automate and replace humans with machines. There is also an environmental benefit to taxing consumption, particularly if rates are adjusted to discourage the most environmentally damaging products.

16.3   Summary

In a community that is responsible for the well-being of its citizens, it makes economic sense to ensure that everyone who can work does work, even if people outside the community offer to do the work for less. This only ceases to be true if the *extra* cost of having your citizens work as opposed to just getting benefits, is so great that it exceeds the value of what they make. So in a family for example, it doesn't make economic sense to get your children wash the dishes if they use such copious amounts of detergent and hot water that the cost of their extravagance exceeds what it would cost you to pay a maid to do the work.

Communities that look after their citizens, raise taxes to do so. Governments need to be careful that these taxes don't push up the prices of goods and services produced within the community compared to those imported. Taxes on income do exactly that and are a problem when competing with countries with lower wages or lower income taxes. To avoid this problem, sales taxes like VAT are preferable because they fall equally on local and imported goods.

Chapter 17

The Tragedy of the Commons

This chapter is about the difficulty of looking after something that is shared by many people, if it is left to each person to make their own choice and there is no collective governance. The standard economics description of the problem is 'the tragedy of the commons'. The concept is an important one for understanding how leaving everything up to the market can produce disastrous results that are very far from what most people would have wished for – and often the complete opposite. Further detail beyond the brief description in this chapter, is readily found on the web.[55]

17.0.1 The mechanism and examples

Common land is land not owned by any one person, and over which people have certain common rights, such as to allow their animals to graze there. The description 'commons', has been extended to refer to all of the Earth's resources that are owned by no-one and thus in a sense by everyone, such as the air and the oceans: the 'global commons'.

Economists speak of the 'tragedy of the commons', because when many people use or damage a resource over which none of them have effective ownership or control, then there is little incentive to conserve that resource. An example that illustrates the concept is a village common upon which several people graze their cows. Even if it becomes badly over-grazed, nobody is likely to withdraw their own cows, because if they did, assuming everyone else's remain, their cows would lose out completely while the reduction in over-grazing would be small or negligible. By contrast, if a single farmer owns land where cows graze, he or she is able to remove all of them to let the grass recover, and gets the benefit from doing so.[1]

Figure 17.1: It's easier to avoid over-grazing if it's your own field rather than common land.

The tragedy-of-the-commons concept is useful because it can be applied not just to common land but to anything that has to be shared between many people or countries. We mentioned the concept in Chapter 13 where we described the economy's environmental impacts, since damage to our global environmental commons is an enormous problem. The damage includes depletion of the planet's resources, destruction of ecosystems, species extinction and pollution.

Externalities

A related economics concept is that of 'externalities'. These are costs imposed on others during production or consumption that are not paid for by either producer or consumer and therefore may be ignored by them. When a business damages the global commons it is an example of an externality. There are other externalities

---

[1]While this is an easily understood example of the 'tragedy of the commons' concept, I recently read that villagers in the past were in fact often able to manage their commons effectively. However, that was presumably because they were few enough in number to be able to cooperate and thus exercise control.

with more localised effects – an example being a business that is causing a noise pollution problem that only affects its immediate neighbours.

Cars, externalities, commons, and game theory

The concepts of the 'tragedy of the commons' and of 'externalities', particularly apply to the rise of the private car. Choosing to own and use a car, uses up finite resources, contributes to global warming and makes the environment polluted, noisier and dangerous (examples of 'externalities'). But if you cannot influence other people's choices you may as well own one yourself.

Figure 17.2: Private cars – a 'tragedy of the commons'. [WMC]

The logic is as follows: as a consumer, you cannot choose what everyone else does, only what you do. If you choose not to have a car, you get the worst outcome: you lose its speed and comfort, and assuming everyone else keeps theirs, you still have to suffer the consequences of global warming, pollution, and the blighting of the streets that are your local 'commons', since with millions of cars, the absence of yours makes only an infinitesimal reduction to any of these harms. So you may as well keep your car and gain the personal convenience; in the very extremely unlikely event that other people spontaneously give up their cars then you'll gain even greater benefits by having emptier roads and an improved environment thanks to the absence of their cars. This is shown in Table 17.1. In game theory the situation is expressed by saying that the dominant strategy for any individual is to keep their car.[2]

	What Everyone Else does	
	If they keep their cars	If they have no cars
Benefit to You if you keep your car:	*Bad Environment* *High Comfort*	*Good Environment* *High Comfort*
Benefit to You if you have no car:	*Bad Environment* *Lower Comfort*	*Good Environment* *Lower Comfort*

Table 17.1: A good environment is only possible if everyone acts collectively to get rid of their cars.

Losing the local 'commons'

Calling the roads 'commons' may seem odd until we remember that up to the early 20th century the roads in our towns and villages, although not common land, were a sort of shared public space, used by children to play, street traders, pedestrians, hand-carts, and the occasional horse and cart. With the arrival of the motor vehicle and particularly cars, this shared space was progressively taken away from its traditional users. Sometimes laws were passed to directly limit the freedom of pedestrians (like the jaywalking rule in the US), but mostly it has been the menace of injury or death from being hit by motor traffic that has driven away other users – each person who chose to buy a car added to the threat.

Particularly heartbreaking is the resulting loss of independence and space for unsupervised outdoor play, suffered by children. Time outside in quiet spaces is known to be important for mental health and especially for that of children; its loss is believed to be contributing to a rapid decline in adolescent mental health.[41] In 1960's Britain a six-year-old child could walk to school unsupervised (I was one such); no child that age would be allowed to do

---

[2]Note that there are some personal advantages not mentioned above to not owning a car. Driving everywhere instead of walking, cycling or using public transport, is likely to lead to poor health. Car users can be exposed to higher pollution – they breathe air contaminated by the cars in front of them. Cars are also expensive. Unfortunately, given the inexorable rise in car ownership worldwide, these factors don't appear to be uppermost in people's minds.

so in the UK today. It was then a pleasure to wander with family and friends, several abreast, in the country lanes at the edge of our town, but few would want to now – streams of fast moving cars will squeeze you in fear of your lives onto the verge, where you are obliged to pick your way over the litter and debris chucked out of or fly-tipped by the less responsible occupants of the passing vehicles.

Children playing, 1950. [INTERFOTO / Alamy Stock Photo]

Figure 17.3: Children used to play in the streets, but are now denied them by motor vehicles.

Some will argue that Britain's roads have actually become safer. It is true that by 2022 there were far fewer road deaths in Britain than there were in the 1960s, as can be seen in Table 17.2, and this even though there were a great many more motor vehicles (40.7 million, compared to 8.5 million in 1960). We know that for car occupants, safety has improved substantially thanks to seat belts, airbags, and huge investment in roads and road-safety features such as crash-barriers and traffic controls.

Road usage by cyclists in 2022 was a little under half what it was in 1960 (3.9 billion miles travelled compared with over 8 billion in 1960 [59]), so you would expect a drop in fatalities, but that doesn't account for the much larger fall shown in Table 17.2. What may explain the fall is that those who continue to cycle have become a great deal more wary, venturing forth almost for combat, with helmets, high visibility clothing and bright LED lights; meanwhile

Year	Pedest-rians	Cyclists	Motor-cyclists	Car Occu-pants	ALL Road Users
1960 :	2,708	679	1,743	1,840	6,970
2022 :	385	91	350	788	1,711

Data source: [56]. Note 'ALL Road Users' includes some others apart from the four listed. **Worldwide about 1.2 million people a year are killed on the roads.**[57, 58] Note that walking and cycling are not by themselves dangerous: pedestrians and cyclists die because they are run over by motor vehicles.

Table 17.2: Road deaths in Britain: death tolls came down as other users abandoned the roads to the car.

former less-determined users such as children and the elderly, have abandoned cycling. Pedestrians on the other hand were no better equipped in 2022 to defend themselves against vehicles than they were in 1960; therefore the fall in deaths seems likely to be at least in part because pedestrians use roads less freely and in particular, as noted earlier, children are far more restricted, seldom ever playing unsupervised in the streets.

Whatever the actual risks, today's congested roads have become such hostile environments that their former more vulnerable users – pedestrians and especially children – approach them with caution or avoid them altogether. When local councils in Britain propose any small restrictions on traffic, the measures are frequently denounced as a "war on motorists". But if there has been a war, then with over 195,000 pedestrians killed in Britain since records began to be kept in 1927, it was and is a war on pedestrians, which the cars have largely won since they now dominate a space that once-upon-a-time belonged to others.

An insidious loss of a public space or utility that takes place over several decades as has happened with roads, is very hard to oppose for multiple reasons. Among these is the tragedy-of-the-commons explanation (in this case, the commons being the shared space of the roads), which means that as individuals we cannot choose to block or reverse the change. But another is simply that few of us can remember or have ever experienced anything different: most people will recall that there was (already) traffic when they were children and only notice that there is 'a bit more' traffic now. How then can people make a choice if they barely know that there is one? For most town dwellers, the same will apply to things like clean air and silence (freedom from noise pollution) – we seldom experience them any more, and don't know what we are missing.

17.1   Consumer Choice

Free-market ideology says that what happens in the world should be left as far as possible to consumer choice. But the example of the decision on whether or not to own a car demonstrates that frequently there is no real choice, because you cannot as a consumer choose an alternative transport system based on few or no cars unless almost everyone does, which is not going to happen spontaneously and would require collective action. We can make such choices only as citizens.

With many environmental issues the dilemma facing humanity is even worse in that the costs of some of our actions will be borne not by anyone alive today, but by future generations. In such environmental areas, government intervention to promote well-being by collective action is therefore essential, however difficult it may be to obtain the political consensus for the necessary policies.

17.2   The 'Tragedy' in a Local Economy

Apart from the resources of the global commons, something else we share with others is the local economy of the area where we live. People usually live out their lives in the country where they were born. They have a common interest with their fellow citizens in the prosperity of that country, and unless they are always on the move, in the prosperity of their region and town as well. However, in a globalised free market something similar to the tragedy of the commons occurs, in that people have little or no incentive to try to protect that common prosperity.

Workers clearly have an interest in the continuing success of a local business that employs them. However, as consumers they are unlikely to affect their employer very much by their buying choices, since their spending must be spread across many products and the amount they spend with their own employer is likely to be small. The outcome is that it is perfectly rational to take decisions as a consumer that are against the interests of the business that employs you and the interests of other local businesses that employ friends, family and others in your local community.

For example, imagine you work in a large clothing factory. One day you decide to buy a shirt and find that one made by your factory is twice the price of a similar imported shirt from a country with far lower wages. Not buying the shirt from your factory will make only a tiny difference to your factory's sales, while buying the cheaper one is a big saving for you.

Figure 17.4: The 1970's Buy British campaign did little to stem the tide of cheap imports. [WMC]

Inevitably many others will make the same choice, and give their custom to distant competitors instead of local or national businesses. Sometimes countries try to counter this by running campaigns to persuade people to buy national produce – there was a Buy British campaign in the 1970s – but these are rarely successful as the temptation to make substantial savings by buying cheaper goods is strong, especially for those on limited budgets.

Economists generally argue against 'protectionism' – the favouring of local products, usually achieved via tariffs on imported alternatives. However, it seems reasonable to have some sort of protection for local economies against a 'race to the bottom' competition to see which country can slash wages by the most.[60] Consumers cannot implement tariffs, so some sort of government action is required, as discussed in Chapter 16 where we considered market impact on communities and their responsibilities. Whether and to what extent, countries should protect their domestic production, is very much a live debate. The European Union has tariffs on agricultural imports to protect farmers within the block. One of the arguments made in favour of the UK leaving the European Union was that Britain could then remove those tariffs and import cheaper food from around the world. There are many issues here, such as the future viability of UK farming, the environmental cost of shipping food from far away (referred to as 'food miles'), and security of supply if the dependence on imports is increased. So far the results don't seem overly positive: global food prices have soared with prices in the UK increasing by at least as much as in comparable EU countries, and UK farmers have faced new problems brought on by the changes.

17.3 Summary

Businesses have little incentive to protect the environment or resources because the benefit is only obtained if most or all of them do so; acting alone they incur the costs but get only a small or negligible benefit. Consumers find themselves in a similar situation in circumstances where their buying choice will make no significant change to the environmental harm caused by a product unless almost all consumers do the same.

A similar situation arises with the prosperity of businesses local to an area. The workers employed in those firms are unlikely as consumers to protect them by their individual buying choices, and will be inclined to buy products they see as best-value, wherever they are from.

These are examples of how it is difficult or impossible to look after something shared by many people, by relying on individual choices. A problem known as 'the tragedy of the commons'. Only acting together via some level of government, offers a solution to such situations.

Chapter 18

Theory of Comparative Advantage

A standard concept in economics is the theory of 'comparative advantage'. The theory asserts that countries will be richer if they trade together and each specialises in areas in which they achieve the most favourable levels of productivity (output per person) compared to the other countries, even if those levels are not actually better than those of the other countries. The purpose of this chapter is to explore whether this is always the case and therefore the best guide to policy for a country. We shall see that there are other factors to take into account, and that if you want a robust national economy that provides near full employment, a rich variety of skilled and unskilled jobs, and is not dependent on a few cash crops, then comparative advantage should not be the only consideration.

18.1   Background of the Theory

The theory of comparative advantage was developed by the British economist David Ricardo in 1817 in order to explain why it is worthwhile for two countries to trade even when one country's workers are more efficient at producing all of the traded products than workers in the other country. He demonstrated that if two countries are both capable of the same two products, but with different **relative** amounts of labour, then each country can increase its overall consumption by exporting the product for which it has a comparative advantage while importing the other product.

The American economist Paul Samuelson, who won the Nobel Memorial Prize in Economic Sciences in 1970, was once challenged to name one theory in all of the social sciences that is both true and non-trivial. Several years later, he responded with David Ricardo's theory of comparative advantage, saying:

> "That it is logically true need not be argued before a mathematician; that is not trivial is attested by the thousands of important and intelligent men who have never been able to grasp the doctrine for themselves or to believe it after it was explained to them."[61]

Well we can't discuss the theory without understanding it. So let's first attempt to illustrate it with an example, in which work is shared out between two people instead of between two countries. Many of us will have experienced trying to share out work with someone in the most effective way given differing abilities, as happens in this fictional example:

> *Lola and Juan run a restaurant together. The main work to be done is cooking and cleaning. Lola is faster at both things: she's 4 times quicker at cooking than Juan and 2 times quicker at cleaning. What then is the best policy for how they divide up the work, if they want to get the most done? It's not hard to see that Lola should concentrate on the cooking until there is no more to be done, and Juan should concentrate on the cleaning. The reason is that although Juan is slower at both, he's 'comparatively' better at cleaning than cooking – only 2 times worse instead of 4 times. Had Juan been slower by an equal amount at both cleaning and cooking, there would be no advantage in Lola concentrating on one or the other in terms of getting more done.*

Figure 18.1: How should you divide cooking and cleaning between Lola and Juan, when Juan is slower at both?

Let's now introduce the trade part of the comparative advantage theory:

> *Lola and Juan amicably split up. Lola keeps the original restaurant and Juan opens a bar next door. He offers to do some cleaning for Lola in exchange for her doing some cooking in his bar. For 1 hours cleaning by Juan, Lola isn't willing to give half an hour's work because in half an hour she can do as much cleaning as Juan does in an hour and would be no better off than if she just did the cleaning herself - but she is willing to give 20-minute's work. As she is 4 times faster than Juan, what she cooks in 20 minutes would have taken Juan four times that, which is 1 hour and 20 minutes. Both benefit by the trade: Lola gets cleaning done that would have taken her 30-minutes by doing 20-minutes cooking for Juan, and Juan gets cooking done that would have taken him 1-hour 20 minutes by doing one hour of cleaning for Lola.*

If we replace our restaurant couple Lola and Juan, with two countries FastCountry and SlowCountry both capable of producing bicycles and chairs, where workers in SlowCountry are less productive, taking 4 times longer to make a bicycle but only 2 times longer to make a chair, then we can see that as a whole, the two countries can produce more of both products if SlowCountry concentrates on chairs and trades chairs for bicycles with FastCountry as needed. We say that SlowCountry has a 'comparative advantage' in producing chairs. You could express the idea colloquially by saying "SlowCountry is worse than FastCountry at making both bicycles and chairs, but less worse at chairs".

Hopefully that gives the basic idea of the comparative advantage theory. For further explanation, refer to any standard macroeconomics text or Wikipedia.[62] We'll now proceed to discuss its applicability.

18.2 Assumptions and Limitations

While the theory undoubtedly does explain many real-world trade choices made by businesses and countries, it is based on assumptions that don't always apply. These assumptions include:

1. Labour is the only input into production.

2. Specialising in a product won't decrease employment.

3. Workers can seamlessly transfer between producing the various goods.

Let's look at these assumptions, and after that, examine some other limitations to the theory.

Assumption 1. Labour is the only input into production

Many countries depend heavily on agricultural production, especially some of the world's poorest. Land is therefore an input into production and may change the calculation of what it is best to produce. To demonstrate this we will visit FastCountry and SlowCountry again where they are debating the merits of growing two different crops (both imagined ones to keep the numbers simple): ReddFruit and BlooBeans. It takes more work to grow a kilogram

240

	Labour Hours to produce each kilogram of:		Exchange Rate, within each country	International Exchange Rate, for trading between countries
	BlooBeans	ReddFruit		
FastCountry:	1 hour	3 hours	1kg of ReddFruit for 3kg of BlooBeans	1.5kg ReddFruit for 3kg of BlooBeans
SlowCountry:	4 hours	6 hours	2kg of ReddFruit for 3kg of BlooBeans	

Table 18.1: An example of 'comparative advantage'.

of the succulent ReddFruit than it does to grow a kilogram of the nutritious BlooBeans. On the other hand ReddFruit is more productive: the yield in terms of kilograms per hectare of land per year, is higher than for BlooBeans.

Initially we will analyse only **labour productivity**. We assume that within each country they are willing to exchange products based on how much labour over the growing season it takes to produce them. In FastCountry, it takes 3 hours of labour to grow a kilogram of ReddFruit, and one hour's labour to grow a kilogram of BlooBeans. Accordingly, in FastCountry's market square, the rate they are traded at is: 3kg of BlooBeans for 1kg of ReddFruit.

The corresponding figure for SlowCountry are 6 hours to grow 1kg of ReddFruit, and 4 hours to grow 1kg of BlooBeans. So in Slow-Country, they trade at: 1.5kg of BlooBeans for 1kg of ReddFruit.

If the two countries begin to trade with each other, then a producer of a kilogram of ReddFruit in SlowCountry discovers that if he takes them to FastCountry he can swap them for twice as many BlooBeans as he would get in SlowCountry: 3kg instead of 1.5kg. However, the BlooBean traders in FastCountry quickly realise that if they came to SlowCountry they could swap that 3kg for 2kg of ReddFruit instead of the 1kg they are getting back home. So after a while the trade internationally is likely to settle at a rate somewhere between the two national rates, for example as shown in Table 18.1, at 1.5kg of ReddFruit for 3kg of BlooBeans (*which works out as 1kg of ReddFruit for 2kg of BlooBeans*).

The figures given above and in Table 18.1, show SlowCountry as having a comparative advantage in ReddFruit, because although it is less productive in producing both crops than FastCountry (i.e. it takes more labour hours to grow them), the difference is less in the case of ReddFruit. The theory of comparative advantage tells us that it is therefore advantageous for SlowCountry to concentrate on making ReddFruit and trade some of them with FastCountry to get BlooBeans. To illustrate this, consider how many BlooBeans a worker in SlowCountry can obtain with 36 hours of labour:

(1) **By growing BlooBeans:**
    ```
    36hrs ÷ 4hrs/kg = 9kg of BlooBeans.
    ```

(2) **By growing ReddFruit and trading them:**
    ```
    36hrs ÷ 6hrs/kg = 6kg of ReddFruit, which is
    traded with FastCountry for 6kg × 2 = 12kg of
    BlooBeans.
    ```

So by picking option (2), and benefitting from comparative advantage, a worker can end up with 12kg of BlooBeans, instead of 9kg. FastCountry also benefits from the exchange.

So far so good, but what if we now take **land use** into account as well as labour? The two crops both require agricultural land to produce them. Suppose that to grow a kilogram of BlooBeans requires only a third the area of farmland than that needed to grow a kilogram of ReddFruit. Let's say you have an area of land the right size to grow the 9kg of BlooBeans described above. However, having heard about the theory of comparative advantage you decide to switch to growing ReddFruit on that land. You will only be able to grow a third as much on the same patch, so:

On land that could produce 9kg of BlooBeans, you can only produce a third as much ReddFruit, which is 3kg. When traded with FastCountry, that gets:
```
3kg × 2 = 6kg of BlooBeans.
```
(*Note: The labour used is only 18 hours (3kg × 6hrs/kg), instead of the 36 hours needed to grow BlooBeans on the same land.*)

So you did less work, but you have ended up worse off in produce (6kg BlooBeans instead of 9kg) than you would have done if

Grow:	Result	Labour Required	Labour Cost (paid in BlooBeans at 0.2kg per hour)	Profit for Landowner (BlooBeans after labour deducted)	Profit Share of Landowner
3kg of ReddFruit and trade them for 6kg of BlooBeans	6 kg BlooBeans	18 hours	3.6kg	2.4kg	40%
9kg of BlooBeans directly	9kg BlooBeans	36 hours	7.2kg	1.8kg	20%

Table 18.2: The biggest profit for a landowner could come from choosing a crop that reduces overall national production.

you'd stuck with growing BlooBeans yourself. Of course, it would be different if you had lots of spare unused land, you could just cultivate a larger area. But in practise both for individual farmers and for countries, land is finite. Even in countries with some wild areas left, you may not want to encroach on them for environmental reasons.

Assumption 2. Specialising in a product won't decrease employment

In the example above in which land is a limitation, we saw that growing ReddFruit on a plot of land and trading it for Bloobeans got you only two thirds as many Bloobeans as if you had grown them directly, but on the other hand needed in total only half the labour (18 hours instead of 36). So the option you choose may depend on your priorities.

A small-scale farmer with no other source of employment, may prefer to grow the BlooBeans directly and get more crop even though it means working twice as hard. But the calculation is different for a landowner who hires the labour: depending on the local wage costs, it could be more profitable to produce a bit less but for a considerably smaller wage bill. From the landowner's point of view, the choices for that piece of land could look like those set out in Table 18.2.

Note how the landowner gets a bigger profit with the first option rather than the last option. Yet the first option produces the lowest quantity of actual product! So from a landowner's point of view, the biggest profit may be available from choosing a crop that substantially reduces their labour costs even though it also reduces overall national production. That may be advantageous to the landowner but worse for the country as a whole if there isn't alternative suitable employment for the displaced workers: they suffer, and the country suffers if it has to support them in some other way or deal with social problems arising from high unemployment.

If these arguments seem obscure, here's the same idea, expressed as a story (the details, including productivity of oil palm versus other crops, are for illustration only, not factual):

> *The agricultural island nation of Econolandia identified oil palm as the crop it could grow with the best comparative advantage in terms of labour per unit of output. Accordingly, it dedicated the whole island to growing oil palm. Unfortunately the work on the oil-palm plantations only required 20% of the workforce, leaving the rest unemployed. Taxing the oil-palm workers to support the unemployed, or forcing the oil-palm plantations to employ extra people unnecessarily, would ruin the comparative advantage that was the whole point of concentrating on oil palm in the first place! So the islanders switched back to a mixed agriculture that includes crops for local consumption, and produces more food per unit of area. Everyone is now employed and the total production of food is greater, although since far more people are working, output per unit of labour is lower.*

Assumption 3. Workers can seamlessly transfer between producing the different goods

The theory assumes that workers can readily switch between producing the various products. Sometimes that might be true but how often? Even agricultural crops can require different skill sets, let alone if we expect a coal miner in their 40s or 50s to suddenly switch to computer programming, or expect a nail technician (finger nails in a beauty salon, not steel nails) to become a farm labourer. A new job may require qualifications that take years of education and training to acquire, for which there may be no funding and which may be hard to undertake in later life. Then there is geographical location: switching jobs may require a move to a very different area – perhaps from the countryside or a provincial town to a metropolitan area where accommodation is harder to come by and expensive. It may also involve separation from family and friends.

The assumptions are not necessarily valid

We have shown that it is quite possible for assumptions 1 and 2 not to be met. In particular if there is limited land for crops, focussing on the one with a comparative advantage may result in less overall production and less employment. Assumption 3 is also a challenging requirement – it might take a generation to educate a population in the newest technologies, and if the only jobs available require an extremely high educational and intellectual level, they may be open to only a small minority.

For many of the world's poorest countries, exporting agricultural products is a major way that they earn foreign exchange to pay for imports – so called 'cash crops'. So they are very likely to look for the crop that has the highest comparative advantage and therefore earns them the most. Individual landowners are also likely to choose the most profitable, without regard to any loss of employment on their land or lower overall national production. If the society is an unequal one, it's also likely that landowners want the foreign exchange to pay for imports of the expensive luxury goods seen in richer countries, so that they can enjoy a lifestyle that is out of the reach of the majority of their compatriots. In doing so, landowners are simply responding to the market incentives to better their lot – as most of us do – and not necessarily acting with bad intent or illegally. However, if the government of such a country wanted to look after **all** of its citizens, it might choose to put a limit on the quantity of land used to grow cash crops for export, and instead require that more land be used to grow staple foods. Where cash crops are grown, the government could ensure that they help pay for the import of essentials – for example supplies needed for public transport or health care. The import of luxury goods can be restricted by applying higher taxes to them, the revenue from which can finance public spending.

> In Costa Rica, the government levies very high import duties on cars. So for wealthier Costa Ricans, it's possible to own a car, but they will make a substantial contribution to the national budget to do so.[63]

Limitations

Apart from the assumptions questioned above, there are other reasons why comparative advantage should not be the only guide to best policy for a country if it leads to the concentration on a few goods or cash crops. Some of these limitations are:

1. Concentrating on fewer products makes you vulnerable. If competitors begin to undercut you and weaken your trade advantage, you have fewer alternatives to switch to.

2. Increasing the proportion of externally traded goods makes you more exposed to trade swings in the prices of commodities.

3. Concentrating on a small number of the most profitable crops could lead to large areas of monoculture. This is a problem as monoculture results in a devastating loss of habitat for other plant and animal species. Monocultures are also at greater risk from disease, pests and unfavourable weather.

4. There may be less job satisfaction if there is less variety and less opportunity to practice advanced skills. Work is how we spend much of our lives and some jobs are pleasanter or more interesting than others. If the products that have a

comparative advantage tend to require mostly unskilled, low-tech jobs, focussing on them could lock a country into an economic dead-end as well as providing no attraction for the youngest and brightest to stay.

Figure 18.2: Monoculture: an oil-palm plantation. [WMC]

18.3 Summary

The standard economics theory of 'comparative advantage' should not be the only guide to what a country should choose to produce because it is based on assumptions that may not be met, and takes no account of several real-world limitations.

In particular, other finite resources apart from labour should be taken into account, such as land. There is no benefit to switching to a crop that requires less labour if it needs far more land – land that you don't have – and the result is less yield per unit area. Nor does focussing on a product which has a comparative advantage help a country, if it displaces labour that cannot find any alternative employment.

Dedicating an economy to the production of only a limited range of products has several other disadvantages – such as the problems associated with crop monoculture, vulnerability to changes in weather or global prices, and a narrower range of job opportunities making it harder to retain the brightest and highly skilled in the country.

Nevertheless, in poorer countries with high levels of inequality, business owners have an incentive to focus on the production of export goods even if it results in less employment and less sustenance for the general population, because doing so earns the foreign currency with which they can buy the trappings of a first-world affluent lifestyle.

Chapter 19

Inequality

The main purpose of this chapter is to consider the economic effects of very unequal levels of income and wealth. However, let us first take a little time to try to understand why inequalities emerge and what purposes they might serve.

How societies structure themselves must be subject to evolutionary pressures, just as the forms taken by biological organisms are. Some ways of organising society will prove better than others at enabling a community to expand, prosper and fend off competitors. Note that by 'better' we mean only in terms of a community's survival, and not whether a community is kinder, more just, or more agreeable to live in. Most of us don't like mosquitoes or scorpions, but we understand that evolution selects for characteristics that enable an animal to survive, rather than for things that make them attractive and cuddly in our eyes. The same goes for societies. Some societies with pretty unpleasant characteristics, may nevertheless be 'successful' in terms of lasting and expanding; their disagreeable characteristics may be part of what makes them successful.

Considerable levels of inequality have existed in most societies throughout history, so it's very likely that an unequal society has at least some advantages over a more equal one.

19.1 The Value of Hierarchy

A society is more likely to succeed if it can establish:

- An ability to take decisions as a group and act as one.

- Respect for a set of rules and norms that promote the greater good of society.

- Loyalty to the society and its chosen leaders such that citizens are willing to adopt society's goals as their own, devoting and on occasion sacrificing their lives to those ends.

A totally flat structure with nobody having any more authority than anyone else, is unlikely to have these characteristics. To see why, just imagine trying to reach agreement between fifty people if everyone has an equal right to speak, let alone between thousands or millions. A community capable of taking decisions as one, will be able to undertake ventures in many walks of life and especially in the fields of production and war, that a chaotic all-for-themselves society could not. Even if many of the decisions taken are wrong, provided that some of them are right it gives a more united society a huge evolutionary advantage over a disorganised one.

Figure 19.1: Success is more likely with clear decision-making. [WMC]

If a society with some sort hierarchy and leadership is needed, will it do to have one educated king leading a nation of serfs?

250

Clearly such an arrangement would be fragile: hierarchies need to be layered. A king establishes a trustworthy set of courtiers by giving them privileges, not by treating them in exactly the same way as he would any other serf. To see how that layering is done, it is illuminating to visit a mansion or palace that has become a museum: often there will be descriptions of the varied roles of the former servants and an opportunity to see their working conditions and accommodation. The most senior servants normally have significant privileges, giving them an incentive to be trustworthy and loyal.

So we have a layered hierarchy that encourages loyalty near the top. But there will be many people at or near the bottom: how can they be persuaded to obey the rules? Almost everywhere in the past and in many places still, one way to persuade them is by repressive and brutal laws. In England, hanging or transportation to penal colonies was the punishment for stealing a sheep until well into the 19th century. But a king's soldiers cannot be ever present to catch all infractions. How much more effective it would be if the population internalised the rules: even if the king is not watching you, an omnipresent God always is – and more fearsomely than modern CCTV, because God knows your very thoughts. Thus a society can be much more confident that laws will be obeyed if it develops a religion that backs up the earthly laws with an intense sense of right and wrong. Religion can supply a feeling of comfort and community to those who conform, plus the promise of reward in the afterlife; meanwhile the threat of God's judgement and eternal punishment, hangs over transgressors.

Religions go further than just obedience to the king and not stealing from the rich. They provide a shared belief system, an extensive code of conduct and public rituals for life's key events. Such things provide an evolutionary advantage over societies without them, promoting greater unity and reducing the scope for conflict between ordinary members of the community.

Kings and religions can do even more than provide rules and rituals: they can inspire loyalty and devotion. I imagine that there are extensive studies of how this comes about. Presumably at some

Christ Between Saints Peter and Paul, Hieronymus
Wierix. [The Met]

Figure 19.2: Religions can provide a code of conduct.

level it's hard-wired since we can observe that other primates are
also social animals and loyalty to a lead individual is common among
many mammals. We are a creature that has a long childhood during
which we depend heavily on our parents to provide both love and
comfort as well as authority and punishment. It seems that as
adults we are able to project these feelings onto kings, priests and
even nation states. In Christianity both God and priests are referred
to as 'father'. Kings are sometimes said to be the 'father of the
people'. Nations and homelands are referred to as the fatherland
or motherland.

Even for those at or near the bottom of society, there is a benefit
to accepting a hierarchy – it's not just fear of the law or of God
that leads people do so. Those with the least are often the most
vulnerable to having what little they have stolen, or being the victim
of violence. They have reason to welcome a hierarchy that can

impose law and order. Harsh laws can provide a degree of security and safety, provided that they are implemented in a predictable and consistent way so that citizens know how to comply with them. Feeling safe when you walk down the street is a genuine freedom, even if that safety is thanks to a strict dictator.

So a degree of inequality is an evolutionary advantage for a society if it provides effective leadership and collective action. Throughout most of history, inequality was also a necessity if a society was to support an educated class, because only a few people could be spared from the hard manual labour needed to produce basic essentials. It was an advantage to have architects, writers, artists, scientists, philosophers, administrators and political leaders, even though society could only support a small group of such privileged intellectuals.

Modern society in developed countries requires far less labour to produce life's basics. Thanks to the industrial revolution we are now able to support a much larger middle class and a wide opportunity for higher education; perhaps one day robots and automation will free everyone from hard work, but not quite yet. Where loyalty to a monarchy and religion is weaker, we have created loyalty to institutions such as the law, the courts, the constitution, and to concepts such as human rights, liberty, democracy – and we have also created larger and more effective police forces.

19.2   The Value of Liberty

We said that a society is more likely to succeed if it can establish:

- An ability to take decisions as a group.

- Respect for a set of rules and norms.

- Loyalty to the society and its chosen leaders.

Those requirements suggest that a society based on some sort of dictatorship – fascist, communist or monarchic – ought to perform best. Yet that is not what we observe over the last century. Instead, the majority of the most technologically advanced countries have moved towards universal suffrage and greater individual freedoms. A possible explanation is to suppose that modern society has new requirements in addition to those listed above. Success now requires an educated population able to understand and use new technology. A consequence of having an educated population may well be that they are less disposed to accept an authoritarian government or an authoritarian religion – the greater liberty being a by-product of requirement for more education. Alternatively it may be that success as a society actually depends on greater individual liberty, and not just on high educational attainment: liberty that allows the population to have the confidence and freedom to advance science and technology, and to be creative in applying new knowledge to commerce and art, as well as to science itself. A browbeaten, fearful population – however many exams they have passed – may struggle to compete with a society which allows more individual freedom.

Figure 19.3: An educated population is necessary to understand and use industrial technology. [WMC]

Yet liberty and democracy sit uncomfortably with the increasingly extreme inequality of wealth that poorly-regulated free-market capitalism is giving rise to. What will happen if large parts of the population become dispensable because of automation – how will society evolve then? In so much as the segment of the population displaced by automation is one of the most marginalised, governments led by the wealthy may go for containment: warehousing them in cheap accommodation, with cheap food, cheap info-entertainment and cheap hi-tech policing (CCTV, tags, databases). Automation is also beginning to threaten the jobs of the more privileged and influential professional classes as well. With the ability to monitor and control populations using computers putting more power into the hands of governments and dictators, it is hard to see any guarantees about the future shape of society.

Figure 19.4: Technology provides new methods of social control.
[WMC]

19.3   Economic Effects of Inequality

Now we turn to consider the economic effects of unequal levels of income and wealth. We made the case above that some degree of inequality is probably inevitable if a society is to have structure and order. It also may make possible a more pluralistic society: wealthy individuals have the ability to make major cultural or business investments, resulting in more varied initiatives than if everything was left to the state. However, extreme levels of inequality distort how the economy works with negative effects for most people and especially for those who own no means of subsistence and depend entirely on the wealthy hiring them to provide goods or services, and if not hired, face poverty or starvation.

19.3.1 Waste and excess

Inequality affects what gets produced. People with low or modest incomes spend most of their money on basics such as food, clothing, accommodation, etc., plus a few small luxuries. The very rich however, easily cover their basic needs and have on top of that, vast amounts of money to spend on luxuries. This creates a market for expensive and often very wasteful products such as private jets, limousines, yachts, extensive air travel and even space tourism.

Figure 19.5: Inequality creates a market for luxuries. [WMC]

19.3.2 Unemployment

Inequality gums up the economy because unlike poorer people, the rich do not need to spend all of their income. For economic activity to be maintained at a steady level, we need people to spend what they earn, buying and consuming the goods and services the economy produces. Poorer people are obliged to do this because they only have enough money for basic essentials. By contrast, the rich do not need to spend their whole income on consumer goods and services; they may choose to save, or choose to acquire assets that already exist – but doing either means less demand for the labour of ordinary people.

19.3.3   Ownership of assets

When rich people have more money than they need, they don't usually keep it as cash, but choose instead to 'invest' it in some way. This typically involves buying assets that make money, or lending money at interest. Assets can be property such as houses, or businesses, or company shares. Often this is not done directly but by placing the money in financial institutions that make the investments for you.

Buying things that already exist from other rich people, whether houses, company shares or paintings by old masters, doesn't cause any new production apart from the transaction costs, it simply shuffles the money to another rich person - transaction costs being whatever small amount of money has to be spent on the administration of the sale, etc. There is no guarantee that the rich person selling the asset will spend the money on consumption – it may just sit in their bank account or be used to buy some other existing asset.

When the rich buy assets from ordinary people or from the state, it is likely that a temporary increase in consumption and therefore production will occur. If the population at large sell their houses to the rich, it's probably because they want the money for day to day spending. If the state sells assets, like airports or power stations, it is likely to use the money to pay for current government spending. But unfortunately whether it is individuals or the state selling off their assets to the rich, and despite any short-term extra spending, the public end up worse-off in the medium to longer term, because:

- The less the public own in terms of housing, the more they will have to pay in rent to landowners.

- The more that public utilities and services fall into private hands, the more the public will be charged for them, and the poorer the pay and conditions of the staff.

The overall effect is to create a growing rentier class on the one hand and on the other, a class of ordinary people who own little or nothing either as individuals or collectively via the state. The second group are therefore increasingly in hock to the rentiers for everything –

housing, employment, services, loans. It's a vicious circle since the more exploited and dependent the general population become, the less able they are to escape financially.

19.3.4 Inequality grows more inequality

Without regulation, inequality inevitably grows. The income of the poor goes entirely on day to day spending, while the rich can easily afford their daily expenses and still have money to spare which they can invest in acquiring assets such as property to rent or business shares, that will then earn them an even bigger income. It's a positive feedback loop: money grows more money. Wealth buys influence too. The rich can own or finance social media, newspapers, TV, lobbyists and politicians, to ensure that government policies favour their business interests; they can more easily use the courts to further their interests than most people, because they can afford the legal costs.

The only counterbalance is popular opinion: protest and political movements that demand that the government limits the level of inequality through such measures as taxes and minimum-wage laws. Wiser heads among the wealthy classes, influenced by realism or compassion, may attempt to head off defeat at the ballot box – or worse still, revolt – by bending to those popular demands to some degree. After the Second World War, right-of-centre political parties in Europe, mostly accepted that the state should provide universal health care and education plus other social benefits – what was referred to in the UK as the 'post-war consensus'.

19.4 Summary

Social evolution is likely to favour orderly, structured societies, with a degree of hierarchy, over anarchic undirected ones. Even for individuals near the bottom-of the pile, there is a value in hierarchy if it brings order and security. A society with some wealthier individuals can also be a more plural one if it means that business and cultural power are not monopolised by the state.

However, social evolution is not all one-way in the direction of order – it also favours prowess. Societies that educate their populations, and that facilitate social mobility and permit free expression, will be more creative and better able to make use of the brightest and most capable individuals. Those factors have become more valuable in the modern age, given the growth in importance of science and technology, and the fast-moving demands of competitive markets for innovative and eye-catching products.

Extreme inequality results in extreme poverty at the bottom end of the spectrum. It causes the world economy to be structured around the desires of the rich, with demand in the economy depending on their inclination to consume. Extreme inequality means that what society '**wants**' in our *Wants, Resources, Work-Effort* model, is largely set by the very rich – if a lack of 'wants' is what limits production (i.e. resources and work-effort are available, only demand is lacking), then it is because the wants of the rich have been met, but not the wants of everyone.

In a free-market economy, inequality will grow more inequality unless government acts to limit it. This happens because there is a positive feedback effect: the possession of wealth makes it easier to acquire more of it and easier to influence policy. Popular opinion expressed through protest or the ballot box is the only obvious counterbalance.

Chapter 20

Planned Economies

Reacting to the injustices of capitalism, socialists and communists sought to abolish it and put in its place a planned economy. They believed that as well as eliminating the gross inequalities of capitalism, a planned economy would also remove the inefficiencies of capitalism such as unemployment and cyclical booms and slumps. Following the 1917 Russian Revolution these ideas were put into practice in Russia and subsequently the rest of the USSR, and after WW2 in Soviet Bloc countries across Eastern Europe and elsewhere.[1]

20.1 Problems of Planned Economies

The experience of planned economies in the Soviet Bloc countries was that while they did remove some of the problems of capitalism, they created or accentuated other problems. Major among these were remote and poorly informed decision-making, ineffective quality enforcement, monopoly of economic power and corruption. They are worth discussing in more detail:

---

[1]USSR – Union of Soviet Socialist Republics, the communist state founded in 1922 and dissolved in 1991, within which Russia was the largest republic.

a) The difficulty of reaching good decisions or any decision at all

Capitalism contains a great deal of autonomy under which many thousands of managers in different companies and at the different levels of each company can take decisions based on their local and specialist knowledge about who to buy from, who to sell to, who to employ, what to make, methods to be used, etc. These managers are less likely to be fooled or kept in the dark than some distant bureaucrat, more likely to react quickly being on the spot, and probably better motivated because of their greater independence of action and greater stake in the success of the business (the likelihood of higher pay if it is successful and redundancy if it isn't). Business autonomy also means that many people in society are able to take the initiative to develop new products or services, not just a single bureaucratic hierarchy.

Figure 20.1: Trotsky described how Soviet leaders struggled with the problems of quality control in a planned economy. [WMC]

b) Lack of mechanisms to enforce quality, reward good performance and punish poor performance

Soviet companies were directed to buy from supplier A and sell to customer B (who was in turn obliged to buy from them). Therefore, they had to accept what A chose to supply whatever the quality, and had no motivation to treat their own customers any better.

On a personal level it seems that keeping your job was often just a matter of complying with bureaucratic or Party norms rather than genuinely trying to do it well. Rationing and quotas are also a disincentive: there is no point in trying to earn more if your ability to buy depends not on whether you have money but on having enough ration coupons which are given to all irrespective of their work. The quality problem was recognised but difficult to solve – the Russian revolutionary Leon Trotsky commented in the 1930s:

"Why is production lowered in light metallurgy in the face of colossal investments? Because, replies Pravda, 'the separate branches of a single combine are not co-ordinated with one another according to their capacity.' Yet the task of co-ordinating branches has been solved by capitalist technology. And how much more complex and difficult is the question of the inter-co-ordination of independent enterprises and entire branches of industry!"

"The administrative hue and cry for quantity leads to a frightful lowering of quality; low quality undermines at the next stage the struggle for quantity; the ultimate cost of economically irrational 'successes' surpasses as a rule many times the value of these same successes." *– Leon Trotsky.[64]*

In the capitalist west, governments also wrestle with the problems of maintaining quality in large state organisations not subject to market discipline. Large private companies that have internal functions that are not easily measured or costed, face similar quality issues. The best way we know of for tackling such problems appears to be an open culture in which independent regulators, opposition parties, journalists and individuals within and outside the organisations concerned, are all free to raise issues and criticise performance. Experience suggests that hierarchical one-party states tend not to offer such checks and balances.

c) Monopoly of power and suppression of individual liberty

An economy run as a single planned entity implies centralisation and a monopoly of economic power. That makes it easier for regimes to become dictatorial and oppressive, with curbs on individual freedoms. As an individual in a pluralist free-market economy, if you fall out with one employer, or they dislike your opinions, then you might hope to find another who is not aware of your dispute or at least takes a different view. In a planned economy where the state is the only employer, there is nowhere else to go. While it is true that private employers have been known to maintain and share blacklists – of trade union activists for example – that is still a very long way from having a monolithic state in control of almost everything from your job to the flat you rent.

While being denied appropriate employment and marginalised or worse, is a personal tragedy for the individual concerned, it also wastes that person's abilities and so weakens the economy. It is quite likely to be the cleverest individuals with strong independent views, who get branded dissidents and excluded, making the loss to society all the greater.

d) Corruption – who gets what depends on planners, not just ability to pay

When decisions about the allocation of products or services are made by planners rather than the market, there is scope for corruption. For example if a bureaucrat is responsible for deciding who gets housed and in which apartment, then there is a clear opportunity for bribery. Similarly, whenever a product is sold below true value, i.e. at less that people are willing to pay for it, a risk of corruption exists, since by definition, someone is willing to pay the true value and therefore may offer it, in the form of the nominal value plus a bribe. For those reasons, in areas where a society uses planning or rationing, controls are required to minimise corruption – but unfortunately as discussed in (b) above, monolithic hierarchical states tend to lack those checks and balances.

20.2 Strengths of Planned Economies

Perhaps unsurprisingly, a high degree of government planning appears to be an effective strategy when a country wants to focus on a limited number of goals, especially during wartime. While the Soviet Union with its planned economy, ultimately failed, it did however – though very brutally – industrialise rapidly and turn itself into a military superpower during and post WW2. Similarly, a focus on healthcare and education by Cuba's communist government has brought exemplary standards in those sectors, comparable to those of countries with much higher GDPs. The governments of capitalist powers are also not averse to planning when they need its advantages. The USA and UK both resorted to extensive direction of their economies during WW2 and in the Cold War armaments and space race that followed it.

Figure 20.2: Colossus computer: computers, the internet and web, were all developed with public funds. [WMC]

In the capitalist countries state funding and state institutions often do the heavy lifting that gets new technologies started. When we think of the internet and the web, we think of the private corporations that provide the computers and smartphones we use to access the internet, and the corporations that provide services available such as Google, Facebook, and many many more. But the internet and the World Wide Web themselves were both developed with government funding and within government funded institutions,[2] as indeed were the first computers.[3] Many high-tech start-up companies are based on research carried out in publicly-funded universities. We may label countries like the USA or UK as 'capitalist' or 'market economies' but in practice they are 'mixed economies' with a great deal of state funding and direction, particularly in areas related to defence.

20.3 Attractiveness of Planned Economies

When the USSR collapsed in 1991, one of the most striking things was how little active popular support it appeared to get from Soviet citizens. Compare that lack of street protest in support of a continuation of communism with what happened in the UK in 2016 following a narrow referendum vote in favour of leaving the European Union. In the UK there were huge pro-EU rallies of hundreds of thousands of people, plus a continuous protest in front of the British parliament over several years. The comparison is all the more remarkable given that the USSR was the product of a historic communist revolution, while the EU had previously been seen by most Britons as just a rather dull bureaucratic institution (judging by the low turnouts in elections to the European Parliament), until they realised what they were about to lose.

One possibility is that even if planned economies are actually better at providing the basics of life like education, health care and jobs (and perhaps better for the environment, if less consumerist), they are nevertheless difficult to sustain because they are undermined politically by the temptation of consumer goods available under capitalism. It could also be the case that capitalism is more

---

[2]The internet emerged from the earlier ARPANET developed by the US Advanced Research Projects Agency. Tim Berners-Lee invented the World Wide Web in 1989, while working at CERN (*Conseil Européen pour la Recherche Nucléaire*).

[3]The first two electronic computers, ENIAC and Colossus, were built during WW2 in the USA and UK respectively, as part of the war effort.

economically virulent: driven by the market requirement to innovate, it generates both more consumer goods and more advanced military technologies, making it able to out compete a planned economy psychologically and militarily.

20.4 Capitalism and Communism Compared

The strength of capitalism comes from the freedom it offers people to make their own decisions within a framework of rules. This is an economic freedom not to be confused with political liberty. Free markets and free enterprise do not necessarily require democracy; they can exist under dictators, and today even exist under communist governments – notably in China. This economic freedom means that:

- Individuals are free to start small businesses. Many remain small, but between them, the thousands of such companies successfully fulfil many local or specialist needs. Some grow into large companies.

- Large companies are free to make major investments in novel products, such as the iPhone and Tesla's electric cars.

With this freedom goes responsibility and the possibility of failure. The small-business owner may lose his or her money, the lazy worker is unlikely to be very successful.

One could argue that since the vast majority of people don't practice the freedom to set up a business, it cannot be a very important freedom. But for society to benefit it is not necessary that a freedom be practised universally. Only a few people become novelists, but society would be quite different if that freedom were suppressed, or limited to state licensed and approved writers. This is also true of inventors and entrepreneurs. There are over 4 million registered companies in Britain, which represents a rich variety of economic decision-making. Furthermore, in a market economy we all have significant freedoms as consumers in influencing what gets made, and as employees in deciding who we will work for: freedoms which were much more limited under Soviet communism.

My own brief experiences of communism were visiting the USSR in 1989 and Cuba in 1992, in both cases travelling from Nicaragua where I was working at the university of engineering. Nicaragua was then one of the poorest countries in the Americas, and emerging from war. It had been experimenting with socialist policies but retained a market economy.

In just a few days spent in Soviet Russia I was struck by the contrast between the country's ability to build passenger jet aircraft like the one I'd arrived in, an impressive and efficient metro, and the handsome university buildings I visited – let alone spacecraft and space stations – and yet at the same time, shops were often dismal and sparsely stocked. In a cafe on Moscow's prestigious Gorky Street, I was served a lukewarm coffee in a cracked cup on a dirty table, while at the airport when I left I couldn't even get that as the one cafe had already shut for the day. By contrast, even then in Nicaragua, you could always find markets selling fruit and snacks, small cafes and bars, and so forth.

The trip to Cuba three years later, was with a Nicaraguan colleague, to visit a sister university that had provided support to Nicaragua. We spent most of our time on the university campus. Research efforts were closely focussed on the country's needs. We saw projects on biotechnology to develop improved crops, and on developing energy-efficient methods in industry, among others. Work was underway to construct two factories to manufacture products developed by the university. We spent time with students since we had met a Nicaraguan student studying there, which allowed us some very relaxed and wide-ranging discussions. We also had direct experience of Cuba's effective health service, when my colleague needed a doctor.

A minor frustration was that I was desperate for some fresh fruit as the canteen where we were staying had none, nor did we see any in shops. Eventually we picked some oranges from trees in a tourist hotel, most of which seemed to be going to waste on the ground. The difficulty of buying a fruit provoked continual thoughts along the lines of "why not allow people to plant a few bananas and sell them off a barrow?" As it happened, the shared private taxi we took back to Havana stopped on the motorway to allow passengers to buy plantain from campesinos (farmers or farmworkers) carrying bunches on their bicycles.[4]

Figure 20.3: Cuba: stopping on the motorway to buy plantain.

Our visit was during a time of economic turmoil following the collapse of the Soviet Union, and Cuba was suffering a severe economic crisis. Cubans spoke of a "double blockade": the intensified U.S. blockade plus the collapse of commerce with the wrecked economies of their former Soviet Bloc trading partners. The country was able to import only about a third of its petroleum needs and had given priority to agriculture. To compensate the government had imported a million Chinese bicycles that we saw everywhere, and set up a bicycle factory. One lecturer who we had known when he worked with us in Nicaragua and had been somewhat overweight, happily ascribed his now slimmer and fitter figure to the switch to cycling for the commute to work. It seems that he was not alone since there are studies showing a large decline in the rates of death from cardiovascular disease and diabetes, during this period. The government also encouraged the planting of allotments (reminiscent of the UK's wartime 'Dig for Victory' campaign); there was one in front of the small block of flats where the faculty dean lived.

I came away from Cuba, fascinated and impressed, as well as very grateful to our hosts – but asking a lot of questions about what is practical and what is desirable in terms of state control of the economy, and also how that might vary with the industrial level of a country. Whatever one may think of its

---

[4]In recent years Cuba has in fact introduced reforms allowing an expansion of the private sector including independent farmers, and its GDP has grown substantially.

regime, Cuba remains an extraordinary experiment in government planning and direction.

My own very limited experiences recounted above, do tend to support the view that in a planned economy it is difficult to identify the need for and organise the supply of small local facilities like cafes and fruit stalls, or to maintain quality of service. Of course there are other considerations: we need to recognise that some of the services in poorer free-market countries are being provided by desperate people who earn only a wretched living, for example by selling a few bananas to drivers waiting at traffic lights. Also, in such economies, it may be that while services are readily available, only the relatively rich can afford them, for example eating a good steak in a decent restaurant. Yet I'm convinced that there were then (as now) plenty of small businesses in Nicaragua that did succeed in making a reasonable living while also fulfilling the needs of local people in ways that central planners would find hard to do.

The above observations suggest that countries do better with: *a system that combines a strong public sector which sets overall direction, with a degree of economic autonomy and freedom that allows decentralised decision-making and enables small businesses to fulfil local and specialist needs.*

Communism was a system designed by intellectuals and planners that was imposed on what became the USSR quite suddenly and with an almost religious insistence that the system and its theories could not be questioned. That left little space for changes in response to 'user dissatisfaction'. Capitalism is not really a 'system' in the same way – rather it evolved over centuries. Capitalism has its theorists, but they came along after the system was already in place and may be regarded as commentators rather than designers: capitalism would have existed without them. Capitalism's 'rules' are the product of adaption to pressure from many different sectors of society, which is not to say that it doesn't strongly favour wealth and privilege.

The lesson seems to be that: *it is better to have a system that can evolve, and on that basis it would seem better to seek one which could evolve gradually from what we have now.*

20.5 Summary

The history of the 20th century tells us that government direction is required for many of humanity's greatest achievements, whether landing on the moon or universal health care. On the other hand it also tells us that it is desirable to have a system that preserves economic autonomy and freedoms, and that those countries that attempted to eliminate the market completely, found themselves with a new set of problems.

So if we seek to change our economy to reduce the injustices and damaging social and environmental effects of free-market capitalism, we should remain aware that revolutions tend to be horribly expensive in both life and money, and the outcomes far from certain. Accordingly, it would seem wise to try to attain any new system by building on and gradually modifying what we have.

Where we choose to increase the use of planning and state-owned enterprises, then to minimise opportunities for corruption we should ensure democratic checks and balances are also implemented.

Further Reading. A book written in the 1980s when the Soviet Bloc still existed, examines the problems of economic management in the communist countries and what we can learn from them: The Economics of Feasible Socialism by Alec Nove.[65] It seems curious now to read about an economic system that has gone from those countries, yet we can still learn from their experience.

Chapter 21

Long Term Investment and Discounting the Grandchildren

This chapter is about making good decisions about the long-term future and in particular about an economics accounting method called 'discounting'.

21.1 Maximising Long Term Economic Benefits

It is reasonable to expect that economic policy should aim to make life better for ourselves and our descendants. By 'better' we usually mean some combination of:

- More or higher quality goods and services – taken in the broadest sense to include everything from housing to health-care, from entertainment to the quality of the environment.

- Less work and more agreeable work.

We have already discussed how scientific and technical progress expands human capabilities, enabling us to do more. But taking the level of technical knowledge as a given at any moment in time, how should we make investment decisions – how can we judge what sorts of things should we choose to build for the best future outcome in terms of our standard of living?

> *The absolute limit on how much stuff we can have is when we have accumulated so much that all our hours of work are taken up with maintaining and replacing what we have and there is no time left to make anything extra.*

It is important to remember that even so-called 'capital' items eventually wear out. The word 'capital' is only a convenient distinction between things which last a longish time (like a tractor or building) and things which last a shortish time (like a tankful of diesel). So an economy that chose to build more and more roads but made no advances in road-building technology, would eventually reach a limit at which the rate of loss equals the rate of gain – the miles of road that fell into disrepair every year, would be the same or greater than the miles of new road built.

Every product requires labour to produce it, to maintain it over its lifetime and to dispose of it. If you add up that labour and divide by the product's lifetime you get a figure for the average amount of work required to make the product available for a year of use. If we can reduce that by technical advances, we will be able to either have more products available to use, or have the same number of products but work less to get them.

The best policy is not always obvious. You might feel that making a solid table that will last one hundred years is better than making a lighter one that will last only twenty-five years. But if the solid one takes more than four times the effort to build, then the total work over one hundred years would be less if you chose instead to build a lighter table every twenty-five years.

Rapid technological change also makes it pointless to build for a long life if the product is likely to become obsolete and therefore discarded after a fairly short time. For example, there is little sense in designing a computer to last thirty years given the rate at which users are obliged to change to newer models because the older ones cannot run the latest software. Even where something still does its job – such as an old fridge or an old car – it may nevertheless be better to replace it if newer models are so much more efficient that they are significantly cheaper to run and less damaging to the environment (although emissions that result from manufacturing the new model and disposing of the old, should also be included in the calculation).

On the other hand if we want to improve the lot of humanity, we should take care that investment in long-lived goods does not ignore benefits and costs that will occur in the distant future – more than 50 years hence say – because buildings, bridges and the like can last hundreds of years, as we see with medieval buildings and Victorian railway viaducts. If we build houses that we expect to last a century or more, and we put in the extra effort required to minimise their heating requirements (by good insulation, passive solar, etc.), we will be saving future generations from having to carry out the far greater amount of work required to either retrofit insulation later, or construct and maintain the extra power generation capacity needed to heat the substandard housing we left them.

The standard economics method for judging investment decisions about long-lived items, is *discounting*, and we shall look at it more closely because there are cases where it has been used to justify some very doubtful decisions. But before we get into the detail, here is a little thought experiment:

> *Imagine that your grandparents from you mother's and father's sides, live in nearby towns not too far from yours. We'll call them the Discounters and the Bequestors. You gave both a set of keys to your house so that they could check on it while you are on a holiday.*

> *On arriving home, you find that the Bequestors have left you an unexpected present in the living room: a beautiful piece of furniture. There's a letter attached explaining that they were having one made for themselves, and that it didn't cost too much extra to extend*

> *the pleasure to you by making a second one. On moving to the kitchen, you discover that the Discounters have also been in your house and have ripped out your washing machine and stolen it! Replacing it and repairing the damage they caused is going to cost you a small fortune. They've left you a note explaining that an economist had advised them that driving over and taking yours would be far cheaper than buying their own.*

How would you feel about your grandparents after this? Are the Bequestors foolish for wasting money on a present that brings no benefit to them, while the Discounters demonstrated wisdom and financial responsibility by saving themselves the expense of buying their own washing machine? The Discounters 'discounted' the cost to you of replacing the washing machine since they don't have to pay it and your distress doesn't impact them given the distance away that they live. The **discounting** we are concerned with in economics also attaches a price to distant costs or benefits ... but distant not in <u>miles</u> as in our thought experiment, but in <u>time</u>.

The thought experiment illustrates that there is a moral aspect to discounting. Both a gift and a theft are similar insomuch as they involve a transfer of wealth between two parties, decided upon by only one of them. But there, for most of us, the similarity ends.

21.2   Discounting Technique

When making investment decisions, economists want to compare alternatives by putting a monetary value on them. A difficulty is that investments may deliver the benefits at different times. Economists solve this by adjusting the value of future benefits, putting a lower value on them the further off they are. If I promise you £100 in a years time, that is assumed to be worth less than an offer of £100 today – but how much less? A way to put a figure on it is to use the typical *real* rate of return available elsewhere such as from banks: suppose that it is 5% per year, then if I put £100 into the bank today I should get back £105 in a year's time. So if I offer you a choice of either £100 today or an investment that may return least a bit over £105 in a years time, then waiting a year could be worth it, but for exactly £105 or anything less, it isn't: you will do just as well spending the £100 today or putting it in the bank.

Note that we use the 'real' rate of return for these calculations, i.e. adjusting for inflation. In the example above we've assumed zero inflation so £105 in a year's time is worth more (buys more) than £100 would today. If inflation were instead 10%, then £105 in a year's time would be worth **less** than £100 today and we'd be worse off in real terms – so in that case we'd want an **actual** rate of return of 15.5% to give us a **real** rate of return of 5%.

Using this approach, economists adjust future costs and earnings to what are supposed to be the values we would put on them if we were going to pay out or receive the money today. With a little maths, we can see that in the example above, if £100 today is worth the same as £105 in a years time, then £100 in a years time is worth £100 × 100 ÷ 105 = £95.24 today. The interest rate used in this calculation is called the 'real discount rate' and needs to be the real rate of return, i.e. adjusted to remove the effects of inflation.

Is there anything wrong with the discounting technique? Probably nothing if only comparing investments for a modest few years into the future, e.g. should I buy machine A for my factory or buy machine B which costs more but will last longer. The problem arises when comparing very long term investments of several decades or even centuries. In such cases discounting gives too little weight to distant future benefits, and even worse, virtually ignores distant future costs.

21.3 Discounting Bequests or 'Gifts'

Our bequests are the things we leave behind for the benefit and enjoyment of those who come after us: our legacy, or our 'gifts to the future'. Many investments do indeed last for decades or centuries, and are passed on from generation to generation. The house I live in is now 97 years old, and many nearby houses are well over 100; the local railways were built 160 years ago or more.

Table 21.1 shows what value we would assign today to a future cost or benefit of £100 when evaluating different investments, assuming a real discount rate of 2.2%. So for example if our project is expected to produce £100 of benefit (at today's prices) in ten years time, we'll value that at £80.44. If the cost or benefit is even further into the future, we scarcely value it at all: if it is two-hundred years ahead we value it at just £1.28 and after a little over four-hundred years, at a negligible 1 penny (£0.01).

Years into the future	Discount future costs/benefits by	Value to be assigned today to that future £100 benefit or cost
0	1.00	£100.00
1	1.02	£97.85
10	1.24	£80.44
50	2.97	£33.68
100	8.81	£11.34
150	26	£3.82
200	78	£1.28
300	684	£0.15
425	10,390	£0.01

Table 21.1: At a discount rate of 2.2%, beyond 50 years, the costs we load onto our grandchildren are largely ignored.

So the problem with discounting future benefits is that it places almost no value on the legacy that we leave future generations. I used to commute to work over a brick railway viaduct built in 1837. It's a vital part of UK rail infrastructure carrying frequent high-speed electric trains. Happily for us, the Victorian engineers built it to last – already almost 190 years. Had they adopted the accounting methods of recent decades they might have built something far less durable: there are concrete structures built only 60 years ago or less that are showing their age like the flyover pictured in Figure 2.5.

Figure 21.1: Wharncliffe viaduct: built 1837 and still in service. [WMC]

Decisions regarding energy for housing and transport, offer further examples of thinking only in the short-term and not about our legacy. In the 1960s the UK invested heavily in developing oil and gas wells in the North Sea, knowing full well that these resources would be exhausted in a few decades. The 'natural gas'[1] from the North Sea, was promoted for heating buildings. Yet also in the early 1960s, the architect Emslie Morgan built a pioneering heavily-insulated school building, heated mainly by passive solar energy.[2] Had the UK chosen back then to invest in solar technology and require new buildings to be so well insulated that they used only minimal energy, we would be continuing to reap the benefits today and would go on doing so for the entire future lifetime of those buildings. Sadly that did not happen and the UK's building stock is poorly insulated. As a result with gas prices spiralling, and much of our gas imported as the North Sea fields dwindle, many households in the UK are struggling or unable to pay their energy bills.[3]

---

[1]Called 'natural' to distinguish it from the 'town gas' used previously which was made from coal.

[2]St George's Secondary School in Wallasey, Merseyside

[3]Gas prices rose rapidly in the UK and globally in 2021 and 2022, with a

21.4 Discounting Thefts

Undervaluing distant future <u>benefits</u> is a great shame – we shall have to hope that future generations will be grateful for what we did leave them, and not think overly much about what we did not. But unfortunately, discounting also allows planners to ignore future <u>costs</u>. To do so on a large scale is a theft from future generations. No amount of financial jiggery-pokery should be allowed to hide the crime, because when our descendants have to shoulder the burden, it will not be reduced by the passage of time, but require just as much in terms of labour and materials as it would take now. The discounters will tell you that we can leave a fund that will grow over the years such that it pays for the future work – but that misunderstands money. Money does not and cannot transmit wealth from one whole generation of humanity to the next, only real wealth does so – things like infrastructure, farms, nature, knowledge and art. Money is a zero-sum game when passed from one generation to the next: if one fund is made bigger, then another has been made smaller by the same amount.[4] All that money does is pass down to the next generation, the *distribution* of stuff among humans, not the total *amount* of stuff in the world. The amount of actual stuff passed on, such as land and other assets, stays the same, and money just affects who owns it.

21.4.1 The nuclear steal

An example of discounting theft is the burden imposed by the civil nuclear power industry on our descendants. Since the dismantling of reactors takes place many years into the future, planners can discount and thus largely disregard the costs imposed on future generations who will get no benefit from the electricity that was generated by the plants decades or centuries before they were born. Worse still, by using discounting, the costs of storing and guarding

---

knock on effect on electricity.

[4]A 'zero-sum game' refers to a situation where one person's gain is another's loss, so when you sum all the gains and losses the result is zero.

radioactive waste for millennia are deemed negligible, and almost completely ignored.

To work out the cost of electricity from a normal (non-nuclear) power plant we add up the lifetime costs to build and run it, and divide by the total electricity it is expected to produce. But the government and nuclear salesmen have a problem: nuclear also has a huge cost at the end of a reactor's life, to dismantle it and store the radioactive waste for many thousands of years. This is where the magic of 'discounting' comes in and abracadabra shrinks those costs to a fraction of their real size, thus concealing the appallingly high cost of nuclear-generated electricity. Proposed discount rates vary; I have used a rate of 2.2% for the examples in this chapter (in Table 21.1 and the graphs) because the UK government used that rate when attempting to make the case for new nuclear plants in its 2008 'White Paper on Nuclear Power'. Referring to the 'size of the fund needed to pay for back-end costs, including the costs of decommissioning and waste management' it says:

> "As a part of the total levelised cost of new nuclear power these back-end costs are relatively small, although there is significant uncertainty attached to them. We also make a conservative assumption of 2.2% (in real terms) on the rate at which the fund grows over the accrual period." – *White Paper on Nuclear Power.[66]*

A discount rate of 2.2% implies that we could invest in a fund that would grow by that amount above inflation and would therefore yield a 3-fold increase in its real value in 50 years time to pay for the shutdown costs. But nuclear plants are not dismantled the year they are shut: the work is spread out over several decades and can exceed 150 years from when the plant was built as illustrated in Figure 21.2, by which time our notional fund would supposedly have grown 26-fold. That allows the planners when they propose the construction of a nuclear plant, to divide costs expected that far into the future by 26, ignoring all but 4% of them.

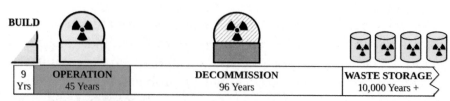

NUCLEAR LIFECYCLE

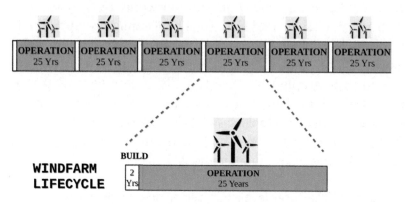

WINDFARM LIFECYCLE

Figure 21.2: The Nuclear 'lifecycle' versus wind.
Future generations must pay the costs of dismantling defunct reactors and guarding radioactive waste for thousands of years. No such issue exists for renewable technologies like wind.

The nuclear lifecycle shown in the figure above, is based on an actual UK power station Hunterston B, as is the projected decommissioning duration.[67] The waste storage duration of 10,000 years is based on proposed compliance periods for the Yucca Mountain US repository, but these have been challenged and guarantees for at least a million years are now requested.[68] The operating period quoted for a windfarm is a typical expected turbine lifetime and may well be extended (the world's first 1MW turbine has operated for 45 years at Tvindkraft). Wind turbines can be refurbished, or replaced with larger and more powerful models (re-powering); gaps are shown for this in the diagram, although a rolling programme replacing a turbine at a time seems more likely.

The radioactive waste fuel from a nuclear power plant, and the radioactive parts of the reactor when dismantled, must be guarded for many thousands of years. If discounting is applied to costs so far into the future, they become a derisory sum: impose a cost of a billion Pounds on our descendants a thousand years hence, and it gets discounted to just 35 pence – less than the price of a small bar of chocolate.[5]

To provide some context, the UK's Nuclear Decommissioning Authority (NDA) in the year 2022-23 had an annual budget of about £3.7 billion, £2.5 billion of which is spent on Sellafield, the major UK site for nuclear waste processing and storage. The NDA looks after 17 nuclear sites across the UK, with more than 800 buildings to be demolished, and it has 17,000 employees across the estate.[69]

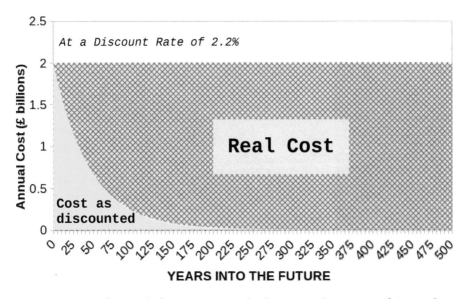

Figure 21.3: Annual future costs decline to almost nothing when discounted.

Let's suppose that we are estimating the expense of work to be carried out over a few hundred years with a real annual cost of £2 billion in today's money (a modest assumption since the NDA

---

[5]Using a 2.2% real discount rate.

currently spends considerably more than that). What would we estimate the annual and cumulative costs to be if we apply a discount rate of 2.2%, and how would that compare with the real future costs? Figure 21.3 shows how discounting an annual £2 billion cost, makes the estimated annual cost decline rapidly to almost nothing, even though the real annual cost has remained exactly the same (again, in today's money).

How the total cost rises year-on-year is shown in Figure 21.4. Notice how the discounted total barely changes after 100 years, and at the end of five hundred years is only a tiny fraction of the real total.

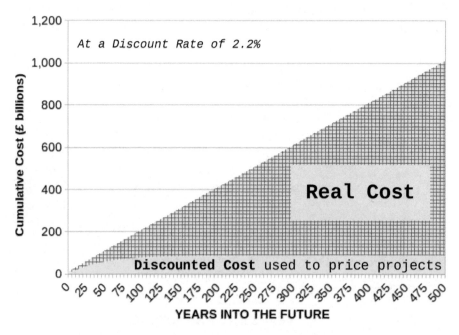

Figure 21.4: Discounting allows the total costs of work extending far into the future to be cut to a derisory amount.

Exactly how much nuclear decommissioning and waste processing will be required is uncertain. A UK parliamentary report mentions a cost to taxpayer of £132 billion to decommission the UK's civil nuclear sites, with work not completed for another 120 years.[70] In any case, the UK is building a new nuclear plant at

Hinkley point, so for as long as reactors continue to be built and for about 150 years afterwards, there will be decommissioning work and waste to be handled.

Even when humanity abandons nuclear fission power plants, the underground repositories are meant to be kept secure for hundreds of thousands of years. Who is going to monitor them? How many employees will be needed and how big a budget: what fraction of the NDA's current 17,000 employees and annual £3.7bn will be enough? There must be some critical minimum below which the requisite skills and equipment cannot be maintained. Let's say only a tenth of that amount is needed, costing £0.37 billion a year, and we'll assume that the UK's long-term storage site is completed in 100 years time. Monitoring then begins and continues for some thousands of years – how will the real costs and discounted costs stack up over time (again, using a real discount rate of 2.2%)?

Years of Monitoring	Real Total Cost	Discounted Total Cost
100	£37bn	£1.692bn
200	£74bn	£1.884bn
500	£185bn	£1.908bn
1,000	£370bn	£1.908bn
25,000	£9,250bn	£1.908bn

Table 21.2: The real costs of monitoring waste for thousands of years could be trillions, but when discounted becomes so small that beyond 200 years it barely changes. (rate used: 2.2%)

The results are shown in Table 21.2. Alarmingly, discounting appears to let us almost completely ignore a cost of trillions of Pounds (note that almost any discount rate likely to be used would have that effect over such long time periods). Perhaps the real costs are too high because we assumed an unrealistically high annual spend? Well by comparison, the UK has an organisation called English Heritage which also takes care of relics from the past: prehistoric sites,

Roman ruins, medieval castles and so forth, some of which are over 2,000 years old. To look after these sites English Heritage spent about £121 million in 2020-21. Although that's a bit under half of the £370 million (£0.37bn) that we assumed above for nuclear waste surveillance, it is still in the same ballpark, and English Heritage's sites are a great deal simpler given that they do not contain tons of lethal radioactive waste with its associated technical complexities and security risks! So it is hard to believe that guarding and monitoring nuclear waste sites and fixing defects, won't cost at least as much and possibly much more. The solutions offered to the nuclear waste problem appear to rely on magical thinking: wishing reality was other than it is. Two examples follow.

Magical Thinking 1. The technical fix

Some argue that technical advances make everything cheaper, so surely it will get cheaper to deal with old reactors and waste, won't it? In fact experience shows otherwise: the cost of coping with the nuclear legacy we already have is spiralling. Future safety standards are likely to be more stringent than today's, pushing costs up further.

In the UK, dealing with the nuclear debris so far accumulated was estimated at £48 billion in 2002; the estimate had risen to £124 billion by 2019, and in 2022 analysis by independent experts suggest it could reach £260 billion.[71, 72, 73] In the USA, Yucca Mountain in Nevada was selected in 1987 as a suitable site for the national geological repository of nuclear waste. The project was abandoned in 2010 – at least $14.5 billion had been spent, with some estimates nearer $20bn.[74, 75] The UK, USA and most other countries that have nuclear power plants as well, still have no solution for long-term storage; the waste remains sitting on the surface at power plants or in related facilities.

The reason for these out-of-control costs is that nuclear is an unusually intractable technology because of the combination of radioactivity, toxicity and security risks (catastrophic accidents, terrorism, weapons of mass destruction, dirty bombs). Those risks

combined with the small numbers produced (only a few hundred reactors have ever been built worldwide), the long construction times
(up to ten years or more) and the need to store waste for more or
less eternity, mean that reactors can never be mass-produced in the
way that televisions and cars are, and will never be cheap.

Magical Thinking 2. The clean-up fund

Another fantasy is that we will solve the problem for future generations by not just discounting future costs, but by actually starting
a fund that really does grow at 2.2% a year in real terms, and will
sit there safely for hundreds and eventually thousands of years, and
will be big enough when the day comes to pay for all the work.
There are three problems with this:

1) It is madness to believe that our countries and institutions
   will be stable enough for such a fund to be maintained such a
   long way into the future. Just look at the history of the last
   one hundred years, let alone the last one hundred thousand.

2) Experience shows that nuclear energy companies are more
   likely to be desperate for government bailouts than flush with
   funds that they can put aside for the future. Even if created,
   few such funds are likely to survive long given the horrendous dismantling and waste costs. The UK's nuclear power
   company British Energy established a fund in 1996, but the
   company had to be bailed out by the taxpayer in 2002 to avoid
   bankruptcy.[76] France's nuclear company EDF also has billions of euros of debts and the French government plans to
   fully nationalise it in 2024.[77] So in practice there are no
   funds, only liabilities, and it is present and future taxpayers
   that will have to pay the ballooning nuclear costs.

3) More fundamentally, even if a fund was established and maintained for centuries to come, it would make no difference to
   the fact that we are passing a material burden to future generations. As referred to earlier in this chapter, money does not
   transmit wealth from one generation of humans to the next,

it only transmits how the actual wealth – land & property – is shared out among that next generation. If you decide on a very lavish funeral you could assure your children that it won't cost them anything because you've put part of your savings into a fund to pay for it – but while they may or may not begrudge you the expense, they'll certainly realise that had you opted for something more modest, most of that money would come to them instead of going to the undertaker. So it is with radioactive waste: no financial scheme can change the fact that if we oblige future generations to spend time dealing with our horrendous garbage, it means that they cannot use that time to work instead on something positive that would benefit them.

Climate desperation

The threat of climate change has led some to say that we must throw everything at the problem of lowering carbon emissions, even atomic plants. It's an argument I'd have sympathy with if we really were 'throwing everything at the climate problem', but we are not, very far from it. We are riding around in SUVs, expanding aviation, launching space tourism, failing to insulate homes, promoting rampant consumerism, and blocking renewable energy schemes such as (in the UK's case) on-shore wind and tidal energy, to name just a few examples. The fastest and cheapest way to drive down fossil-fuel use is to invest in energy saving and renewables. Nor does nuclear help as a back-up for renewables: for that you need inexpensive generators that are mostly held in reserve and can be run-up swiftly when needed. Nuclear by contrast has to be run at high capacity all the time because that's the only way to justify the enormous build cost. Cheaper, simpler and safer would be just to keep some of the gas power stations we already have for emergencies; eventually to fuel them we could use biogas or gas synthesised with spare peaks of renewable electricity. In terms of 'keeping the lights on', even minor accidents and maintenance can take reactors offline for months or years, as can hot weather – half of France's reactors were off in the summer of 2022 because of maintenance and problems cooling them during the summer.[78] And then there are the accidents ...

Cost of accidents

There is considerable debate about how many people have died as a result of nuclear accidents, but let us put that to one side, since what we can all agree on is that nuclear accidents are <u>very</u> costly. About 1% of all the reactors ever built have suffered catastrophes: Windscale (military, UK), Three Mile Island (USA), Chernobyl (Ukraine) and three at Fukushima (Japan). These accidents rank among the most expensive in history, and they have not ended – they will continue to impose heavy costs for years to come. Since Fukushima in 2011, most of Japan's 54 reactors have been switched off, and for several years <u>all</u> of them. Italy and Germany have shut all their nuclear plants, prompted by public reaction to respectively the Chernobyl and Fukushima accidents. Should there be another major accident in Europe it could easily result in the closure of much or all of Europe's entire remaining nuclear fleet. A leaked 2007 study by France's Institute for Radiological Protection and Nuclear Safety (IRSN) is said to have given an estimated worst-case cost for a major accident of €5.8 trillion, or over three times France's then GDP – such a disaster would be likely to result in financial and societal collapse.[79] These are astonishing financial risks and are part of the reason why nuclear is uninsurable for all but a small liability that would cover only a fraction of the costs of a Chernobyl or a Fukushima. It is today's and future taxpayers who are paying for the disasters, and even pay for those in countries other than their own – several European countries including the UK contribute to the ongoing costs of securing Chernobyl.[80]

Probability of accidents

What about the probability of an accident? Very low probabilities are quoted by the nuclear industry, based on complex and rather abstract calculations of failure modes. The UK government suggests that "the potential for a major accident in the UK – the meltdown of the reactor's core along with failure of the containment structure – is one in 2.4 billion per reactor year".[81, 82] Well there are roughly 450 reactors operating in the world today, so worldwide, instead of one failure every 2.4 billion years we ought to expect 450 times that, or in other words:

$$Worldwide,\ One\ Failure\ Every = \frac{2.4 \times 1000,000,000}{450}\ years$$

$$= 5.3\ million\ years\ (approx.)$$

One major accident worldwide every 5.3 million years still sounds incredibly infrequent – is it believable? The answer from our experience so far is a resounding '**NO**': we've already suffered FIVE major reactor accidents and nuclear power reactors have existed for only seventy years. That works out as an average of **one accident every fourteen** years, not one every 5.3 million years. Others have made similar observations, as with this study: *'How safe is nuclear power? A statistical study suggests less than expected'* published in the *Bulletin of the Atomic Scientists*.[83]

On page 194 of Walter C Patterson's excellent 1976 book 'Nuclear Power', he explains the risk of reactor meltdown if the cooling system fails, which remains a danger even after the reactor has been shut down, since radioactive decay continues to produce considerable heat.[84] That was what happened at Fukushima: seawater from the tsunami caused the back-up diesel generators that powered the cooling pumps to fail. I don't know how many times I have heard nuclear proponents insist that the UK cannot suffer such an accident because we don't have tsunamis. If a truck carrying nuclear waste crashes in Australia to avoid a kangaroo, will we also be told that no truck in the UK will ever crash because the UK doesn't have kangaroos? Unfortunately other animals – and other cooling system failures – are available. The war in Ukraine has put at risk the Zaporizhzhia nuclear power plant, which has been forced at times to rely on emergency diesel generators to maintain cooling, with supplies of diesel fuel also a concern.[85, 86]

It's hard to understand how anyone could ever have taken the decision to hand such a legacy to our successors. When the atomic energy industry started it was part of a desperate race to acquire atomic weapons at the outset of the Cold War. The UK's first power plant Calder Hall, was primarily intended to produce plutonium for the UK's atomic weapons programme. Immediate military advantage may therefore have overridden long-term considerations. Today we are assaulted by multiple fears: of climate change, of AI taking over, and the ongoing threat of nuclear war. Perhaps as a result, we don't believe in our hearts that we'll have any descendants in a couple of hundred years' time let alone in a thousand: we don't care about the long-term future because we don't think there is one.

Nuclear power further reading

There many government reports about nuclear but since they are usually written to justify a nuclear-power policy, they require painful dissection. The two books below are accessible and stand the test of time. Patterson in particular explains topics such as fast breeder reactors that are still being argued about today. The Voodoo Economics report is clearly relevant.

- Nuclear Power by Walter C Patterson.[84] Patterson's book is a rare animal: a technical book by a nuclear physicist written for the lay reader.

- Small is beautiful by E F Schumacher.[1] Part II, Chapter IV. Nuclear Energy – Salvation or Damnation.

- Voodoo Economics and the Doomed Nuclear Renaissance by Paul Brown.[71]

21.4.2 Theft of the ecosystem and biodiversity

The science is settled: human activities are causing a rapid warming of our planet, the consequences of which are a threat to future generations of humans and other species of animals and plants. For anyone who doubts that statement, please browse the subject on the websites of the UN, NASA, or any reputable university or scientific body. In recent years, leading economists have spoken out on the need to address the problem and explained that action now will be less costly than acting later and trying to mitigate the damage.

Unfortunately politicians have not caught up. For most of them, the economy means 'growth', delivering more 'stuff' to consumers and more profit to investors ... and it's only when the economy is prospering in those terms that there will be any cash spare to spend on some 'green' measures. As a consequence, we are denying future generations the ecosystem and biodiversity that should have been their birthright: it is wanton vandalism and theft.

We have known about the scale of the damage caused to the natural world by human activities since at least the 1960s, The Club of Rome published The Limits to Growth in 1972 and the world became aware of climate change in the 1980s (it seems the oil companies knew about climate change much earlier and concealed it) and accepted the need to combat it at the 1992 United Nations Conference on Environment and Development. But over the same period almost every government has poured investment into fossil-fuelled transportation. An entire network of wide multi-lane highways has been laid down during the last fifty years, and it's still growing. The same goes for air travel: new airports, new terminals, cheap flights. Yet we knew decades ago, that road and air travel consume far more energy per passenger-mile than travel by railway, tram or buses, and they are also harder to electrify meaning that the energy had to come from oil. In the UK in 1974 a book 'Changing Directions' was published by The Independent Commission on Transport, which covered almost all of the ills of mass-motoring which we are now only too aware of (accidents, pollution, noise, effect on local shops, impact on pedestrians and cyclists), and pointed out the perils of dependency on oil, which as well as damaging and polluting the environment, was recognised as a finite resource expected to decline in the 21st century, with most supplies in the hands of distant and potentially unstable or unfriendly regimes.[6][87]

Essentially we've spent fifty years building a system that we knew at the outset could not last a hundred, without collapsing and possibly taking us with it. That would remain true even if most cars were electric instead of petrol or diesel. We knew it back then, and we know even more now. Nevertheless, governments compete to get car plants located in their respective countries and do nothing to challenge the worldwide shift to even more damaging (but more profitable for the manufacturer) over-sized vehicles.

Is it so difficult to appreciate that most people on the planet are likely to aspire to the levels of consumption that they see the world's middle and upper classes enjoy – especially since it is actively marketed to them? And that being so, that governments should estimate and plan for a level of consumption that is sustainable if replicated worldwide. How curious it is that despite our scientific sophistication, we are not only less capable of building for the distant future than the ancient Egyptians, Greeks or Romans, or the medieval cathedral builders, but are even unwilling or unable make such simple calculations and work out how to run our economy without laying waste to the planet. Truly, the thinking has stopped too early.

21.5 Summary

When we know that something is required for the long term, we should value **benefits** in the distant future more highly than the current economic technique of discounting does. In that way over decades and centuries, humanity will be more enriched.

We should **NEVER** discount major **COSTS** that we impose on future generations, because they will have to pay the full amount when the time comes. Leaving a bequest for our descendants constitutes a gift; taking something from them is theft.

Nuclear-power assessments in particular, should include the full

---

[6]If you are a transport planner or just interested, this extraordinary little book, packed with both wisdom and data, is still worth reading.

undiscounted cost of all the work to dismantle stations and to guard waste over the centuries and millennia to come, as well as the high probability of further expensive accidents, and balance that against the value of fifty odd years of rather expensive electricity now. Not to do so is immoral, and over the medium to longer term, poor economics. Fortunately renewable energy alternatives are already cheaper and far quicker to build.

Similarly, we should consider the full cost of the burden of climate change on our descendants and take urgent action now to decarbonise and to preserve the natural world.

Chapter 22

The Finance Sector

22.1 Introduction

So far we have focussed on the production of goods and services as the core of what an economy is about and tried to avoid relating everything to money, because real wealth is made up of the physical products of farms and factories – such as wheat, eggs, bicycles and televisions – and of services such as transport, telecommunications, education, healthcare, entertainment, and so forth. By contrast, the financial sector offers no physical products and few services that people would want as ends in themselves – unless you consider playing with money and investments as entertainment. Yet such is the power of money, it's all too easy to believe that the financial sector is a major or even the principal source of wealth; certainly large parts of the GDP are ascribed to it.

"In 2021, the financial services sector contributed £173.6 billion to the UK economy, 8.3% of total economic output. The sector was largest in London, where around half of the sector's output was generated." – *House of Commons Research Briefing.[88]*

But consider this thought experiment: What would set humanity back the most: The loss of the financial sector's offices and expertise or the loss of all farms, factories, mines, schools, hospitals, etc. and associated technical knowledge. In the former case some sort of clumsy system of rationing and barter would have to be established to share out what was produced until a more sophisticated finance system could be rebuilt. In the latter case most people would rapidly starve or freeze to death, and humanity would be thrown back into the Stone Age.

Where then does the extraordinary wealth that the financial sector appears to generate, really come from, if it doesn't itself create it? The answer is that sector has to be viewed as a producer of administrative services used by individuals and companies, and what is being administered is the ownership of wealth: cash, the titles to assets of various sorts (shares, bonds, property, land) and the earnings from those assets. In return for its services the sector takes a cut of that ownership, thus acquiring a share of the wealth produced elsewhere by the wider economy. Additionally, wealth generated by assets is channelled through and reported by the finance sector. So for example if you invest in a fund that buys shares in several companies – in manufacturing, mining, telecommunications or whatever – then those companies will pay dividends into your fund out of the profits they make, and the finance company that manages your fund will report that it has grown; the finance company didn't create that wealth, the wider economy did.

That is not to say that administration doesn't contribute towards production: enterprises of any sort from factories to universities all require administrators. Likewise, finance also needs administration and money is key to the operation of a modern economy as the way in which we share out what is produced and exchange assets such as property. However, the world's financial centres do far more than provide a monetary system. Their rules and operation are part of how the economic game is played, and as such they bias the economy towards the needs and interests of the very rich.

- For most of us who work for a living, money is limited to its basic role: it is the way in which we are given a share in the goods and services produced by the economy in return for our labour – goods and services which we need or want for our own consumption.

- However, for those people or organisations with substantial wealth, money does much more than the basics: it also makes it easy to exchange assets that you do not intend to consume yourself but are buying and selling in order to make a profit. Those assets could be goods that you acquire to re-sell as an intermediary or speculator and that will eventually be consumed, or they could be assets that are not consumed such as the ownership of property or businesses.

The finance sector has a strong influence over the direction of the economy because people or organisations in control of large amounts of wealth are economic decision-makers. They can use that wealth to acquire the assets and labour needed to create new businesses; similarly, they can break up businesses they no longer value by selling off the assets and terminating the employment of the workers. As well as deciding what businesses should exist, they can choose where those businesses are located. They can buy and sell goods, assets and currencies, to speculate on their future value. They can influence slumps and booms, by either spending less than their income (adding to their savings) and thus causing a drop in demand and economic activity, or by doing the opposite and increasing demand and economic activity.

The finance sector is not the only economic decision-maker. Economic decisions are decentralised in a free-market economy; government and large companies are also major players. Nor is it necessarily a bad thing that wealthy individuals or organisations have the ability to make major business or cultural investments; it may for example result in more varied initiatives than if everything was left to the state. However, investment decisions made by the sector are driven by the potential for profit, and therefore likely to show scant concern for any negative consequences for the workforce or the environment. In Chapter 6 we described the consumer going out to shop as being like an eighteenth century gentlemen or lady, waited on by a variety of distant servants of whom they know little or nothing. Likewise, for the finance sector, moving millions of dollars from one company to another and between different countries, is a matter of a moment on a computer trading screen, and equally remote from the real-world outcomes in terms of what gets made where and by whom and under what conditions. Unfortunately the desire for high profits incentivises businesses to search out the most exploited workers in the least regulated environments, with the minimum of taxes or other social responsibilities, and to engage in political lobbying or interference to make sure that those conditions don't improve.

As discussed in previous chapters, production levels in modern industrial economies are mostly limited not by *resources* or *work effort* but by *wants*, and the wants that count are those of the rich. Unable to spend all their income on consumption, they desire opportunities to grow their accumulated savings through trade and investment, and the financial sector's decision-making is driven by that want. This chapter explores some of the consequences; it doesn't attempt to explain the operation of the financial sector, which would be beyond the scope of both this book and my knowledge. However, just as it is possible to observe the negative effects of casinos and gambling without being an expert bookmaker, it ought to be possible to make some observations about the effects of financial markets without being a trader.

22.2 The Need for a Finance Sector

22.2.1 Specialisation needs trade and trade needs money

A modern technological economy is not possible without specialisation, as was discussed in Chapter 10. Specialisation is not possible without ownership and trade: the farmer exchanges the ownership of some of the grain harvest, for ownership of shoes produced by the cobbler; those basics were discussed in Chapter 3. While some trade is possible by direct swap (barter), that rapidly becomes unwieldy and an economy needs money as described in Chapter 5. In order to recognise and record ownership, and issue money, an authority is needed, and in modern societies that is normally the state.

22.2.2 Markets for assets, commodities and currencies

The finance sector is built on top of the fundamental concepts of ownership and money. It provides basic banking services familiar to most people, like the personal and business accounts that enable people to manage their money and make payments. Beyond that it provides marketplaces for the ownership all sorts of assets and commodities, such as land, shares in companies, coffee and petroleum. Money itself can be traded, for example between different currencies or trade in debt.

22.2.3 Speculative financial products

Increasingly complex financial 'products' have been created as the financial sector grew. The basis is usually some sort of speculative financial promise. Insurance is a promise made by the insurer in return for a payment, that they will cover losses if some event should occur; a sort of bet on the future. Similarly, markets allow traders to buy or sell a certain quantity of a commodity to be delivered at a specified future date or simply commit to doing so at an agreed price, creating a futures contract which can also be traded. Typically, these 'financial promise' products reduce risk and uncertainty for those who buy them (the shipowner is covered if the ship sinks, the farmer knows the price that next summer's crop can be sold at); instead the seller takes on the risk in return for a probable profit.

22.2.4 Investment decisions

Basic to capitalism is that the financial sector seeks out opportunities to invest capital in productive businesses, by the issue of shares or via loans. In this way the sector is taking economic decisions about what the economy should produce. Such decisions are not only taken by the finance sector but also within companies themselves which often make investments using retained earnings from the business.

Even an almost entirely planned economy like that of the former USSR needs some financial services, such as banking. Others however, are less important or likely to be absent. For example if all major assets – ships, factories, etc. - are owned by the state, then there is no point in insuring them since he state has deeper pockets than any insurance company, which in any case would presumably be owned by the state.

22.3   Casino Capitalism

While financial services have a legitimate role in a market economy, a great deal of what goes on in financial centres appears to be far beyond what is required to support the productive economy, and has been dubbed by critics as 'casino capitalism'. The sector has grown disproportionately compared to the overall economy. In the USA the financial services sector contributed 2.8 percent to GDP in 1950, which rose to 4.9 percent in 1980 and 8.3 percent in 2006.[89]

The foreign exchange or forex market has grown to be the largest financial market. Most of this currency trading is speculative since it wildly exceeds the actual currency exchanges needed to finance international trade – by about 80 times over. Annual foreign exchange trades are over $2400 trillion, while the value of global trade in actual goods and services is only about $30 trillion a year.[90, 91] Such levels of speculation have not gone unnoticed and have resulted in calls for a tax on conversions of one currency into another with the intention of discouraging short-term speculation and providing a useful source of government income. The idea is known as a 'Tobin tax' after the economist who proposed it.[1]

---

[1]A Tobin tax is a tax on currency conversions in order to discourage short-term currency speculation. The idea is named after economist James Tobin. He is said to have been influenced by Keynes, who in 1936 proposed a transaction tax on dealings on Wall Street, to reduce excessive speculation by uninformed financial traders.

22.3.1   Surplus cash looking for a return

Based on the 'Wants, Resources, Work-Effort' model, it is not surprising that the financial sector has become more prominent. We now have historically extraordinary levels of production in the world thanks to technology. Since the market tends to concentrate wealth, we also have extraordinary levels of inequality. As a result, the world's mega rich have so much money that they cannot spend all of it on personal consumption (they have 'run out of wants'). Because cash depreciates they are continuously searching around for investments where they can place their surplus cash and make even more. This could be by buying ownership of productive resources such as land, housing or businesses, or by loaning the money at interest. They know that playing in the market is a gamble, but it's hard to resist the lure of profits, and an entire industry of account managers, advisers and so forth has grown up to encourage them. These financial experts don't just advise on investments but are also masters in tax avoidance.[2]

The graph shown in Figure 22.1 shows how, as GDP and inequality have increased in the USA, the financial sector has grown to be a larger proportion of the economy. The graph is consistent with the theory that the financial sector has grown in prominence because there is both far more wealth in total (GDP), *and* it is increasingly concentrated in the hands of fewer people, resulting in them having more spare cash with which to play.

---

[2]Tax *avoidance* is taking advantage of legal methods to reduce the amount of tax paid, of which there are many if you have enough money to make it worthwhile. By contrast, tax *evasion* is illegally not paying tax due.

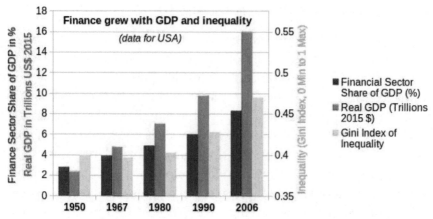

Data sources: GDP [92, 93]; Gini index and inequality [94, 95, 96, 97]; Financial Sector Growth [89]; conversions made to 2015 US dollars where needed.

Figure 22.1: More production and more inequality means the rich have more to play with in the finance 'casino'.

22.3.2 Who plays in the casino?

It's not only the very rich that participate in financial markets – part of the world's middle and better-off working classes also do so to some extent. Anyone with a private or company pension, a savings account with a bank or building society, a unit-trust, or similar, has their money invested for them by financial services companies, either as loans to borrowers or by the purchase of stocks and shares. Few however, will have any involvement in how their funds are managed; their investments are likely to be pooled with those of many others, so even if someone is interested in how their money is invested, he or she is unlikely to have influence over the managers of the financial services companies in charge of the funds.

However, making speculative investments in financial markets is not attractive unless you have plenty of spare cash, because:

- If you only have modest savings, you dare not put them at risk since they are your buffer against eventualities such as losing your job, medical expenses, or having to replace an expensive possession. Accordingly, you are likely to invest only in safe options such as the savings accounts of high street banks, which may be offering only low rates of interest (at the time of writing, often below 1%).

- If the sum you can invest is small the returns are also likely to be small, making the effort barely worthwhile, if for example, you stand to earn no more than you could save simply by skipping a few takeaway coffees.

Most people haven't enough to stake

Across the world, wealth is concentrated in few hands. The diagram in Figure 22.2 based on data from the World Inequality Report 2022, shows how the poorest half of the global population barely owns any wealth at all, possessing just 2% of total world wealth.[98]

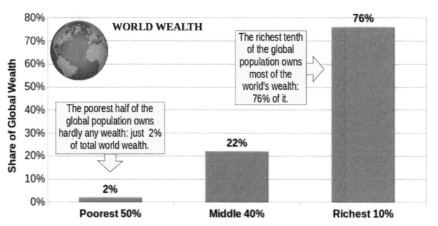

Share of Global Wealth owned by world's poorest 50%, the middle 40% and richest 10%

Figure 22.2: Wealth is concentrated in few hands globally.

Contrast that with the richest 10% of the global population, who own 76% of all wealth. Not only is that 38 times more, but since it is spread over 5 times fewer people, it means that on average people in the top 10% are 190 times wealthier than those in the bottom 50%. Of course inequality continues within these subgroups, so for example within the top 10%, wealth ranges from the rich to the astronomically rich.

Even in the USA, despite it being one of the world's richest countries, most people do not have substantial financial assets. The median value of net household assets at financial institutions was only $5,803 in 2017 – to spell that out, it means half of all US households had that or less, with some owning nothing or in debt.[99]

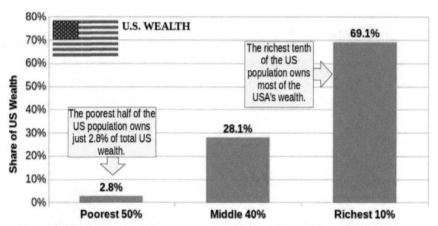

Figure 22.3: Within rich countries, wealth is also concentrated in few hands.

If we consider household net worth which measures not just cash in the bank but all of a household's assets including the value of houses, cars, etc. but subtracting money owed, then the median net worth in the U.S. was $121,760 in 2019.[100] Wealth really is concentrated at the top, as Figure 22.3 shows. In the first quarter of 2023, 69 percent of the total wealth in the United States was owned by the top 10 percent of earners, while the lowest 50 percent of earners only owned 2.8 percent.[101] So even in the rich USA, the majority possess too little to indulge in financial speculation. However if you are in the top 1% for U.S. household net worth – implying that you have at least $10.3 million – then you can comfortably do so.

The situation in the UK is similar: one survey found that 40% of UK adults have less than £500 in savings, while another revealed that over a quarter of adults have no bank savings at all.[102] Furthermore, pension wealth in a country like the UK is highly skewed to the wealthiest in society, with most private (non-state) pension wealth owned by the richest and little or nothing owned by the rest. Data from the UK Office for National Statistics shows how pensions wealth is shared between individuals when split into 10 equally sized groups (deciles), from those with the most in their pension savings to those with the least.[103]

- One-tenth of the UK population held more private pension wealth than all the rest put together.

- The top 10% held 64% of all private pension wealth.

- The bottom half of the population had less than 1% of all private pension wealth.

- Median private pension wealth in the top decile was £637,500 compared with £0 in the first three deciles, £1,200 in decile four and £7,800 in decile five.

It's frequently said that voters in the UK should be happy to see companies making large profits and substantial payouts to shareholders, rather than say paying higher wages, because we all have a stake in the financial sector via our pension funds. As the above statistics and the graphic in Figure 22.4 show, this largely untrue because most of the population have little or no private pension wealth and nothing much in the way of savings either. This is very probably the situation in other countries that similarly lack a comprehensive earnings-related state pension.

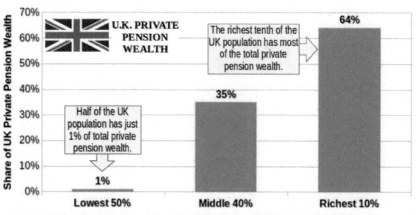

Share of UK Private Pension Wealth held by lowest 50%, the middle 40% and richest 10%

Figure 22.4: We're told "the finance sector looks after your pension savings" – but most of us barely have any.

22.3.3   The casino takes its cut

All this shuffling around of loans, shares, bonds, currencies, options, etc. may contribute little to real production, but it does enable the financial sector to make a lot of money out of the wealthy who come to play in its 'casino' by taking a cut, just as actual casinos do. And just as with actual casinos, the true source of that wealth is not in the casino but outside it, in the productive economy that is based on offices, factories and farms, on science and education, on arts and entertainment, and on the workers, professionals and managers in all those sectors. It's said that if you work in a chocolate factory you are probably not short of chocolate; unfortunately same rule seems to apply to the people who manage our money.

So what evidence is there that the large and growing cut of the world's wealth taken by the financial sector is undeserved and often of no benefit or even a positive harm to the majority of the population? Well rather a lot – as we shall see in the remainder of this chapter.

22.4 The Casino and the Public Good

The finance sector serves those with money – the world's rich. Among the world's rich are a lot of the people who work in the finance sector, being well-placed to influence 'appropriately' the rewards they themselves receive. While accepting that certain financial services are necessary, allowing the financial sector so much control over the economy appears damaging from the point of view of the wider public, for reasons such as those that follow.

22.4.1 Amoral capitalism

The finance sector pools the wealth of many and decides how to invest it. The rate of return (profitability) is generally the only criteria, apart from not losing the capital. There is also a tendency to prefer short-term profits, since as we have seen, long term benefits are 'discounted', i.e. valued less. The consequences of this sole focus on short-term profit are:

- A willingness to invest in products that are harmful to health, whether alcohol, junk food or cigarettes, restrained only by what is legal.

Figure 22.5: Profit from doing harm. [WMC]

- A willingness to invest in products that damage the environment, such as toxic chemicals, fossil fuels, and aviation. Again, restrained only by what is legal.

- No concern for the treatment of workers: slavery was an acceptable investment well into the 19th century, as are today investments in companies using sweatshop labour with wretched working conditions and pay.

- No responsibility for the community or country where the savings came from, the money flows away to wherever in the world the profits are highest.

- A willingness to profit from the sale of weapons and security apparatus to oppressive regimes.

- No concern for the future consequences of investment decisions. Accordingly, making money out of selling arms to doubtful regimes or out of fossil fuels, are seen as profitable investments, even though in the longer term such activities may or will impose costs that substantially outweigh the profits, if for example they lead to war or to climate breakdown.

22.4.2   Tax avoidance and ill-gotten gains

The wealthy are usually keen to hang onto their money. The finance services sector not only provides them with opportunities to invest and speculate, it also assists them in keeping their cash and profits out of the reach of government tax authorities. In some cases it helps them hide their wealth from any prying eyes through convoluted chains of ownership and banking secrecy protection; valuable services, especially if you have acquired your wealth through doubtful or illegal means. The UK seems to specialise in these activities which have been likened in the book 'Butler to the World' to a financial version of the services provided by a discreet butler to his wealthy master.[104] In terms of taxes, we are talking about major chunks of the economy, not just the occasional casual worker asking to be paid in cash for a job. The scale of tax avoidance is spelt out in the book 'Treasure Islands: Tax Havens and the Men who Stole the World', and by the Tax Justice Network.[105, 106] Among the things that they signal, are:

- More than half of world trade passes, at least on paper, through tax havens.

- Around $12 trillion, a quarter of the world's wealth, goes untaxed in tax havens. If banks and companies were included, the amount would be at least twice that.

- The IMF estimated the balance sheets of small island financial centres added up to $18 trillion – about a third of world GDP at the time of the estimate.

- Over a third of world trade happens within multinational corporations.[107]

We even tolerate the evasion of taxes and regulations by the shipping fleets that transport the world's goods. A BBC article described how the tiny country of Panama has the largest shipping fleet in the world, exceeding those of the US and China combined. The attractions for foreign ship-owners of registering their vessels in Panama are said to include avoiding the stricter marine regulations that exist in their own countries, being able to employ cheaper labour, and that as foreign owners they pay no income taxes.[108]

22.4.3 Irresponsible risk-taking

The finance industry makes extensive use of bonuses and commission. This incentivises the sale of financial products to people for whom they are not suited. An infamous case was the sale of subprime mortgages in the USA to borrowers who had no realistic possibility of paying them, which led to the 2008 global banking crisis. In the year before the crisis, one in five people given a subprime mortgage was defaulting within 10 months. Sales people got their commissions and the bank executives who oversaw the disaster got their huge salaries and bonuses, while governments and the taxpayer had to pick up the tab and bail them out to avoid a banking crash. The bailouts in response to the financial crisis cost hundreds of billions of dollars.[109, 110]

In the UK, the government was obliged to rescue the Royal Bank of Scotland from collapse. RBS had grown into the world's biggest bank through a wave of questionable takeovers under its boss Fred Goodwin. Ten years later, the UK Office for Budget Responsibility estimated that saving RBS cost the public £27 billion.[111] Goodwin quit with a reported £2.8m lump sum and inflation-adjusted pension of £342,000 a year.[112] Worldwide, apart from in Iceland, few bankers went to jail for their misdemeanours; they mostly got off scot-free, their personal wealth intact.

Figure 22.6: The 2008 banking crisis: irresponsible risk-taking?
[WMC]

The financial sector generally pushes for deregulation and the ability to offer highly geared financial products (which enable the making of large bets by laying out a far smaller sum than the total that would be lost if the bet fails). Yet it is good regulatory checks and balances that might have avoided the sort of crisis that occurred in 2008, and increasingly obscure financial products appear likely to contribute to instability.

22.4.4 Rentier and parasitic capitalism

Socialism for capitalists

In the socialist classic 'The Ragged Trousered Philanthropists', the capitalist owners of the Mugsborough town gasworks have a problem – it has become loss-making, they'd like to offload it, and they hatch a cunning plan to do so:

'Sell out!' replied Grinder with a contemptuous laugh in which the others joined. 'Who's going to buy the shares of a concern that's practically bankrupt and never paid a dividend?'

'Who's to buy?' repeated Sweater, replying to Grinder. 'The municipality of course! The ratepayers. Why shouldn't Mugsborough go in for Socialism as well as other towns?' – *from The Ragged Trousered Philanthropists by Robert Tressell.[113]*

This is not far from reality. Britain's railways were built as speculative ventures in the nineteenth century by private companies, and often did yield large profits. After the Second World War however, they were close to bankruptcy. The railways were nationalised in 1948 and compensation paid to the owners.[114] But fast-forward to the 1990s and the railways were privatised again, under the Railways Act 1993. How was that possible given that no railway in the whole of Europe made a profit, and that included British Railways, even though it was one of the least subsidised?[115, 116] The answer is that capitalism has found a new way to make a profit out of public services that are not by themselves profitable. The new private rail companies, in addition to fare income from passengers, are also paid by the government to provide a rail service, and hey presto, are thus profitable. It is as if the government is a customer as well as the passengers. When the nationalised British Railways used to receive payments from government to supplement its fare income and make it solvent, the money was referred to as a subsidy and the company condemned as loss-making, though it actually cost the government less than the payouts to the new private operators.

This pattern is now widespread. Work that was previously carried out by employees of national or local government, is farmed out to private companies who charge the state whatever is required to make the service and themselves profitable. In some cases the companies are natural monopolies like the UK water companies, and can charge the hapless customers directly. In others the only 'customer' is the government, which contracts the companies to provide services that the public don't pay for at the point of use, such as some NHS (the UK's state healthcare) services.

This is hardly the free competition lauded by Adam Smith. Large corporations lobby a single customer – the government – for contracts that contain the profit built in. There is a clear risk of an unhealthy revolving door where former politicians in the government land jobs as executives or advisers in such companies and vice versa.

Another costly example is the UK Private Finance Initiative (PFI). Traditionally if the state wanted a hospital or road, it financed it out of taxation and paid a private company to build it. In order to escape the initial capital cost, the UK government began offering contracts by which a private company would build the hospital, road or whatever, and maintain it for several decades in return for regular payments. Unsurprisingly this turned out to be far more expensive in the long run. The scheme has been described as 'The great PFI heist' and by a senior banker as a "fraud on the people".[117] The Guardian newspaper reported that an initial £13bn of private sector-funded investment in new hospitals would end up costing the NHS £80bn by the time all contracts end.[118]

Suppress the competition

When the state provides an attractive service that competes with the private financial sector, the latter are not slow to cry foul. Following the 2008 financial crash, the UK government nationalised certain banks in exchange for the government protecting them from the billions of Pounds worth of toxic assets that they had foolishly or unwittingly acquired. A year or two later I was amused to hear a radio interview with a banking executive that went something like this: 'we must get these banks back into private ownership, because it's a major problem'. 'What is the problem?' the interviewer asked. 'Well' came the reply, 'since they don't have to pay dividends to shareholders, they are offering much better savings and loan rates to customers'. The executive didn't seem to spot the irony that his message to the public was that they should support privately-owned banks so that they can receive a worse service! But he got his way, and the banks referred to have now been returned to private owners.

It's not the first time in the UK that competition from a state-owned bank was unwelcome. The National Girobank was a public sector bank set up by the Labour government in 1968 and run by the Post Office.[119] It was innovative and successful, introducing computerised payment systems in the UK for the first time, and was the first bank to offer free banking to the UK public, including free cheques and deposits. At its peak, one pound in every three deposited in cash at UK banks was deposited with the Giro. But the Conservative government of the 1980s, probably under pressure from the banking sector, privatised the bank in 1989, and it was subsequently absorbed by other financial institutions.[120]

Scorched earth capitalism

One way to make a quick profit is to engage in what is referred to as asset stripping. You buy a business that is relatively cheap because it is not overly profitable, but does however, have extensive assets, typically property. The property can be re-mortgaged or sold, or if still required, rented back.

Figure 22.7: A Debenhams store. [WMC]

News reports describe the demise of the UK retailer Debenhams. They say it was purchased by private equity firms in 2003, which sold off freehold properties, making substantial returns, and a few years later sold the firm on, now loaded with over £1bn of debt; the chain eventually going into liquidation in 2020 with the loss of several thousand jobs.[121, 122]

We should not however, be too quick to condemn business practices that offend us. The incentives within our economy are to make as much money as you can, provided that you stay within the law, and most of us are happy to buy attractive competitively priced products – jeans, smartphones, chocolate – without extensive research into the conditions of the workers who made them. In fact society tends to admire and be fascinated by the very rich without being overly concerned about how they got the money. If you doubt this, consider the box office hit film Pretty Woman. The hero Edward played by Richard Gere, is rich, handsome and sophisticated (he likes opera!) ... and ... an asset stripper. Admittedly he's 'reformed' during the course of the film, but then he's apparently made so much all ready he can afford to be.

22.4.5   Competence and efficiency

While a large part of the world's population have little or nothing in the way of savings, there are many especially in the world's richer countries, who are not among the world's super wealthy but do have some modest financial investments either via savings accounts or private pensions or both. Sometimes people might be barely aware of their stake in the financial markets, as for example if they have a pension managed via their employer. How well are they served by the financial sector?

Savings

If you invest in a pension scheme or unit trust offered by a financial institution, you will typically find that there is a 'fund manager' who decides how your money is to be invested from day to day, choosing which combination to hold of company shares, government bonds and cash, based on their expertise. One way to judge their success is to compare the performance of the portfolio they choose for you with the overall average for the stock market. Alarmingly there are studies suggesting that most professional fund managers fail to do better than the market average and even more embarrassingly, that randomly picking shares – a strategy dubbed 'monkey with a pin' – often does better than the 'professionals'. In some experiments, real monkeys or chimps did the picking, by for example throwing darts into a list of shares. Some of those experiments are described in a book 'Monkey with a Pin', which also quotes financial advice that 'around 80% of all actively managed funds undershoot the stock market average over the long term'.[123]

Figure 22.8: For once, paying peanuts and getting monkeys, may not be a bad plan.

There are more than 2,000 different unit trusts and similar investments called OEICs, available to investors in the UK.[3] A quick search on-line suggests that mutual fund managers make an average of $436,500 a year.[124] Multiply that by 2,000 and we get a total not far off a billion dollars to pay UK fund managers. If a random strategy can be equally effective, this may be a case where we really would be better off paying peanuts and getting monkeys!

When it comes to economic prediction, it's not just lowly fund managers who don't do too well. During a briefing at the London School of Economics about the toxic debt mountain that caused the

---

[3]Unit trusts and OEICs (open-ended investment companies) are ways to invest collectively in a portfolio of companies and other assets.

2008 market crash Britain's Queen Elizabeth asked the assembled experts the obvious question: "Why did nobody notice it?"

Pensions

Several European countries have national pension schemes that are the only pension a citizen requires as they include an element proportional to lifetime earnings, and therefore on retirement provide a reasonable fraction of the salary that the retiree was accustomed to. The UK however, opted to encourage private pensions, provided either by employers or directly to individuals by a financial institution. This was despite having an earnings-related state scheme for some years (now closed). There remains a basic state pension, but it is set at a flat rate, unrelated to earnings.

Accordingly, the UK has a plethora of private and company pension schemes, apparently about 5,500 'defined benefit' schemes that guarantee a certain level of pension, and 29,500 'defined contribution' schemes that give the retiree a pot of money which they then can use to purchase a pension (an annuity) from a financial services company.[125, 126] These 35,000 or so pension schemes require trustees, administrators and account managers. Furthermore, they can be affected by the bankruptcy of the employer or of the financial institution that provides them and manages the money (although some protection against workers losing everything if their employer goes bankrupt has been put in place in recent years). If you change jobs you can be left with a hotchpotch of multiple employer-pensions and difficult decisions about whether to try to combine them.

The cost and complexity of having so many private schemes assuredly provides lots of work for the financial services companies that manage the schemes, but raises questions about how much of the workers' contributions are absorbed in costs compared to a straightforward universal state scheme. Furthermore, the piecemeal nature of pension provision means that if a scheme has problems, the workers or retirees affected are largely on their own, rather than being able to count on the solidarity of fellow citizens and together form a substantial pressure group.

I have my own experiences of private schemes collected from multiple employers. One scheme failed, losing a substantial proportion of the money saved. Another lowered the predicted pension from the value they had quoted annually for decades, claiming an error in the original calculation. With a third it took six months and scores of phone calls and emails to get them to make a simple transfer, at the end of which they wrote saying that they'd transferred the money to ... the wrong company! It transpired that they hadn't in fact done so but had used a letter to another customer as a template and failed to change the details.

It is sometimes argued that private pensions are preferable to state pensions because they are truly funded via the pensioner's saved pot of money, whereas the state pension is just funded by government taxation. 'Therefore' the argument goes, the state pension is just a 'smoke and mirrors' government promise that if we pay taxes when we are working to support today's pensioners, then we will be supported in turn by the next generation of workers; a sort of promise between generations. This argument fails to notice that the saved pension pot is also a promise: namely that the next generation will recognise and respect our title to the money or assets, rather than just seizing them now that we are old and weak. Furthermore, if a private pension pot is used to buy an annuity, then all you have is yet another promise of a pension until death, but this time from a finance company not a government. A promise made by a stable democratic government is rather likely to turn out to be the safer bet, especially since state pensioners are a large group with a shared interest and the vote.

However, the worst thing about this huge teetering edifice of private pension schemes, is that it fails to provide any pension to part of the population and only a small top-up to the state pension for much of the rest. It really serves only a wealthy minority. In the UK:

- One third of people expect to retire with only the state pension.[103]

- Almost half (46 per cent) of UK business owners – or 1.3 million people – have no private pension savings, according research from Prudential.[127]

- The best-off tenth of the UK population in terms of private pension wealth, have more than all the rest put together.[103]

22.4.6 Poisoned politics

The financial sector has undue power and influence over governments through control over financial flows and through political lobbying, personal connections and favours. Governments are pressed to deregulate, privatise and overlook tax evasion – all contrary to the public interest. This is described very effectively in a section *Effects on political system* in an entry on *Financialization* in Wikipedia, an extract from which is quoted below:

"Some, such as former International Monetary Fund chief economist Simon Johnson, have argued that the increased power and influence of the financial services sector had fundamentally transformed American politics, endangering representative democracy itself through undue influence on the political system and regulatory capture by the financial oligarchy.

In the 1990s vast monetary resources flowing to a few 'megabanks' enabled the financial oligarchy to achieve greater political power in the United States. Wall Street firms largely succeeded in getting the American political system and regulators to accept the ideology of financial deregulation and the legalization of more novel financial instruments. Political power was achieved by contributions to political campaigns, by financial industry lobbying, and through a revolving door that positioned financial industry leaders in key politically appointed policymaking and regulatory roles and that rewarded sympathetic senior government officials with super high-paying Wall Street jobs after their government service. The financial sector was the leading contributor to political campaigns since at least the

1990s, contributing more than $150 million in 2006. (This far exceeded the second largest political contributing industry, the healthcare industry, which contributed $100 million in 2006.) From 1990 to 2006, the securities and investment industry increased its political contributions six-fold, from an annual $12 million to $72 million. The financial sector contributed $1.7 billion to political campaigns from 1998 to 2006, and spent an additional $3.4 billion on political lobbying, according to one estimate." *– from an entry on 'Financialization' in Wikipedia.[128]*

22.5 Summary

The financial sector administers the ownership and trade of goods and assets. It earns an income by, in effect, claiming a share in those goods and assets managed.

Technology has enabled extraordinarily high levels of production in recent decades and markets have concentrated wealth in fewer hands. The mega-rich have so much money that they cannot spend all of it on personal consumption, having 'run out of wants', and therefore search for investments where they can place their surplus cash. The world's financial sector has swollen to serve this wealth mountain, providing not just basic banking services but operating like a vast casino. It takes little responsibility for negative real world impacts such as :

- Amoral investments – Profit being the main criteria, investment decisions disregard the pay and conditions of workers, loyalty to country and community, and harm to people's health and the environment.

- Tax avoidance – The sector facilitates tax avoidance and financial secrecy. As a result the wealthy escape their responsibilities and wider society is the poorer.

- Irresponsible risk-taking – High salaries and the widespread use of bonuses and commission, incentivise dangerous economic risk-taking, causing great expense to governments and taxpayers, while sector executives seldom suffer any penalties.

- Rentier and parasitic capitalism – Democratic governments are expected to supply various public services that cannot be provided by the normal operation of the market. Typically, state or municipal enterprises used to carry out this work, but in recent years many such services have been contracted to private businesses with governments then paying both the costs and the investors' profits; increased costs to the taxpayer, a loss of service quality and inferior employment conditions, often result. The financial sector lobbies against competition from the state in areas like high-street banking and earnings-related pensions, where state provision would in fact benefit the public. Short-term asset-stripping of long-established companies is allowed and even lauded.

- Competence and efficiency – The claims to expertise by city fund managers are dubious given the often as-good or better performance of tracker funds or random 'monkey' strategies. The proliferation of private pensions schemes creates a large and pointless overhead of administration that has to be paid for by members of the schemes.

The finance sector doesn't produce end-products, nor advance science and technology. It is not the only source of capital – most corporations are no longer funded by share issue but raise finance internally or by borrowing. Thus, a question mark hangs over the finance sector: how many of its activities are necessary and how many risky and expensive gambling? These are not new concerns and periodically governments attempt to separate investment and retail banking, in order to protect day-to-day banking from highly risky investment activities. The majority of the population would seem to be poorly served by a sector that mainly looks after the rich, has no moral compass except short-term profit, and is all too willing to evade social responsibilities. The sector also has undue power and influence over governments, through its control over financial flows, and via political lobbying and personal favours. Governments are pressed to deregulate, privatise, and overlook tax evasion – all of which is contrary to the public interest.

Chapter 23

Inflation and Money Supply

I was uncertain whether even to include a section on money, prices and inflation. They are subjects which economists have studied extensively, winning Nobel Prizes for their theories. The main theme of this book is that in our modern highly-productive economy, an 'economic balance' is both possible and likely to occur at a point which leaves a large part of the population under or unemployed, and that the main contemporary solution proposed for this – to continually increase growth and consumption – is for environmental reasons undesirable and probably impossible. With respect to that theme, inflation seems merely a technical issue.

On the other hand, controlling inflation – if need be by restricting the money supply – often appears to be the principal concern of political leaders and economists. They focus on inflation at the expense of not one but two elephants in the room: that the economy fails to deliver for a large part of the world's people, and that it is wrecking the planet we live on. Invariably the 'solution' that is proposed is the 'tighten your belts so that we get more growth' recipe, despite the fact that it never seems to bring a definitive cure. Accordingly, this chapter attempts to review the causes of inflation, the 'restrict money supply' analysis and the derived policy responses that are intended bring inflation down.

We took an initial look in Chapter 5 at what sets the value of money, and at various changes in the economy that may cause prices to change. Prices will always shift about to some extent with changes in what products are seen as fashionable or desirable, and with fluctuations in supply (such as the availability of seasonable fruit and vegetables and variations in annual crop yields). In this chapter we are not interested in those ups and downs in the prices of particular products, but in general and sustained price increases.

23.1   Causes of Inflation

Printing Money.   The value of money depends on how much of it there is in circulation compared with the amount of goods the economy produces, as we saw in Chapter 5. Therefore, printing extra money is a straightforward cause of inflation and the cure is equally straightforward – stop doing it! Nevertheless, some governments resort to printing money out of desperation (as I saw first hand in Nicaragua – see the illustration of an overprinted banknote in the Preface). Most governments in modern times do slowly print extra money over time, since firstly they are willing to live with some inflation, and secondly because advances in technology increase productivity and so tend to decrease the prices of manufactured goods, offsetting the inflationary effect of the extra money. Note that with modest inflation over a long time period, while thanks to more automated manufacture the prices of some manufactured goods may increase only slightly or even fall, prices of other goods can be expected to rise substantially if the labour to make them has not decreased, or if the supply is finite (such as of land, or paintings by old masters).

An economics text will typically distinguish two types of inflation: **'demand pull' and 'cost push'**. We'll look at those next, and then consider **'wage-price spirals'** – a sort of argument about sharing out what is produced.

Demand Pull is explained as occurring when the demand for goods and services exceeds their supply, due to increases in consumer or government spending, or in investment spending. But this appears to be just stating the obvious – the question is where are people getting that extra money from? In a stable economy the value of money adjusts so that what people earn matches what is for sale. So the only way people could spend more than they earn is by dipping into their savings (or borrowing other people's savings), which could produce only a transitory increase in demand (although a shift in preferences could cause a rise in the price of products that have become more fashionable, but balanced presumably by a fall in the prices of those that are now less favoured). To produce sustained inflation, the source of the money would have to be extra 'new' money, so we would be back to printing money, and if that is what is happening then it should be named as the cause with 'demand pull' merely the obvious effect.

Cost Push refers to an increase in production costs, causing producers to raise prices. Now we are onto something: we know that a product's price generally reflects the amount of work required to make it. We can easily imagine changes in the real world that would result in more work being needed, such as a growing scarcity of mineral ores or the exhaustion of soils. Even if extra workers are recruited, they must be taken from some other activity. Thus cost rises will ripple through the whole economy. Essentially the entire economy now produces less, and the value of the money in circulation must therefore decline. Some of these real-world 'shocks' may be related to political events rather than physical ones: a government decides to stop or limit access to resources under its control, or a war makes access impossible.

Argument – Wage-Price Spirals. A quite different potential source of inflation is argument between humans about how to divide up what is produced, or to put it another way: how much our respective jobs deserve to be paid, and also, how much business owners should get. During this discussion we should remember that we can equally name this phenomenon a **Price-Wage** spiral: businesses are very happy to put up prices if they are able to (because say, the product they sell is in short supply), which will motivate the rest of the population to seek compensatory wage increases if they can.

As far as wages go, naturally enough many of us are easily persuaded that we deserve higher pay. Indeed, many groups of workers do have a strong case: they may be on such poor wages that they struggle to get by, or they may observe that compared to other jobs of comparable skills, training and responsibility, they are less well rewarded. We frequently hear such arguments in news-stories about labour disputes. There are others who don't have to argue their case, because they are in the comfortable position of being able to influence or set their own salaries.

What happens when a group of workers seeking to increase its share, succeeds in doing so? The money has to come from somewhere, so the business(s) employing them will have to pass on this increase in costs by increasing prices, or in the case of the state, by increasing taxes. When that happens the rest of society becomes worse off – logically so, given that if total production is the same, then an increase in one group's share must cause a reduction in the share received by others. On seeing the increased prices, other groups that now feel worse off as a consequence, may in turn, demand higher wages to compensate, which, if granted, cause further price rises that set off yet more wage demands. This is known as a 'wage-price spiral'. Governments tend to be very concerned about this phenomenon whenever a large group of workers is fighting for increased pay, but a lot less interested when business owners or members of high-status professions, quietly award themselves substantial pay increases.

What sets off a wage-price spiral? In principle, it could be simply ambition or greed. But a likely trigger for workers to struggle for an increase and perhaps take industrial action such as striking, is that they have suffered a real-terms fall in their standard of living:

either an actual wage cut, or their wages have stagnated and failed to keep up with inflation (i.e. with businesses putting up prices). These are certainly the typical arguments that you hear when you listen to news reports about labour disputes.

Apart from general inflation that affects everyone, particular groups sometimes find that their wages are falling behind. Two common reasons why certain groups of workers may become worse off in industrialised countries like the UK and US, are:

- Automation has reduced demand for labour in their sector, or generally.

- Better transport and communications is enabling firms to shift work to lower-wage countries (or firms from those countries are attracting business away with their lower wage costs and thus lower prices).

In both cases, world business taken as a whole is able to produce the same amount of goods as before, while using less labour (through automation) or paying labour less (by producing in lower-wage countries). Also in both of these cases, the bargaining position of labour to negotiate wage increases is weakened. Given a competitive world market, employers are under pressure to resist increases: if they don't lower costs by automating or using cheaper labour, they will lose out to competitors at home or overseas who do, and if as a consequence the business fails, the jobs will go anyway. As the economist J K Galbraith commented: "It has never been sufficiently observed that strong trade unions require, above all, strong employers. Nothing so weakens a union's claims as the workers' need to keep the employer in existence."[129] Accordingly, while these changes do make people worse off, they do so by driving down wages or making workers unemployed; they also drive down prices.

Another possible candidate for starting a wage-price spiral is a *genuine fall* in how much the world can produce, as described under Cost Push, due to a resource becoming scarcer or some other restriction in supply. People from all levels of society can potentially feel aggrieved if the real value of their pay goes down, and inclined to respond, by attempting to get themselves a compensatory increase; a wage-price spiral may then ensue. However, if less is being produced, then somebody has to lose out. So when the dust settles it will be those in the strongest position that win the compensatory increases, and those least able to defend their income who will take the hit. One would hope that government would step in to protect the weakest and most needy – though that depends on what the current leaders find politically convenient.

Some resources are strictly finite, such as land. A growing world population means that land has to be shared between more people, inevitably making land scarcer and therefore more expensive. Other resources, even if not strictly limited in the way that land is, may nevertheless be hard to expand as fast as the population is growing.

An additional problem for workers in older industrialised countries is that the recent rapid industrialisation in countries like China and India, means that not only are there more people in the world, but they also have more goods to offer in exchange for the world's scarce resources. So whereas once, a country with grain that wanted to swap it for cars, had the choice of trading only with Europe, the US or Japan, now it can also trade with South Korea or China. With more people bidding for the grain, the buyers will have to offer more in return and the price will be higher than it otherwise would have been. As well as other countries catching up or overtaking in technological and industrial development, there are plenty of further possible reasons why the terms of trade may become less favourable for a country, such as political instability and greater exposure to external competition due to cheaper transport or the removal of trade barriers. These issues are very pertinent to a country like the UK. In the 19th century the UK was the 'workshop of the world' and people beat a path to its door to buy its manufactures, permitting the country to obtain much of its food by trade rather than growing it. But now China is the workshop of the world, and the UK a minor player by comparison. For the moment the UK's long-term relative decline is concealed by the fact that while its slice of world GDP is much smaller, the cake is much bigger. However, one day the UK may struggle if it finds itself bidding for food or raw materials that have become scarce on the world market, against other countries that now have as much or more to offer for them.

23.2 Rationing by Price

We have to accept that if there is genuinely less of something to go around, whether because of resource scarcity or population growth, then some sort of rationing must take place. What the market does is ration by price. Money is a sort of general ration-coupon which entitles you to a share of the economy's output in a flexible way: you can only have so much stuff but the mix of products is your choice. Nevertheless, it is rationing: if there is a shortage of wheat, there must be a cut in consumption, which is achieved by the price rising until some of the population eat less or cannot afford it at all. Rationing of certain essential products may be necessary during a crisis to prevent the wealthier buying the lot and the rest of the population going without any; for example, during World War II, most foodstuffs – butter, eggs and so forth – were rationed in Britain.

Despite its apparent unfairness, rationing by market price is generally to be preferred except in extremis. Formal rationing of individual products is unpopular and creates a host of new problems: the bureaucracy involved, who gets to decide, corruption, a reduction of free choice, and a loss of the price signal that would have encouraged suppliers to raise production and consumers to economise.

23.3 Dealing with Inflation

How should inflation be dealt with? First let's summarise what appear to be the more important of the causes of inflation described above. We have:

1. The government printing extra money.

2. Increased costs due to resource scarcity or reduced access to resources.

3. Arguments about the sharing out of what is produced, resulting in a wage-price spiral.

4. Population growth meaning that there is less per person of finite resources like land.

5. The terms of trade deteriorating for a country or local producers because of external competition, especially from newly industrialising countries.

Apart from (1) for which the solution seems obvious (stop doing it), it is an interesting and varied set of problems. Faced with resource scarcity (2), we'd want to identify which vital resources may become scarce and look for ways to reduce dependency such as substitutes, alternative sources or economising. Democratic countries will surely want to tackle the sharing issue (3) through a public debate aimed at reaching some sort of criteria for setting relative wages that are widely seen as fair ... or so one would like to think. Population growth (4) demands a strategy for bringing it under control and meanwhile managing the demand on finite resources as best we can. Global competition and automation (5) mean that we need a long and hard international conversation about how to sustain local economies within the global marketplace and avoid a race to the bottom in terms of employment and working conditions.

23.3.1 Solution: squeeze the less well off

The actual policy promoted by many economists and politicians in the UK and elsewhere, does not appear to be any of the above. It's much simpler: 'squeeze the less well off'. As described above, inflation is the market rationing something by raising its price: if there is a shortage of wheat or petrol, someone has to have less, and so the price rises until people consume less or cannot afford it at all. So if you want to reduce the amount by which prices rise, all you have to do is take away some of the population's money so that they have less to spend in the first place. For the best effect you want to take the money not from the wealthy but from large numbers of the more ordinary and poorer citizens; that's because the wealthy are less likely to cut their consumption of basic goods like food, and even if they did, since they are fewer in number and don't necessarily consume much more of basic foodstuffs per person than the average, the reduction in demand would be smaller.

One way a squeeze can be implemented is by adjusting interest rates. In the UK the Bank of England are currently implementing a policy of raising interest rates to deal recent high levels of inflation. They say that the main causes of the current inflation are: the pandemic and fewer people available for work afterwards, and the impact of Russia's invasion of Ukraine on energy and food prices. They explain the problem and their policy to deal with it on their website.[130] The theory of the causes of the inflation are identified as follows:

"There are two main causes of inflation."

"One is sometimes called 'cost-push' inflation. This can occur when there is a fall in supply of a product or service, which causes its price to rise. For example, after Russia's invasion of Ukraine, the supply of gas from Russia fell significantly. This in turn meant that price of gas – which is a key source of energy in the UK – rose significantly. That pushed up on inflation both because households consume energy directly (in the form of domestic gas and electricity supplies) and also because higher energy costs make it more expensive for businesses to produce many other goods and services.

The other is referred to as 'demand-pull' inflation. This is when there is an increase in the demand for something relative to its supply. For example, if there is too much money in the economy, that can lead to more demand for goods and services than there are available, which pushes up on prices and inflation.

Recent high inflation in the UK has been driven mainly by 'cost-push' inflation. That happened first after the supply shortages due to the Covid pandemic and the invasion of Ukraine. And more recently, fewer people available to work after the pandemic is also 'cost-push' inflation. It pushes up on wages and businesses costs and prices."

The Bank explains that their target has been set by the government:

"The UK government sets us a target of having low and stable inflation. As the UK's central bank, the best tool we have to slow down rising prices is interest rates."

The Bank then explains how they believe that the policy works:

"How do higher interest rates help to slow inflation?

Interest rates on mortgages, loans and savings are at their highest level for many years.

The reason for that is we are using interest rates to slow price rises in the UK. We have put up the UK base interest rate 14 times over the past two years.

Higher interest rates increase the return on savings. They also make the cost of borrowing more expensive.

Higher interest rates help to slow down price rises (inflation). That's because they reduce how much is spent across the UK.

Experience tells us that when overall spending is lower, prices stop rising so quickly and inflation slows down. That has started to happen in the UK. We need to make sure it continues to happen.

People have told us directly that they are finding higher mortgage and loan payments very hard. They also ask if higher interest rates are the best option we have.

The answer is yes. The UK government sets us a target of getting inflation to 2%. And interest rates are the best tool we have to slow down price rises. We know that interest rates are an effective tool for managing inflation, because they have been used successfully across many countries and circumstances. They are effective in influencing the amount of spending in the economy, and therefore inflation. And we can see that they are working now." – *extracts from: Bank of England Explainers 'Why have interest rates gone up in the past two years and when will they come down?'.[130]*

The Bank insist that this policy is effective – but why does it work? After all, it doesn't seem to change the total amount of money, but only means that people who owe money have to pay more in interest to the people they borrowed it from. Wouldn't the creditors spend the extra money they receive from debtors, and so cancel out the debtors' reduced spending? It seems that to a large extent they don't, and that's not really much of a surprise: wealthy creditors are by definition people with savings that they haven't spent – giving them a bit more isn't likely to create more things that they want to buy; a theme of this book is the problem of creating enough 'wants' to persuade the rich to part with their money. Debtors on the other hand are unlikely to have spare cash; if they are made to pay more in interest payments, then what they have left to spend on food or petrol goes down. Commonly their largest debt will be a mortgage on their home; at the time of writing, it looks likely that the *annual repayments on UK mortgages will increase by several billion Pounds.*[131] The Bank of England itself mentions that people say they are "finding higher mortgage and loan payments very hard".[130]

In the UK there will be many who are unable to get onto the housing ladder and some may be inclined to view those who have bought a flat or house as the lucky ones, even if they do have large mortgages. Unfortunately however, the rise in mortgage interest rates appears also to lead to rent rises, as explained by an article on the National Residential Landlords Association which says: "Almost two thirds of private landlords expect to see their mortgage payments increase over the next 12 months with warnings that this trend will lead to higher rents."[132, 133] UK government statistics show that rents are rising.[134] The graph in Figure 23.1 shows how both rents and mortgage rates increased in the UK, in response to increases in the bank rate. The effect on mortgage holders has a lag as some have fixed rate mortgages: they will be impacted later when their fixed rate deal ends and they have to negotiate a new fixed-rate deal or move to a variable rate.

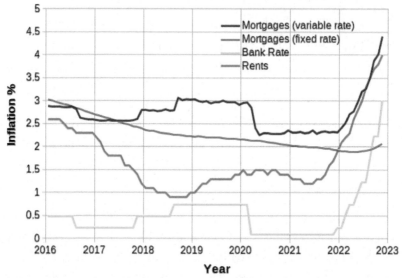

UK private rental prices saw the largest annual percentage increase in November 2022, since records began in 2016. Data sources: [134]

Figure 23.1: Mortgage interest and rents, rise together.

The policy of raising interest rates, affects primarily the less well off as they are more likely to have mortgages or other debts, or to be renting. Rents are influenced by the mortgage rate since private landlords often have a mortgage on their properties, and in any case will want to obtain a return comparable with savings account rates. Debtors owe the money to the better off who by definition are those with more assets. So interest rate rises, increase payments of interest and rent by the less-well-off to the better-off, who are less likely to spend the money, and thus demand is reduced.

In summary: Inflation due to a resource becoming scarcer (or people more numerous) is the markets' way of rationing the resource – by increasing the price until some people are unable to afford as much or any. Inflation can be reduced by transferring money away from large numbers of ordinary people, reducing their ability to afford the product and bid up its price. On the flip side, wealthier people who are not in debt, benefit from higher interest on their savings and lower inflation. Whatever gloss is put on the policy, the sacrifices are not equal.

23.3.2 Dealing with scarcity

Raising interest rates to squeeze debtors, as described above, sounds very unfair. Yet not all savers are wealthy. Those in retirement often have pensions that are not or only partly, indexed linked (raised in line with inflation). Unchecked inflation rapidly diminishes the value of such pensions and does the same to any small pot of savings people may have. High inflation is very damaging economically and politically. So if there is a genuine scarcity of a product that is a basic essential, are there any other options? Some that I'm aware of are:

1. *Subsidise the product:* the state pays part of the high market price. A recent example was the UK government's Energy Bill Support Scheme which gave every household a £400 discount on their energy bills for winter 2022 to 2023. International gas prices were very high at the time due to the war in Ukraine, and there was a fear some households would be unable to heat their homes.

2. *Ration the product:* give each citizen the right to only a limited quantity of the product – such schemes are familiar from the wartime experience of the UK and many other countries. More recently in 2023, a shortage of fruit and vegetables in the UK led some supermarkets to limit how many items shoppers could buy – not more than two cucumbers per customer

for instance – a curious scheme since it was so obviously easy to evade, but perhaps the public behaved responsibly or at least were made to think more about our dependence on other countries for food.

3. *Distribute the product:* issue citizens directly with a quantity of essential goods. Nicaragua during its years of blockade by the USA, had a period when state salaries were so low that employees were also given a packet of basic foodstuffs. At that time Nicaragua was one of the poorest countries in the Americas, it was coping with a war as well as a blockade, and was receiving donations of food from sympathetic countries which it could use in this way. More shocking is how in the 21st century, many of the citizens of rich countries are unable to afford enough food at market prices and increasingly have to rely on schemes that directly give them food, such as food banks and free or subsidised school meals.[1][135, 136, 137] Such schemes don't tackle the inflation as most food is still sold normally at market prices, but do provide some protection for the poorest by giving them access to free or subsidised food.

All these schemes have drawbacks but perhaps the worst in economic terms is (1): a subsidy. If a resource like gas is scarce, someone will have to use less. By subsidising the price to UK customers the government took away some of the incentive on UK citizens to reduce their consumption, meaning that others in poorer and more vulnerable countries will have had to do so. It is also a very expensive policy which UK taxpayers will eventually have to pay for – the subsidy even going to wealthy families who didn't need it.

---

[1]The Trussell Trust, which supports the largest network food banks in the UK, had around 35 food bank centres in 2010/11. By 2023 it had just under 1,400 centres; there were also at least 1,172 independent food banks. The British Labour Party is promising to provide free breakfast clubs for all primary school pupils if it wins the election due in 2024. The US Supplemental Nutrition Assistance Program, previously referred to as 'food stamps', aims to provide children and low-income people with access to food.

Since gas and electricity supplies to each customer are metered, it would have been far better to oblige energy suppliers to restructure their tariffs and allow each customer a basic quantity of gas and electricity at a reasonably modest price, with the cost per unit then rising after that, the more that you consume. Such a policy would have protected poorer consumers while also providing a strong incentive to heavier users to save energy and insulate their homes. Astonishingly at present, tariffs often work the other way around with a fixed standing charge that customers must pay even if they use nothing – in effect, those who use more pay less per unit! Unfortunately schemes of this nature to ensure everyone can access an essential minimum, are not applicable to most products as our consumption of them is not metered: nobody keeps a count of how many cucumbers or tomatoes each of us buy (although if you usually patronise the same supermarket and have a loyalty card, they may have a pretty good idea). The most satisfactory solution remains aiming to ensure that everyone has a sufficient minimum income to purchase life's essentials at market prices.

23.3.3   Natural rate of unemployment

Some economists believe that the economy has a natural long-run equilibrium and a natural level of unemployment corresponding to it, and that going below that unemployment level results in inflation. Unemployment is considered necessary in order to curb the workforces ability or willingness to demand higher wages which are considered a source of inflation due to a wage-price spiral. Evidence that there is a link between inflation and employment was claimed by the economist Bill Phillips in a 1958 paper and based on the relation he observed between unemployment and wage rates in data for the UK covering the period 1861 to 1957. Most economics text books refer to the 'Phillips Curve' but the extent and cause of any relationship is still debated.

A 'natural rate' of unemployment is said to occur when the economy is operating at its 'long run equilibrium'. That equilibrium in turn, is said to be at a level at which total demand is equal to long run total supply. The argument appears unhelpfully circular "long run equilibrium is when demand and supply are in equilibrium for the long run". Surely what we want to know is: what determines that equilibrium? Chapter 8 in this book set out to answer that question: the level of production is determined by the wants of business owners plus the goods (i.e. wages) they have to provide to the workers they need to employ. Seen in that light, *there is no 'natural' rate of unemployment or 'natural' equilibrium.* There is only the messy end result of what the owners can be persuaded to want, the number of workers needed to make it and what they are in a position to demand, and what resources owners and governments consider it politic to provide to those with insufficient employment or none (either to support them or to provide security and policing to keep them in check). It is perfectly possible for a country with a high level of inequality, to have very large numbers of unemployed people, should its business owners not find a use for them in the production of goods that those owners desire, either to consume directly or to export in exchange for desired foreign goods. The worst affected are the landless poor as they cannot turn to subsistence agriculture to sustain themselves.

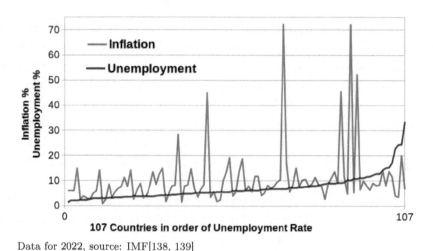

Data for 2022, source: IMF[138, 139]

Figure 23.2: Across 107 countries, inflation does not appear to be lower where unemployment is high.

Nowadays unemployment and inflation data are available for many countries. Figure 23.2 shows the unemployment and inflation rates for over a hundred countries (those I managed to find data for) in 2022. It does not show any tendency for inflation to be lower in countries with high unemployment. If anything, the opposite appears to be true, with some of the highest inflation rates in countries that also have high unemployment. In the case of those countries that have both horrendously high unemployment levels and high inflation as well, are we to suppose that unemployment is still below its 'natural rate' and needs to be increased further to cure the inflation? ... an approach that seems reminiscent of medieval blood-letting.

Figure 23.3 shows most of the same data (some outliers removed) with inflation plotted against unemployment. Again there is no indication that high unemployment correlates with low inflation – the trend line shows a weak correlation for the opposite.

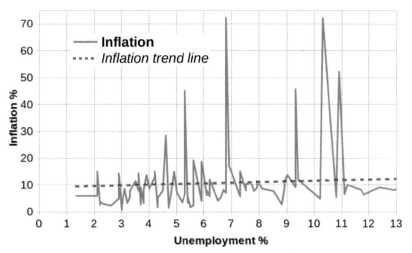

Data for 2022, source: IMF[138, 139]. To expand the graph, 8 outliers with unemployment over 13% that were included in Figure 23.2 have been removed.

Figure 23.3: Inflation versus unemployment for 99 countries.

23.3.4 Curbing a wage-price spiral

We have discussed the case that there is a genuine resource short-age that is the source of inflation. What if the main problem is a wage - price spiral: are there any approaches other than deliberately increasing unemployment to put downward pressure on wages? If we see the problem as an argument between humans about how economic output should be shared, then arguments have two so-lutions: impose a solution, or reach an agreement. If you want to reach agreement rather than just endeavour to force down pay by the threat of unemployment or some other pressure, then it's a matter of a lot of talking. The UK multinationals I first worked for back in the 1970s and 80s, had lengthy negotiations with the staff trade unions about salary grade structures and pay scales, cover-ing details such as qualifications required to enter higher grades, annual progression, and small variations in entitlements. In the UK today, there are a number of pay review bodies which are "in-dependent advisory non-departmental public bodies who provide evidence-based advice and recommendations to governments across the UK on levels of pay for their respective remit groups" cover-ing public sector workers such as the armed forces, health service employees and school teachers.[140]

However, reaching an agreement seems more likely if workers see the process as open and society as fair. The Gini Index measure of inequality grew very rapidly for the UK in the 1980s during the Conservative government of Margaret Thatcher, and the UK is now one of the most unequal in Europe. The population are also likely to be aware that a cap on the huge bonuses bankers can be paid was scrapped in 2023, that the prime minister is a multi-millionaire with a penchant for travelling within the UK by helicopter or jet, and that many who govern the country were born into wealth, attended elite fee-paying private schools, and have taken full advantage of their family and school connections. Accordingly, UK citizens may take some convincing that they live in a fair society with an equi-table distribution of income and wealth.

One approach to creating more openness and perhaps having a better chance to convince workers that a pay agreement is fair, is involving workers in decision-making. Workers are represented in company boards across most of Europe but not in the UK. The British Trade Union Congress (TUC) is in favour of worker representation.[141]

However, there is a debate as to whether workers and their unions should take responsibility for the running of the companies in which they work. Some would prefer to restrict themselves to fighting for the best pay and conditions obtainable and not compromise themselves by involvement in management decisions. That tends to be the view of the far left who favour a revolution and socialism as the solution to all problems. They believe in making what are referred to as 'transitional demands' which are demands that cannot be realised in the current economic system and are therefore a way to break it; they are unwilling to consider the complexities of how production would be shared out in a post-revolution society, or even to believe that any sharing would be necessary. For fifty years or more, far left groups in the UK and USA have put their faith in such a strategy while elected right wing governments have successfully weakened the position of workers and their unions, and ramped up inequality. It's difficult not to conclude that designing a workable and realisable set of radical reforms would have been a better objective ... although of course a more tedious and complex one.

23.4   Summary

Major causes of inflation are the government choosing to print extra money, a real-world change that reduces how much can be produced such as a resource shortage, and struggle among groups in society to increase their respective shares of what is produced creating a wage-price spiral. Population growth and increasing competition for resources are also factors. Population growth makes us all on average poorer in terms of land and other finite resources. When a resource becomes scarcer, some sort of rationing must occur: the market by its nature, rations by price – prices rise until the population consumes less. If this is unacceptable because the poorer cannot afford basic essentials, then alternative rationing schemes have to be considered that are targeted at the products concerned.

Most western governments and their national banks have controlling inflation as one of their principal objectives. The usual method employed to lower inflation is to take demand out of the economy by raising interest rates (the bank base rate). This works by obliging a large part of the population to pay more in interest on loans such as mortgages, or in rent (since rents tend to be related to interest rates), and as a result they have less to spend on other goods. The extra that they pay goes to those who are wealthier – creditors or landlords – who since they are wealthier, are less inclined to spend the additional money that they receive.

Government subsidy as a way to limit a price increase, appears inadvisable as it removes the incentive to economise or seek substitutes, and denies supplies to poorer countries. Growing inequality and poverty even in wealthy countries like the UK and USA, have created pressure to distribute some basics such as foodstuffs, outside of the regular market, via schemes such as foodbanks and free school meals. Formal rationing presents many inconveniences and openings for corruption, so ensuring the poorest have enough to obtain what they need at market prices is preferable.

Many economists say that there is natural long-run equilibrium for an economy and a corresponding natural level of unemployment. Earlier in this book it is argued that there is no guarantee that equilibrium will occur at anywhere near an acceptable level of unemployment, since employment depends on what business owners want and how many workers they need to employ to get it. Some economists also believe that there is a trade-off between unemployment and inflation, higher unemployment being a way to bring down inflation; widely varying unemployment and inflation rates across the world's countries do not seem to bear this out.

Rather than using unemployment as a way to depress wages, reaching agreements on a fair distribution of what is produced, would appear a better way to prevent a wage-price inflation spiral. But that would require citizens to feel confident about the openness of negotiations and the fairness of the result – conditions which look distant in today's UK and USA where inequality is far higher than it was fifty years ago in the 1970s.

Chapter 24

What We Have Learnt and Where We are Heading

This chapter begins with an overview of the analysis in the preceding chapters. It then makes some predictions based on that analysis, about what is likely to happen if we continue as we are and leave too much to market forces. We shall also briefly review some of the major threats humanity faces, but which our current economic model distracts us from tackling.

24.1 Overview of the Analysis So Far

All animals have to 'produce' goods and services to cover their needs, the 'economy' is the system by which they do that. The actual amount produced is limited by which of the three ingredients required for production runs out first: **wants**, **resources**, or **work effort**.

While past societies may have been unable to produce all the things they wanted even working flat out, or were limited by scarce resources, instead with today's technology what mainly sets the level of production is not the availability of labour or resources, but **demand**, i.e. what society **wants**. By what 'society wants', we mean what society wants *as whole and as currently organised*. So what our current society 'wants' is very largely what the rich and powerful want; the needs of the poor and the powerless carry little weight. The evidence that it is a *lack of wants* that limits production in the modern economy, is the huge effort that goes into dreaming up new products, advertising and selling – all of it in order to persuade people to want more.

Human economies function on the basis of rules, which may be formal, custom or tradition. Fundamental among these rules is the notion of ownership, since that makes trade possible, and trade in turn allows us to compare values. Marx believed that the value of a thing depended on the work it took to make it; in practice other scarce resources such as land, can also influence value. Resources taken from the environment around us are 'free' because the environment isn't a human being and asks for nothing in exchange.

Free-market economies have a 'private sector' of independent businesses. Consumers can choose who they buy from. Such economies decentralise economic decisions. Producers move into fields where there is more demand; consumer choice incentivises better quality and lower prices. Markets do match supply to demand but only to financial demand. The increasing complexity and variety of products means that consumers cannot easily judge quality or safety, and need regulation to protect them from potentially harmful products.

What takes place in a free market is the exchange of goods and services by a series of complicated swaps, in each of which both parties want to make the trade. Money hides the complex chains of swaps involved. A change in what one person or business wants can have a knock on effect on the rest of the economy much greater than the initial change, as can a change in resource availability. There is no 'natural level' of economic activity: the level of production depends on what the different actors in the economy want and may be limited by the wants of one of them to a lower level than is wanted by others.

In a free-market economy, most of us play three different roles: as **workers**, as **consumers** and as **citizens**. Our double lives as both *workers* and *consumers* mean that our political interests as *citizens* can be contradictory.

Earning a living as workers is a sort of 'game' in which most of us can offer only our capacity to work in exchange for the things we need. But there are some privileged players who also bring to the game their ownership of the places where goods and services are made. In return for our work in these places, they give us a proportion of what gets made in them. The rules of a free-market economy tend to concentrate wealth in a few hands

Long term change to the **maximum** an animal can produce results from changes in its **capabilities** due to evolution or, especially in the case of humans, due to learnt knowledge. Capabilities at a given moment of time are fixed: we cannot 'decide' to have the skills or technology of the future, although we can try to stimulate learning and innovation. Continued growth requires managing humanity's accumulated knowledge and handing it on to the next generation. Growth as measured by GDP includes any economic activity including work to mitigate harms such as pollution.

Growth in human capabilities explains long-term growth in economic output. It doesn't explain the cyclical behaviour of the economy, with periodic falls in output even though there is no interruption to technical progress. The three-ingredient model clarifies that booms and slumps can be expected in a market economy because positive feedback accentuates movement in either direction, and that boom peaks are not necessarily the maximum possible output level of the economy.

Connecting local economies by improved transport can weaken employment conditions in a high-wage high-technology area if it brings labour competition with a lower-wage hinterland, while at the same time result in low-tech artisans being out-competed by more automated factories. Connecting economies obliges businesses to be present in multiple markets, thus increasing transport use.

Population increase plus growth in consumption per capita, creates unsustainable pressure on the natural world. But the current market economy requires growth in order to provide jobs. There is no obvious solution to this conundrum except government regulation of some sort.

The market economy shapes the society we live in. For the

worker there is an increasing impermanence in employment and in required skills. The consumer and citizen face a barrage of marketing and products, designed to maximise desire and addiction, and with little consideration given to potential physical and psychological harm.

Much that is valuable in life is out of the reach of private individuals and can only be supplied collectively as public goods. Such provision is threatened by neoclassical economic philosophy that values only individual private spending.

Some would object that our economic system has not failed but is very successful in Western Europe, the USA and Japan: poorer countries have simply failed to emulate it properly. But poorer countries are part of the global economy and have structured their economies to serve the needs of the global rich. The wealthy in poorer countries are typically not satisfied with the limited range of products their own workers can produce: they want the best the world market can provide. They therefore dedicate their nations' economies to the production of cash crops or anything else in demand on world markets, that can be exchanged for imported luxuries. Among the imported products will inevitably also be advanced weapons systems and other instruments of control needed to maintain the privileges of governing elites in the face of extreme inequality and poverty.

Nor is it the case that the citizens of richer western countries have experienced a steady and general improvement to their lives. Among these countries you can find growing levels of inequality, failing public services, and formerly prosperous areas that have become rust-belt towns. In many cases the incomes of the working and lower middle classes have stagnated for decades.[142]

24.2 Given the Analysis, Where are we Heading?

What will happen if we continue to let market forces largely determine the level of production and types of product that get made, in a grossly unequal world? Based on the analysis in the preceding chapters and on current trends, here's what appears likely to take place in the free-market economies that participate in the global market:

- Rising productivity due to technical advance means that fewer workers are needed and implies high levels of under-employment and unemployment.

- The decline in material resources from the combination of a growing world population and higher consumption levels, will limit output in some areas. However, the economy's drive to produce may just shift the pressure onto other not-yet-exhausted resources.

- To compete on cost, firms will minimise labour costs, replacing secure jobs that had sick pay and pension benefits with casual 'gig economy' jobs.

- To compete on cost and quality, firms will impose greater monitoring and control on their workforces.

- The pressure to compete in order to at least survive and if possible grow, will mean that firms continue to generate a plethora of new technologies and products, intensifying the advertising that is colonising public and private life.

- The pressure to get employment in a world with a surfeit of labour will push down wages and conditions. Anxiety among children and their parents about the qualifications needed to have a chance of success in the labour market, will continue to grow.

- Driven by the desire for profit and the need to compete inter-nationally, employers will push for lower taxes on corporations and on employment. Governments will be tempted to give in, since they are in a competition with other countries to bring or retain investment.

- Faced with lower wages and fewer employment opportunities, workers will press for lower income tax, and both they and those not in employment such as pensioners and the unemployed, will favour lower taxes on consumption (in the UK that would be, lower VAT, lower fuel duties, etc.), and lower local taxes (council tax in the UK).

- Diminishing tax income will lead to a deterioration in public services.

- The more extreme free-market economists will back opening domestic markets to cheap foreign produce manufactured to lower quality and environmental standards, and argue that this helps the poor by lowering prices – even though such a policy undercuts domestic business and puts all countries in a 'race to the bottom' in terms of wages and standards.

- The poverty and job insecurity experienced by the poorer part of society combined with the flaunting of extreme wealth by the rich (and made very visible by advertising), is likely to lead to greater 'anti-social behaviour' or crime, and thus to greater expenditure on security, policing and the further development of security equipment using technologies like CCTV and artificial intelligence (AI).

- Concern for the environment and other threats that don't appear 'immediate', will be weakened by the population focussing on day-to-day survival, by companies interested only in profit, and by government which almost always has as its first priority the promotion of growth.

24.3 We Are Not Addressing the Real Threats

Humanity is not dealing with major and urgent threats to our existence. We fail to focus on these threats, in no small measure, because we have an economic system which puts everyone from individuals to corporations to governments, under the continual pressure of competing in order to survive economically. The need to buy food today or pay the mortgage tomorrow, inevitably trump trying to tackle difficult and longer-term global problems; we cling to the hope that those problems are still a few years away and that we can delay a little longer.

Unfortunately the threats we face have never been so serious. It is no coincidence that they are happening now: it is because they are largely related to the same technological revolution that has created our modern economy and the explosion in human numbers that it has facilitated.

Figure 24.1: The Bulletin of the Atomic Scientists identifies existential risks such as nuclear war and climate change. [WMC]

Shocked by the atomic weapons that their work had helped create, Einstein and others, founded the 'Bulletin of the Atomic Scientists' to warn of threats to humanity.[143] The Bulletin continues to inform; it maintains a *doomsday clock* to visualise how close we are to apocalypse:

> The Doomsday Clock is set every year by the Bulletin's Science and Security Board in consultation with its Board of Sponsors, which includes 11 Nobel laureates. The Clock has become a universally recognised indicator of the world's vulnerability to catastrophe from nuclear weapons, climate change, and disruptive technologies in other domains.

Other groups of scientists make similar assessments. In the UK, the 'Centre for the Study of Existential Risk' is an "interdisciplinary research centre within the University of Cambridge dedicated to the study and mitigation of risks that could lead to human extinction or civilizational collapse".[144] In an article written for the BBC published in February 2019, scientists at the centre put the most probable risk for 2019 as a "severe pandemic such as flu".[145] The COVID-19 pandemic started later that year, being first reported in December.

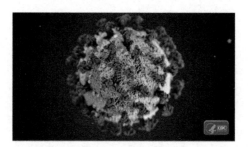

Figure 24.2: Coronavirus. [WMC]
If you didn't expect a pandemic, you weren't listening to scientists.

Some people argue that although there are risks on the horizon, humanity has in fact never had it so good. Harvard professor Steven Pinker might be considered by some to give support to this view in his books 'The Better Angels of Our Nature: Why Violence Has Declined' and 'Enlightenment Now: The Case for Reason, Science, Humanism, and Progress'.[146, 147] He points out that life has been getting better for most people based on a variety of statistics, including that people are living longer and healthier lives, and are less likely to be murdered or die in conflict. However, while the statistics are fascinating, it is plain that we should temper such optimism with concern for what is currently happening in the physical world around us, even if the impacts of forces such as climate change don't yet seem too severe. Reason also tells us not to ignore potentially devastating risks such as all-out nuclear war, merely because so far we have been lucky.

> *Should the crew on an ocean liner study the horizon for icebergs, or study statistics about how ocean travel is becoming safer?*

Professor Pinker's work highlights the sorts of factors that may have led to past reductions in violence. We have the opportunity to learn from such research what sort of behaviours and institutions we should support and promote in the future.

A further reason to be careful about extrapolating favourable statistics into the future is that a collapse often follows a peak. This is discussed in 'Collapse: How Societies Choose to Fail or Survive' by Jared Diamond.[148] The book is mainly concerned with the demise of historical civilizations, but Diamond also argues that humanity faces many of the same issues, with possibly catastrophic future consequences.

> *If you consume a food store meant to last you a month in just two weeks, life seems pretty good during those first two weeks.*

Scientists have warned of the threat of climate change for over thirty years with increasing alarm.[149] Global heating is causing droughts as rains fail, rivers dry up, and glaciers that once fed rivers melt. Crops fail directly because of drought or because they are not adapted to the new extreme temperatures. Extreme weather also threatens our infrastructure: electricity, water supplies and transport. Unfortunately market forces do not provide adequate incentives to stop the activities that cause the damage or to prepare for changes that are seen as being in the 'distant' future.

Apart from direct threats to humanity, there is the destruction of the natural world. Scientists believe that during our geological epoch the Holocene, which started about 10,000 BC, other species are disappearing due to human activity at somewhere between a hundred and a thousand times the normal rate. That puts us at the centre of a 'mass extinction' event, like the one that wiped out the dinosaurs.[150] Since we are totally dependent on nature for oxygen and food, if we destroy too much then we will also become extinct. Even if we stop short of that and humanity or some fraction of it manages to survive, they will be living in a largely barren world, devoid of the natural beauty of the wild animals and plants we have hitherto lived alongside.

Awareness of these issues is growing, but effective action lags far behind because the logic of our economic system prioritises making money in the market and financial survival, over all else.

24.4 Summary

The free-market economy has failed to provide a reasonable standard of living worldwide because it cannot generate enough demand or 'wants' to create full employment. The poor have many things that they want and indeed need, but an economy based solely or mainly on private enterprise and markets recognises only the wants of those who possess something tradable to offer in exchange – in other words, only monetary demand is recognised. When the rich spend less than their income because they have satisfied most of their wants, then the economy slows.

Attempting to maintain employment through growth is a failing strategy. The advance of automation puts a downward pressure on employment. The weak position of global labour with employers moving jobs to the lowest-wage areas, likewise subdues potential demand for goods from workers and therefore employment levels.

Nevertheless, to induce those with money to spend, much of the economy is focussed on generating endless growth in things to want and consume, pushed at the public by intensive advertising. This is a poor way to provide employment as high consumption damages the environment and many of the products are of no benefit to humanity and often do harm.

The intense competition in the market economy shapes the society we live in. For the worker there is increasing impermanence, and for the consumer, a barrage of marketing designed to maximise desire for products even if they are harmful. For citizens and politicians, short-term economic prosperity outweighs facing up to long-term dangers.

Consuming our way into full employment is not an option. Humanity already faces existential threats due to the current level of consumption and growth in population. While most of the environmental damage is caused by the wealthiest consumers, the aspiration to consume at these levels reaches far beyond them. Extending the existing consumption levels of the world's middle classes to everyone worldwide, is incompatible with retaining any chance of preserving a habitable planet.

So our economic system, while associated with an astonishing pace of technical advance, is flawed – especially so in terms of social justice and sustaining the environment. In Part Two we will consider what we might do to tackle the flaws.

Part II

A Fairer and More Sustainable Economy

Chapter 25

Changing Direction: Introduction

The last chapter of Part 1, Chapter 24, described the near future we can expect if we continue to let uncontrolled market forces largely determine the level of production and the sorts of products that are made ... and it's a bleak prospect.

> Reacting to the latest findings of the Intergovernmental Panel on Climate Change, the UN Secretary-General insisted that unless governments everywhere reassess their energy policies, **the world will be uninhabitable**. Unless action is taken soon, some major cities will be under water, Mr. Guterres said in a message, which also forecast "unprecedented heatwaves, terrifying storms, widespread water shortages and the extinction of a million species of plants and animals". – *from United Nations News.[149]*

We now move on from the analysis of the existing market economy laid out in Part 1 and turn to look at ways in which we could change direction and head for a rather better future than the one we appear to be facing. In an overpopulated world that is undergoing a storm of technological change, and on top of everything else is armed to the teeth, improving the outlook won't be easy. Yet humanity ought to be able to do so much more if we could only set

Figure 25.1: "some major cities will be under water". [WMC]

our mind to it. Of course 'setting our mind to it' is a major part of the problem, and we shall need to modify structures and incentives so that we are encouraged along a new path rather than battling a headwind every step of the way. Key will be changing the way our economy works so that we are in control of the market rather than letting the market control us. So the chapters that follow contain policy suggestions based on the economic analysis in Part 1. They assume that to achieve a better world, the goals of policy should be:

- *An environmentally sustainable world that tackles climate change, pollution and the destruction of nature.*

- *A fairer world where everyone has the opportunity for a reasonable life.*

Most people probably share these goals, although of course not everyone does. If your aim was to be fabulously wealthy and lord it over the impoverished but cowed masses, in a world that is fast becoming arid and lifeless, then there is nothing to stop you from using the economic analysis in this book to design some very different policies (although I hope you won't).

I should emphasise that while the chapters to come will contain policy ideas, they do not provide or pretend to provide, a detailed set of proposals that are feasible in legal, political and financial terms. That is a challenge for all of us.

25.1 The Logic

The logic of the policies that will be described in the next chapters is summarised here as a set of **requirements**. All of those requirements follow from this first statement:

It is essential to moderate human impact on the environment

*Note: an **environmentally sustainable world** is put as our overarching requirement because on a dead planet 'fairness' is meaningless. Humans have survived under all sorts of horrible regimes – while there's life there's hope. However, below we shall add the second goal of **a fairer world** as being necessary to achieve the first, as well as something we would wish for.*

It follows that ...

- We need to control and moderate global consumption of stuff and energy.

- Moderating consumption will require global agreement.

- Global agreement will require greater equality between nations, since poorer nations will not accept remaining poorer than the richer ones indefinitely.

- Greater equality is necessary between individuals as well as between nations, if measures to limit consumption are to be seen as fair and gain public support. Therefore, **fairness** is added as a **second goal**, for practical as well as ethical reasons.

- Both automation and moderating the production of stuff, reduce the amount of labour needed. Therefore, employment in services that do not produce material goods is required, or a universal basic income must be provided.

- In order to finance the salaries of people who don't produce stuff (e.g. pensioners, those working in services provided for free such as healthcare and education, those paid a universal basic income), the production of stuff must be taxed in some way. That puts up prices and reduces the competitiveness of manufacturing as it is essentially paying the salaries and pensions of all workers, not just of its own. So a country that follows this policy must regulate its trade with others that do not, or failing that, at least impose the relevant taxes in such a way that imported and local manufactures are equally affected, e.g. by taxing sales, not wages.

- We need to build long-term sustainable investments that improve the quality of life and reduce human impact.

- We need to reduce the impact of farming: the space occupied, the energy used, and pollution. We need to limit hunting and fishing.

- We need to limit world population, ideally reducing it as that increases the level of the sustainable standard of living that can be offered and reduces human impact on the environment. Greater space per human would improve the quality of life, by allowing more spacious houses and cities, and more national parks and wild spaces.

- To gain acceptance of lower consumption levels, we need to curtail the propaganda in favour of consumption. Advertising operates as a public misinformation service, promoting consumption as the way to be healthy, happy and successful. We shall want the opposite message to dominate.

- Similarly we need to provide alternatives to material consumption that are sustainable and provide interest and fulfilment.

- We need an education and a philosophy that explains and supports the above goals.

25.2 Policy Overview

Based on the above requirements, a set of policy suggestions are listed in the bullet points below, aimed at achieving or at least moving towards the desired fairer and more environmentally sustainable world. In the chapters that follow these ideas are explored one by one, and the reasoning behind them explained.

- **Livelihoods – providing the means to live**

    - Provide jobs for all who want them. Share out work.
    - Services will in many cases need to be cheap or free, or purchased with a different currency that can be spent on services but not material goods.
    - Remove taxes from employment.
    - Tax unearned income and the super rich.
    - Tax undesirables: pollution, energy, resource use.
    - Promote fairness in the distribution of basic goods, if necessary rationing them where supply has to be limited.
    - Invest for the long term.
    - Align economic boundaries with government boundaries, since governments with economic responsibility must also have some economic control.
    - Encourage resilient local economies, e.g. favour local businesses via dual currencies (local plus national).

- **Reducing environmental impact and protecting the natural world**

    - Manage population.
    - Reduce impact of farming fishing & hunting.
    - Reduce impact of industry.
    - Adopt sustainable lifestyles – encourage moderation in household consumption.

- **Public support, participation and well-being**

  - Promote community and political participation. Encourage support for international cooperation and agreement.

  - Provide ways to take local spending decisions locally.

  - Curb advertising – replace with genuine and accountable public information.

  - Limit inequality.

  - Make available pleasures that are environmentally sustainable – arts, nature, sports, crafts, social life.

  - Improve quality of working life: working conditions, variety & interest, job security, sick pay, pensions.

25.3 Summary

Unrestrained market forces are provoking environmental damage and levels of inequality that endanger humanity. A change of direction is urgently needed. This chapter proposed two main goals – an environmentally sustainable world and a fairer world – and derived some requirements from those goals.

Based on those requirements and the economic analysis in Part 1 of this book, a set of policy ideas were then outlined. The next three chapters discuss the suggested policies.

Chapter 26

Changing Direction: Livelihoods

Near the start of this book in Chapter 2 we defined the economy as being the system by which people produce and consume the goods and services whose primary purpose is to enable us to live. In other words, the purpose of the economy is to provide us all with a livelihood. Unfortunately it very plainly fails to do so: across the globe there are many millions who live a hand to mouth existence in unsatisfactory and sometimes appalling conditions.

This chapter is about providing those livelihoods. It suggests that we do this by providing enough jobs so that everyone able to do so can earn a living by working – as opposed to having too few jobs and needing to support large numbers of unemployed. There also needs to be a mechanism to provide an income to those who are unable to work or retired. Already there are not enough jobs in production, and the combination of further automation with the need to limit consumption for environmental reasons, means that there are likely to be even fewer in the future. Therefore, we need to create additional jobs in services that have little or no environmental impact, and which although not viable commercially and thus need to be offered subsidised or free, are of value to society.

The latter part of this chapter deals with the taxation needed to be able to finance the incomes of those unable to work and of those employed in the non-commercial service jobs. It suggests that taxation should fall mainly on consumption, not on employment (i.e. not on wages), because we want to encourage the provision of work. In addition, given the tendency of wealth to concentrate, taxation of very high incomes and wealth is required in order both to raise revenue and to tackle extreme inequality.

26.1 Jobs for All

Not enough jobs

In Chapter 2 we said that the amount the economy can produce will be limited by what it runs out of first:

- **Wants** – the existence of categories of stuff that people want more of, like food, clothes, cars, mobile phones, TVs, etc.

- **Resources** - to make the stuff out of.

- **Work Effort** – people to make the stuff.

The mass of ordinary people have tended to be happier if it is *work effort* that is most in short supply, because since everyone is needed, it is likely to be possible to extract a better deal from employers than just a basic subsistence wage. The 1950s and 60s in Western Europe and the USA were such a time. Unfortunately should *wants* or *resources* be the limit on the economy, then free-market capitalism fails to provide an acceptable life for a large part of the population. Currently, *wants* are the main limit on production (there isn't enough consumption to result in full employment), although running out of *resources* is a growing concern for the future.

Why provide jobs – won't robots do everything in the future?

There is a great deal of speculation that eventually robots will do all the work and humans can be paid to do nothing. Nevertheless, the best way to share out wealth for the foreseeable future, is to ensure that it's possible for everyone able to do so, to earn a living by working. That is so because:

- **There remains a great deal of work to be done, despite the progress of automation.** It would be better to share out that work, otherwise we will end up with a minority still working who have to maintain others who are idle – a recipe for resentments.

- **Work remains one of the main ways people find structure and meaning in life.** If we are ever to move away from that, it would be best to do so in cautious steps.

We should also bear in mind that when an employer installs a robot, it is not because they want to pay the displaced workers to sit at home doing nothing – it is so that they don't have to pay those workers at all. Working people have political and economic power because their labour is needed, and potentially they can withdraw it – but a 'kept' population without work, is powerless. A robot economy controlled by private business owners and a handful of technocrats, is not in the interest of the majority of us. If there is to be a transition to a largely robot-run economy, then we should use what power we have to press for widespread popular participation in that economy and strong democratic control over it.

We can't consume our way to full employment without destroying the planet

Within the free-market economy, to maintain full employment, we need the level of production to be limited by the available *work effort*, not by *resources* or *wants*. Currently, the economy does not operate at its maximum level because it is limited by *wants* – the world's rich do not spend all their money. In theory, we could solve this problem by boosting wants; we could either:

1. Find more things for the rich to want. This implies more consumption, especially of luxuries. Or ...

2. Share out money more equally across the population (tax the rich), and hope that once poorer people have more money, they will want to spend it. This should increase consumption of more ordinary goods, not just luxuries.

However, neither of these two solutions is advisable because our planet cannot support ever-increasing consumption. In a previous period in history when the world population was much smaller, solutions like these based on increasing consumption, might have been viable, but with the explosion in human numbers they would cause too great a level of damage to the environment. They also don't help us if in the future, resource scarcity becomes the limit to what the economy can produce.

We need to <u>lower</u> productivity!

The conclusion is that we must choose to operate the economy at less that the maximum output level, in order to conserve resources and reduce environmental damage. Doing so will leave us with surplus work effort, i.e. more workers than work to be done. The choices are then:

1. Have a proportion of the workers employed full-time in production, and the others unemployed. Those working in production would need to produce enough goods for their own consumption and for that of the unemployed.

2. Have some workers employed full-time in production as in option 1, and employ the others in services that do not result in production of goods nor damage the environment in other ways. Those working in production need to produce enough goods for their own consumption and for that of those working in services.

3. Share out the available work so that everyone is employed but working shorter hours – or the same hours but less efficiently!

All of these three solutions in a sense, lower the overall productivity of economy in terms of manufacturing. In options 1 & 2 above we have required manufacturing workers to produce not only what they need to survive, but also to provide goods for the unemployed or service workers. In option 3 we are employing and paying more workers than necessary. None of these options are likely to be welcomed by manufacturing businesses because normally the objective of the free-market capitalist is to pay the workers the minimum in terms of goods that they need to survive; that is how a business makes its products cheaper and therefore more competitive or profitable. However, business can generally accept regulation provided it applies to all and leaves a 'level playing field'. Achieving this is easier within one country and more challenging with international trade. In an international context, option 3 is difficult, and for options 1 and 2 it depends whether businesses are taxed on labour or on sales; we'll say more about taxes later.

Accordingly, if we are to apply any of the three productivity-lowering solutions above, then **regulation** is needed to oblige all businesses to comply; they cannot adopt such solutions voluntarily because they would lose out to others who don't. It also requires **international cooperation** or **trade controls**, because otherwise businesses in a country that adopts such measures will lose out to competitors in countries that don't. Unfortunately politicians (at least those in the UK) have convinced themselves that pay rises must be funded through productivity increases and see no other path than competing with other countries in a race to the bottom.

We do not have to pick just one of the solutions above, but can use some combination of the three. For fairness, it's probably best to ensure that everyone able to work has the opportunity to do so, which means that we may need to create jobs in areas where the market provides too few, or share out jobs. In terms of creating jobs, option 2 (providing the extra employment needed in services) is important, because there are many services that are clearly needed but are not adequately provided by our current economy; we will examine why the market cannot provide them next.

Figure 26.1: Maximising productivity can put countries in a 'race to the bottom' in environmental standards and workers' conditions.

Services will need to be cheap or free, or use a different currency

If services are genuinely needed, why do we need government regulation to provide them, why not just leave the market to do so? This was discussed in Chapter 13 where we described the economy's environmental impacts; we will briefly summarise the argument again here:

- Services are likely to form only a small part of an ordinary worker's consumption. This is because businesses have no incentive to pay more than the minimum, and in a world with surplus labour, that will be something approaching subsistence – so only enough to buy basic material goods like food, housing, clothing, and the odd electronic gadget. Production workers paid at this level cannot hire a service worker, since the service worker also clearly needs at least subsistence pay, and the production worker's pay is only enough for their own subsistence.

- The very rich can afford numerous service workers, but they will not want more than a certain number of servants, so the total amount of employment is limited.

But hold on! The above applies to things as they are – but we are going to regulate the economy, so we can arrange things differently. Let's suppose that half the workers are production workers and half are service workers. Couldn't we pay all workers twice subsistence pay, and they can then spend half of it on subsistence goods produced by the production workers and the other half on buying services from the service workers? The difficulty with doing so is that there is no obvious way of enforcing that pattern of spending. The extra services we need are mostly either public services such as improvements to the environment, or things that we know people struggle to plan and set aside sufficient funds for such as care of the elderly. Experience shows that if you pay people double, they are likely to spend much of it on personal consumption – more stuff, more TVs, cars & foreign holidays – not on public benefits like the local park. That's why all countries fund the army, the police, the fire service, etc. through taxation, not by hoping that the public will want to buy their share of policing or whatever at the local supermarket. It's also the case that many of the poorest people live such a hand to mouth existence that they struggle to find money for immediate necessities like buying food or paying the electricity bill, making it almost impossible to save for a pension or pay health insurance – that is why decent governments ensure that everyone has access to a minimum pension and to public health care, and do not rely on people purchasing them individually.

The implication is that if you want to provide a large number of additional services as a way to create employment, then they will have to be mostly free or heavily subsidised and paid for out of some sort of taxation. However, where a service is something that can be sold to individuals, we could consider a dual currency scheme. Workers would be paid in two currencies: one to be used to buy material goods that have an impact on resources and the environment, and the other only usable to buy services that are judged to be environmentally neutral or beneficial, such as a haircut, an appliance repair, or domestic help. In some places community organisations known as 'transition towns' are experimenting with alternative local currencies which often tend to be biassed towards the exchange of services.[1]

Jobs for All – conclusion

Our economy should enable everyone to work who can, and provide for those who cannot. Since restricting consumption for environmental reasons is likely to mean there is not enough work for everyone in producing saleable goods and services, we shall need either to share out such work as there is, or preferably create extra work in services that are provided to the public free or heavily subsidised. There are plenty of worthwhile services that we could choose to provide in this way. Government regulation will be required to organise this and ensure that unfair competition does not occur due to some businesses and countries shirking their responsibilities to maintain employment while others shoulder them. To fund additional employment in services, we shall need taxes ...

26.2 Taxation

The background

Governments finance themselves through a range of taxes. The UK where I live is fairly typical. There are consumption taxes like VAT (Value Added Tax) which adds a percentage to the price when something is sold to the consumer – currently the standard UK rate is 20%, so if you buy an item costing £1, you will actually pay £1.20; although prices in the shops generally already include the tax, so you may not be aware that the £1.20 price includes 20p VAT. For certain items, consumption taxes in the UK vary from the standard rate, being charged at higher rates on petrol and on certain luxuries such as alcohol & cigarettes, and at a lower or zero rate on some other items - for example foodstuffs. The other major tax that the populace see is income tax, charged on an individual's earnings on a rising scale; the UK income tax bands for the tax year 2022-23 are shown in Table 26.1.

---

[1]For more about transition towns, see: *https://transitionnetwork.org*

Band	Taxable income	Tax rate
Personal Allowance:	Up to £12,570	0%
Basic Rate:	£12,571 to £50,270	20%
Higher Rate:	£50,271 to £150,000	40%
Additional Rate:	over £150,000	45%

Note: The rates only apply to income in that band. So if you earn £20,000 you pay 0% on the first £12,570 and 20% on the rest.

Table 26.1: UK income tax rates 2022-23

There are other taxes in the UK of course. It is said that the art of taxation is to spread it out over a variety of taxes so that no one tax appears so large as to be felt too onerous or too worthwhile evading. In 2020, the United Kingdom had a tax-to-GDP ratio of 32.8% compared with the OECD average of 33.5%.[151] In some European countries the ratio is above 40%.

A very large part of UK taxation comes from income taxes and from social security contributions which are also deducted from earnings, totalling between them about 48% of the total tax take.[151]

'Business' and 'Social' sectors

To understand the rate of taxation required, imagine the economy as grouped into two parts:

1. ***The Business Sector.*** Everyone who lives off the production of saleable goods and services (food, TVs, cars, entertainment, haircuts, etc.), whether by working in or owning these businesses. Usually these are private-sector businesses, although not always. The business sector earns money from its sales and uses that money to pay the people who work in it. Money is the way that the goods are shared out: how much you are paid determines the share of the produce that you can have.

2. ***The Social Sector.*** Everyone paid by the state and not producing goods for sale, which includes workers providing services that the public receive free (e.g. police, fire service, education, etc.), and people not working who are receiving the state pension, unemployment pay, etc. The social sector doesn't earn money from sales – it is supported by taxes on business, with the money raised used to pay social sector workers, who are thus able to buy a share of the goods produced by the business sector. The services produced by the social sector, being free, are not shared out by money, but in other ways, typically by need – so the amount of education services your family receives from state schools depends not on payment, but on how many children you have and their educational needs.

The business sector has to be taxed in order to pay those in the social sector. The tax rate (the percentage size of the tax) depends on the relative sizes of the two sectors: if the social sector is small, so will the tax rate be. In today's industrialised countries the social sector has become sizeable because of the needs of modern society.

The effect of taxes on the business sector is to force the private companies within it to provide goods and services for the rest of society, not just for its owners and workers. This is not a one-sided deal. By paying its taxes, business is buying an educated healthy workforce, public infrastructure, and the whole legal and security framework within which it operates.

Note: Communist countries where the state owns all businesses, don't in theory need taxes to finance the social sector. Since the state owns the businesses, it already owns all of their income (although the state might still choose to have taxes for accounting reasons, as do state industries in capitalist countries).

Problems with income tax

Income tax problem 1. Consider the case that automation advances to the point where just one worker is needed by the whole business sector, operating the factories of the world from a central console. What should that worker be paid? If he or she is paid only a normal wage adequate to buy a normal household's needs, then where will the taxes come from to sustain the entire of the rest of the population, who will need to be paid either a universal basic income (if they don't work) or a wage to work in services?

An employer only needs to employ enough workers to produce the goods the employer wants to consume plus whatever goods are required to pay the workers (the goods manufactured being sold/exchanged for the variety of other goods desired). In the case that just one worker can produce everything, you need to somehow force businesses to produce and distribute goods for the rest of the population? Suppose that you pay a universal basic income to the rest of the population that is sufficient for them to buy what they need from the businesses. Where will you get the money to pay that basic income? Plainly, since the factory only needs one worker, the money paid to everyone else to allow them to buy goods, needs to be raised by taxes. In other words almost the entire price of the goods would need to be taken as a sort of sales (consumption) tax in order to provide the universal income. If you were to wish to do this via income tax you would have to pay the one worker in the factory an immense salary and then take almost all of it in tax to use for the universal income of the rest of the population. Imagine what that might look like – even if the business sector employs not one worker but 50% of the workforce, that still implies a 50% income tax rate. An example may help – in this example we shall assume that wages are the same in both business and social sectors:

> Suppose all the products of the business sector sell for a total of $100bn. That money is used to pay the gross wages of everyone (workers and owners) who live off the business sector, but as it is taxed at 50%, their net wages total $50bn, and the other $50bn goes to the government. The government uses that $50bn to pay the wages of everyone who live off the social sector. Note that the gross wages in the social sector are also $100bn but since they are also taxed at 50%, the government only actually has to pay out the net wages, totalling $50bn.

If in the future the business sector only requires 10% of the workforce, that implies a 90% income tax rate. Logically this does no harm to working people – on the contrary, it is actually forcing private owners to produce far more goods and employ and support far more working people that they otherwise would do. However, having a 90% deduction shown on payslips may be a psychological and political problem. It provides a target for unscrupulous or ignorant politicians to argue that the government is robbing people, when in fact the tax does the **exact opposite**, forcing business to provide goods for the whole population, and not just for the owners and a handful of workers, with everyone else being left destitute.

Income tax problem 2. There is another issue with income tax when it is a major part of taxation and therefore a major part of the gross wage of workers. Businesses have to pay workers enough so that their net wage (after taxes have been deducted) is at least enough for basic subsistence. If income taxes are high, that means that the gross wage businesses have to pay is considerably higher than the net wage, meaning that the price charged for products has to be higher and the business is less competitive. Two problems arise from this: unfair competition with businesses in low-tax countries, and an increased pressure to replace people with machines:

- *Unfair Competition:* A business based in a country that maintains an extensive welfare state financed via high income taxes, may find itself in competition with others based in countries that provide few benefits to their population and accordingly have low income taxes and therefore cheaper labour costs. The countries that try to do right by their population by providing good public services, then face seeing their local businesses going bankrupt, or migrating to places where labour costs are lower – often at least in part, because the workers there are denied decent public services. Consumption taxes avoid this problem since they can be charged equally on local and imported goods.

- *Pressure to replace people with machines:* When businesses

376

pay higher gross wages because they include income tax, the potential saving of replacing workers with machines is correspondingly greater: no wage or income tax is paid to a machine. Some economists argue that this is a good thing as it provides a strong incentive to automate and make businesses more productive. However, if those displaced are unable to find other work and require state support, they will be poorer; the overall economic effect may also be negative. There is as well a negative social effect if customers or co-workers are obliged to interact with a robot instead of a human.

26.2.1 Tax consumption not labour

Consumption taxes are the answer – but are they regressive?

Consumption taxes solve the above problems. Even if automation became total so that no workers were needed, you could just pay the population enough to purchase the output of the factories – whether as a universal income, or as wages for service work, obtaining the money to do so from a consumption tax that would be approaching 100%.

A criticism of consumption taxes like VAT[2] is that they are 'regressive' by which is meant that they weigh more heavily on the poor than the rich. By contrast a 'progressive tax' is one where the tax rate increases as the taxable amount increases, so that richer people pay a higher percentage in tax and not just a higher total amount. Income taxes are typically progressive, the UK tax bands shown in the table earlier in this chapter being an example. I'm not sure how strong the argument really is that consumption taxes are regressive as opposed to just neutral; I believe it is based partly on the idea that the poor will spend almost all their income on purchases upon which they have to pay tax, while the rich will save or invest some of their income – that being not subject to sales tax. On the other hand, a larger proportion of the spending of the

---

[2]Value Added Tax – the sales tax used in the EU and the UK.

poorest may be on food, which in the UK at least is exempt from the sales tax. A positive argument for consumption taxes is that they may be more difficult for the rich to evade – while it is well known that the rich find numerous ways to avoid income tax.

In practice, if consumption taxes become the main part of taxation, it matters little if they are viewed as neutral or slightly regressive, because the way that the tax income is distributed can be progressive: it can be used to guarantee full employment and provide a basic income to those who cannot work.

26.2.2 Tax unearned income and the super rich

We saw in Chapter 6 where we described life in the market economy, that someone who is already wealthy has a significant advantage in getting even richer, because: (i) they can save and invest a larger proportion of their income, whereas someone on the breadline has nothing spare to save or invest, (ii) as well as any earned income, they benefit from unearned income from investments, limited only by the size of their fortune, (iii) they can afford professional advice, (iv) they can make riskier but more profitable investments, (v) they can more easily evade tax, and (vi) if rich enough may have significant contact with and influence over government. The rich also have opportunities to provide each other with mutual support, as for example when corporate 'remuneration committees' made up of wealthy men decide what other wealthy men should earn.

It all adds up to an example of positive feedback: the richer you are, the richer you get. Some examples of this trend (from an Oxfam Briefing Paper 'An Economy for the 99%' [10]), are:

- Since 2015, the richest 1% has owned more wealth than the rest of the planet.

- The incomes of the poorest 10% of people increased by less than $3 a year between 1988 and 2011, while the incomes of the richest 1% increased 182 times as much.

- A FTSE-100 CEO earns as much in a year as 10,000 people in working in garment factories in Bangladesh.

- In the US, new research by economist Thomas Piketty shows that over the last 30 years the growth in the incomes of the bottom 50% has been zero, whereas incomes of the top 1% have grown 300%.

Therefore, if unchecked, the free-market leads to extreme inequality. A small minority of people on the planet are astonishingly wealthy. Wealth refers to what you own, not your income, although great wealth is naturally likely to be associated with a high unearned income from property, shares, and interest.

"The ten richest billionaires saw their wealth more than double from $700bn to $1.5 trillion between March 2020 and November 2021. They now own six times more wealth than the poorest 40% of the global population, some 3.1 billion people." – *Oxfam Views and Voices.[152]*

The case made in the previous section about reducing or removing taxes on employment, applies to the normal jobs of the bulk of the population. However, high taxes remain a good way to discourage ridiculously high salaries. Reducing inequality also requires taxes on unearned income and on excessive wealth. A world in which global consumption is kept to a sustainable level can have some comfortably wealthy people but cannot afford the insanely wealthy whose consumption of resources is off the scale.

26.2.3   Is taxing the rich unfair?

Is it unfair to tax the incomes and wealth of the very rich? We can readily accept that it is natural for humans to want to compete and to better themselves – we share such behaviour with many other animals. So it would be both wrong and fruitless to try to stop people from reaping rewards from ability, initiative and hard work. But that doesn't mean that we can't or shouldn't apply some limits to economic competition, just as we do in sport. Winning at sport may result in a handsome financial reward, but you don't get to enslave your opponent and take possession of all their worldly goods – even the title and trophy are often only the winner's for a year until the next time the competition is held. In any case, great wealth is often not or not only due to personal merit, but because the operation of the market tends to concentrate wealth – it can do so merely by the positive feedback of wealth creating more wealth, without necessarily any malpractice, although other non-meritworthy factors may of course play a part, such as inherited wealth, luck, cronyism, and crime.

Nor should we suppose that everyone who can be labelled rich is against some level of redistribution. We are all human, and every human has some idea of fairness and justice. Many of the world's famous radicals have come from the more privileged classes, and that should hardly surprise us given their greater access to education and leisure to study – particularly in past centuries when much of the rest of society was oppressed, barely literate, and worked to the bone just to survive.

It is very much in the interest of the wealthy as well as the rest of us, to support economic policies that lead to a stable and safe world. The evidence is that more equal societies are happier and more secure. Quite a number of the world's richest people appreciate this and try to turn their fortunes to good use. At the meeting of the World Economic Forum in Davos, Switzerland, one UK millionaire said:

> "It's outrageous that our political leaders listen to those who have the most, know the least about the economic impact of this crisis, and many of whom pay infamously little in taxes. The only credible outcome from this conference is to tax the richest and tax us now." – *quoted in: Millionaires at Davos say 'tax us more', BBC Business News.[153]*

There is in fact a movement of millionaires calling for higher taxes under the banner of In Tax We Trust. On their website they say:

> "Trust is built through accountability, through well-oiled, fair, and open democracies that provide good services and support all their citizens. And the bedrock of a strong democracy is a fair tax system."

> "As millionaires, we know that the current tax system is not fair. Most of us can say that, while the world has gone through an immense amount of suffering in the last two years, we have actually seen our wealth rise during the pandemic – yet few if any of us can honestly say that we pay our fair share in taxes." – *In Tax We Trust.[154]*

Some argue that taxing the wealthy will stifle enterprise or reduce investment, although with very little evidence for either. The opposite is more likely: the world's richest and happiest countries typically have relatively high levels of taxation and public spending.

Apart from these arguments, levels of inequality across the world have become so grotesque that if we want to apply resources to solving the problems that face us, we have little choice but to co-opt some of the huge private wealth that has accumulated in recent years. As 'Tax We Trust' say:

> "Until participants [at Davos] acknowledge the simple, effective solution staring them in the face – taxing the rich – the people of the world will continue to see their so-called dedication to fixing the world's problems as little more than a performance."

> "History paints a pretty bleak picture of what the endgame of extremely unequal societies looks like. For all our well-being – rich and poor alike – it's time to confront inequality and choose to tax the rich." – *In Tax We Trust.[154]*

Taxing those with the broadest shoulders is not seeking to make enemies of anyone nor create a society of total equality with everybody walking around in identical chairman Mao suits. It is simply economic realism, necessary to bring about a stable and sustainable world that benefits all of us, and that will still contain significant variations in wealth and income.

26.2.4 Selective taxes

Higher taxes are already used in many countries to discourage harmful behaviours such as smoking, while taxes are sometimes lowered on essentials or things considered desirable – books are exempt from sales tax in the UK. Clearly there is scope to try to achieve environmental goals via selective taxes while also raising needed revenue. However, preventing people by prohibitive pricing from doing things that are either essential (heating their homes) or at least very familiar (holidaying by car or plane), seems unfair. The end effect would be that the world became a playground for the rich who can easily pay the higher prices. Accordingly, some sort of individual allowance or ration could be a better alternative. Environmental taxes and rationing are considered in Chapter 27 which deals with policies for the environment.

26.3 Will Taxation Suppress Demand and Reduce Employment?

Politicians regularly call for tax cuts as a way to boost the economy and thus increase employment. So it may seem surprising and initially hard to believe, that the opposite is true: taxation actually increases economic activity through the government spending it makes possible. The reason is that higher taxes oblige business owners to produce more, because in addition to the production necessary to provide for themselves and cover their workers wages, they must also produce extra to pay their taxes to the government. Those taxes are then used to pay the wages of those in the state sector, creating employment and demand for goods. Regardless of whether the taxes are applied to consumption or to labour, they have the effect of increasing the cost of labour because business must pay at least a subsistence wage; both types of tax oblige businesses to pay higher gross wages to ensure that the net wage is equal to or higher than a subsistence wage.

We saw in Chapter 8 that discussed labour supply and demand, how increasing the cost of labour for all businesses, increases the amount of workers that business owners need to employ in order to produce for themselves and for their workforce. It's not really such a strange concept. The same idea was described by Henry Ford in the early 20th century when he reduced the working week of his workers from six days to five for the same pay – essentially a pay increase. Here is how he explained it:

> "The people with a five-day week will consume more goods than the people with a six-day week. People who have more leisure must have more clothes. They must have a greater variety of food. They must have more transportation facilities. They naturally must have more service of various kinds."

> "This increased consumption will require greater production than we now have. Instead of business being slowed up because the people are 'off work,' it will be speeded up, because the people consume more in their leisure than in their working time. This will lead to more work. And this to more profits. And this to more wages. The result of more leisure will be the exact opposite of what most people might suppose it to be." – *Henry Ford.[155]*

If you want to see how this works mathematically, what follows is a simplified model of what is going on. To start with, we'll consider how many workers the owners of businesses need to employ to supply what they want for themselves and a basic subsistence wage to their workers. The quantities need to be for some set amount of time; let's say they are *per day*. To keep it simple, we shall assume that all workers get the same wage and produce the same amount.

So the production needed to supply the business sector both with what the owners want to consume, and to cover the wages of the number workers employed in the sector, is:

$$ProductionNeeded = OwnersWants + (N_{Prod} \times Wage)$$

We already worked out a formula for the number of workers that owners will need to employ in a closed economy: see equation (8.2)

Quantity of goods wanted by the owners:	*OwnersWants*
Quantity of goods needed by a worker for subsistence (i.e. net wage):	*Wage*
Quantity of goods produced by a worker:	*WorkerOutput*
Number of workers employed in production (i.e. in the business sector):	N_{Prod}

in the example of a country estate given in Chapter 8. Using that formula, the number of production workers needed N_{Prod} is given by:

$$N_{Prod} = \frac{OwnersWants}{WorkerOutput - Wage} \qquad (26.1)$$

The above equation (26.1) is hopefully fairly intuitive. The owners get the 'profit' from each worker, being what a worker produces minus a worker gets paid, i.e. $WorkerOutput - Wage$. So the number of workers they need is the total wants of the owners divided by the profit from a single worker. The scenario is illustrated in Figure 26.2

If government imposes a tax, whether it is on incomes or on consumption (added to the wages of the worker or taken off their output), then businesses will have less profit per worker. To compensate for that so that they can still receive their wants, the owners will have to employ more workers. This means we have to modify the formula we had in equation (26.1) for workers needed, to include the effect of tax, and it becomes as shown in equation (26.2) below:

$$N_{Prod} = \frac{OwnersWants}{WorkerOutput - (Wage + Tax)} \qquad (26.2)$$

Note that the 'Wage' in this equation remains a real or 'net wage', i.e. what the worker actually gets after tax, and their nominal or gross wage could be higher if taxes are levied on workers incomes rather than sales. Note also that we assume that at least in the long term, businesses have to pay a higher gross wage to cover the tax, rather than try to reduce real wages of the workers;

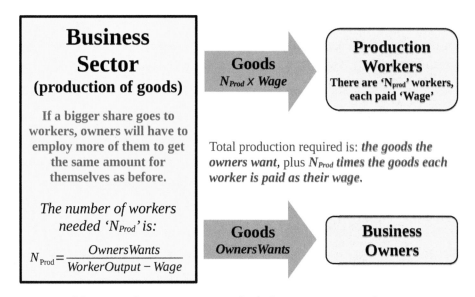

More workers are required if they consume a larger proportion of what they produce.

Figure 26.2: Workers needed in the business sector, if it operates alone, i.e. without a publicly-funded social sector.

that is because while businesses always try to pay as little as they can, they do normally have to make net-pay be at least a certain minimum amount, since workers have to live.

You cannot take more out of a business than it actually produces, so $(Wage + Tax)$ cannot be more than what a worker produces $WorkerOutput$, and needs to be rather less to leave enough for profits to supply the owners' wants and provide them with a reward and incentive. If you don't want to let the owners have anything, you'll have to nationalise all businesses or turn them into workers' cooperatives – that brings a different set of issues.

What will be the employment share between the business and social sectors?

We can also explore what proportion of employment will need to be in the business sector. To keep this simple we will treat all those who live off the business sector as a single group (workers plus owners), and assume an average pay of $Wage$. Let's suppose that the total output across the whole economy corresponds to an average consumption per person of $AverageConsumption$. As before, the output per worker employed in the business sector is $WorkerOutput$. We will call the total number of workers employed or supported by both business and social sectors N_{All}.

Total output is the same as total consumption, and total consumption is simply N_{All} multiplied by average consumption per person. So in order to supply that amount of manufactured goods to everyone, employment in the business sector N_{Prod}, needs to be:

$$N_{Prod} = \frac{N_{All} \times AverageConsumption}{WorkerOutput}$$

And the percentage of people who need to be employed in production (i.e. in the business sector) is:

$$PercentInProduction = \frac{N_{Prod}}{N_{All}} \times 100\% \tag{26.3}$$

$$= \frac{AverageConsumption}{WorkerOutput} \times 100\% \tag{26.4}$$

You hardly need the detail to understand the result in equation (26.4). We are simply saying that if for example a worker in the business sector can produce enough for two people (so, twice average consumption), then you would only need 50% of the workforce employed in the business sector. But it's an important result because it shows us very clearly that if we have to limit the average consumption per person $AverageConsumption$ because of environmental limits, then as automation increases output per worker $WorkerOutput$, the percentage employed in the business sector must fall. We can easily imagine that output per worker $WorkerOutput$ in the business sector might reach four times an acceptable sustainable world average consumption, in which case the business sector would only need to employ 25% of the world's workers, and we should aim to employ the other 75% in the social sector, implying an overall tax rate of 75%.

Could taxes really be so high?

The suggestion that taxes may need to be very high to provide the jobs and services we need may to some people seem surprising. In fact this is the direction that most advanced countries have moved in over the last century or more, and many of the world's richest countries already have tax rates of approaching or over 40% of GDP, and government expenditure approaching or over 50% of GDP (the difference being made up by borrowing). For example in Europe, France, Denmark, Belgium, Sweden, Finland, Italy and Austria, all have tax revenues that exceed 40% of GDP, and these are among the most prosperous and pleasant places to live in the world.[151, 156]

Is it fair on the business sector to support the rest?

It may seem that the business sector 'produces everything' and the rest of the population are living off it. Certainly some politicians like to remark that "it's the profits of private industry that support the public services". Plenty of us, when we see what we pay in tax, can be tempted to think that we'd like to keep that money and could spend it better ourselves – and far-right politicians are very ready to encourage that attitude. But subject their case to scrutiny and it falls apart – like complaining about gravity because you don't like lifting things, without having given a moment's thought to how without it, ourselves, and everything else not tied down including the atmosphere we breathe, would float off into outer space.

The anti-tax pundits would have us believe that a private hospital, private school and toll road, are all productive economic assets because they make profits, while their state-funded counterparts are all drains on the economy. The truth of the matter is that we do in fact 'spend all of our money' – but some of it we spend individually or as families, and some of it we spend collectively by paying taxes that finance the public services that we benefit from. We can equally say "it's the services provided by the social sector that create the conditions in which industry can operate". The interdependency of business and social sectors is illustrated in Figure 26.3. The collective spending provides the basis for a comfortable modern life and underpins business activities too.

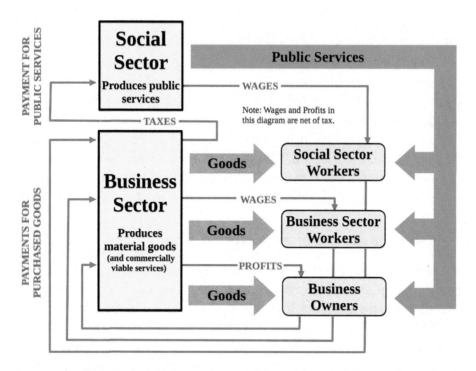

Figure 26.3: The business and social sectors: supply goods we buy individually, and services we buy collectively.

Perhaps you have a small business and are unconvinced that public spending is a vital part of the economy? Well try this thought experiment: Your fairy godmother has given you wish and your request is "*When I wake tomorrow let there be no more state and no more taxes*" – imagine now what would happen next ...

> *On waking up the following morning, you find that your car has been stolen, your business looted and set on fire; there are no police, no firefighters to help - gone also are courts and prisons. The toilets are blocked (no sewers)*

and rubbish is piling up in the street - no refuse collection! Mind you the street is just dirt – all the roads, bridges, street lights, traffic lights, parks and museums, have gone. There are no public schools or hospitals, no vaccination programmes against infectious diseases, no controls on food hygiene or building safety. Anarchy sets in with scores of gangland and fundamentalist militias battling it out. Local production collapses, all shops are looted or empty, no imports or exports as no traders want to come near. Eventually foreign powers seize bits of the country where there useful resources, there being no defence forces to stop them, and also take to bombing areas that they suspect of being the hideouts of drug barons or terrorist groups.

How could any business function in such circumstances? Yet this description of horrors doesn't take much imagination. You only need to think of countries that have suffered periods of weak and ineffective government (sometimes referred to as 'failed states'). Refugees flee such places, often heading when they can towards countries with strong effective states and high taxes, e.g. to countries in Western Europe, or to Canada or the USA (the USA being fact a relatively high tax country, despite some oddities such as its attitude to public health care when compared to most other rich nations).

The reality is that we all consume the 'free' services produced by the social sector, and once basic individual consumption needs are satisfied, these free services become more important. They are just as much part of the economy as the business sector, the only difference being that they need to be purchased collectively.

26.4   Borrowing and Debt

Governments often borrow in order to finance their expenditure – is this a better option than taxation? Right wing politicians tend to frown on borrowing, and warn of a terrible burden of debt that will be left to our children to pay off. Yet curiously they usually say nothing about the wonderful credit that they and their rich friends who lend the money are leaving to their own children who will be the recipients of those repayments (since for every debtor there is a creditor). Centre-left politicians, in the UK at least, tend to favour borrowing, especially in periods of low interest rates meaning that borrowing is relatively inexpensive.

In practice governments of all stripes have been happy to borrow. For the right, lending money to the government is a relatively safe way for themselves and their wealthy friends to earn interest on their cash; it creates scope for tax cuts which can be substantial cuts for the rich, as well as small but politically popular cuts for the wider population. For example:

> During Ronald Reagan's presidency, the federal government debt held by the public nearly tripled in nominal terms, from $738 billion to $2.1 trillion. The U.S. moved from being the world's largest international creditor to the world's largest debtor nation.[157, 158]

Reagan spent money from this borrowing, on the military, and cut taxes for the rich:

> Reagan increased public expenditure, primarily on the Department of Defense, which rose (in constant year 2000 dollars) from $267.1 billion in 1980 to $393.1 billion in 1988.
>
> In 1981, Reagan reduced the maximum tax rate, which affected the highest income earners, and lowered the top marginal tax rate from 70% to 50%; in 1986 he further reduced the rate to 28%.[157]

For the left, government borrowing enables increased spending on government programmes, without having to do battle with the rich and powerful in order to finance the spending from increased taxation instead. It's a soft option which delivers benefits today at the cost of placing a greater burden on ordinary taxpayers in the future. An example is the 1997-2010 UK Labour Government's use of 'PFI':

> The Private Finance Initiative (PFI) is a scheme whereby private firms are contracted to build and manage public projects. Traditionally, to construct a public facility like a hospital, the government pays the builders and then takes over the completed hospital and maintains it, financing the construction by taxation or borrowing. Under PFI the government escapes the up-front construction cost by signing a deal with a private consortium to both build the hospital and then run it for a period of typical 20 years or more, in return for annual payments. In essence this replaces the up-front taxation or government borrowing that would have financed the construction, with much more expensive borrowing from the consortium who build and run the hospital.
>
> The result is that many public bodies have been lumbered with huge long term payments for years after facilities were built. For example: PFI investments of £618m in Wales up to 2007 have created a public sector liability of £3.3bn.[159]

It's difficult not to conclude that the public would be better served by governments that use taxation rather than borrowing to raise revenue. Perhaps borrowing is valid when governments want to ask the whole population to forgo consumption for a period due to an emergency, as has occurred during wartime.

Figure 26.4: A War Bond [WMC]

Several governments issued 'war bonds' during the First and Second World Wars, motivating citizens to buy the interest-bearing bonds through patriotism. Perhaps it is time for a Climate Bond. Government borrowing also makes more sense if it is aimed at providing a safe home for the small individual savings of ordinary citizens, and not as a way of putting the bulk of the population in hoc to the very rich.

26.5   Invest for the Long Term

As discussed in Chapter 21, governments should, where appropriate, invest for benefits in the long and very long term. These will accumulate, making life progressively better. They should avoid as immoral, any investment that causes long term harm, and NEVER use 'discounting' to ignore damage to future generations. Some examples of where 'the thinking stopped too early' are:

- For 70 years the world has poured billions of dollars into a transport system based on cars and planes, despite knowing that oil reserves are finite and would probably be largely exhausted within a century or less, and knowing at least for the last 35 years, that burning them was wrecking the climate.

- In the 1960s a school was built in England that was heated mainly by solar energy; it's described in section 21.3 page 277. No effort was made to extend this technology which offered a permanent solution to heating buildings. Instead, investment went into North Sea oil and gas, with a transition to gas domestic heating, even though it was known that UK gas reserves would last only a few decades.

- Also in the 1950s and 60s the UK and other countries took an axe to their rail networks. From 1955 to 1971 the UK lost over 56% of its passenger railway stations: 3,164 of them.[3] This happened even though it was known that rail was easier to

---

[3]See the book 'Changing Directions', page 30 Table 2.2.[87]

electrify, easier to automate with the new computers, safer, more energy efficient, cleaner (once electrified), and better suited to mass transit. Worse still was that in most cases the track bed was not preserved as say a cycle or footpath, in case it was ever needed again, but fragmented and sold off. Over 5,000 freight depots were also shut, leaving only a few hundred.

- Nuclear power investment has taken place since the 1950s and still continues despite the benefits in electricity generation lasting only a few decades, while the astonishingly long-term costs harm future generations for millennia to come.

- Because of the 1970s oil shock, electricity generation using solar CSP technology (Concentrated Solar Power, using mirrors to generated steam that drives turbines) was developed in the US and Europe. Some of the plants operated for decades, but investment in the technology stalled as soon as the oil price fell, even though oil reserves are finite and the damage caused by fossil fuels was already known.

Figure 26.5: Abandoned station in Devon, 1968: the UK lost over half of its railway stations.

26.6 Governments with Economic Responsibility Need Economic Control

To introduce this section, imagine that you were given the job of 'Safety Officer' on a ship, and the following happened:

> *The owners explain that your duty is to ensure that everyone onboard is safe and comfortable. A few days into the voyage you realise that the captain and other officers are risk-taking lunatics. They took onboard insufficient fuel and provisions, happily steam at full speed through treacherous waters, ignore essential repairs, and several times have thrown overboard people that get in their way. You are expected to somehow save these random victims and, in the event of a major accident, everybody! Assuming that you survive the first voyage, you will probably tell the owners that you cannot do your job unless you have some control over what happens on the ship, and the cooperation of a captain and crew.*

Governments in countries with free-market economies have a similar problem to that described in the above story. Many of them take extensive responsibilities for their citizens, considering it their job to provide a safety net for those unable to make a living in the market and providing a wide range of welfare services such as education, healthcare, social services, pensions and support for the unemployed. Yet at the same time they leave a large part of economic control of the country in the hands of global financiers willing to take outrageous risks for short-term profit (as they did when they crashed the banking systems of the USA and Europe in 2008), and of owners of private companies who show no loyalty to their workforces or their home country, and enthusiastically market harmful products to the populace if there's money in doing so. To be fair to the financiers and company owners, the risk taking and lack of loyalty are not necessarily just the result of lunacy: the nature of competition in the global free-market, incentivises or even forces companies to take decisions that have negative consequences for the country where they operate. In the news as I write are events at a UK based shipping company:

> On 17th March 2022, P&O Ferries sacked almost 800 UK seafarers with no prior warning, and replaced them with foreign agency workers paid less than the UK minimum wage. P&O Ferries said: "We took this difficult decision as a last resort ... we concluded that the business wouldn't survive without fundamentally changed crewing arrangements". P&O was a famous British shipping company founded in the early 19th century; the P&O Group including P&O Ferries, was sold to a Dubai-based parent company in 2006.[160, 161]

It's easy to condemn both the previous owners (who sold this venerable UK company) and the current Dubai parent company, for lacking any care or loyalty to the long-standing UK workforce. Yet it could be true that in a competitive market the company would have gone bankrupt had they not taken this cruel decision to replace their workforce with a cheaper one.

This story and many similar ones, demonstrate that in a world with global markets and an overall surplus of labour, just leaving economic decisions to the market all too often implies a '*race to the bottom*' in which competition drives down the living standards towards those of the most miserable workers on the planet. It has already led to extensive de-industrialisation in places that once had strong economies. This was discussed at greater length in Chapter 12 about the effects of connecting economies.

There is a view that left to itself the market will sort everything out. The idea is that countries like China and India will eventually have economies like those of the USA and Western Europe, and Chinese workers' wages will reach US and European levels instead of undercutting them. But in a world with surplus labour and growing automation, there is no reason to suppose that workers' wages will ever match those of the golden years in the US and

Europe following the Second World War (*during those years, there was a labour shortage that strengthened the bargaining power of US and European labour, since at the time it was not practical to shift manufacturing to less-industrialised countries on anything like the scale that happens now*).

It does not appear feasible for governments to fulfil the responsibilities they have for the welfare of their citizens, if they don't also have some control over how the economy operates.

Some people suggest that we should welcome the shift of manufacturing to poorer countries because we need to help them industrialise and partake of the good life that those of us in the rich west enjoy. Unfortunately it is rather hard to believe that the corporations that have shifted production to Asia have done so, not because they can pay wages that are a fraction of what they would have to in the US or Europe, but because in their hearts they are motivated by the ideals of an aid agency! Perhaps the shift may indeed speed up industrialisation to a degree, but what would really help workers anywhere and everywhere would be a demonstration of how to run the economy and politics of a country in a way that puts the well-being of workers and citizens first, rather than using them merely as a disposable means to an end. As things are, today's boom-town all too easily becomes tomorrow's rust-belt city, when automation or cheaper labour elsewhere, takes away the jobs that were once plentiful.

Where poorer countries are run by privileged elites – whether elected or not – there is clearly an incentive for the elite to structure the economy to maximise exports to the industrialised world so that they can purchase the goodies of a first-world high-life: the cars, the planes, the luxury goods, the foreign travel. In some cases this might be accompanied by a strategy to industrialise and raise the standard of living of all citizens, not just the elite – but there are no guarantees. We have seen that the global economy can and does settle at levels where there is enough industry to supply the whole of the global elite's wants, yet without reaching global full employment. If that happens many countries in the world, particularly those that are poorly connected or lack the size to support any significant industry, will remain impoverished places where people eke out a living in maquiladoras[4] or cash-crop agriculture to sustain the lifestyles of the national elite.

For the reasons above and those laid out in Chapter 16 where we considered the impact of the market on communities and their responsibilities, we can conclude that *where a level of government (whether national, regional or city) has some economic responsibility for the livelihood of its citizens, it ought also to have some economic control, in order to guarantee local employment.*

Exactly how this might be done is beyond the scope of one book, but with modern electronic payment and stock control systems, there must be things we can try – given the will to do so. Community organisations in various countries have experimented with local currencies with the aim of keeping money circulating within a town rather than 'leaking out of it', but as far as I'm aware, schemes have seldom had the backing of government. If governments created a dual 'services' currency, as discussed earlier in this chapter, a locality aspect could be included such as assigning the currency more value if spent in the town where it was earned. With larger organisations and businesses, government could require stakeholder representation; they could also insist that global businesses pay local taxes based on their sales volumes in that jurisdiction. We have to start exploring these and other ways of protecting communities, because a global free-for-all means that it's not just money and livelihoods that drain out of an area, but knowledge, expertise, interest, and hope.

26.7 Summary

We can provide decent livelihoods for all by providing work for everybody able to work and an income to those who cannot or

---

[4]Factories owned by foreign corporations in poorer countries where wages are lower, typically given favourable tax treatment by the host country.

are retired. There won't be enough jobs in the production of stuff and of commercially-viable services, because: (a) automation will eliminate many jobs, and (b) the volume of production will need to be constrained to limit environmental damage. The extra jobs must therefore be created in services that don't damage the environment and are subsidised or free.

To finance the additional jobs plus the incomes of those unable to work, we should tax consumption (which we need to limit), rather than employment (which we wish to stimulate). However, very high incomes and wealth, should be taxed to raise revenue and to achieve a measure of redistribution given the extraordinary levels of inequality reached in recent years. Higher taxation on products that are unhealthy or damage the environment is worth considering, although in some cases such as fossil fuels, rationing is a better option as it shares the resource out fairly rather than having it monopolised by the rich. Governments will need to manage taxation and trade to ensure fair competition, so that their efforts to protect employment and the environment are not undermined by other companies or countries who do not take on that responsibility, and that workers are not condemned to a 'race to the bottom'.

Chapter 27

Changing Direction: Reducing Environmental Impact and Protecting the Natural World

27.1 Introduction

As humans we want an economy that offers each of us a livelihood; how we might achieve that was the subject of the last chapter. In this chapter we turn to the task of allowing the rest of nature a livelihood as well. To do so is in our own self-interest because we are totally dependent on the natural world that we are a part of.

We are also motivated by the beauty and wonder we find in nature and a sense of duty to preserve that beauty both for its own sake and so as not to deny its pleasure to future generations of humans. Given the wholesale destruction of the natural world by our economic activities, there is not much time to lose.

> *Around 1 million animal and plant species are threatened with extinction:* *more than ever before in human history.[162]*

> *Insect populations: a 75% decline in the last 50 years.[163]*

Cross River Gorillas: *only 100 to 250 left.[164]*

British Hedgehogs: *97% wiped out since 1950.[165, 166]*

Why are we having such a dramatic effect on the natural world? It is because there are more humans on Earth than ever before, and we consume more per person than ever before.

Our IMPACT = Population x Consumption

<u>More</u> people consuming <u>more</u> stuff means <u>more</u> pressure on the Earth's resources and <u>less</u> space left for wild animals and plants.

Our growing numbers and growing consumption affect nature in multiple ways:

- **Habitat loss**. Our farms, cities, industries and roads occupy so much space that there is little left for wild plants and animals.

- **Exploitation**. We consume some wild plants and animals directly – by felling trees for timber, by fishing and hunting.

- **Climate Change**. The Earth is heating up and its climate changing, due to the emissions from burning fossil fuels. Many organisms won't be able to adapt to this rapid change and will decline or go extinct.

- **Pollution**. Industry, farming, mining and the extraction of oil, result in toxic chemicals being released into the environment; sometimes deliberately so in the case of herbicides and pesticides. Consumption also pollutes through the burning of fuels and the discarding of garbage and waste.

Less obvious is that our main economic system – free-market capitalism – has an **inbuilt drive to continually grow consumption**, because doing so is necessary for businesses to grow their profits and for workers to maintain their employment and thus their livelihoods.

"But" you might ask, "isn't that desire for consumption and growth something normal?" Well certainly we can assume all living creatures tend to expand their numbers – evolution is plainly going to select that trait over one where an animal can't be bothered to reproduce itself. We can also imagine how evolution could select for traits like curiosity, adventurousness and inventiveness which we humans have in abundance and which are what enable us to develop the avalanche of new technologies now hitting us. Yet it is not true that we were always so driven. Humans lived for hundreds of thousands of years as hunter-gatherers until we developed farming and industry. Many anthropologists believe that hunter-gatherers actually worked less than we do today – once they had caught or gathered enough they could and did rest.[167] Today however, things are very different: with our market economy, we have to work our socks off and run to stand still, for fear that if we don't our business will go bankrupt or we'll get the sack. And this happens despite the fact that we have an abundance of so-called 'labour-saving' technology that our cave-dwelling ancestors could not have dreamed of.

A market economy has an inbuilt drive to continually increase consumption

Businesses want growth to increase profits and **workers** want growth to keep their livelihoods.

There is no denying that the relentless pressure placed on us by our economic system has transformed the world. But if we want to preserve our planet and our sanity, we will have to put a limit on it.

Concern about the environment has mushroomed since the 1960s and there is now abundant material available about the damage we are doing and possible solutions, from numerous environmental groups, scientific organisations, government bodies, the United Nations, and others (*for more information beyond what is covered in this chapter, please refer to such sources*). Unfortunately, despite this abundance of information, governments and politicians show little awareness of the predicament we face, preferring to see the environment as just another special interest group to be placated: get a photo opportunity inaugurating a solar panel installation or an EV charger, and job done.

What is needed is far more radical: to solve environmental problems we have to modify our economic system so that perpetual growth isn't the only way in which people can be provided with livelihoods. But one reason for politicians' inaction is that they don't accept or don't understand, or don't dare to contemplate, that our economic system requires modification; it's just too big a challenge for them. They insist that we continue to need more and more growth, and try to placate environmentalists by sticking the word 'green' in front, every time they mention 'growth'. Yes we should shift to so-called 'green' technologies and products which are less environmentally damaging, but if we keep on consuming more, it will cancel out most of the gains.

The remainder of this chapter suggest some measures to deal with the climate emergency, the loss of biodiversity, and other environmental problems. Three areas are covered: consumption, population and protecting nature. But again, please bear in mind that these are only pointers.

27.2   Limit Consumption

Technological development has enabled tremendous growth in the amount and variety of products that humans consume. The result is far greater damage to the environment than in previous epochs. To limit and reduce the damage we will have to limit consumption. Of course individual consumption varies widely, with the rich typically consuming far more. So we should pay more attention to the higher consumers, although that will still be a very large number of people: it will include the majority of those living in the richer countries and much of the world's middle classes, wherever they live.

27.2.1 'Green technologies' are not enough

An attitude prevalent in the world's richer countries is that we can solve environmental issues like global warming, by finding 'green technologies' that let us carry on doing all the things we currently do: green cars, green heating or air conditioning, green aeroplanes, and everything made out of recyclable materials. It's wishful thinking, unless we assume that the poorer countries of the world will always stay poor and never aspire to these luxuries. Most 'green technologies' still use significant amounts of raw materials and energy – the 'green' claim is applied to anything that uses less, even if it's not all that much less. If the whole world reached the level of consumption of the rich countries, the huge increase in cars, planes, air-conditioning, etc., would blow out of the water any savings obtained by having greener versions of those products.

27.2.2 Electric cars – a 'green technology'?

In the UK as in other rich countries, cars are widely seen as an 'essential' that we could not contemplate being without, despite the fact that widespread car-ownership is a phenomenon of just a few decades. In the United Kingdom in 2022 on the occasion of Queen Elizabeth II's platinum jubilee, it was estimated that 77% of UK households owned one or more cars; 70 years earlier in 1952 when the queen was crowned, that figure was only 12.5%. Go back a bit further to when my own grandparents were born in the late 19th century and there were of course no cars at all. In large parts of the world it is still the case that cars are a luxury of a wealthy minority.

However, let's suppose for a moment that cars really are essentials, and somehow we managed to raise car ownership across the whole world to UK or US levels. Global emissions from car use would grow as illustrated in Figure 27.1, where the first column shows actual emissions in 2020 and the 2nd and 3rd columns are estimates of what emissions would be if every country had either UK or US car ownership levels (assuming that cars are fuelled in the same way as in 2020, i.e. mostly by petrol or diesel). As can be seen, we would face disaster: emissions would be five times greater if the whole world reached the US car-ownership level; oil consumption would also soar causing reserves to swiftly run dry. Emissions from just cars alone would be almost as much as current CO_2 emissions from ALL sources (which were about 36 $GtCO_2$ in 2020).

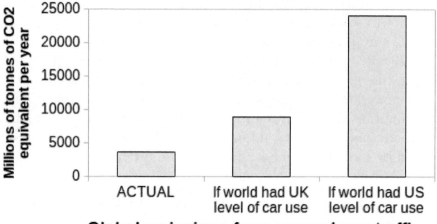

Global emissions from car and van traffic

Sources: emissions - world(2022), UK(2023, US(2021, includes light-duty trucks as US equivalent of van category) [168, 169, 170]; population [171].
The data is for what cars and vans emit in-use; emissions from their manufacture is not included.

Figure 27.1: Global emissions from car and van traffic could grow sixfold if everyone adopts the usage levels of the USA.

There is worse! The emissions data above is for what cars emit *in use*, i.e. when they are driven. However, substantial emissions are produced when vehicles are *manufactured* and when they are *disposed of* at the end of their life. We need to add those in to get the *'whole life'* emissions that vehicles are responsible for. Larger heavier cars result in considerably more emissions during manufacture than smaller lighter ones, as well as requiring more fuel in use, so the fashion for SUVs is particularly unfortunate.

> *Whole life emissions* are emissions from *manufacture* plus *use* plus *disposal*

But here comes the magic 'green technology' solution: make

all cars battery-electric vehicles (EVs), and then there won't be any emissions! It sounds great but sadly just isn't true, because the 'whole life' carbon emissions (from manufacture to disposal) of battery-electric vehicles (EVs) while generally less than those of oil fuelled vehicles, are certainly not zero.[172, 173, 174] There are two main reasons for this. The first is that the manufacture of any vehicle produces a lot of emissions, and more in the case of EVs because of the emissions associated with making the batteries. The second is that the electricity to charge EVs has to be generated somewhere and much of the world's electricity is still generated from burning fossil fuels; even if generated by renewables, building and maintaining that renewable generation will cause emissions. So a shift to EVs is beneficial compared to continuing to use fossil-fuelled vehicles, but it's no panacea and is not a sustainable solution for worldwide personal transport. The message is clear:

> **The modest reductions in carbon emissions that can be obtained even by a complete switch to EVs will be cancelled out and reversed if global car ownership continues to rise.**
>
> *China's car population went from 78m in 2010 to 301m in 2021, an increase of 3.7 times. At this growth rate, the reduction in carbon emissions of changing every car in China to an EV would be cancelled out in just two years.*

We can hope that technology will improve, but the idea that it will **ever** be cheap and kind to the environment to provide every adult on the planet with a metal box weighing over a ton to travel around in, at speeds of up to 100mph, replete with five or more comfortable chairs, air conditioning, heating and a sound system, is completely fanciful, and aiming for that is a sure-fire way to destroy the environment we depend on.

Affordability of cars

In practice cars are likely to remain unaffordable for much of the world for the foreseeable future, so adopting transport strategies based on them is inequitable. In less-industrialised countries only a small elite have ever been able to afford cars – for the majority the expense far exceeds their income, as Figure 27.2 shows. Building infrastructure for cars is subsidising the privileged. Affordable private transport for almost everyone worldwide, would need to be based on bicycles and lightweight electric vehicles such as ebikes.

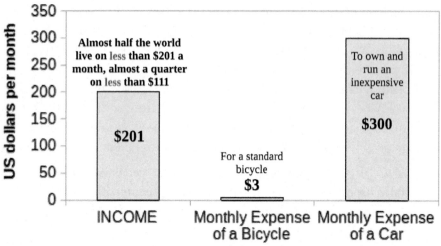

In 2019, almost half of the global population lived below the US$6.85 per day poverty line ($201 a month).[175] Average 2021 UK household expenditure on motoring is $484 a month and lowest decile is $225, so the $300 shown is at the low end, but in some countries costs may be less.[176] A basic bicycle can be purchased in China for around $150 and in the UK for $220; spread over 5 years that is a monthly cost of $2.50 to $3.70 (a 5-year life is a low assumption since bikes can last 40 years or more, but allows for maintenance costs).

Figure 27.2: For most people in the world, the cost of running a car exceeds their income; bicycles however, are affordable.

I fear some people will find this unpalatable 'hair-shirt' stuff: yet another environmentalist who wants to wind the clock back to the horse age! Not so: it is simply an attempt to be realistic about what is possible if we assume that we need to head towards a fairer world with a similar standard of living available in all countries. Perhaps some future generation will be able to largely de-carbonise production and get the world population down to below 1bn instead of today's 8bn, whereupon they can have all the cars and all the air travel they want. As for 'winding the clock back' and 'hair-shirt', there is nothing old-fashioned about lightweight electric vehicles and excellent public transport, and many of the world's cities are discovering that far from being a sacrifice, the quality of life is better in urban areas not dominated by cars, where it becomes a pleasure to walk, cycle or use a tram.

But to give ourselves a fighting chance of a decent future, we must make our aim finding a way to live comfortable and satisfying lives without costing the Earth. How could it make sense to do anything other than that? The alternative is to consume our way into the abyss like there is no tomorrow, and in the process ensure that there literally isn't.

27.2.3 Tax undesirables: pollution, energy & resource use

Products that are unhealthy for the consumer

The UK has a long tradition of high consumption taxes on tobacco and alcohol, justified at least in part because these products are harmful to health. However, the great majority of products that are harmful to health have largely escaped any additional taxation – products like the junk food that contributes to the nation's obesity epidemic. After decades of inaction, a levy called the 'Soft Drinks Industry Levy' was introduced in 2018 that obliges companies to pay a tax of 24p per litre of drink if it contains over 8 grams of sugar per 100 millilitres, or 18p per litre if it contains between 5 and 8 grams. The intention is to encourage companies to reformulate their soft drinks and many have done so. Such taxes would seem to be a good idea if they encourage consumers to switch to better quality foods, and manufacturers to produce them. An important factor is that these products are not essentials – in fact you are better off not consuming them at all, or consuming healthier alternatives.

Products that damage the environment and the wider population

How far should governments use tax or other charges to discourage the use of environmentally damaging products that pollute or contribute towards global warming, in a similar way to the use of tax to discourage smoking, unhealthy foodstuffs, etc.? One such proposal called the 'Fuel Price Escalator' was adopted in 1993 in the UK; it is intended to increase steadily the tax levied on petrol and diesel every year (known as 'fuel duty'). It is fiercely opposed by the motor lobby and understandably unpopular with the car-owning public. It is also perceived as unfair since poorer drivers will be priced off the road long before the richer ones are. As a result the government backs down every year – the last rise was in 1999 over two decades ago and since then rises in fuel duty have routinely been cancelled.

As for fossil fuels used in homes, domestic gas and electricity[1] in the UK have a reduced VAT (sales tax) rate of 5% (compared to the standard VAT rate of 20%), and as I write there is public pressure to reduce those further – perhaps to zero – to mitigate the impact of unusually high world energy costs on consumers.

The problem is that transport and home heating are seen understandably as essentials. Of course if you go back to the 1950s, most UK citizens did not own a car; it's not just that they walked, cycled or used public transport instead – they simply travelled less. But since then we have spent decades changing our lifestyles so that we increasingly rely on the car – extending the distances we are willing to commute, travel to shop, or send our children to school. Similarly, in the 1950s we heated only one or two rooms in the house and scraped the frost off the inside of our bedroom windows when we got up. Now we've adjusted to central heating and uniformly warm houses.

So it is that if we increase the price of fossil fuels sufficiently to discourage use, we will push a significant part of the population

---

[1]Part of UK electricity is generated by burning gas and thus results in carbon emissions.

into giving up modest comforts that they have got used to, and make it a struggle for them to afford their daily commute or heat their houses. This is not only unfair, it is not very effective, as the rich are the heavier users of fossil fuels, not the poor. Yet in order to tackle global warming and pollution, we do need to create incentives that reduce fossil-fuel use and encourage the development of energy saving technologies and alternative sources of energy such as renewables. Thus it is highly desirable that we do charge more for fossil fuels, because as well as discouraging use, this creates a stronger incentive for developing energy saving technologies and alternative sources of energy such as renewables. How can this be done fairly?

27.2.4 Fairness will require some rationing

Increasing prices through extra taxation or charges, should not be the only way to discourage use of products that damage the environment. Fossil-fuel consumption is already grossly unequal. If we consider air travel, it is only a minority who fly and an even smaller minority who fly frequently.[177, 178]

Of the world's population:

> 1% fly so often that they caused *half of all aviation emissions* in 2018.

> 80% have never flown at all.

For the UK:

> Most flights are made by relatively few people (15% of passengers made 70% of all trips in 2014).

> Many don't fly at all (48% of people did not fly abroad in 2018).

We can only imagine the impact if everyone started flying as much as the world's richest do.

Figure 27.3: 80% of the world's population have never flown. [WMC]

We could even double the price of aviation fuel by taxing it, and the rich would mostly still carry on flying willy-nilly. Much the same applies to vehicle fuels; wealthier drivers are so little put off by the price of fuel that many of them are buying large gas-guzzling SUVs merely to drive around in cities.

Therefore, the fairest and most effective proposal for limiting fossil-fuel consumption is some form of carbon allowance. Each individual would have an annual allowance which they would use when purchasing fossil fuels directly or when travelling by vehicles that consume fossil fuels such as ships, aircraft, and diesel buses and trains – perhaps using a carbon debit smart card like the mock-up illustrated in Figure 27.4. Electricity use would also be counted to the extent that it is part-generated by burning fossil fuels. Such a scheme would barely affect the less well off, since they are already limited by what they can afford; in fact it could benefit them financially if they were allowed to sell any unused allowance. The rich on the other hand, could be allowed to top up, either by buying unused allowance from others, or buying extra allowance from the state at a significant rate. A system of this sort spares the poorest from a financial hit, and by making them able to sell unused ration gives them a financial benefit and thus an extra incentive to reduce their use. At the same time the system implements what amounts to a higher fuel tax on heavy users since they have to purchase extra allowance – the rates for which could be staggered, rising with greater use, giving the rich as well, an incentive to reduce their use. An article in Nature Sustainability describes the concept of personal carbon allowances and their role in achieving climate mitigation targets.[179]

Fairness will require that the nations that are the largest per-capita emitters reduce their emissions the fastest and eventually all nations converge on a net-zero level. This concept termed 'Contraction & Convergence' was developed by the Global Commons Institute (GCI) and has been adopted by the UN COP on Climate Change.[180]

Figure 27.4: A carbon allowance would be fairer than rationing by price; a debit card like this mock-up might be used.

A comprehensive study of how the UK could decarbonise called ZeroCarbonBritain was published in 2007 by the Centre for Alternative Technology (CAT) in Wales. It analyses emissions sector by sector, proposes how we can reduce energy consumption and generate the energy that we do need by renewable sources. CAT have published several follow-up reports since then.[181]

27.3 Manage Population

At any level of consumption, there will be some limit to the number of humans that can live on a finite planet. The same technological advance that has enabled a tremendous growth in the amount of products that humans consume, has also enabled a population explosion. We have a double whammy: <u>more</u> people consuming <u>more</u> stuff.

For most animals, what they consume is simply what they eat – they don't live in houses full of furniture and electrical goods. So for example, if you want to know how much the world's entire population of zebras consumes, you could get a rough estimate by multiplying what a typical individual zebra eats by the number of zebras in the world. Estimating the consumption of the world's humans is not so simple because as well as food we humans consume a huge variety of other things, and as a result, individual consumption can vary wildly from that of oligarchs to that of street beggars. Accordingly, when discussing how much the whole human population consumes, we need to be sensitive to the fact that the consumption of a handful of the very rich can have more impact than that of a far larger number of the world's poor.

However, while acknowledging that some humans consume far more than others, it remains inescapable that huge increases in the global human population are inevitably going to increase total human consumption. As population grows, the global upper and middle classes grow in number as well as the poorest, and pretty much everyone aspires to a consumer lifestyle once they start seeing that lifestyle portrayed on television or observe their better-off neighbours adopting it. Also, some aspects of consumption are in fact fairly uniform across quite a wide range of incomes, since we all have only one stomach, cannot drive more than one car at a time, generate a similar amount of sewage, and so forth. Accordingly, while accepting that individual human consumption levels vary greatly, we humans remain subject to the simple logic that applies to any animal:

$$IMPACT = Population \times Consumption$$

Therefore if we want to limit human impact, we should try to limit the population size as well as the amount individuals consume.

27.3.1 Already overpopulated

Humans are using ecological resources as if we lived on 1.75 Earths.[2]

The world is already suffering the impact of overpopulation. Many countries are now so overpopulated that they are incapable of feeding themselves or of producing enough energy without fossil-fuel imports.[182] Overpopulation makes it far harder to supply even a modest standard of living worldwide. It makes some countries very vulnerable.

Table 27.1 gives an idea of the pace of change. Notice how in the 1000 years from 0AD to 1000AD, population levels barely changed, then over the next 800 years world population increased about threefold, and in just over 200 years from 1800 to 2022, increased eightfold. For someone in their 70s alive today, there are well over three times the number of people on the planet than when they were born in the 1950s. Imagine how much easier it would be to both protect the environment and at the same time provide a good standard of living, even if the population had just remained at 1950s levels at three times less than now, let alone were it eight times less as it was in 1800. Human numbers on Earth must ultimately be limited – it would be madness to let famine, disease and war do the job, rather than sensible planning.

Since the 1970s both of the world's most populous countries, China and India, have made efforts to control population. China's 'one child policy' is usually criticised in the West as an assault on liberty, although it is also acknowledged to have been effective and indeed criticised for being so: it's said that it will result in too few working age people to support the elderly. India's efforts in the 1970s are criticised for involving forced sterilisation and have also been less effective than China's as the population has grown far faster and now exceeds that of China.

From 1950 to 2023 China's population increased by 2.6 times, and India's by 4 times. A finite planet faces us with some difficult

---

[2]It is estimated that we consume 1.75 times more resources than nature can provide sustainably.[182]

Year	World	Britain	China	India	Egypt
0 AD :	300	1.5	50	60	6
1000 :	310	2	60	75	5
1800 :	980	12	340	200	4
1900 :	1,650	46	437	303	10
1950 :	2,570	50	547	359	20
2023 :	8,045	68	1,426	1,429	113

Figures are rounded and for the more distant past are very approximate as estimates vary. Data sources: [171, 183, 184, 185, 186, 187]
Most of the population growth shown in the table took place in just the last couple of centuries, much of it in recent decades. Figures for the more distant past are ballpark only as estimates vary.

Table 27.1: Population of the world and of selected countries over the last 2000 years [millions].

choices. Limiting families to one child may seem harsh but had China grown instead at India's rate of 4, it would now have an extra 751m people and be on course for an even higher eventual total later this century. China struggles to feed itself as it is, turns increasingly to food imports, and is purchasing agricultural land in other countries.[188, 189]

> "It takes about 1 acre to feed the average U.S. consumer. China only has about 0.2 acres of arable land per citizen, including fields degraded by pollution."[190]

China has only 0.21 acres of arable land per person and is losing land as cities encroach on it.[191] Had the population increased since 1950 as fast as India's, the extra 751m would have given China a population of 2.18bn people instead of the actual 1.43bn, and the arable land per person would be only 0.14 acres – or less if the cities to house the extra people covered up farmland. We don't know for sure what would have happened as a result, but such a large reduction in land per person would have clearly threatened the ability of the country to feed itself.[3]

27.3.2   Won't the education of women halt population growth?

It has become fashionable to argue that we don't need to have a population plan because rising living standards as countries industrialise and rising levels of women's education, tend to bring down birth rates. So does that mean that we don't need to do anything? It would be wonderful if that turned out to be the case, but it makes no sense not to have a plan in case it's needed. Having no backup plan would be like ignoring a fire in your house because you think it may with luck burn out by itself – at the very least you want to be on standby with an extinguisher or pail of water in case you're wrong. We should therefore set targets for future sustainable population levels, and implement and track measures to meet them, of which women's education can be one.

27.3.3   Is talking about population 'eco-fascism'?

Another fashionable argument is that talking about population, is a form of 'neocolonialism' or 'eco-fascism'. However, overpopulation applies just as much to the UK and other industrialised countries, as it does to countries such as China or India or Egypt. The UK is heavily overpopulated and unable to feed or fuel itself; it is vulnerable to interruptions in supply chains, global shortages, and to long term decline in the value of its exports and its world market share (as the rapidly-industrialising economies of China and elsewhere grow) reducing its ability to pay for the required food imports.

A WWF-UK report says that *the UK must reduce its production and consumption footprint by three quarters by 2030* to meet planetary limits.[192] The UK is now home to almost 70 million

---

[3]China suffered what is said to be the world's largest famine between 1959 and 1961 with the death of tens of millions of people – its cause is largely attributed to the policies of the Great Leap Forward launched by the Chinese Communist Party, with drought also being a factor.

people ... and over 33 million cars! The rapid population growth is shown in Figure 27.5: the population is over six times more than it was just over two hundred years ago in 1800. Unsurprisingly, it is also about two centuries since the last time the UK was self-sufficient in food; today in the UK, we only produce about 60% of our food.[193] For its own security and comfort, as well not consuming beyond its share of global resources, Britain would do well to decrease its population over time to a more sustainable level.

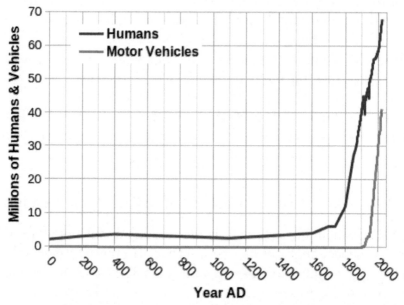

Number of motor vehicles for GB, then UK from 2014. Data sources: [194, 195, 183]. Cars and vans predominate: of the 41.3 million motor vehicles in 2023, 33.6 million were cars.

Figure 27.5: Human and motor-vehicle growth in the UK.

Regarding former colonies and countries in the global south, an open and honest discussion of the physical limits that face us all as humans on this planet, does not force any government to do anything. But the well-being and sustenance of those countries' own citizens requires that governments plan for the resources to feed them. Some such countries have undergone far faster growth than Britain. The population of Egypt for example has grown over ten times since 1900 to 2022 (10 million to 106 million). Today it is dependent on grain from Ukraine and has problems with supply due to the Russian invasion of Ukraine.

Food security was one of Egypt's priorities on its agenda for the 2022 UN COP 27 climate change conference held in Sharm El Sheikh, Egypt. The Egyptian Minister of Agriculture in a speech to the senate, said that Egypt has achieved self-sufficiency in many crops and commodities, especially vegetables and fruits, but he pointed out that Egypt has limited arable land, and that the amount of agricultural land per capita has declined to 350 square meters from 4,200 square meters in earlier times.[196] That is a spectacular twelvefold drop in the amount of farmland per person, and since Egypt hasn't changed its size, is presumably mostly the result of there now being ten times more Egyptians, trying to live off the same land.

Egyptians consume a lot of bread but are only able to produce about half of the wheat they need, the other half being imported. They aim to grow more, but increasing demand due to the rising population, combined with the negative effects of climate change on crop growth and availability of fresh water, make it unlikely that they can become self-sufficient.[197] A growing population also tends to encroach on what farmland there is, as cities expand and more roads and airports are built. On top of that, climate change may render some farmland unusable due to drought, heat, or rising sea levels.

27.3.4   Is population control possible?

The design of population policies is beyond the scope of this book. There are organisations dedicated to campaigning on this issue such as the UK-based charity Population Matters, of which the renowned naturalist Sir David Attenborough is a prominent supporter.[198] But we can affirm without any doubt that economic planning must take into account that we live on a finite planet and as a consequence, we need to consider what a sustainable population level would be for the world as a whole, and for the individual countries we live in.[199] Once that we accept that population is an issue, society can examine the drivers of population growth such as for example:

- Concern about who will care for us when we're old if we don't have enough children, or that we'll have too few economically active young people in the workforce to support retirees;

- The desire in many cultures to have sons rather than daughters and therefore either having more children until a son is obtained, or selectively aborting daughters and as a result producing a gender imbalance;

- Cultural or religious rejection of family planning;

- The oppression of women and lack of educational and employment opportunities.

By examining the above drivers of population growth, we can think about ways to mitigate them. In countries where a decrease in population is achievable soon or is already happening, we can research and plan how to manage it well, ensuring for example that the elderly are cared for. Family planning and birth control can be made available with incentives and disincentives to encourage smaller families rather than large ones. We should also highlight the potential benefits of a falling population – the extra space, the reduced pressure on resources, an end to the housing crisis. With a return to 1950 population levels, China would have 2.6 times more arable land per person, India almost four times, and Egypt over 5 times, while Britain would free about 25% of its housing stock and preserve its green space. Yet instead of being celebrated, the smallest dip in population is treated as a cause for alarm.

Ultimately I return to education, and choices in a finite world. Everyone can understand the cruel choice that faces a lifeboat crew if there are more people in the water than they can pick up without sinking the lifeboat and drowning everybody aboard. We face the same choice with human numbers on Earth – the difference is only that it's harder to know what the limit is, and that there won't be a sudden 'sinking' but piecemeal degradation, with suffering at multiple locations on the planet and over many years. Happily however, we are not talking about leaving people to 'drown' but merely bringing into being rather fewer people, which is something that we do all the time. Even the most conservative cultures promote chastity before and outside of marriage. Were we really anxious to ensure that all potential humans were brought into existence, then we would send our children out to procreate the moment they reached puberty.

27.4 Protecting Nature

In the short to medium term, global population will continue to rise and so almost certainly will global consumption; furthermore we should welcome a rise in consumption by the world's poorest, since what they consume currently is inadequate for a decent life. Accordingly, there will be no respite for nature for many years to come if we simply wait for human impact to reduce as a result of declining human numbers or from lower average consumption levels. So we need to act now to protect the natural world, by changing or ceasing some of our economic activities. We should focus on areas where our impact is most devastating and changes to our consumption habits or technologies could make a substantial change. However, as discussed earlier in this chapter, we should be cautious with 'green technologies' that offer only modest reductions in harm and are in reality just an intent to sell us more 'stuff'. Furthermore, we should remember that finding ways to reduce the impact of the current human population buys us time, but if the population continues to grow, that reduction will be short-lived.

While the goal is clear enough, the detail involved in understanding the environmental impact of the whole range of human economic activities and finding ways to reduce that impact, is plainly enormous. Fortunately there are many academics, scientific institutions, UN bodies, environmental charities, and so forth, who study such topics. What follows are therefore just a few general areas in order to give at least a taste of the sort of things we may wish to consider.

27.4.1 Reduce impact of hunting and fishing

The direct hunting of animals – and that includes fishing which is hunting at sea – threatens the existence of numerous species with many already having gone extinct. Hunting on land for food provides a negligible amount of food and should end – except in special cases of traditional communities (provided it is adequately regulated), or where it is clearly sustainable and perhaps even necessary for culling purposes. Hunting for trophies or for animals used as ingredients in so-called 'traditional medicine' (but invariably quack cures), brings no genuine benefit to humanity and should stop (although there is an argument that limited sustainable trophy hunting is a way to finance game reserves).

Fishing is a type of hunting – the catching and killing of wild animals – but we seem to have fewer feelings for fish than for land animals. It differs from hunting on land in that it is still a major source of food since the seas are so large, whereas on land only a few large wild spaces remain. The oceans also suffer from being part of the global commons and are therefore subject to the 'tragedy of the commons' effect – the scenario that since nobody owns them, nobody has an economic interest in preserving them. Regulation is required to protect fish stocks and to protect areas of ocean from damage – for example by bottom trawling or pollution. That is easier in national waters, and more complex in international waters.

An example of destruction of a fishery is the fate of the Atlantic north-west cod fishery off the coast of Canada. It had been fished for centuries and fish were so plentiful that from the seventeenth century to the beginning of the twentieth century, sail boats crossed the Atlantic from Europe to fish for cod. The reliance on sails and the use of hook and line fishing methods, limited their catch to sustainable levels. Then in the twentieth century, steam-powered trawlers replaced the sailing boats. They caught many more fish and their trawl nets damaged the seabed. In 1992 the fishery collapsed after years of overfishing. It is not clear if it will recover.[200, 201]

Whaling has also been disastrous. Antarctic Blue Whales have been 97% wiped out, going from 125,000 mature individuals in 1926 to about 3,000 in 2018, and are *critically endangered*.[202] The

Figure 27.6: Limit hunting and fishing. [WMC]

population has recovered very slightly since commercial whaling was banned in 1986. Unfortunately Japan, Iceland and Norway continue to hunt and kill certain whale species.

While whales have some protection, fishing continues apace. We urgently need to limit it to sustainable levels by measures such as quotas, ocean reserves, and finding substitutes (such as plant protein alternatives).

One example where a change of habit would help is the use of fishmeal. Salmon are carnivorous and farmed salmon are fed fishmeal made from wild fish. It would be far more efficient to forget about salmon farming and eat the wild fish directly. It would also most likely be healthier since farmed salmon are kept in crowded conditions, prone to disease and treated with antibiotics – added to which, animals higher up the food chain (carnivores) tend to concentrate pollutants.

Scientists from the University of Cambridge, using data from Scotland for 2014, compared the volume of wild-caught feed fish to the volume of farmed salmon that was harvested. They found that 460,000 tonnes of wild-caught fish were used to produce 179,000 tonnes of salmon. Furthermore, 76 percent of the wild-caught fish were species that are commonly eaten by humans, such as anchovies and sardines. Applying those figures to the whole world, the scientists estimated that if people were to eat the wild-caught fish directly instead of using them for salmon-feed and then eating the salmon, almost 3.6 million tonnes of fish could be left in the sea each year, and more fish would be available as a human food source.[203]

Fishmeal is also fed to cattle, sheep, pigs and poultry. Again it would be far more efficient to eat the fish directly and not feed it to another animal that we then eat. The use of fishmeal is said to contribute to over-fishing, and following the BSE[4] scandal, there was also a question mark over the wisdom of feeding fish-meat to herbivores that do not naturally consume animal flesh.[204, 205]

They were probably infected a few years earlier by eating feed derived from the parts of sheep, cows

27.4.2   Reduce impact of farming

Farming has an immense effect on nature because of the space it occupies. The amount of the Earth's land surface used for farming has gone from about 7% in the year 1700 to about 40% now (being most of best land).[206] That means that many wild plants and animals have lost the habitat they lived in.

> Habitat loss is main threat to 85% of all threatened and endangered species. – *International Union for Conservation of Nature.[207]*

How farms are managed also affects nature. Traditional farmland operated with horses and with little if any use of chemicals, provided habitat for a wild plants, birds and small animals, in hedgerows, meadows and among crops. But the introduction of herbicides, pesticides and modern farm machinery during the 20th century eliminated many of these. Large tractors and harvesters are more easily operated on large open fields, so hedgerows were

---

[4]An outbreak of bovine spongiform encephalopathy (BSE), a fatal cattle disease, occurred in the UK in the 1980s. The cattle were believed to have been infected by feed derived from the remains of other animals including cows, in effect, obliging herbivores to be carnivores and cannibals.

removed. Herbicides and pesticides directly kill wild plants and insects, which in turn means that birds and animals that lived off those plants and insects, also disappear. The groundbreaking book Silent Spring by Rachel Carson, documented the environmental harm caused by the indiscriminate use of pesticides.[208]

The most dramatic way to reduce the space taken up by farmland would be to reduce the amount of meat and dairy products in our diets. This is because about two-thirds of farmland is used for meadows and pastures for grazing livestock.[209] Additionally, some of the one-third that is cropland is used to grow crops that are fed to animals: almost 80% of the world's soybean crop is fed to livestock.[210] In energy terms it is far more efficient to eat plants directly rather than feed them to an animal and eat the animal. As a result a shift to a plant-based diet is unlikely to require more cropland to provide plant replacements for the meat, and may even require less.

There is little doubt that a mainly plant-based diet can provide adequate nutrition, so the main obstacle to reducing meat consumption is cultural. An additional challenge would be to provide alternative livelihoods for people who formerly worked with livestock or in meat processing. However, if convincing people to eat less meat proves difficult, there may be another solution in the near future. Already it is possible to grow meat in a laboratory, and with far less land and energy requirements than keeping animals. We may be on the cusp of laboratory-grown meat technology moving into commercialization. People could then continue to eat meat but with a far lower environmental impact. Another possibility is the farming of insects which requires less land and energy inputs for a given amount of protein; cultural acceptance of eating insect-meat may be a block.

Apart from meat, there are some technical developments that could reduce the land area required for certain vegetable and fruit crops. Some are now being grown in 'vertical farms' where stacks of trays like multiple layer shelving units, contain the crops – each layer being illuminated with LED lamps. This technique allows a high density of crop, multiple crops per year, protection from weather and pests, and automated control and handling.

A substantial reduction in the space required for farming, by for example a shift away from meat consumption, might permit less intensive farming practices since extra land would be available to grow crops. This could allow more organic farming with less use of herbicides and pesticides, even if yields per acre were lower, and the setting aside of more space for wildlife. There may be other ways to help reduce herbicide and pesticide use, such as the use of robotic technology to precisely apply them where needed instead of general spraying.

A reduction of the space required by farming would leave more space for the natural world and makes for a richer more attractive planet. It also enables countries with limited agricultural land to grow more on what they have and thus become more self-sufficient and resilient.

27.4.3 Reduce impact of industry

The damage caused by industry is mainly in the extraction of resources and in the creation of pollution and waste, including the emission of CO_2 and other greenhouse gases. Industrial processes are numerous and complex, although the issues are often well known to government regulators, scientific bodies and environmental organisations. Solutions usually require regulation, typically either to prohibit the harmful activity or product, or to impose costs on it so that industry has an incentive to find alternatives. In economics terms this means controlling or charging for 'externalities' – costs imposed not on the business or customer but on others and the environment. The problem is that business considerations of staying competitive, and the desire for growth, tend to outweigh protection of the environment in the minds of political leaders and of a good many of the general public too.

Resource extraction

Resource extraction damages areas of both land and sea, for example the extraction oil from tar sands, oil wells at sea, different types of mining. Extraction pollutes the surroundings in various ways: escaped product (such as oil spills and gas leaks), waste (such as mining spoils), chemicals used during extraction (as with fracking). Since fossil-fuel extraction is a major cause of the damage, policies to de-carbonise energy production via restrictions and pricing, will help to reduce the impact of resource extraction.

Product manufacture

Industry generates carbon emissions that cause climate change due to its use of energy, and sometimes directly as part of a process, like that of cement manufacture – the cement industry contributes seven per cent of global anthropogenic CO_2 emissions.[211] Governments have to impose carbon pricing or quotas, designed to be strong enough to meet or exceed UN targets.

Industrial processes generate many polluting chemicals, some deliberately because they have a use, and some as unwanted by-products; there can also be hazardous biological and radioactive waste. Governments already have regulations covering industry, built up over many decades as hazards emerged. However, many materials are not covered that should be, and the variety of potential hazardous materials is likely to grow ever faster because of scientific advances. We can imagine a future in which artificial intelligence and robot laboratories continuously design and create novel chemical and biological products to assess their potential (if this is not already happening!). How can government regulation possibly hope to keep up, given that we want to shut the stable door before the horse bolts (or in this case the laboratory door before the novel bacteria escapes and turns out to be a plague)? Governments will need to intervene earlier with measures like:

- Require industry to register all emissions so that over time a full picture emerges of the current state of play, and so that damage caused can be tracked.

- As current emissions are better understood, set regulations where required.

- Introduce a requirement to register the creation of any new chemical or biological materials, with a process to carry out a safety assessment before they can be marketed. The point being to move from a paradigm in which you can produce what you like and we only regulate if it later turns out to be hazardous, to one in which you can't produce something new until at least some checks have been made, and subsequently the effect of introducing the material is monitored.

Novel products

Apart from regulating hazardous substances, governments should consider regulation covering the introduction of any novel product where the effects of the product on its users, society and the environment, need to be thought out; essentially requiring a sort of risk assessment (as discussed in Chapter 14, section 14.3.4), and subsequently monitoring outcomes if the product is permitted. Currently manufacturers can make anything they like, provided it doesn't contravene existing legislation, which typically covers only the more obvious and well established dangers (smartphone manufacturers must ensure that their products don't electrocute users but do not have to concern themselves with psychological damage). As a result, issues tend to be discovered only when use of a product is already widespread. Legislation is then too late to stop the product's introduction, and may well be weaker because it will face lobbying by a now established customer base and supply chain.

1 in 2 young people listen to unsafe levels of sound through personal audio devices, with 1.1 billion globally at risk of hearing loss.

Numerous products are launched with little thought about the consequences. An early spin-off from the nuclear industry was glow-in-the-dark clock hands; later these were found to be emitting radiation at levels deemed unsafe. Personal audio devices (smartphones, MP3 players, etc.) are typically able to generate sound levels in headphones or earbuds that will cumulatively damage hearing; the World Health Organisation estimate that 1.1 billion young people globally are at risk of hearing loss due to unsafe listening practices.[212] A recent example in the UK could be the electric scooters that are becoming a common sight despite not being legal (except in certain licensed trials) either on the road or the pavement, and whose safety is questionable (although they are a fascinating form of lightweight transport).[213] Another is the sale of drones: in the UK there is legislation covering drones but the potential for nuisance, danger, and criminal or terrorist use is clearly there.

Technology can bring losses of which we are only dimly aware for much of the time. In a remote location you might look up at night and be awestruck by the canopy of stars above you that was once the birthright of all humans, but in modern towns has been replaced by a haze of contaminated air and light pollution. Similarly, the hum of electrical appliances and white-noise of moving traffic, form a background noise so ubiquitous that we tend to only notice it if for some reason – perhaps a power outage – it stops, and we hear birdsong. To observe this is not to be anti-technology, only to argue in favour of being aware of the balance of gains and losses, and making conscious choices about what technology we have and where we have it.

The future will undoubtedly bring an ever-greater volume of potential new products whose 'benefits' will be enthusiastically marketed in the same way that we were told that providing computers to our children would make them into IT gurus, and not warned that some might hole up in their bedrooms playing non-stop computer games or become prey to paedophiles and abusive porn merchants from anywhere on the globe – or that vaping was promoted as a health product to help smokers quit, but then quickly expanded into selling colourful flavoured vapes that attract young children and threaten a new public health catastrophe.[214] Unless we exercise control over what can be made and sold, many products that are introduced will be found to be damaging to the environment and harmful to humans, but often only when it's too late to easily restrict them.

Products in-use

As well as being directly responsible for harm caused during product manufacture, industry is also indirectly responsible for pollution and environmental damage caused by its products when in use. Imposing regulation on product manufacturers is more effective than campaigns aimed at pressing consumers to take precautions during product use and disposal; consumers are likely to be unaware of the risks, or at any rate unable or unwilling to do much about them. For example if paints or other DIY and household chemicals contain problem pollutants, policing their use is a hopeless task; they need to be removed from the market and where necessary, substitutes found.

Many electrical goods such as TVs and microwaves, when seemingly switched off are actually in a standby mode and unknown to their owners are still consuming what can be a significant amount of electricity, given that households typically own several such items. Campaigns to persuade people to switch off at the wall plug are a hopeless strategy – the whole pointy of standby is user convenience. The right approach is to oblige manufacturers to ensure that any standby current is truly minimal. The European Union is bringing in regulations to achieve just that.[215]

Product disposal – a 'circular economy'?

Industry's products also generate waste when they are disposed of after use. As well as polluting the environment, valuable and sometimes rare materials that went into the products are likely to be lost. Three solutions to the disposal problem are:

1. Minimise consumption of products, so that there's less to dispose of.

2. Make products out of natural materials like wood, paper and cotton, which will 'naturally recycle' by rotting down.

3. Create a 'circular economy' in which products are disassembled and their component parts re-used or recycled.

The first two solutions are the ones humans have used throughout most of our history, and we know that they work. Our ancestors were fewer in number and possessed and consumed far less stuff. Most of what they did have was made of natural materials so usually little remains – nature completed the circle.

The third solution, the 'circular economy', has become a popular concept in recent times because it seems to offer a way that we can deal with our intractable modern waste and still carry on consuming as usual. The idea is that instead of a 'linear' economy in which products are made, used and discarded into landfill, we want products to circle back into being used again in some way. The most immediate way is to ensure products are repairable so that when broken they are not discarded but fixed and returned to use. The next is to promote re-use – essentially a second-hand market. Then comes refurbishing: giving the product an overhaul, replacing worn parts, etc., as a bicycle shop might do to prepare a second-hand bike for re-sale. A further stage for some products is re-manufacturing, in which a product is re-worked, usually by the manufacturer, and brought to a state almost equivalent to a new product. Finally there is recycling, in which the product is broken down or dismantled and the materials it's made of are recovered for re-use. All of this sounds attractive, but is far harder to achieve than the first two solutions. Briefly, here are a some of the reasons why:

Repair. Products are often designed in a way that makes them cheaper to manufacture but hard to repair. Perhaps that can be addressed by regulation to some extent and the EU parliament is looking at 'right to repair' legislation to get manufacturers to take more responsibility for making their products repairable. A bigger problem is that automated manufacturing carried out in low-wage countries has made new products so insanely cheap that repair is often more expensive than buying new, especially in richer countries where the repairer will require a higher-wage to live. Making the use of materials and energy more expensive, relative to the cost of labour, would help; adjustments to taxation might be a way to do that.

Refurbishing. Has the same issues as repair. As well as the labour cost being likely to make refurbishing costly, spare parts are frequently not as competitively priced as the whole unit. I was told by the manufacturer of a fridge I owned that just to replace the door seal required a whole new door costing about two thirds of the price of a new fridge.

Re-manufacturing and recycling. Only a product's manufacturer is likely to have the know-how and equipment to re-manufacture. That may also be true for the recycling of complex products that require disassembly to component level to recover the materials they are made of. We have created an extraordinary global supply chain that assembles products from materials and components gathered from all over the world and delivers them to consumers, also scattered across the world. The whole process is aptly summed up by the philosopher Bertrand Russell's definition of work as *"altering the position of matter at or near the earth's surface relatively to other such matter"* or *"telling other people to do so"*.[5] So reversing the chain to return discarded products to the manufacturer for disassembly and then re-use or recycling, is something like asking for all the work of 'rearranging matter on the Earth's surface' that it took to create and deliver the product, to be done again, but this time backwards.

Clearly, reversing the manufacturing process is not cheap or simple, and energy and materials would be consumed in doing so. I once visited the production line for a diesel engine fuel-injection pump: shiny new metal parts and bolts were assembled in a smooth repetitive operation by a mainly female workforce wearing clean work overalls. If you've ever tried to fix an old car or other machinery, you'll appreciate the contrast: the bits are covered in oil and ac-

---

[5]"Work is of two kinds: first, altering the position of matter at or near the earth's surface relatively to other such matter; second, telling other people to do so. The first kind is unpleasant and ill paid; the second is pleasant and highly paid." from In Praise of Idleness by Bertrand Russell

cumulated filthy crud, screws have rusted solid, bolt heads shear off, it's seldom smooth and repetitive, and your overalls don't stay clean. So disassembly can be harder than assembly. Furthermore, some manufacturing processes are irreversible: asking to do them backwards is like hoping to 'un-bake' a cake and retrieve the eggs you made it with.

These words are not to argue against trying to achieve some 'circularity' via re-use and recycling, but to suggest caution before accepting business-as-usual projects because of 'circular economy' claims made by the constructor. In a conversation with an elected representative, I quoted research showing that tall buildings have higher embedded carbon per unit of floor area than low to mid-rise alternatives, as well as higher emissions in use.[216, 217] He replied suggesting that the 'circular economy' was a way around the problem – but what on earth can that mean in this case? Tower blocks have a shorter average lifetime than traditional brick buildings, and when demolished will leave concrete rubble, chipped or broken windows & bathroom fittings, and obsolete electrical equipment. There is nothing you can do that compensates for the greater embedded and in-use carbon inherent in a tower block. Of course with any building you may be able to improve sustainability with features like insulation or solar panels, but that is irrelevant since they can equally and more easily be applied to lower-rise buildings.

Creating a degree of circularity even in more mundane items will require a great deal of change: to start with, motivating end-users to return items for re-use or recycling. Deposit schemes can create an incentive to do this – the price includes a deposit that is repaid when the product is returned to the manufacturer (probably via the shop or supplier it was purchased from). There needs to be pressure to ensure that products are built of materials that can be separated and recycled. A policy of refurbishing or re-manufacturing might increase the incentive to manufacture locally rather than on the opposite side of the world, in order to shorten and cut the cost of what are now both supply and return chains. Making products repairable and re-usable might favour smaller-scale craft manufacture, and might also encourage the use of traditional materials, since it is likely to be more feasible for a local artisan or DIYer to modify or repair wooden furniture, doors or windows, than factory-made metal or plastic equivalents.

Product standardisation is also a key to repair or re-use – both of the whole product and of the component parts. Glass and plastic bottles would be easier to re-use or recycle if they were limited to a fixed range of standard sizes and materials. You often notice in the bathrooms and toilets of modern offices and public buildings, that an originally-fitted, elegant but non-standard door closure has broken, and a traditional bolt has been roughly screwed on in its place, or that a clever automated tap has failed and been replaced with a more standard model that doesn't match the other fittings. Presumably with so many product variants on the market jostling to differentiate themselves, spares of the original components often become too inconvenient or expensive to source, or are no longer obtainable.

Unfortunately the free market's wonderful variety is the enemy both repair and re-use. Re-use implies maintaining stocks of second-hand products or components somewhere, checking them, cataloguing them, and making them available to buyers. These tasks are greatly complicated by the multiplicity of products and product versions, so again, standardisation would help. Maintaining such inventories will also be costly – should manufacturers or retailers do it, and how will it be financed?

A circular economy is then a worthy aim for those products that we feel we really must have, but it is complex and likely to be costly; reading some of the EU's proposals in this area give an idea of the scale of the task.[218] Far simpler, quicker and cheaper is to minimise consumption and where possible to build products out of natural materials that nature itself can recycle for us.

27.4.4 Adopt sustainable lifestyles

The changes that are necessary to hunting, farming and industry, mean that we will also need to change the way we live. If we reduce the amount of land dedicated to livestock, then we must eat less meat (unless there is an artificial alternative). Reducing the production of harmful pesticides means that we have to accept insect damage to our fruit and vegetables. Reducing emissions means that we have to modify our houses, travel less and generally consume rather less 'stuff'.

Measure	Co-Benefits
Building and retrofitting houses to use minimal energy for heating or cooling.	Major and permanent reduction in household bills; clean air.
Use of electricity as the only 'fuel' for most land transport.	Cleaner air; more reliable vehicles.
Urban environments that encourage walking, cycling, and ultra-light electric vehicles.	Improved health thanks to exercise and cleaner air; safer streets and thus greater freedom for children to play; space freed up for parks and recreation; lower transport costs.
Replacement of fossil fuels with renewable energy.	Cleaner air; greater energy security; increasingly cheaper than fossil fuels; better & healthier jobs than those in fossil-fuel extraction.
Mainly plant-based diet with low meat consumption.	Improved health; potentially lower food costs.

Table 27.2: Environmental measures and associated co-benefits.

We must aim for a lifestyle that is sustainable if shared by all countries; it would be unjust to do otherwise, and it is unrealistic to expect other nations to live sustainably if we refuse to. The biggest challenge is likely to be convincing the world's wealthier citizens to accept a more modest lifestyle than the one they have grown used to in the age of profligate fossil-fuel consumption. One of the ways to do this may be to identify associated or knock-on benefits that will occur if an environmental or emissions-reduction measure is taken. Referred to as 'co-benefits', these additional benefits may help win support for a measure if they are more visible to the public or of more immediate value to them, e.g. a policy to reduce car travel offers the co-benefits of less pollution and safer, more peaceful streets.

Fortunately there are rather a lot of co-benefits to the actions that are required to combat climate change and protect the environment. Table 27.2 lists a few examples. We'll talk more about co-benefits in the next chapter.

Hoping for a radical change in public habits by public education schemes alone is wishful thinking. For years in the UK people were asked to avoid disposable plastic shopping bags, but to little avail. However, when a five pence charge per bag was mandated, their use plummeted by 85%.[219] Such small measures to incentivise behaviour change, have been denoted as 'nudges'; we shall need a lot of them!

27.5 Summary

Humans are totally dependent on the natural world that we are a part of. Green plants produce the oxygen in the air that we breathe; all of our food comes from other life – from plants or animals. While we might be able to cling to existence in a severely degraded environment, choosing that path is an enormous gamble since the Earth's ecosystem is complex, and we do not know how much damage we can do without pushing it over the edge into collapse. In any case most of us find beauty and wonder in nature and do not want to live in a degraded and impoverished environment – although sadly many of us already are, often to a greater extent than we appreciate given how modern lifestyles distance us from nature.

Consumption levels and human numbers have grown so much, that we are now the main cause of environmental destruction. The major mechanisms are:

Habitat loss – leaving too little space for wild plants and animals;

Exploitation – hunting and fishing;

Climate change – catastrophic heating caused by CO_2 released by burning fossil fuels;

Pollution – toxic chemicals, garbage, pesticides.

To reduce the impact of humans we need to limit our consumption and our population size, and find ways to protect nature. To lower consumption, 'green' technologies by themselves are not enough. Often the gain is modest and is wiped out in just a few years by growth in consumption and population – for example, the reductions in carbon emissions due to the introduction of electric cars are being swiftly cancelled out by growing vehicle ownership and the fashion for larger vehicles.

Justice requires that consumption levels across the world converge, with richer citizens reducing their consumption from current levels since their lifestyles generally exceed what would be a sustainable level for all. Governments can use taxes to discourage consumption by increasing prices, but when dealing with essentials like heating and transport, some sort of individual allowance or ration would be a fairer mechanism.

World population has grown almost fivefold from 1900 to 2022, with some countries experiencing increases of as much as tenfold. To limit human impact, we have to limit the population size as well as the amount individuals consume. The logic is inescapable but it has become unpopular to even admit the reality of:

$$IMPACT = Population \times Consumption$$

One argument made against having a population policy is that rising living standards and the education of women, will automatically bring down birth rates. Another is that even discussing population is attempting to shift blame onto poorer countries whose growing populations, given their lower consumption levels, actually cause less damage than those of richer countries. Yet the fact remains: there must be some limit to the number of humans that can live on a finite planet. If we exceed that limit, famine, pestilence and war will adjust the numbers for us. Perhaps it will be enough to accept the need for a limit to human numbers, educate people about that, provide some simple incentives, and ensure people have the wherewithal in terms of family planning. But not to have any plan or concern at all, is to put our head in the sand and trust in magic. We all see this clearly enough in more mundane circumstances: we would readily accept that the number of people who can board a boat may have to be limited if we don't want it to capsize and sink. The only difference is that since the Earth is a lot bigger, the precise limit beyond which disaster will ensue is unknown.

Regardless of what the global population and level of consumption may be, we should not put off trying to protect the natural world and minimise the harm caused to it by economic activity. Some things are particularly damaging, and we can relieve the pressure on nature by either doing them less or not at all, by finding substitutes, or occasionally by technological breakthroughs. Reducing the consumption of meat and fish by adopting a largely vegetarian diet would allow more of the land and the oceans to be conserved as wild spaces, as would the development of sustainable lab-grown meats. Agreements are needed to preserve global commons such as the atmosphere and the oceans, to prevent over-exploitation. Industry must be given strong rules and incentives to reduce pollution and resource use, and eliminate carbon emissions. We have to develop sustainable lifestyles that citizens and societies are attracted to and find satisfying.

Chapter 28

Changing Direction: The Politics

28.1　Introduction

Our dominant economic system of free-market capitalism, has an inbuilt drive to grow the amount of consumption. Businesses want consumption growth because they want to grow their profits. Workers want consumption growth because they want jobs.

Continual consumption growth combined with a growing population, is playing havoc with the natural world, damaging it so severely that our future existence is threatened. We looked at policies to provide decent livelihoods in Chapter 26, and at policies to tackle the environmental crisis in Chapter 27. The current chapter is about the *politics* of a change of direction: how do we convince people to accept and work for the changes needed. It's a huge topic and this chapter should be seen as notes and ideas, and not as a set of definitive solutions.

28.2 Multiple Challenges

Convincing people of the need to change our economic system has many aspects to it.

> *How can we persuade people to prioritise a long-term environmental crisis that is hard to visualise since its effects vary and are scattered in time and place, over their more immediate economic and consumer goals?*

The current needs of providing employment and financing state-spending on services, combine to pressure governments to maintain growth. As a result, longer term goals of tackling the climate and ecological emergency are kicked into the future, despite dire and urgent scientific warnings. Growth is also the politically easy way to offer to improve the lot of the poorer part of society: "we will make the whole cake bigger and then everyone's slice will be bigger, however rich or poor they are". Few governments are brave enough to propose alternatives to growth, such as redistribution from the rich to the poor, because the rich are influential and usually well represented in the government itself as well as in business and the media.

The nature of the modern market economy makes life feel like a struggle for most people. Even in affluent western countries, many individuals are either unemployed or stuck in insecure and exploitative jobs, and the situation is even worse in poorer parts of the world. Understandably, people grappling with economic and sometimes physical survival, find these immediate concerns more urgent than environmental issues. Furthermore, rising expectations mean that yesterday's luxury is seen as today's necessity. Changing lifestyles reinforce this shift. For example, in much of the world having a smartphone and internet access have become almost essential for work, education and social life – or at least are perceived as such. As a result, even those who are not on the breadline and are far better off in terms of consumer goods than previous generations, can still find themselves constantly striving to earn enough to afford the things that are now considered basic expectations – so they too are susceptible to the message that "we cannot afford the green stuff".

> *How can we convince the world's wealthier citizens to accept not only no growth but a reduction in their consumption to a sustainable level?*

For the world's wealthiest citizens, action to protect the environment requires not just a temporary pause in growth but a radical reduction in how much they consume. But such has been the success of free-market capitalism in promoting consumption that it's not just the very rich but the global middle class too, who have become accustomed to unsustainable lifestyles. These lifestyles are unsustainable because they not only directly cause harm but also set a standard that the rest of the world aspires to. International agreements on protecting the environment will never be accepted by less industrialised countries if the richer countries don't accept a convergence of consumption levels, and clearly the target level everyone needs to converge to must be a level that is sustainable if adopted worldwide. That means that in the richer countries we have to somehow convince large numbers of people to use cars and planes less, and generally consume less overall.

> *How can we make an alternative to the current perpetual-growth consumerist model, attractive?*

Is it even politically feasible to get support for a transition to a more modest standard of living? It's said that the Romans kept the population content with 'bread and circuses'. Our modern-day equivalent is an ever-growing flow of consumer goods; capitalism may produce very unequal societies, but that inequality is less upsetting if your own wealth in terms of car ownership, package holidays, electronic gismos and so forth, has grown, even if not as fast as that of the richest. Slowing or halting growth threatens to take away those consumer goodies while offering nothing in return. Although there are periods in history when in the face of an immediate threat such as war or a pandemic, people have accepted sacrifices to their living standards, the difficulty with the environmental crisis is that it plays out over many years and affects different places at different times, which makes it hard for people to see it as a crisis and hard to see a clear goal or 'victory' to aim for.

The remainder of this chapter explores what might help gain the necessary public support for tackling environmental issues, looking at:

Education. A growing understanding of environmental issues will help people to appreciate the urgency of taking action, and to resist pro-growth consumerist arguments.

Participation. People are more likely to try to bring about change if they feel that democracy works: that they have some control and can take part in developing and implementing solutions.

Co-Benefits. Many of the measures needed to tackle environmental issues automatically bring other benefits, such as clean air, better health, and jobs in new green industries.

Vision. For the longer term we need to picture a better future to work towards, and outline an attractive sustainable lifestyle that fills lives with interest without requiring excessive consumption.

28.3   Education

Survival on our crowded planet, tackling the climate emergency and managing powerful new technologies, will require many changes to the rules and regulations we live under. It will be all too easy for people to see this as the 'interfering' government, scientists or environmentalists, endlessly telling people what they 'ought' to do. People are more willing to support policies when they understand their purpose and context.

Accordingly, we need to ensure that citizens don't only hear about individual measures, but also become familiar with the bigger picture: the basics of ecology and the implications of living on a finite planet. This education can start in school and needs to continue in adult life. We should also have citizenship programmes at school that go beyond classroom lessons, incorporating participation in real forums where children's voices can be heard.

Providing the environmental education required is an uphill struggle because there are loud voices engaged in what we could term *'de-education'*. For example:

- *Advertising designed to persuade people of the benefits of products that in reality have few or no benefits, or are positively harmful.* Examples of such products include tobacco, alcohol, junk food, gambling and SUVs. Advertising is fairly straightforward to regulate as the brands must identify themselves in the adverts; some countries do already have restrictions on the advertising of certain products – notably tobacco.

- *The propaganda output of media, think-tanks and lobbyists, financed by vested interests.* Corporations and the mega-rich who are determined to maintain gross inequality and fight off any restrictions on their businesses, conduct a misinformation war. Both the tobacco and oil industries deliberately undermined the evidence on the harm that their products do for decades, even though their own scientists knew it to be true.

- *Fake news and conspiracy theories.* Before the internet such material had to be printed – the cost of printing was a disincentive and the publisher could be held responsible for libel. By contrast, you can post on the web for free and the platforms that are essentially the equivalent of publishers, deny all responsibility for content.

28.4 Participation

Given the complexity of the future we face and the necessity of getting support for what will be contentious policies, we need people to participate in society not just as 'workers' and 'consumers', but also as informed and active '**citizens**'.

28.4.1 The current model of participation in democratic politics isn't adequate

Democratic participation across the globe is currently quite minimal. Most people do no more than vote in elections, and do so based only upon what they hear via the media, much of which pushes the views and interests of its owners, and upon what they come across on social media, which is hardly a source of reliable information and often an echo chamber of prejudice and paranoia. Very few attend detailed debates or discussions, or have access to policy experts. Elections dominated by the popular press can degenerate into a beauty contest about which party has the most likeable leader.

Those few members of the public who do join a political party, get the opportunity to participate in campaigns – especially to get the vote out at election time – but have very limited input into policy, let alone what policies actually get implemented. These observations are unashamedly based primarily on my own experience in the UK. Unashamedly because from what I have read and from what I have seen in those countries I have visited or had the good fortune to live in for a while, I find it very difficult to believe that there are many places in the world where the majority of the population are continuously and vigorously engaged in democratic politics.

What is more, being a member of a party isn't enough; to get to know what's going on and have some influence you have to attend meetings – perhaps two to three a month. That still may not be enough because at those meetings, which are often bound by procedure, you may well be faced with a strange dance between competing factions who have held their own pre-meetings to decide their 'position' and how they intend to intervene in the official meeting, making it very hard for an outsider to fathom what is going on. For those who become party activists, it can be hard to stay the course over many years without suffering 'burn out' through either exhaustion, or disillusion when hoped-for progress seems elusive.

28.4.2 Continual mobilisation is not sustainable

There is little evidence that it is feasible to sustain extensive public participation in political parties over many years, given how they currently operate. Nor perhaps should we expect it, even under the most favourable circumstances. Countries that have had popular revolutions do not maintain those peaks of fervour for years afterwards – people revert to their daily concerns.

Since we cannot realistically expect a large part of the population to become permanent political activists, we need to find other ways to enable and institutionalise popular participation.

28.4.3 Alternative political-participation models

Citizens' assemblies

A Citizens' Assembly is a representative group of citizens selected at random from the population and given the task of learning about and making recommendations on an issue. An assembly typically meets several times over a period of some months, hearing from relevant experts and from interested parties with differing views, and with enough time to discuss issues properly and formulate some recommendations. It is up to elected politicians whether to follow the recommendations. To make more use of citizens' assemblies, we would need to be able to call people to serve and if necessary give them paid leave from work.

Countries with jury service co-opt their citizens to participate with the justice system. Serving as a juror is considered an important public duty and trial by jury is seen as a hard won right that should be protected. Jury service provides a clear model for involving the public in civic duties.

Thus we could consider creating citizens' assemblies that co-opt participants in a similar way to jury service, with paid time off work to serve. They could be a regular duty undertaken various times throughout life. The assemblies could address issues at various levels from local government to national and international issues.

Citizens' assemblies have been used very successfully in Ireland, notably to consider abortion rights.[220] One of the key elements was that their work was publicised: contributions and speeches to the Assembly were made available online and its recommendations were published. This provided useful and informed input to the subsequent referendum. In the UK, the Citizens' Assembly project, the RSA[1] and others, offer information about how assemblies operate, give details about those that have been held in the UK, and provide a handbook for local authorities 'How to run a citizens' assembly'.[221] The UK parliament (as opposed to the government) ran a citizens' assembly on climate change: it produced valuable recommendations, which unfortunately were largely ignored by the government.[222]

There is no reason why even quite young children couldn't take part in appropriately structured citizens' assemblies, which are after all, advisory bodies that are not directly responsible for decisions.

Citizens' assemblies are a more satisfying way of participating in politics that traditional party meetings, because they are non-confrontational, with real and extended discussion and access to experts. There is also the expectation of delivering a set of recommendations that will be taken into account by government. Most participants in the assemblies that have been held, value and appreciate the experience. Unlike jury service, participants are able to question experts in a natural manner, rather than listening passively to barristers and witnesses.

Local versus global

Despite modern communications, people still strongly identify with place. They are probably more likely to participate in governance if it is physically near them.

London was originally a series of villages that merged into one another and those town centres and high streets still exist. However, in the name of efficiency, local government was reorganised in the 1960s into larger local councils covering multiple town centres, with

---

[1]The royal society for the encouragement of arts, manufactures and commerce.

the result that for most people the council is more distant and located in a different centre to the one where they live.

The same complaint about distant government can be heard where there are campaigns for a region of a nation state to break away completely and become an independent country, though usually mixed with a potent element of nationalism. Something like this was heard in the UK Brexit debate, in which British nationalism was combined with complaints about being governed by far away Brussels. There may be a case for smaller local government and devolving powers to the lowest practical level, if it facilitates more participation, even if more expensive. However, the Brexit referendum and the UK's subsequent exit from the EU does give us two warnings:

1. Creating borders where there were none is messy and unpleasant because many individuals and businesses will have organised their lives base on the ability to move seamlessly across the now-divided areas.

2. The process can generate years of acrimonious argument and negotiations (which in the UK, 7 years on from the Brexit vote, still show no sign of ending).

No doubt every case is different, but given that the climate crisis is upon us and needs our full attention globally, we should surely be cautious about taking on too many conflictive issues unless they are truly unavoidable.

One thing however is certain: while people may identify most with their own locality, tackling the environmental crisis requires global vision and global cooperation. In fact, it's hard to see how humans can survive for much longer without some sort of *global governance*, because it's not just the environment and climate change that we have to worry about. Scientific advance is creating a stream of powerful technologies capable of unleashing havoc and possibly our extinction, if they are unregulated. Chapter 24 referred to the *Bulletin of the Atomic Scientists* founded in 1945 by Albert Einstein and scientists involved in the development of the atomic bomb.[143]

The group has been warning the public about technological risks ever since, and signalling what they see as the most worrying. To nuclear weapons we can now add things like deliberately-engineered deadly viruses and the misuse or uncontrolled development of artificial intelligence (AI), as well as climate change. The Bulletin's 'Doomsday Clock', shows symbolically how close humanity is to disaster.[223]

To regulate dangerous technologies, global laws, globally agreed and globally enforced are needed. So somehow we have to devise a system that combines the required global governance with devolution and local participation. This would suggest building on global institutions like the United Nations and on bodies that facilitate regional cooperation such as the European Union, while also devolving to an appropriate level what can be locally decided.

Individual action and campaigning

Individual actions are comforting but have only a fraction of effect of government policy. No amount of exhortation to recycle or save energy would have the impact of the plastic bag tax and investment in offshore wind. So as citizens we have to campaign to:

- **Get politicians to act** – of whatever party;

- **Generate public support for politicians who do take action** – and for the measures they implement.

However, lobbying and campaigning can be a frustrating as it's hard to achieve something concrete. Complementing it with practical activities may help build groups and maintain moral. The 'transition town' movement sets out to do that.[224] The idea is that any group of concerned citizens can launch a 'Transition Initiative' and begin to prepare their town for the future, without necessarily waiting for support from local government (although such support is of course welcome).

28.5 Co-Benefits as Motivators

Tackling climate change requires us to stop burning fossil fuels and to protect and expand green spaces such as forests which absorb carbon. The primary purpose of doing so is to reduce the amount of the greenhouse gas CO_2 in the atmosphere. But we have a problem. Even if we were phenomenally successful in lowering the CO_2 concentration, many people will barely notice. CO_2 is an odourless gas that is harmless to breathe at the levels it is found in the atmosphere. Success at halting or reversing climate change would play out over many years and the evidence of success won't be that obvious to the public. We'd have to say:

> *"Remember that disaster we said would happen? Well now it won't."*

> Or more realistically: *"Those extreme weather events we warned of, are happening rather less than predicted."*

They are difficult messages to convey. Sadly the best way to convince the public of the seriousness of climate change would be to let it rip until the catastrophe affects almost everyone. But that's not an option we want to pursue.

Fortunately however, ending the use of fossil fuels, expanding green spaces and cutting CO_2 emissions, have other beneficial effects, such as clean air and better health. We described in Chapter 27 how these associated benefits are referred to as 'co-benefits' and listed some of them in Table 27.2. Co-benefits are seen as a possible way to help motivate people to support environmental action.[225, 226] We'll now look at some of them and at their value as motivators.

28.5.1 Lower fossil-fuel and energy use

Fossil-fuel extraction is a dirty business leaving slag heaps and oil spills. Transport to the end-user is often over long distances and causes further spillage and pollution. When the fuels are burnt they not only release the greenhouse gas carbon dioxide, they also pollute the air with smoke, with smaller particulates not visible to the naked eye, and with toxic gases such as nitrogen oxides, sulphur dioxide and carbon monoxide.

Getting off fossil fuels means finding alternative energy sources and reducing the amount of energy we use. The main alternative sources of energy are the renewable technologies of wind and solar, which although inevitably having some emissions and pollution associated with their manufacture, are once installed, almost completely clean in operation. The expectation is that electricity generated by renewables, will replace the oil and gas used for industry, transport, heating and cooking. Where the economy is electrified in this way, operational emissions will be largely eliminated. Unlike oil pipelines and tankers, electrical transmission cables never leak pollutants. Similarly, there are no combustion emissions given off by electric motors, heaters or cookers.

Reducing how much energy we use requires a reduction in car use and car ownership. The manufacture and use of road vehicles and particularly cars (as they are so numerous) is a major demand on energy and would be completely unsustainable if all countries had car ownership at the levels of the richest nations. Ways to reduce car use include reducing the need to travel by ensuring people are able to live near their jobs and near the facilities they need (schools, shops, leisure, medical, etc.), promoting active travel (walk or cycle instead of using a car), and the use of public transport.

Lowering car use lowers air pollution (even electric cars still give off tyre and brake dust) and has additional benefits if it results in active travel as part of daily routine. Even just a walk to the bus stop or railway station is positive for health in populations that are otherwise becoming over sedentary. Restructuring towns so that the need to travel is reduced also has benefits, such as shorter and less stressful commutes, with correspondingly more leisure time, and more sense of community (if you live near your workplace or school, it's easier to socialise with fellow colleagues or students). Safe walking, cycling and public transport facilities also extend mobility and independence to those with no access to a car; we should remember that in households that do own a car, there are often family members who cannot use it, notably children.

28.5.2 Green spaces and nature

Protecting and expanding green spaces to soak up CO_2 has co-benefits for those living near them. They can enjoy the natural spaces and the greater abundance of wildlife, while forest cover mitigates flooding as it absorbs water and holds together the soil. However, to have a serious impact on CO_2 emissions, we need to protect the world's remaining great forests. That requires a political campaign because the number of people who directly experience benefit from their protection may be modest, given that those forests tend to be distant from the bulk of the world's population centres – if they weren't they'd already have been cut down.

28.5.3 Making co-benefits visible and tangible

So we have: cleaner air, improved health from active travel, better green spaces, the creation of green jobs. Surely implementing the measures that bring these benefits should be a 'no-brainer'? Yet while these benefits are real and mostly measurable, they are not 'in-your-face' visible. In particular, measures that restrict car-use or increase its cost by say, road-pricing or higher taxes on the most polluting vehicles, often elicit a furious response from drivers, who immediately notice that their commute is more inconvenient or expensive. But unfortunately, they and the wider public do not so easily observe the reduction in air pollution and the corresponding slowing in the insidious damage to their and their families' lungs, that such measures bring about.

I fear the same is true of many of the co-benefits of tackling climate change: they are not very visible to the public. For example this is a list of co-benefits cited in respondents to a CDP-ICLEI[2]

---

[2]CDP is a charity that runs the global disclosure system for investors, companies, cities, states and regions to manage their environmental impacts. ICLEI (Local Governments for Sustainability) is a global network working with local

questionnaire:

> Disaster preparedness. Disaster risk reduction. Economic growth. Ecosystem preservation and biodiversity improvement. Enhanced climate change adaptation. Enhanced resilience. Greening the economy. Improved access to and quality of mobility services and infrastructure. Improved access to data for informed decision-making. Improved public health. Improved resource efficiency, quality & security (e.g. food, water, energy). Job creation. Poverty reduction/eradication. Promote circular economy. Resource conservation (e.g. soil, water). Security of tenure. Shift to more sustainable behaviours. Social community and labour improvements. Social inclusion, social justice.
>
> *– from 'The co-benefits of climate action'.[225]*

It's not that these aren't real and genuine benefits, but how tangible and immediate are they to the populace? It is not easy to imagine a family member returning home from work or school and announcing with any excitement: *"Hey, the Council have just enhanced resilience / greened the economy / promoted a circular economy."*

So as well as working hard to communicate the need to tackle climate change and the associated co-benefits as effectively as possible, we should also try to design policies which bring benefits that are **immediate and tangible step-changes**. For example, a small reduction in cars on a road achieved by partially restricting traffic, is barely detectable without carrying out a survey and counting how many cars pass by, whereas fully pedestrianising a road instantly changes it from a hostile, polluted, dangerous place, to something where it's pleasant to stroll with your children. You **can** imagine a family member returning home and excitedly saying: *"Hey, the Council have just pedestrianised the High Street".*

By the same logic, when changes are necessary to tackle climate change that bring some restriction or cost, they should be designed

---

and regional governments committed to sustainable urban development.

so that those negative effects are **more distant, less obvious and more incremental, than are the benefits of the change**. To illustrate this, two example cases are described below, both of which concern measures that discourage car use. In the first, the benefits sufficiently outweighed the more distant disadvantages, and residents voted for it. In the second case it was not so clear-cut and the measure encountered much greater opposition.

Example 1: Residents-Only Parking

In London's suburbs, many streets have no off-road parking and car owners park on the street. Until the 1980s in London, you could park almost anywhere in the suburbs, but as the numbers of cars soared, streets near popular destinations became packed with the cars of visiting non-residents. This occurred around many suburban Underground stations (London's metro), because commuters could park on a street near the station for free and then continue by rail to the city centre, which was advantageous for them as parking in the centre was already difficult to find and expensive, but inconvenient for local residents who could not find space to park their own cars. People living in the affected streets began to ask their local councils to implement residents-only parking, whereby residents pay an annual fee for a permit to park in the controlled zone where they live. What then happened was that the commuters began parking in streets just outside the controlled zones, and that combined with continuing growth in vehicle numbers, meant that more and more streets requested residents-only parking. As a result, zones with restricted parking have grown to cover much of London's suburbs.

What is curious about this evolution of parking controls, is that being either charged for parking or unable to park at all at your destination, is a major motivator for people to choose walking, cycling or public transport, instead of driving. So a process backed by car owners for the selfish (though understandable) reason that they want to stop others parking in their home streets, has produced a traffic reduction scheme. The immediate tangible benefit of being able to park in one's own street, overrode the more distant restriction of it being harder to park elsewhere.

Example 2: Low Traffic Neighbourhoods

During the Covid pandemic, London councils were told to reduce traffic in residential back-streets and encourage active travel by creating what are called Low Traffic Neighbourhoods (LTNs). This was achieved by blocking off certain streets to make it more difficult for through traffic to use the area as a rat-run (short-cut). It also meant that residents in had fewer routes in and out of their area and had to drive a longer way around for some journeys. Pedestrians, cyclists and emergency vehicles were able to pass the blocks. The schemes certainly worked in terms of reducing traffic, but most met strong opposition and often fury from residents with cars because of the inconvenience when they had to drive a more circuitous route. Many were removed after councils gave residents a vote on whether to retain them.

However, the outcome might have been different with a small adjustment. Some residents said that they would accept a scheme, provided that their own cars were exempt – something that is not difficult to arrange through automatic number plate recognition (ANPR) cameras (and because registration of residents' vehicles is already commonplace given the many residents parking schemes). Allowing this exemption might seem contrary to the objectives of the policy, i.e. to encourage residents to use their cars less. However, as with residents parking, there would be a domino effect driven by self-interest. By supporting an LTN from which they are exempt in their own street, drivers lose nothing and immediately benefit from the quieter street. But over time as LTNs spread and since the exemption only applies to their own local LTN, there would be fewer short-cuts through residential streets available across the whole city, thus discouraging driving and encouraging active travel.

The suggestion for how the LTN scheme could have been modified may sound a bit Machiavellian, but in a sense it only compensates for the disastrous and unjust 'tragedy of the commons effect'. Disastrous because it drives up car ownership since citizens have little incentive to give up their car as they lose its benefits and get in return only a negligible general reduction in traffic (just one less car). Unjust because citizens are effectively denied the option of choosing fewer or no cars in their suburb, even if they don't own one themselves.[3] The modified LTN scheme as outlined above reverses the dilemma because voting for it gives a driver the option of an immediate benefit in their own street, and voting against gives an immediate loss with no guarantee that the rest of the city's neighbourhoods will follow suit and continue to allow short-cuts and rat-runs through their areas.

In summary, the message then is: make co-benefits visible and immediate, make restrictions intangible and distant, reverse the tragedy-of-the-commons effect so that the 'selfish' choice that directly benefits an individual or their family is also the environmentally positive one that brings a public good, rather than the environmentally destructive one that destroys the public space.

28.5.4 Job creation and a fairer society, as co-benefits

Job creation and a fairer society are often mentioned as being among the potential co-benefits of tackling climate change. Job creation could occur for two reasons:

1. Regulation to force a shift to technology with zero net emissions, may oblige the use of more labour-intensive technologies.

---

[3]Reminiscent of the choice offered in a restaurant I visited years back, when one of our group asked if we could sit in a no-smoking area. The waiter shrugged and replied "you don't have to smoke if you don't want to".

2. If a government decides to enforce a rapid transition, a lot of work will have to be undertaken in a short period.

Hopes that green technologies will bring about a fairer society, revolve around their distributed nature. It's believed that they will create large numbers of medium-skilled jobs scattered across the country, such as modifying buildings, installing solar panels on roofs, etc., as opposed to a handful of highly skilled jobs in a few huge power plants. It is also hoped that ownership may become more distributed, via for example the cooperative ownership of wind farms or household ownership of solar panels.

Note however, that it is government action which produces the job creation. The market left to itself would only take up green technologies if they were cheaper than the existing alternatives, and cheaper usually means requiring less labour, i.e. fewer jobs. Assuming that the government does invest and creates some green jobs, there is no guarantee that they will be enough to soak up all unemployment; some of those jobs are also likely to disappear over time, as the transition boom passes and automation advances.

Full employment and a fairer society are worthy goals and attractive benefits, but there is no reason to suppose that they are intrinsic co-benefits of green technologies. There are many other labour-intensive and dispersed activities in the economy, from maintaining streets to installing domestic gas boilers, and they have not brought about full employment. We could easily end up with green infrastructure being predominantly owned by large corporations and private landlords, with society no fairer than it is now.

Yet, we do need job creation and a fairer society to be part of tackling climate change because we cannot continue to base our economy on perpetual consumption growth as the only mechanism to create employment. That means implementing the sorts of policies discussed in Chapter 26, and applying them to the whole economy, not just green technologies. Doing so will offer major co-benefits to those who are currently unemployed, in precarious work or overworked; however, others who don't benefit directly may view the changes only as unwanted new regulations or taxes.

28.5.5   Justice and 'co-negatives'

Unfortunately, not only is there no guarantee that co-benefits will include job creation and a fairer society, it's also the case that many of the measures to tackle climate change will have side effects that are in some way negative for part of the population, or at least are seen as such. So as we engage in what will be a wholesale transformation of the economy, we need to ensure that the burden of the changes doesn't fall on the less well off.

The poorest mustn't take the hit.

Many people own or depend on businesses that are based on cheap fossil fuels, mass car ownership, air travel, and excessive consumption. Even in the relatively rich countries, large numbers of people are categorised as 'just about managing'. Restrictions on car use worry shop owners in case customers cannot park, plumbers and electricians who rely on a van, and those whose commute to work is difficult without a car.

Using price increases via taxes or duties as the method to discourage consumption of fuels inevitably hits the less-well-off hardest, while the wealthiest who can afford the increase with ease, carry on consuming. Rationing would be fairer, though perhaps shock people more. Policymakers have their work cut out to design measures that make the benefits outweigh the negatives for as many as possible and especially for the least well off.

28.6   A Future Beyond Consumerism

While there may be co-benefits associated some of the measures required to tackle climate change, the environment will always be under threat if our economy remains based on free-market consumerism. Nor will such an economy provide secure livelihoods for all. So for the longer term we have to design an economic model and sustainable lifestyle that allows people to have satisfactory and fulfilling lives without requiring excessive consumption. In thinking about that better economic model, we should note that there are two major arguments against consumerism:

1. The world cannot sustain the environmental damage it is already causing, let alone what would happen if everyone consumed at the levels of today's rich.

2. When consuming becomes the main focus or goal, it does not lead to a fulfilling or happy life.

The first argument is the one that runs through much of this book and is pretty much straightforward and irrefutable; it does not say that consumerism is bad, just that with the current population on planet Earth, it is not sustainable. The second argument is more open to debate: clearly humans do have a strong acquisitive urge, but at the same time, sages throughout history have advised us to value more than just material possessions. So while the first argument obliges us (or should do) to moderate our consumption, the second gives us hope that doing so might not be all sacrifice, but instead offer alternative and sometimes greater pleasures. That's important because if we want a transition to a more sustainable world, we need to make it as attractive as possible; accordingly, this section is about those alternative pleasures. Of course we cannot prove that say, riding a bicycle will make you happier than driving a big gas-guzzling truck – and indeed for some people it probably won't be true. However, at least we can try to build a future that isn't just a hair-shirt version of the present but something that is not only sustainable but also rather lovely.

"Anyone who has visions should go to the doctor"[4]

In what follows, I fully accept that people's visions of the future will vary ... and some can be dangerous! However, we do need some ideas about what we are aiming for. We'll start by looking at what we know about what makes for a happy and fulfilling life. That also involves looking at what makes us miserable: the things which we'd like to mitigate or remove.

---

[4]Said to be a popular phrase of the former German Chancellor Helmut Schmidt.

28.6.1 What makes us happy

Traditional wisdom

Philosophers and religious teachings throughout the ages have considered what makes a good life. We referred to the four cardinal virtues of Christian theology and classical philosophy in Chapter 14 – prudence, justice, fortitude, and temperance – and we noted how they contrast with the behaviour promoted by a consumerist market-based society. Other philosophical traditions also tend to favour self-control, respect for others and restraint. Confucianism for example, stresses knowledge, learning, responsibility, duty, and social engagement with friends, family and the wider community; good government and the rule of law are also said to be important for happiness. I came across an interesting article that compares ancient Chinese philosophical advice with what modern studies tell us, and it seems that there is plenty of overlap.[227]

Britain's pre-eminent 20th century philosopher Bertrand Russell wrote a book on happiness: The Conquest of Happiness.[228] He doesn't reference any research, but he had a lot of observation and experience to draw on: he studied and travelled extensively, spending time in both the USSR and China, and wrote a history of western philosophy. He emphasises:

- A consistent and constructive purpose in life that enables the development and use of skills, and the value of work (employment) in providing that purpose plus the necessary routine and structure;

- Wide interests and hobbies outside work, which by being absorbing but not obligatory, are restful and distract you from worries;

- Acceptance that we are creatures of Earth and maintaining contact with its rhythms and with nature, especially as children.

Among sources of unhappiness he lists envy, commenting that whereas once people were limited to comparing themselves with

their neighbours, nowadays thanks to the press people can be sus-
picious or envious of people all over the world who they have never
actually met ... and bear in mind that he was writing in 1930 long
before television and modern social media! He argues that too much
excitement undermines health and dulls normal pleasures, and he
recommends that children should mostly get their pleasure from
their environment by their own effort and inventiveness, and only
rarely be offered ready-made excitement that involves no physical
effort (again, one wonders what he would make of today's computer
games and childhoods spent online).

Modern studies

Past philosophers relied on observation and experience. Researchers
in more recent times have applied the more rigorous methods of
science and statistics, but the message to a large extent appears
fairly similar. Beyond a certain minimum for basic comfort and
security, contentment comes not from accumulating material goods,
but from being part of a community and having work, interests or
hobbies that take you out of yourself and give a sense of purpose.

These conclusions might seem strange: many people dream of
wealth, so surely a person who wins the lottery and buys everything they want should be **very** happy. Researchers have found
that this doesn't necessarily follow because humans *adapt* to many
types of change. So a change for the better may make us initially
happier but in many cases we get used to the new situation and our
state of contentment returns to its normal level. Similarly, some
changes for the worse make us sad for a while but over time we
recover. It seems that our response to consumer purchases tend to
follow that pattern. So a new shiny coffee machine increases your
happiness but only for a short while; should it break and have to
be thrown out, your regret is also short-lived (you quickly accus-
tom to using your old Italian percolator again). However, we do
not adapt to everything. Researchers also found that certain types
of change do have permanent effects. For example, ongoing noise
pollution and chronic health problems both have permanent neg-

ative effects on contentment, while good health, individual auton-omy, social embeddedness and a good environment, have permanent positive effects.[229]

So it looks like a more sustainable world doesn't have to be a miserable one. We can be equally happy without so much mate-rial stuff as we are now, and perhaps increase our happiness if the changes we make also improve things like health, the environment, fulfilment at work, and community life.

There is however a fly in the ointment. Researchers also say that material possessions are 'positional' which means that the sat-isfaction we get from them comes from comparing what we have to what others have and feeling that we've done better. Status mat-ters to us so we feel a pressure to have as much or more than our neighbours – often referred to in Britain as 'keeping up with the Joneses'. That possessions are 'positional' presents a problem: if for example we wish to encourage the use of smaller cars (let alone bicycles) that's going to be hard if a part of the population con-tinues to drive around in very large ones. It suggests that we'd need to make small cars the norm so that competitive-minded pur-chasers are happy, provided their small car is a little bit newer or better equipped than that of their neighbours; or alternatively we'd need to find something about small cars that makes them enviable! It also suggests that people will be happier in a more equal society than in one where a section of society is flaunting its greater wealth.

Since most of us pass much of our lives under pressure to study or work, we tend to associate happiness with holidays and idleness. But the evidence shows that meaningful and productive activities contribute to our happiness and that a satisfying career increases our general satisfaction with life. In other words, work is actually good for us, always provided that it is interesting and meaningful. Of course work is not the only source of meaningful activities; happy people tend to have interests that they pursue outside of work or in retirement. Work and non-work activities also socialise us. They are where we make friends and meet partners, and they help us to feel part of a community – all things that are good for our sense of well-being.

Comparing societies: GNH versus GDP

Another way to try to learn what makes a for good life, is to compare countries and see whereabouts in the world people appear to be more content.

Most governments today judge their success by the increase in Gross Domestic Product (GDP) which measures how much is produced and therefore also consumed. It is however a poor measure because it includes all economic activity, which includes activities that are directly harmful, and activities that are only there to protect against or repair harm caused by problems we are unwilling to tackle. So manufacturing gas-guzzling cars, cigarettes and weapons adds to GDP, as does cleaning up after traffic accidents, treating lung disease brought on by pollution or smoking, and elaborate security (locks, cameras, metal detectors) required where crime is common. Furthermore, GDP says nothing about equality of distribution: a country might have a high GDP but almost all of that production be consumed by a fabulously wealthy clique while ordinary citizens live in abject poverty – a state of affairs that will seem familiar to many across the globe.

As a result, there is widespread interest in alternative measures which allow us to compare how well countries are doing in terms of human well-being and environmental impact instead of just production and consumption: a 'Gross National Happiness' (GNH) index or similar. The government of Bhutan has adopted the goal of maximising Gross National Happiness, rather than GDP. A number of organisations have worked on similar measures, observing which societies appeared to be happier and assessing what made them so.[230]

The British think-tank The New Economics Foundation, says that higher levels of life satisfaction are found in countries where more people belong to community groups, where concepts such as adventure, creativity and loyalty are valued more than possessions, and where government is open and democratic. Other factors include the avoidance of extreme poverty, adequate healthcare, and a healthy work-life balance.[231]

When countries are assessed on the basis of Gross National Happiness, those that score highly are not necessarily those with the highest GDPs. This again gives us hope that a society can moderate its consumption and still be attractive to live in, or possibly even increase its attractiveness.

International agreement

If the idea that governments should focus on happiness and fulfilment seems rather fanciful, bear in mind that there is already international agreement about the sorts of conditions humans require for a decent life. The Universal Declaration of Human Rights (UDHR) was proclaimed by the United Nations General Assembly in 1948 as a common standard for all peoples and all nations, and it was later extended with covenants on Economic, Social and Cultural Rights and on Civil and Political rights.[232, 233, 234] It covers things like:

- The right to work in just and favourable conditions.

- The right to social protection, to an adequate standard of living and to the highest attainable standards of physical and mental well-being.

- The right to education and the enjoyment of benefits of cultural freedom and scientific progress.

- Political rights such as freedom of movement, freedom of opinion and expression, participation in public affairs and elections.

So we do not start from zero: almost all countries pay at least lip service to these rights.

28.6.2   What needs to change to bring about the vision

We have seen that the conditions that give a good chance of a happy and fulfilling life, are not so very mysterious or contentious; often they are quite the opposite – simple and rather obvious. However, to achieve them, we will need to change the primary goal of society from maximising GDP to creating a world that is good to live in. We'll need to find ways to regulate and control the economy to remove a lot of bad effects and add in new good things.

Removing the bad stuff – things that make us miserable

Poor health makes people unhappy. Significant causes of poor health are pollution (including noise pollution), lack of exercise and poor diet. Government health programmes across the world often include advice to exercise, eat healthily, and avoid smoking or heavy drinking – but unfortunately the budgets for such worthy efforts are dwarfed by the billions spent on advertising to promote products that damage people's health, generate unhealthy lifestyles and wreck the environment.

Much current economic activity directly damages our health and environment, and thus our happiness. It needs to be regulated or in some cases stopped altogether. Our economic system also increases inequality, which we know is associated with less happy societies: positional unhappiness (envy) creates pressure to consume more, and unfair unequal societies tend to have higher levels of crime and violence.

We'll look in a little more detail at some of this 'bad stuff' that we'd like to remove – advertising, damage to the environment and inequality – and then move on to think about 'good stuff' that we could introduce to make our lives better.

Curb advertising. The bulk of advertising, apart from that in specialist and trade journals, is not really informative but a psychological propaganda campaign to persuade people to consume more stuff. In a world where consumption must be constrained for environmental reasons, this makes no sense. It will lead to frustration and anger when people are no longer able to buy the consumer goods they have been told are essential to happiness. It already creates dissatisfaction in those who could never afford such goods in the first place. We shall need to find ways to curb advertising that promotes consumption, or shift it to promote sustainable goods & services instead.

> *Billions are spent on advertising campaigns for products that damage people's health and wreck the environment.*

Many of the products intensively marketed are actively harmful to the consumer, the planet, or both – for example, junk foods and enormous gas-guzzler vehicles. It is insane that state funded health care systems like the UK's NHS, spend a fortune on treating diseases like obesity, diabetes, heart disease and tooth decay, that are all commonly related to or made worse by poor diet, while at the same time the food industry is spending billions to promote the ultra-processed, high-fat, high-salt and high-sugar foods that are a major cause of the damage.

> The Coca-Cola advertising budget in 2010 was about $2,900 million, the NHS (UK health service) 2011 budget for targeting improvements to the lives of young people (not just diet) was about $6.4 million (£4 million).

Cars are likewise heavily advertised – especially the most over-powered and over-sized (and also most profitable!) models, despite those being the most destructive. Cars are not only a major source of carbon emissions in both manufacture and use, they also pollute our cities, tempt us into an unhealthy inactive lifestyle, alienate us from our neighbourhoods, and intimidate and endanger those who would walk or cycle.

In a free-market economy we cannot expect advertising to voluntarily choose to be ethical, since a company that shows restraint will lose out to competitors who don't. Thus when unrestrained by law, advertising can be truly immoral, targeting vulnerable groups with harmful products. Unhealthy junk foods are skilfully promoted to young children, for example by associating them with popular children's stories or cartoon characters.

Questioning advertising will provoke shrill complaint from business and from that part of the media which lives off it. But if we are in a life and death struggle to bring consumerism under control, it makes no sense to allow businesses to spend billions on propaganda promoting excessive consumption, thus countering and cancelling the education provided in schools who have a far more modest budget.

The sophisticated psychological manipulation used by advertisers was well documented over half a century ago in the book The Hidden Persuaders by Vance Packard, still in print and well worth reading.[39] Various campaigns have sprung up to challenge the worst advertising. Two of them are 'Badvertising', a campaign to stop adverts fuelling the climate emergency such as those for cars, airline flights and fossil fuels, and 'Adfree Cities' which is a network of groups across the UK concerned about the impacts of corporate advertising on our health, wellbeing, environment, climate, communities and the local economy.[235, 236]

Tackle direct damage to the environment and health. A good deal of current economic activity pollutes the environment and threatens our safety. As well as material pollutants such as toxic chemicals, carbon emissions, microplastics and the like, there is noise pollution from traffic, aircraft, etc., and visual pollution such as smogs that block out the sky and distant views.

The unregulated free-market encourages a cavalier attitude to safety: firms can do anything unless or until it is so evidently dangerous that governments feel obliged to enact laws that prevent them, which often takes decades. There are many areas where regulation is weak or non-existent despite obvious harm or danger. Road traffic gets away with far lighter regulation and control than is considered appropriate for the railways, aviation or factories, despite the many violent injuries and deaths it causes.

> Road crashes cause over a million deaths and somewhere between 20 and 50 million non-fatal injuries around the world, every year. Apart from physical injury this causes significant mental distress. Even if you don't suffer an accident you are affected because the fear of accidents and the

intimidating, noisy and polluted environment created by busy roads, has changed the nature of public space. Where young children were once free to play in the streets from infancy and walk by themselves to school, they are now confined to their homes and escorted or driven to school. Walking has been made less attractive and cycling made frightening and dangerous.

Chapter 17 explained how the 'tragedy of the commons' effect means that it is near impossible for individuals to protect public spaces and amenities, and gave as an example the traffic-blight onslaught on our streets and its effect on children's mental health. Collective action through government is therefore required to regulate any economic activity that damages our local or global environment and ensure that harms are minimised or eliminated.

Limit inequality. Without regulation, our current economic model tends to grow inequality, as described in Chapter 19. While those who have nothing to sell but their labour can only earn one income, the rich can earn many times a single wage from the assets they own and thus grow yet richer – a positive feedback phenomena. Apart from the obvious ill that inequality leaves some people in extreme poverty, studies also show that high inequality is associated with less happy societies.

Inequality is associated with less happy societies with higher levels of crime and violence.

The book *The Spirit Level: Why More Equal Societies Almost Always Do Better*, describes how inequality erodes trust, increases anxiety and illness, and encourages excessive consumption.[237, 238] It compares some of the world's richer countries, and shows that for eleven different problems (physical health, mental health, drug abuse, education, imprisonment, obesity, social mobility, trust and community life, violence, teenage pregnancies, and child wellbeing), the outcomes are worse where inequality is higher. High inequality also increases the pressure to consume driven by envy and status. So limiting inequality should make it easier to moderate consumption, giving us more chance of protecting the environment.

Feeling safe from war, crime and random violence is also necessary for a good life. We should aim for economic justice and good governance worldwide, with a world economy that keeps inequality to moderate levels and provides all of us with the opportunity of an acceptable livelihood without the need to resort to crime.

> More than 400,000 people die from homicide each year – in some countries it's one of the leading causes. Less than 1% of global deaths are from homicide, but in some countries it's as high as 10%. Homicide rates vary widely across the world – in the most violent countries, rates are more than 50 times higher.[239]

To achieve a world in which everyone has satisfactory life opportunities, requires a generous, internationalist foreign policy. We cannot solve climate change without global cooperation, and in today's interconnected world we can't expect either to have a stable sustainable economy in our own country if the rest of the world is collapsing around us. Disruption to trade, huge migrant flows and wars, will affect us wherever we live, and be likely to encourage dangerous populism and xenophobia across the globe. So even if we live in a place that is relatively secure and wealthy, it is in our own interest to look outwards and do all that we can for the rest of the world.

Adding in good stuff

Creating a world that is good to live in, shouldn't stop at just removing existing harms – we also want to actively create the conditions that are conducive to the good life. This might sound wildly utopian, although it shouldn't do because in certain settings, it's exactly what most countries do or at least aspire to do.

One of those settings is school. Step into any primary school in the UK and the goals espoused are to do the best for the children not just in terms of the minimum knowledge to make them employable, but to interest them in art, science, history, literature, sport. A sense of community is promoted, children are monitored to keep them safe and healthy, specialist help is available for children with mental or physical difficulties. I assume schools across the world have similar aims, although some may have fewer resources than others to fulfil them.

> "Our passionate team of teaching and support staff go the extra mile to ensure that every child is valued, inspired and engaged." – *from a school website.*

Of course schools don't necessarily achieve all of this, but they try. That is in complete contrast to what happens when the child grows up and emerges into the adult world. Who then will *'go the extra mile to ensure that as adults they are valued, inspired and engaged'*? Apart perhaps from close family or friends, probably nobody. For many, the world on reaching adulthood becomes a struggle to make ends meet economically, with such work as is available, often insecure, repetitive, and poorly paid. What was the point of the 'art, science, history, literature, sport' if all that the economy wants of you is to work long days delivering parcels, or operating a supermarket checkout, or answering the phone in a call centre? And then only until you can be replaced with a robot that is cheaper.

The same contrast is seen with state-run universal health services. You could be homeless on the streets of London with no-one to look out for you – but if you are hit by a car and admitted to hospital, then suddenly you have a warm bed, food, and a team of professionals caring for you.

> *Why not create a society that aims to create a good life for everyone, not just for children in school or patients in hospital?*

So if we are already willing to do the best for people at certain times in their lives, let's extend that and create good lives for everyone, not just for children in school or the sick in hospital. Some people will insist that it is not the job of society to try to enrich the lives of all adults, and instead it should be left to the individual to fend for themselves and choose the sort of lives they want to lead. But in the complex modern global economy with its giant corporations, individuals have too little power to control their own lives – they are obliged to comply with what the economy wants of them and frequently batted from pillar to post like balls in a pinball machine.

To enable people to have good lives, we need institutions which, regardless of someone's wealth or educational level, ensure that they are offered opportunities for secure employment, for ongoing education, for leisure time and leisure activities (hobbies, pastimes, sports), and for participation as a citizen. And we want pleasant healthy places to live. What might this mean in practice? It is up to us collectively to decide that, but to illustrate, here are some areas we might consider:

Working life. We spend much of our lives at work. So for a good life we'd like a good work environment, not just a safe one with reasonable pay and hours of work, but one that offers purpose, interest and variety.

> "... factories or workshops, should be pleasant, just as the fields where our most necessary work is done are pleasant. Believe me there is nothing in the world to prevent this being done, save the necessity of making profits on all wares; in other words, the wares are cheapened at the expense of people being forced to work in crowded, unwholesome, squalid, noisy dens: that is to say, they are cheapened at the expense of the workman's life." – *from How We Live and How We Might Live, an 1884 lecture by William Morris.*[5] *[240]*

---

[5]William Morris was a British socialist who was also prominent in the Arts and Crafts movement in the nineteenth century. Other writings include News From Nowhere which describes as a dream, a future socialist and environmental utopia.

Over a century of astonishing technical advances has passed since William Morris wrote the passage above. But the market economy's drive to reduce labour costs remains much as it was in Morris's day, putting businesses under pressure to pay the minimum and demand long working hours in return. As a result, even if work has become less physically demanding, it still often involves unhealthy shift patterns, long periods sitting or standing, lack of exercise, and boring repetitive tasks.

When I started work in the 1970s, the UK was at the tail end of the post-WW2 full-employment boom and trade union membership and influence was high. My first two jobs were in research centres that belonged to large British industrial companies in the private sector. Both were located on extensive sites that included both factories and offices. The facilities and conditions provided for all workers (shop-floor as well as office) now seem almost a dream. They both had:

- Fixed hours, which meant that you had to arrive on time, but also guaranteed that work stopped for the full lunch hour and promptly at the end of the day. *Your evenings and weekends were completely your own: employers and colleagues didn't try to contact you and given the absence of mobile phones and email couldn't easily have done so even had they wanted to.*

- Permanent jobs, pensions, sick pay, paid holidays.

- Staff and shop-floor trades unions, providing effective and independent employee representation.

- Subsidised canteens serving a choice of good quality lunches;

- Formal tea breaks morning and afternoon, during which work stopped and you conversed with your colleagues – and generally not about work. *In one a fleet of tea trolleys distributed free tea across the site during the tea break; in the other we had provision to brew our own plus a snack-bar cafe.*

- First aid rooms permanently staffed by two nurses, who as well as workplace injuries were happy to treat minor ailments unrelated to work, and also ran first aid courses.

I fear some will scoff at this description. They might say: *"tea breaks, trade unions, and no pressure to work in the evenings ... no wonder that the UK economy struggled in the 1970s"*. However, the modern equivalent office with no formal tea breaks and a lunch that is just a sandwich at your desk, is not necessarily more productive. Walk around that modern office as a manager and notice how many computer screens flick from a holiday booking site or some such to a work task as you approach. And that's assuming staff are actually on-site and not 'working from home'. Surreptitious unauthorised time-out from the job does not offer the proper rest that permitted and clearly demarcated breaks for lunch or tea do, nor is it so beneficial in terms of getting to know your colleagues. Nowadays, staff are cajoled instead to connect with each other via team building exercises – often involving activities with cardboard or Lego that can seem more appropriate for a primary school.

Note however that the situation is very different for clerical or manual staff in jobs where their output can readily be monitored. Professional staff may be able to partially compensate for the loss of formal breaks by finding other informal diversions from their work such as surfing the web. But for clerical or manual staff, the computer or mobile device that they use, rather than permitting them brief moments of 'virtual' escape, may well be giving them a stream of instructions, monitoring them closely and measuring their output.

Comparing modern conditions to the past is not to say that we want to go back to that in every detail, but to remind ourselves that alternatives exist. So what more broadly would we like in a better world? At a guess:

- Job security, decent pensions, sick pay, paid holidays.

- Regular hours that don't encroach on home life.

- Opportunities to work in teams and make friends at work.

- Variety – the chance to change career or retrain.

- Decent facilities – canteen, medical, creches – either by provided by the company or shared among several if individual companies are too small.

- A say at work – independent employee representation whether via a trade union or some other form of workplace democracy.

- Flexible work for periods when needed, e.g. due to child care, or needing to work fewer hours in later life.

- Purpose and interest in our work.

Regarding the last of the above points, we cannot always promise purpose and interest at work, but we should try. For many of the artefacts that surround us, the market will for reasons of efficiency and cost, tend to concentrate not only the manufacture but also the design tasks, in only a few locations worldwide, and will automate away as many of the manufacturing skills as possible. To have more satisfying working lives, we may wish choose to resist these trends and give up some efficiency in favour of retaining skills that we value, and maintaining in our localities or country, opportunities to apply ourselves to creative design whether in engineering or artistic fields, even if the work could be done more cheaply elsewhere or by automating it. It is widely observed that the happiest people both in working life and retirement, are those who have interesting and absorbing activities to structure their days around.

The alternative if we automate everything or concentrate it in a few global mega-factories, is that we end up with very few people who know how to make or do anything. If we nevertheless continue to train our young people in specialist skills at school and university, they may find on graduating that they cannot get jobs locally, except for serving fast food or pressing buttons on machines designed on the other side of the world.

An economy that provides good working lives is more compatible with environmental goals than one in which you are overworked and then compensated for that by consumerism. For those worried about productivity, there is good evidence that well treated employees perform better that those that are treated less well or badly.[241]

Ongoing education. To quote William Morris again, writing in 1884:

> "What I claim is liberal education; opportunity, that is, to have my share of whatever knowledge there is in the world according to my capacity or bent of mind, historical or scientific; and also to have my share of skill of hand which is about in the world, either in the industrial handicrafts or in the fine arts; picture-painting, sculpture, music, acting, or the like" – *from How We Live and How We Might Live.*

Working class movements have long valued the opportunity for ongoing adult education both for the joy of knowledge and for vocational reasons. In the UK, the Workers Education Association was founded in 1903. A Labour government founded the Open University in 1969 to provide distance learning for those who otherwise might not have been able to obtain a university education. Many further education colleges provide part-time and evening courses.

However, much of this sector has become less accessible than it was, as government subsidies have been reduced or withdrawn. For good lives we should aim to ensure such opportunities are available to all. They directly aid the social life of the community and they enable citizens to develop new interests, and also if they wish, new skills that allow them to vary their employment.

Participation in governance. We talked earlier in this chapter about how even in developed democratic economies, participation in politics and governance is really quite minimal, amounting for many to just a cross in a box every few years, and some don't bother to vote at all. As we noted, even those who do join a political party, seldom achieve a clear change in government policy. It is all too easy to become cynical, seeing our democratic institutions as made up of distant elites who ignore public opinion. No wonder the UK Brexit slogan "take back control" was so successful, however hollow it turned out to be in practice.

What though does this have to do with good lives? It matters because sociologists have found that feeling that you have control over your life is associated with well-being, and if instead you feel that you are unable to influence events whatever you do, you fall into a psychological state referred to as 'learned helplessness'.[6] In this sort of state people may become apathetic or depressed and withdraw from engaging with society. As well as being bad for the individual some believe it may be one of the reasons that people turn to authoritarian or populist leaders; since such leaders seldom have constructive solutions that is likely to result only in greater misery and frustration.[242]

Pastimes, recreation, sports and hobbies. A sustainable world economy will require the world's rich and its middle classes to consume less in terms of material goods and energy. But many of their/our current pleasures and pastimes are energy-intensive and involve a lot of stuff. This is hardly surprising since as we have seen, the world's existing economic system is dedicated to creating as many wants as possible to enable businesses to sell more stuff. It has become hard to imagine recreation without money – even though most of us know that a small child can often have more fun with a cardboard box than an expensive toy, we still feel obliged to buy the toy ... and unfortunately given advertising and peer-pressure, the child will likely demand that we do.

Throughout history until the industrial age, a holiday was for most people an occasional day off from tilling the land; a day which you would probably spend with family and friends in your home village, or possibly making a trip to a nearby village, town or beauty spot. Not any more: in the world's wealthier countries, a holiday means boarding a plane – often to a destination thousands of miles

---

[6]A concept originally researched by US psychologist Martin Seligman.

away. It is not wrong to enjoy travel, but the current volume of air-travel is unsustainable even at present levels, let alone if emulated by the whole world. However, we can also question the worth of some of the heavily-marketed modern tourism. Is it really essential for our happiness to be able to fly a thousand miles just to go clubbing, hold a stag or hen party, binge on alcohol, or lie on a beach? If that were so then the 80% of the world's population who have never flown must all be miserable, as must have been all generations of humans that ever existed before the invention of aeroplanes.

More time – less stuff. A future sustainable economy could offer us more free time as compensation for having less stuff. Time allows you to properly immerse yourself in your chosen activity, and there are many pastimes that are sustainable, i.e. don't require much stuff: socialising, walking, gardening, singing, painting, most sports and many hobbies and crafts, are examples.

Long-distance mass air-travel is unlikely ever to be sustainable at current world population levels, but once again, plentiful free time can compensate. Given enough time it is perfectly possible to travel substantial distances overland by public transport, staying in campsites or budget hostels if money is tight, or if it isn't, in hotels or aboard comfortable sleeper trains. Even on a bicycle you can go a long way; some cyclists make extraordinary journeys, crossing countries or even continents. Far more modest rides or hikes can still outmatch, in terms of adventure and experience, a package-tour flight to some bland tourist hot-spot.

Walking in the countryside or 'rambling', became a working class recreation during the UK's industrial revolution, allowing an escape from the factories, mines and mills. Rich landowners had enclosed much of the countryside and people fought for access, notably in the 1932 Kinder Scout Trespass when hundreds crossed land owned by the Duke of Devonshire to reach the highest point in the Peak District in Derbyshire. Popular pressure led to legislation that slowly opened up much of the countryside to walkers. English folk singer Ewan MacColl who took part in the trespass, celebrated it in his song The Manchester Rambler. In his autobiography[7] he describes how he and other young working-class men and women, were able to ramble at minimal cost in the 1930s, using cheap but very basic accommodation.

Kinder Scout in the UK Peak District, scene of the 1932 trespass. [WMC]

Figure 28.1: Access to countryside was a working-class cause during the industrial revolution.

Britain's Youth Hostelling Association[8] was also established at the beginning of the 1930s, to give young working people an unprecedented opportunity to spend leisure time in fresh air and open countryside, by providing affordable accommodation in a network of hostels. There are Youth Hostel Associations in approximately 60 countries around the world.

However, domestic holidays have declined in popularity compared with foreign travel. Of course the attraction of long-distance holidays is not only down to marketing. There is the lure of the different and the exotic, plus often better weather. Costs can be surprisingly reasonable because aviation is very competitive, and pays no tax on its fuel – let alone on the cost of the environmental damage it causes. When you add in the factor that the labour costs and the cost of living in the destination countries are often much lower than in the wealthier home countries of the tourists, it can

[7]'Journeyman – An Autobiography'.[243]
[8]The Youth Hostelling Association or YHA, www.yha.org.uk

even mean that a foreign holiday works out cheaper than holidaying at home.

The challenge for a future sustainable economy is not to deny people pleasures but to provide as much as possible of what they like within environmental limits. So future long-distance holidays could be less frequent but for a greater length of stay (as it is the travel that causes most of the emissions, not the stay), and the journey to get there by train or bus rather than by plane (fortunately a slower journey matters less if your stay is for weeks or months instead of just a few days). In between those occasional longer-distance trips, we should make our towns and countries into good places to be rather than places to escape, so that it's a pleasure to take our shorter holidays nearer to home.

What of other pastimes? I have focussed on leisure travel and holidays because travel and particularly plane travel is a major source of carbon emissions which cannot be eliminated except by not travelling. For many other pastimes it is far easier to imagine low-carbon, low-impact ways of pursuing them. If we tax or preferably ration carbon emissions, the market will adjust.

We also live in the age of computers and AI. People may choose to pass their leisure time in virtual computer-generated worlds ... or for that matter just watching TV. Provided that we can manage to manufacture the electronic devices and power them in a low carbon way, that may be sustainable – although currently server farms are consuming quite a lot of power. What the physical and social effects may be on humans of passing our time in this way is another debate.

The task of finding and creating pleasures in life that don't involve excess consumption and environmental damage, may not be as difficult as we might think, since the evidence is that the cornucopia of consumer products marketed at us and particularly at the better off, doesn't really bring much happiness. The book "Paradox of Choice – Why More is Less" by Barry Schwartz, explores how too much choice can overwhelm us. Most of us understand this from our own experience.[244] If you visit a shop and find two or three types of shampoo, you have the time to read the labels and prices and make some sort of choice. But if there are 40 different types, you cannot be expected to read and absorb all the labels, or even work out the price differences given that bottle sizes vary. So you semi-randomly choose something that you hope will do and emerge from the shop doubting whether your choice was a good one. The phenomena of excess choice was very noticeable in the UK when the state-run utilities were privatised. Suddenly we had multiple gas, electricity and phone companies, each offering a plethora of continually changing 'customer plans' constructed in ways that made them hard to compare. What had previously been simple became bewildering: should you waste chunks of your life on the tedium of regularly comparing them, and now and then switch supplier to try to get the best value, or just stay with whichever you had ended up with? If you did the latter you had the uncomfortable feeling that perhaps you were getting a bad deal – which was very possibly true, as to attract new customers, companies offered better deals to those who switched than to their loyal customers.

Here is William Morris again, writing over 140 years ago on 'the waste of useless luxury' and the free time we would gain if we used labour-saving machines on actually saving labour instead of producing more stuff:

> "At present you must note that all the amazing machinery which we have invented has served only to increase the amount of profit-bearing wares; in other words, to increase the amount of profit pouched by individuals for their own advantage, part of which profit they use as capital for the production of more profit, with ever the same waste attached to it; and part as private riches or means for luxurious living, which again is sheer waste – is in fact to be looked on as a kind of bonfire on which rich men burn up the product of the labour they have fleeced from the workers beyond what they themselves can use."

> "So I say that, in spite of our inventions, no worker works under the present system an hour the less on account of those labour-saving machines, so-called. But under a happier state of things they would be used simply for saving

labour, with the result of a vast amount of leisure gained for the community to be added to that gained by the avoidance of the waste of useless luxury, and the abolition of the service of commercial war." – *from How We Live and How We Might Live.*

How much leisure might we gain if we moderated our consumption of stuff? The book Ecology as Politics written in the 1970s contains an estimate that the typical US citizen spent 1500 hours a year between working to pay for their car and driving it.[245] This works out to an hour for each three and a half miles travelled – approximately walking speed. People without cars in non-industrialised countries, travelled just as fast, but didn't travel as much, and therefore used up less of their time travelling. Cars have resulted in urban sprawl and enabled and encouraged people to accept long commutes to work; they've even created a new reason to travel ... to escape cities congested and polluted by traffic.

In 2006, I researched and carried out a similar calculation. It showed that the average UK household spent about 1 day a week or 20% of its income paying for each vehicle owned. Also, that cars had indeed encouraged more commuting – the average journey to secondary school for example had gone up by over 30% in a decade. I also did some back-of-an-envelope sums on what we could buy with the astonishing £130 billion a year that the UK was then spending on motoring, had we spent it on something else instead. Just £30 billion would have bought enough wind turbines to generate a quantity of electricity equal to that used by all UK homes – the unwanted car factories could have manufactured them. That still left another £100 billion to spend in the first year! The following year there'd have been a further £130 billion to spend – in fact, even more because spending on gas and coal for power stations would have gone down thanks to the wind turbines, and our health system would have been cheaper because there would have been fewer road accidents. Furthermore, none of these calculations took into account the appalling looming disaster of climate change, brought on in no small part by the emissions generated in the manufacture and use of private cars.

Cars are not the only products or services that could fall into Morris's category of 'useless luxuries'. The Covid pandemic and resulting lockdowns revealed that huge numbers of people could stay at home, many not working at all, and yet amazingly the essentials of life continued: food was grown and delivered, electricity, gas and water supplied, rubbish collected. The lesson seems to be that many jobs are not all that necessary – which isn't really surprising given that so much of our economy is devoted to persuading people to want things that never previously existed. Of course, we do want some luxuries, even some fairly useless ones, but our economy doesn't offer us the choice of trading them off for leisure – unless you choose to count unemployment as leisure.

Eating well.   We started this book with food at the top of the list of the primary needs of all animals. It is remarkable that wealthy modern societies – I'm particularly thinking of the UK and US – have managed to create a situation where the diet of many citizens is so poor and unhealthy. The prime reasons for this state of affairs are:

- A food industry motivated by profit that markets highly processed food, exploiting our human weakness for sweet and fatty foods.

- Governments that cost-cut the catering in state institutions such as schools, prisons and even hospitals, by minimising on-site kitchen staff and serving factory-made processed food instead of freshly cooked.

- Fewer works canteens due to fewer large workplaces, plus weaker trade unions, less able to press for such facilities.

- A decline in home-cooking and family mealtimes, for which there are probably various causes, though one is likely to be the pressure for both parents to work full time.

Good food eaten in a convivial atmosphere is one of life's pleasures. A healthy diet and sociable meals also have valuable physical, psychological and social effects. In our hearts we all know this – everyone loves the images so often used in advertising, of extended Italian families sitting around a table of home-cooked food. However, we don't need to rely only on our hearts: multiple studies show marked improvements in physical and mental health when diets are improved. For example, improvements to prison food are reported to cut inmate violence, and children who eat more fruit and vegetables are found to have better mental as well as physical health.[246, 247]

Some countries do retain a stronger tradition of good food. Spanish state schools for example, make the school lunch menus available to parents so that they can see what their children have eaten, often accompanied with nutrition advice for what parents might give their children in the evenings to complement each day's lunch. Michael Moore's 2015 American documentary film 'Where to Invade Next', hilariously compares the quality of lunches served in a French state primary school, prepared by the on-site chef and served on china plates, to the poor fare dished up to US children on plastic trays. Notably in world rankings of obesity, the US has far higher levels than France.[9]

So one of the good things we want is good food, and the time and place to eat it. Wherever the state has a responsibility – whether in schools, universities, hospitals, prisons – it should ensure good canteen facilities are provided. Similarly, large employers should be encouraged or required to provide canteens. Public canteens should be available for those in smaller workplaces that cannot provide their own.

Living well – housing and public spaces. Our home plus its immediate surroundings, is where we spend most of our lives. For a good life we want it to be more than just functional. It should be unpolluted, have clean air and minimal noise pollution. It should have green spaces and attractive architecture. The design

---

[9]There are various rankings, usually similar though not always identical. At the time of writing, one placed the US 14th from the top (most obese), the UK 29th and France 67th.[248]

and layout of buildings should be conducive to community life and conducive to exercise and active travel. It should be easy to make local journeys to work, schools, shops, and medical facilities, by foot, bicycle or public transport. It should be safe for both children and the elderly.

Port Sunlight
Founded by a Victorian industrialist to house his soap factory's workers. Still treasured over 120 years later.

High-rise flats in London built early 2020s
Few tower blocks are loved, and many are demolished within 50 years or less.

Figure 28.2: Shall we build beautiful places to live, or human warehouses? [WMC, Auth]

The European aristocracy of the past understood these criteria and typically possessed a fine town house facing onto a square or boulevard, plus a house in the country surrounded by gardens. Not everyone can live like that but the garden cities movement in the UK attempted to create green and beautiful suburbs for working people – Port Sunlight[10] (pictured) near Liverpool is an example. Sadly even in wealthy countries, the ambition of governments and planners to create quality housing seems to have faded, and soulless dormitories of high-rise flats with little or no green space are spreading across many of our cities, all too reminiscent of how we house factory-farmed animals. Many are expected to live by congested, polluted and noisy roads.

---

[10]Port Sunlight is a garden village built near Liverpool between 1899 and 1914 to house the workers of Lever Brothers, a soap manufacturer. It was influenced by the ideas of William Morris and the Arts and Crafts Movement.

16ᵗʰ Century Student Accommodation   **21ˢᵗ Century Student Accommodation**
Where would you prefer to study, and which will still be here in 100 years time?

Figure 28.3: Student Accommodation. [WMC, Auth]

Ironically, one of the reasons for travel and long-flights to 'less-developed' or 'unspoilt' countries is frequently the desire to escape the noisy congested, polluted and often ugly towns and cities back home. Huge volumes of traffic and the roads and parking to accommodate them have desecrated our towns, and out-of-scale characterless blocks blot the urban landscape.

Figure 28.4: Houses blighted by traffic and tower-block 'developments'.

We know that a good environment and green spaces are beneficial mentally and physically. So we want a good place to live for everybody, not just for the rich. To quote William Morris once more:

"I have spoken of machinery being used freely for releasing people from the more mechanical and repulsive part of necessary labour; it is the allowing of machines to be our masters and not our servants that so injures the beauty of life nowadays. And, again, that leads me to my last claim, which is that the material surroundings of my life should be pleasant, generous, and beautiful; that I know is a large claim, but this I will say about it, that if it cannot be satisfied, if every civilised community cannot provide such surroundings for all its members, I do not want the world to go on." – *from How We Live and How We Might Live.*

There are numerous contemporary reports that stress the value of high quality public and green spaces, free of toxic road noise, and how they improve our mental health and our memory, reduce depression, lower blood pressure, and even boost children's academic performance.[249, 250, 251, 252] It seems they fall on deaf ears.

28.7 Summary

Our economy's drive for continual consumption growth is damaging the environment so severely that our existence is threatened. This chapter explored the politics of how we might convince people to accept and work for a change to our economic system. For many people it's hard to prioritise a long-term environmental crisis over day-to-day struggles to earn a living. For the rich the measures needed are seen as a threat to their wealth and high-consumption lifestyle. But it is unreasonable to expect poorer countries and people to accept the need to moderate consumption, unless the whole world agrees to converge on a sustainable target level of consumption. That implies a reduction for the world's middle classes as well as the rich.

We looked at measures that might help gain the necessary public support: Education, Participation, Co-Benefits and Vision.

Education. A solid understanding of basic ecology and the implications of living on a finite planet, enables people to appreciate the urgency of taking action, and to resist the misinformation generated by advertising, media & think-tanks funded by vested interests, and conspiracy theories.

Participation. People are more likely to try to bring about change if they feel involved and participate in society not just as 'workers' and'consumers', but also as 'citizens'. Traditional participation via political parties alone is unsatisfactory; newer ideas like citizens' assemblies which allow proper engagement and discussion with expert input appear to have more potential. Devolving powers to local areas may help promote citizen involvement, but we must also strengthen regional and global institutions like the United Nations because many economic and environmental issues as well as a plethora of potentially dangerous new technologies, require regulation at a global level. Campaigning should focus mainly on getting government action as individual actions seldom have as much impact – although they may help give a sense of purpose to campaign groups.

Co-Benefits. Many of the measures needed to tackle environmental issues bring other associated benefits or 'co-benefits', such as clean air, better health, and jobs in new green industries. A policy's co-benefits are likely to be more local, immediate and visible than its effect on climate change, and can therefore help win it public support. However, many co-benefits, although real and measurable, may still not be very visible: a modest drop in air pollution won't be much noticed by the public, while drivers however will straight away notice any restrictions on car use that produced it. So where possible, policies should be designed to produce co-benefits that are very tangible, and a gain for individuals who back the policy substantially greater than any loss. We cannot guarantee that all environmental measures will have positive associated effects: some may negatively affect businesses or individuals particularly in economic terms, and we will need economic policies to mitigate that and ensure that the poorest are protected.

Vision. For the longer term we need to picture a better future to work towards, and outline an attractive sustainable lifestyle that doesn't require excessive consumption. From ancient times to modern and across the world, there is a fair degree of consensus on the conditions that make for a good human life, which is at least partly enshrined in the United Nations Universal Declaration of Human Rights. Yet our economic system does not pursue those conditions as a goal, but instead contains an inbuilt drive to maximise consumption and promote any product or service however harmful, provided that money can be made out of it. Through regulation and other means, we need to limit or remove those harms – 'the bad stuff' – and direct the economy instead to producing a world we want to live in – 'the good stuff'. Bad stuff includes poor health, malicious information, damage to the environment, excessive inequality. Good stuff includes a satisfying working life, ongoing education, participation in governing ourselves, ready access to pastimes, sports and hobbies, greater free-time, eating well, and good and beautiful housing and public spaces.

This has been a difficult chapter to write because it is not economic theory but an opinion about how we might push for changes to our economic system and what sorts of goals we might aim for. I've tried to provide evidence for what goals are most likely to be good for human well-being, but inevitably the chapter also reflects my personal opinions. So there is lots to debate. ***But the important thing is that we take charge of the economy and direct it to achieve the aims we collectively manage to agree on.*** The alternative is to leave the economy as a *directionless unregulated free-for-all*, which probably leads at best to some sort of dystopian nightmare – some places in the world probably feel that they've already got there – and at worst to catastrophe.

Chapter 29

Stop the World – Let Me Off

The rapid growth of scientific knowledge and of the technology it makes possible, means that our world is undergoing continuous change. For those of us who have reached at least middle age, the world that we currently live in is very different from the one we were born into; for the old it can be almost unrecognisable. What is to come is likely to be even more dramatic.

Already machines have replaced most of human muscle. Now robotics and artificial intelligence are replacing human dexterity and intelligence for an increasing number of tasks. One constant throughout human history has been that we cannot change the bodies that we are born with; however rich or privileged you may be, you cannot guarantee that your children will be strong or healthy or musical or intelligent or handsome. It is an equality of sorts: it's just as likely that the son of the farm labourer be quick-witted and the son of the Lord of the Manor a dullard, as the reverse. But now we're entering a world where it will be possible to modify the human body and potentially enhance it with powers that humans never had before. This opens up a whole new field of inequalities where the wealthy may be able to purchase characteristics that make them or their offspring into different beings.

One understandable reaction to such unsettling rates of change, might be to plead: *"Stop the world I want to get off!".*

29.1 The Curse of Knowledge

If you want humans to continue to exist for many more thousands of years, it could be perfectly rational to try to stop or reverse our headlong technological development. Some scientists speculate that the reason we do not see evidence of other intelligent life in space is that those beings that develop advanced technology end up destroying themselves in conflicts or environmental meltdown. We humans are already well on the way to doing so: we have weapons of mass destruction such as nuclear, chemical and biological weapons, and on top of that we are destroying the environment we depend on through pollution and climate change.

The most effective way to prevent the development of dangerous technologies would be to edit our genes to remove the ability of abstract thought that separates us from the other primates, reverting ourselves to an earlier stage of evolution – for example to our common ancestor with chimpanzees.[1] After all, life has existed on Earth for billions of years and primates have existed for many millions, so there is no reason why, if we return to being just another primate in the forest, we shouldn't have millions of years ahead of us, just as long as there isn't an unlucky asteroid strike. However, even if it were technically possible to wind back the brains of all humans on Earth to be like those of our furry ancestors, it's hardly likely to be a vote winner ... unless of course the other animals got a vote as well, in which case all bets are off!

The biblical story of Adam and Eve cast out from the Garden of Eden forever, after eating the apple from the tree of knowledge, illustrates our predicament beautifully. We cannot undo what we have learnt, and we are doomed to live with the consequences.

29.2 Just Slow Down?

If we cannot go backwards, could we at least choose to limit technological development to a pace that meant that change over one

---

[1] That would be to as we were, roughly 6 million years ago.

Figure 29.1: Eating from the tree of knowledge. [WMC]

lifetime was only gradual? It does not seem likely as to do so would require policing many thousands of scientific institutions and technology companies across the globe to limit what they do. It would need either an agreement between all major countries or a world government, because no country would want to hold back its technological capabilities while other countries continued to advance theirs. You would also need the majority of the world's citizens to back such a policy, which is unlikely because new technologies are always sold by their most desirable and promising characteristics, not by the problems that they might bring. For example, while writing this I heard about research into the development of artificial wombs that could allow pregnancy to be eliminated: babies would develop entirely within artificial wombs in some sort of laboratory, with if necessary recordings of a mother's heartbeat to comfort them. To many this may seem a horrifying dystopian future, although perhaps a few will find it attractive. But that isn't the point. Such technology will initially be sold not on the basis of eliminating pregnancy but as a way to save very premature babies, and for that there will be considerable support and far less opposition.

All this means that we live in astonishing times. If you transported some Romans from the Year 0 AD to the Year 1000 AD they would find most of the technology in use still familiar. Bring them to the year 2000 and they would be amazed, but after they got over the initial shock, probably able to adapt and find their way around. But for us the world of 1000 years hence is unimaginable, unless we just suppose the worst: that it will be a smoking ruin with a few cockroaches scurrying around. Even trying to think 100 or 200 years hence is extraordinarily challenging.

29.3   Doing Our Best: Regulate and Set a Direction

Faced with such an unknowable future the only thing we can do is to try to do our best. What would that best look like? We know that we are faced with a stream of new technologies, some of which are disturbing like artificial wombs, some of which will have unintended consequences, like the cyberbullying associated with smartphones, and some of which are highly dangerous, like nuclear weapons or experiments with deadly viruses. We also know that in a market economy there is an incentive to develop and sell any product for which there are buyers, regardless of whether it is beneficial or harmful to society or to the planet.

To tackle such problems we must work for stronger world governance, whether that be an actual world government or strong international institutions to which all countries belong. We should expect our governments to negotiate with all other countries to regulate globally where possible, even if there are fierce disagreements over other matters, rather than maintaining a shifting list of friends and enemies based on the latest Realpolitik and commercial interests, and refusing to talk to countries currently assigned to the 'enemy' camp.[2] We shall also have to work for greater equity – a

---

[2]The cynical strategy 'my enemy's enemy is my friend' regularly leads to disaster. Chapter 'Us and them' in Francis Wheen's 'How Mumbo Jumbo Conquered the World' describes some of Realpolitik's post-WW2 failures.[253]

fairer sharing out of the world's resources – because nations and peoples will not accept world governance if it sets in stone gross inequalities between rich and poor countries.

In terms of the economy, as more and more becomes technically possible we will need more and more regulation. Current regulation tends to be aimed at avoiding specific harms: a foodstuff must not contain carcinogens; an electronic device must not catch fire or electrocute its user. This still puts us at the mercy of the flood of new products launched onto the public without any consideration of whether they are beneficial. In the future, regulators could require that new products demonstrate some genuine benefit. Governments could lay out criteria for products that were wanted, for example: foodstuffs that are of clear benefit in terms of health and nutrition; products that contribute to energy-saving and thus assist in tackling climate change. It would require experimentation to find the best framework. The rules could perhaps be looser for small-scale businesses provided that they use sustainable materials and processes, since they are less likely than large corporations to mass-market products or be able to manufacture a new category of mass-consumer product.

The aim would be for citizens to be able to set a direction for what the economy should do, rather than as present, just leaving which products and services are provided to the anarchy of the market and individual choice. For people to support this process requires something more than just parliamentary democracy and a vote every four to five years, which is why we should consider other possibilities such as for example, workplace democracy with employee representation, more local democracy, and citizens' assemblies in which people actively participate in developing policy with access to expert opinion.

29.4   A Shared Set of Values

However participatory we are able to make governance, global regulation will not be successful if imposed on a largely reluctant and resentful public. We need a global shared set of values so that people understand and support the purpose and benefits of regulation. To create and propagate a set of values may seem an ambitious undertaking. Yet major religions have done this for centuries. Across mediaeval Europe every village had a church at its centre where at least weekly the priest reminded the population of the behaviour expected of them.

Figure 29.2: A global set of values: the United Nations Universal Declaration of Human Rights

To promote the new values needed today, should we try to modify existing religions or create a new one? Almost certainly 'no', in both cases. The adherents of existing religions generally believe that their faith's rules are God's rules and therefore not subject to change by humans, let alone by outsiders. Creating a completely new religion would merely create more division in the world. It would be better therefore, through the work of organisations like the United Nations, to promote a set of human values that can be shared among people of any religion or none. Perhaps the major world religions could then agree to propagate those values or at least a subset of them, creating an understanding that there are some things that all humans sign up to, whatever their faith.

Developing shared values is no small undertaking, but what alternative do we have if we want to unite to control our world economy? For an exploration of morality that might help with the task, the book The Righteous Mind is fascinating.[254] The world is beset with divisions and wars, but the way out of conflict is finding common ground on a subject that matters to all, and there could hardly be a better one that protecting the environment of the planet we all depend on. The people we perceive as nuclear-armed enemies clearly do want to preserve the planet as much as we do, otherwise 'nuclear deterrence' would not work and we'd all be long-dead.

29.5 An Economy that Serves Humanity, Not One Served By It

Once we accept the idea of citizens collectively setting a direction for the economy, we can view the free market as a valuable tool but not an end in itself. We can set about designing an economy that offers a livelihood to all and avoids damage to people or to the planet's ecosystems. We can try to keep as much de-centralisation and freedom of enterprise as is compatible with these aims. One country at least, Bhutan, already has a 'Gross National Happiness' (GNH) index alongside the more familiar Gross Domestic Product (GDP) measure of economic performance.

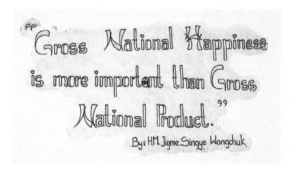

Figure 29.3: Bhutan's Gross National Happiness index. [WMC]

From time to time, governments of capitalist countries do seize control to direct the economy in the face of a threat. The US and UK governments did so during World War II, and not just to provide armaments but also to ensure that their civilians were fed and as far as possible protected. They did so again in the Cold War years when particularly in the US, vast sums were directed into weapons and space technologies in the face of the perceived threat from the USSR. More recently governments acted with unprecedented spending in the face of the covid pandemic.

Figure 29.4: In a crisis, governments need to seize control. [OGL]

In all of these examples, they did not destroy or eliminate their private sector but gave it direction, business being very willing to take the funding. But when the threats recede, these same governments go back to the minimum: they let the market mostly set the direction and regard the government's task as just putting a floor below which people don't fall – a floor that may be wretchedly low, such as food stamps or a miserable level of social security. We should not accept such limited ambition. Governments should be continuously engaged in directing the economy to provide a good and healthy life to their citizens, full of opportunities and interest and in beautiful surroundings.

Why cannot governments direct the economy in this way? We will probably be told that it is because the spending they undertake to counter external threats like Covid, saddles government with debts which are a burden on future citizens. Yet those debts are not a burden for **all** future citizens because governments borrow the money from the world's rich, for whom it's a future **credit**. There is a simple solution: don't borrow the money from the rich, tax them instead. An obstacle to doing so is that those in government are quite often very rich themselves ... or fairly rich with very rich friends; it's highly likely that some of them are among those who lend government money at interest and don't wish it to be taken instead as tax. Nevertheless, such a policy is not necessarily being hard on the world's wealthy. It's an axiom that wealth beyond a certain level does not bring greater happiness – some of the world's billionaires choose to give most of their fortunes away, and countries with high levels of taxation are among the world's happiest.

29.6 To Conclude

The ideas for a change of direction laid out in Part 2 of this book, may seem idealistic – and indeed they are. They should however be viewed as an **aim** – not a prediction or detailed policy. They outline the sorts of things we need to face up to if we don't want our lives and our planet to be wrecked by the unconstrained and anarchic market forces, whose logic was the subject of Part 1. They are also a suggestion that a very much better world – for humans and the other life we share the Earth with – might be possible if we are willing to work for it and work together.

The future is clearly going to be a bumpy ride. To devise policies to make it less chaotic and more agreeable, we shall need to be realistic about how our economy **actually works** and pragmatic in finding ways to control and direct it.

I hope that the analysis and observations in Part 1 of this book will help in that endeavour, and that they have made it very clear that *the idea that public services and environmental protection must be financed by growing consumption, is both mistaken and counter-productive* – being tantamount to financing public-health measures through mass sales of tobacco, alcohol and hard-drugs. I hope also that they help avoid economic theories that are more belief systems than observation, with Marxists on one side tied to a 19th century prediction of a future socialist paradise, and on the other, right-wing economists attached to the Panglossian[3] belief that a totally free market is the 'best of all possible worlds'.

---

[3]In Voltaire's satirical novel Candide, the character Dr. Pangloss teaches his pupils that they live in the 'best of all possible worlds' and that 'all is for the best', despite the reality of terrible events around them.

End Notes

Summary of the Book's Main Argument

Our current market economy can only provide such employment as it does and counteract the loss of jobs to automation, by producing an ever-growing volume of 'stuff' and persuading the better-off to want it. This continual growth in consumption combined with overpopulation is destroying the environment we depend on.

Even at this unsustainable level of consumption growth, the economy still fails to provide much of humanity with a secure livelihood, leaving them in want of life's basics; there is no 'natural full-employment equilibrium' to which the economy tends.

Furthermore, since money can be made more easily out of addiction and dependence than out of restraint and self-sufficiency, much of the consumption growth consists of products with limited benefits or that are actively harmful to health, well-being and community life.

The solution has to lie in government regulation from the local level to the international, with the environment and fairness as the major goals, and preferably with the best democratic and pluralist checks and balances that we can elaborate, and citizen participation in setting society's direction. Only by taking control of the market can we ensure that instead of it dictating to us, it serves us.

Further Reading

Our shared ancestry with the rest of life on Earth

- The Ancestor's Tale: A Pilgrimage to the Dawn of Life.[255]

Growth, Limits to Growth and Economics

- Limits to Growth The 30-Year Update.[3]

- Prosperity Without Growth.[256]

- Small is Beautiful.[1]

- Guns, Germs and Steel.[11]

- Collapse: How Societies Choose to Fail or Survive.[148]

- The Economics of Feasible Socialism.[65]

- For mainstream macroeconomics, there are numerous undergraduate university text books.

Advertising

- The Hidden Persuaders.[39]

- Badvertising website.[235]

Energy and De-carbonising

- Zero Carbon Britain.[181]

- Nuclear Power.[84]

- Voodoo Economics and the Doomed Nuclear Renaissance.[71]

- Reports from: The International Renewable Energy Agency (IRENA).[257]

Climate Crisis

- Reports from: The Intergovernmental Panel on Climate Change (IPCC), the United Nations body for assessing the science related to climate change.[258]

- The Climate Book, created by Greta Thunberg.[259]

- NASA: Global Climate Change - Vital Signs of the Planet.[260]

Inequality, alternative economic goals

- The Spirit Level: Why Equality is Better for Everyone.[237]

- Treasure Islands: Tax Havens and the Men who Stole the World.[105]

Well-being, Happiness

- Happiness: The Science Behind Your Smile.[229]

Reaching Agreement and Shared Values

- The Righteous Mind: Why Good People are Divided by Politics and Religion.[254]

Bibliography

[1] E. F. Schumacher, *Small is Beautiful.* Blond and Briggs Ltd, 1973.

[2] P. R. Ehrlich and A. H. Ehrlich, *Population Resources Environment.* San Francisco: W. H. Freeman and Company, 1970.

[3] D. Meadows, D. Meadows, J. Randers, and W. Behrens, *The Limits to Growth.* Potomac Associates, 1972. Updated in 2004 as 'Limits to Growth The 30-Year Update', Chelsea Green Publishing.

[4] A. Guterres, "Secretary-General's Address to the General Assembly." https://www.un.org/sg/en/content/sg/statement/2021-09-21/secretary-general%E2%80%99s-address-the-general-assembly, September 2021.

[5] K. Marx and F. Engels, *Communist Manifesto.* Communist League, 1848.

[6] K. Marx, "Critique of the Gotha Programme," 1875.

[7] E. A. Shrider, M. Kollar, F. Chen, and J. Semega, "Income and Poverty in the United States: 2020," Tech. Rep. P60-273, The United States Census Bureau, September 2021.

[8] "Nearly Half the World Lives on Less than $5.50 a Day." The World Bank press release https://www.worldbank.org/en/news/press-release/2018/10/17/nearly-half-the-world-lives-on-less-than-550-a-day, 2018.

[9] "Employment in the UK: December 2021." Office for National Statistics, UK, https://www.ons.gov.uk/employmentandlabourmarket/peopleinwork/employmentandemployeetypes/bulletins/employmentintheuk/december2021, December 2021.

[10] D. Hardoon, "An Economy for the 99%: It's time to build a human economy that benefits everyone, not just the privileged few," tech. rep., Oxfam, January 2017.

[11] J. Diamond, *Guns, Germs and Steel.* W. W. Norton, 1997.

[12] A. Smith, *The Wealth Of Nations.* Available from Project Gutenberg, 1776.

[13] "About The Adam Smith Institute website." https://www.adamsmith.or g/about-the-asi, 2023.

[14] C. Giattino, E. Ortiz-Ospina, and M. Roser, "Working Hours," *Our World in Data*, 2020. Working hours: https://ourworldindata.org/working-hou rs, Annual working hours vs. GDP per capita: https://ourworldindata.o rg/grapher/weekly-work-hours-vs-gdp-per-capita.

[15] "Earnings and hours worked, occupation by four-digit SOC: ASHE Table 14: 2022." Office for National Statistics https://www.ons.gov.uk/emplo ymentandlabourmarket/peopleinwork/earningsandworkinghours/datase ts/occupation4digitsoc2010ashetable14, October 2022.

[16] M. Sainato, "This used to be a great job," *The Guardian*, 2021.

[17] D. Nicks, "How Trucking Went From One of the Best Jobs in America to One of the Worst," *The Guardian*, 2016.

[18] TruePrice and Fairtrade, "Assessment of Fairtrade Coffee Farmers' in- come," tech. rep., Fairtrade, 2017.

[19] P. Stewart, "The Coffee Price Crisis: How to Support More Sustainable Livelihoods for Farmers," *Business Fights Poverty*, October 2019.

[20] Charts based on data from: Coffee Production historical,1990 onwards - International Coffee Organization, www.ico.org; Coffee Prices - 45 Year Historical Chart, www.macrotrends.net, then adjusted to 2020 dollars via CPI Inflation Calculator, U.S. Bureau of Labor Statistics www.bls.gov.

[21] E. Ortiz-Ospina, D. Beltekian, and M. Roser, "Trade and Globalization," *Our World in Data*, 2018. https://ourworldindata.org/trade-and-globali zation.

[22] "Exports of goods and services (% of GDP)," 2022. World Bank https: //data.worldbank.org/indicator/NE.EXP.GNFS.ZS.

[23] DataBank, "The Labour Share in G20 Economies," tech. rep., Interna- tional Labour Organization, Organisation for Economic Co-operation and Development, 2015.

[24] M. Guerriero, "The Labor Share of Income Around the World: Evidence from a Panel Dataset.," tech. rep., Tokyo: Asian Development Bank In- stitute, 2019.

[25] J. Denman and P. McDonald, "Unemployment statistics from 1881 to the present day." UK Central Statistical Office, http://www.ons.gov.uk/ons /rel/lms/labour-market-trends--discontinued-/january-1996/unemploy ment-since-1881.pdf, 1996.

[26] "UK Office for National Statistics (ONS)." https://www.ons.gov.uk.

[27] A. Gregory and N. Bartlett, "'Vasectomies are free': Tory party's new vice chair urged jobless to stop having kids or UK would 'drown in wasters'," *The Daily Mirror, on-line*, January 2018.

[28] N. Britten, "Britain has produced unteachable 'uber-chavs'," *The Telegraph, on-line*, February 2009.

[29] Y. Zayed and P. Loft, "Briefing Paper: Agriculture: historical statistics," tech. rep., House of Commons Library, Briefing Paper, June 2019.

[30] "Anthropocene." National Geographic, https://www.nationalgeographic.org/encyclopedia/anthropocene/.

[31] Y. M. Bar-On, R. Phillips, and R. Milo, "The biomass distribution on Earth," in *Proceedings of the National Academy of Sciences of the United States of America*, pp. 473–480, May 2018.

[32] M. Roser, "Mortality in the past: every second child died," *Our World in Data*, 2023. https://ourworldindata.org/child-mortality-in-the-past.

[33] G. Phelps and S. Crabtree, "Worldwide, Median Household Income About $10,000," *Gallup*, December 2013. "The median per-capita income is $2,920".

[34] R. Kochhar, "Are you in the global middle class? Find out with our income calculator.," *Pew Research Center*, July 2021.

[35] A. Tanzi and M. Dorning, "Top 1% of U.S. Earners Now Hold More Wealth Than All of the Middle Class.," *Bloomberg*, October 2021.

[36] L. Elliott, "World's 26 richest people own as much as poorest 50%, says Oxfam," *The Guardian*, Jan 2019.

[37] "40 Jobs in the Middle Ages." Medievalists.net https://www.medievalists.net/2023/05/40-jobs-middle-ages/.

[38] "A Look at Coca-Cola's Advertising Expenses." Investopedia, https://www.investopedia.com/articles/markets/081315/look-cocacolas-advertising-expenses.asp, February 2023.

[39] V. Packard, *The Hidden Persuaders*. Penguin Books, 1957.

[40] "Global Witness reports 227 land and environmental activists murdered in a single year, the worst figure on record." Global Witness https://www.globalwitness.org/en/press-releases/global-witness-reports-227-land-and-environmental-activists-murdered-single-year-worst-figure-record, September 2021.

[41] J. Haidt, *The Anxious Generation*. Penguin Press, March 2024.

[42] "What Bhutan got right about happiness - and what other countries can learn." World Economic Forum https://www.weforum.org/agenda/202 1/10/lessons-from-bhutan-economic-development, October 2021.

[43] Transcript of 2004 interview with economist Milton Friedman, on Fox News. https://www.foxnews.com/story/your-world-interview-with-eco nomist-milton-friedman.

[44] Quoted by the think tank, The Free Market Foundation (Southern Africa) www.freemarketfoundation.com/quotes.asp.

[45] "The National Institute for Health and Care Excellence." NICE https: //www.nice.org.uk/.

[46] P. Bolton, "Education spending in the UK," tech. rep., House of Commons Library, November 2021.

[47] D. C. Black, "Review of drugs." Home Office https://www.gov.uk/gover nment/publications/review-of-drugs-phase-one-report/review-of-drugs -summary, September 2020.

[48] "Consumer spending on tobacco in the United Kingdom." Statista, https: //www.statista.com/statistics/289980/expenditure-on-tobacco-in-the-u nited-kingdom-uk/.

[49] "The economics of tobacco." Ash, https://ash.org.uk/resources/view/th e-economics-of-tobacco.

[50] "Statistics on Alcohol, England, 2018." NHS, https://digital.nhs.uk/dat a-and-information/publications/statistical/statistics-on-alcohol/2018/ part-7.

[51] "Gambling: How much do we spend in the UK?." BBC, 21 September 2019, https://www.bbc.co.uk/news/uk-49731701.

[52] "GROSS DOMESTIC PHILANTHROPY: An international analysis of GDP, tax and giving." CAF Charities Aid Foundation https://www.cafo nline.org/docs/default-source/about-us-policy-and-campaigns/gross-d omestic-philanthropy-feb-2016.pdf, January 2016.

[53] R. Booth, "Britain's top earners giving less to charity while incomes rise," *The Guardian*, Dec 2021.

[54] "Families and households in the UK: 2020." Office for National Statistics https://www.ons.gov.uk/peoplepopulationandcommunity/birthsdeat hsandmarriages/families/bulletins/familiesandhouseholds/2020, March 2021.

[55] Wikipedia contributors, "Tragedy of the commons — Wikipedia, the free encyclopedia." https://en.wikipedia.org/w/index.php?title=Tragedy _of_the_commons&oldid=1173666422, 2023. [Online; accessed 4-September-2023].

[56] "Reported road casualties Great Britain, annual report: 2022." UK National Statistics https://www.gov.uk/government/statistics/reported-road-casualties-great-britain-annual-report-2022/reported-road-casualties-great-britain-annual-report-2022, September 2023.

[57] "Road traffic injuries." World Health Organisation https://www.who.int/news-room/fact-sheets/detail/road-traffic-injuries, December 2023.

[58] "Global Road Safety Statistics." UK National Statistics https://www.brake.org.uk.

[59] M. Keep, "Road cycling: statistics." House of Commons Library, Research Briefing https://researchbriefings.files.parliament.uk/documents/SN06224/SN06224.pdf, June 2013. See also: Department for Transport, Road traffic statistics, 2022 https://roadtraffic.dft.gov.uk/summary.

[60] Wikipedia contributors, "Race to the bottom — Wikipedia, the free encyclopedia." https://en.wikipedia.org/w/index.php?title=Race_to_the_bottom&oldid=1162861283, 2023. [Online; accessed 4-September-2023].

[61] Wikipedia contributors, "Paul samuelson — Wikipedia, the free encyclopedia." https://en.wikipedia.org/w/index.php?title=Paul_Samuelson&oldid=1172455961, 2023. [Online; accessed 4-September-2023].

[62] Wikipedia contributors, "Comparative advantage — Wikipedia, the free encyclopedia." https://en.wikipedia.org/w/index.php?title=Comparative_advantage&oldid=1144677283, 2023. [Online; accessed 4-September-2023].

[63] J. Lopez, "The Pros and Cons of Importing a Car into Costa Rica," *The Costa Rica Star*, February 2012. "Taxes for importing vehicles into Costa Rica are 52.29% for models that rolled out of the assembly line in the last three years.".

[64] L. Trotsky, *The Soviet Economy in Danger*. Pamphlet Pioneer Publishers, 1932.

[65] A. Nove, *The Economics of Feasible Socialism*. George Allen & Unwin, 1983.

[66] "Meeting the Energy Challenge, A White Paper on Nuclear Power." UK Department for Business, Enterprise & Regulatory Reform. Crown copyright. https://assets.publishing.service.gov.uk/media/5a7490ace5274a44083b7b15/7296.pdf, January 2008.

[67] W. G. U. Ltd, "Decommissioning of Hunterston B Nuclear Power Station. EIA Scoping Report," tech. rep., PSIRU University of Greenwich, August 2022.

[68] "Why geologic disposal?." Duration of waste storage https://www.yucc amountain.org/faq.htm#disposal.

[69] "NDA Annual Report 2022 to 2023." UK Nuclear Decommissioning Authority (NDA) https://assets.publishing.service.gov.uk/media/5a7490a ce5274a44083b7b15/7296.pdf.

[70] "The Nuclear Decommissioning Authority's management of the Magnox contract - Understanding and managing the burden of nuclear decommissioning on the taxpayer." UK Parliament, Public Accounts Committee https://publications.parliament.uk/pa/cm5801/cmselect/cmpubacc/653 /65306.htm, November 2020.

[71] P. Brown, "Voodoo Economics and the Doomed Nuclear Renaissance," tech. rep., Friends of the Earth, May 2008.

[72] "Nuclear Provision: the cost of cleaning up Britain's historic nuclear sites." gov UK, 4 July 2019, https://www.gov.uk/government/publicat ions/nuclear-provision-explaining-the-cost-of-cleaning-up-britains-nuc lear-legacy/nuclear-provision-explaining-the-cost-of-cleaning-up-britain s-nuclear-legacy.

[73] S. Laville, "UK's nuclear waste cleanup operation could cost £260bn," *The Guardian*, September 2022.

[74] R. H. Bryan *et al.*, "Report and Recommendations of the Nevada Commission on Nuclear Projects," tech. rep., State of Nevada, November 2019.

[75] "A rare tour of the tunnel that is ground zero for a nuclear waste controversy." CBS, 10 June 2019, https://www.cbsnews.com/news/yucca-mou ntain-nuclear-waste-storage-controversy.

[76] S. Thomas, "Comparison among different decommissioning funds methodologies for nuclear installations. Country Report United Kingdom," tech. rep., PSIRU University of Greenwich, October 2006.

[77] "French government wins court approval for EDF nationalisation," *Nuclear Engineering International*, May 2023.

[78] C. Pitchers, "France's ageing nuclear fleet paints bleak picture for coming winter and near future," *euronews*, November 2022.

[79] W. Richter, "France Predict Cost of Nuclear Disaster to be Over Three Times their GDP," *OilPrice.com*, March 2013.

[80] "Global Threat Reduction Programme: Support for international remediation work at Chernobyl." UK Department of Energy & Climate Change https://www.gov.uk/government/case-studies/global-threat-reduction -programme-support-for-international-remediation-work-at-chernobyl, January 2013.

[81] "The Sizewell C Project. SZC Co.'s Response to the Secretary of State's Letter dated 31 May 2022." gov UK, https://infrastructure.planningins pectorate.gov.uk/wp-content/ipc/uploads/projects/EN010012/EN01001 2-010985-SZC%20CO.%20Response%20to%20SoS%20Information%20R equest_31.05.22.pdf.

[82] "The Future of Nuclear Power." gov UK, DTI https://infrastructure.pla nninginspectorate.gov.uk/wp-content/ipc/uploads/projects/EN010080 /EN010080-003124-Appendix%2014,%20Annex%2005%20Nuclear%20P ower%20in%20a%20Low%20Carbon%20UK_Redacted.pdf, May 2007.

[83] T. Rose and T. Sweeting, "How safe is nuclear power? A statistical study suggests less than expected," *Bulletin of the Atomic Scientists*, vol. 72, no. 2, pp. 112–115, 2016.

[84] W. C. Patterson, *Nuclear Power*. England: Penguin Books, 1976.

[85] "Ukraine's Zaporizhzhya Nuclear Power Plant lost off-site power again, diesel generators providing back-up electricity." International Atomic Energy Agency https://www.iaea.org/newscenter/pressreleases/ukraines-z aporizhzhya-nuclear-power-plant-lost-off-site-power-again-diesel-gener ators-providing-back-up-electricity, November 2022.

[86] "Ukraine accuses Russia of blocking diesel supplies to Zaporizhzhia nuclear plant." Reuters https://www.reuters.com/world/europe/ukraine-a ccuses-russia-blocking-diesel-supplies-zaporizhzhia-nuclear-plant-2022-1 0-12/, October 2022.

[87] H. Montefiore *et al.*, *Changing Directions. A Report from the Independent Commission on Transport*. Coronet Books, 1974.

[88] G. Hutton, A. Shalchi, and M. Ward, "Financial services: contribution to the UK economy," tech. rep., House of Commons Library, Research Briefing, September 2022.

[89] R. Greenwood and D. Scharfstein, "The Growth of Finance," *Journal of Economic Perspectives*, vol. 27, pp. 3–28, May 2013.

[90] T. Segal, "Forex Market: Who Trades Currencies and Why." Investopedia, https://www.investopedia.com/articles/forex/11/who-trades-forex -and-why.asp, August 2021.

[91] "Global trade hits record $7.7 trillion in first quarter of 2022." United Nations Conference on Trade and Development (UNCTAD) Global Trade Update, 7 July 2022. Quarterly trade in goods and services. https://unct ad.org/news/global-trade-hits-record-77-trillion-first-quarter-2022, July 2022.

[92] "GDP (constant 2015 US$) - United States." https://data.worldbank.o rg/indicator/NY.GDP.MKTP.KD?locations=US.

[93] "Annual Gross Domestic Product and real GDP in the United States from 1929 to 2020." Statista, https://www.statista.com/statistics/1031 678/gdp-and-real-gdp-united-states-1930-2019/.

[94] "Gini Index - United States." Data from Gini Index graph from World Bank. https://data.worldbank.org/indicator/SI.POV.GINI?locations=U S. Gini Index for USA: about 41.4 in 2006, about 35 in 1980.

[95] B. Thompson, "The Rise in Income Inequality." Urban Milwaukee, https: //urbanmilwaukee.com/2014/12/08/data-wonk-the-rise-in-income-ine quality/, December 2014. Graph shows Gini Index for USA fell from 38 in 1950 to low of 35 in 1967, then 36.5 in 1980, 44.5 in 2006.

[96] "US Income Inequality: Latest Data." https://datatrekresearch.com/us-i ncome-inequality-latest-data/. Article about release by US Census Bureau of data on local-level income, poverty and health insurance statistics from its American Community Survey.

[97] "Historical Income Tables: Income Inequality." Statista, https://www.ce nsus.gov/data/tables/time-series/demo/income-poverty/historical-inc ome-inequality.html.

[98] "World Inequality Report." World Inequality Lab, https://wir2022.wid. world/executive-summary/, 2022. Aslo cited and described in an article by OXFAM "World Inequality Report 2022: a treasure trove of trends and new data" https://frompoverty.oxfam.org.uk/world-inequality-rep ort-2022-a-treasure-trove-of-trends-and-new-data/.

[99] J. Eggleston, D. Hays, R. Munk, and B. Sullivan, "The Wealth of Households: 2017," Tech. Rep. P70BR-170, The United States Census Bureau, August 2020.

[100] D. D. Treece, "Are You In The Top 1%?." https://www.forbes.com/adv isor/investing/financial-advisor/are-you-in-the-top-1-percent/, 2023. The top 1% of Americans, have a net worth that is more than 85 times the median net worth in the U.S.

[101] "U.S. wealth distribution 2023." Statista, https://www.statista.com/s tatistics/203961/wealth-distribution-for-the-us/. [Online; accessed 6-September-2023].

[102] J. Parkinson, "How much of a savings buffer do people need?." BBC, https://www.bbc.co.uk/news/magazine-35801951, March 2016. Cites surveys by the Money Advice Service and ING bank.

[103] "Saving for retirement in Great Britain: April 2018 to March 2020." Inequality in private pension wealth, ONS https://www.ons.gov.uk/peo plepopulationandcommunity/personalandhouseholdfinances/incomean dwealth/bulletins/pensionwealthingreatbritain/april2018tomarch2020 \#inequality-in-private-pension-wealth, June 2022.

[104] O. Bullough, *Butler to the World: How Britain Became the Servant of Tycoons, Tax Dodgers, Kleptocrats and Criminals.* London: Profile Books, 2022.

[105] N. Shaxson, *Treasure Islands: Tax Havens and the Men who Stole the World.* London: The Bodley Head, 2011.

[106] Tax Justice Network, https://taxjustice.net/.

[107] N. Shaxson, "Over a third of world trade happens within multinational corporations." Tax Justice Network, https://taxjustice.net/2019/04/09/over-a-third-or-more-of-world-trade-happens-inside-multinational-corporations/, April 2019.

[108] A. Swaby, "Why so many shipowners find Panama's flag convenient." BBC, https://www.bbc.co.uk/news/world-latin-america-28558480, August 2014.

[109] Wikipedia contributors, "2008 united kingdom bank rescue package — Wikipedia, the free encyclopedia." https://en.wikipedia.org/w/index.php?title=2008_United_Kingdom_bank_rescue_package&oldid=1173208521, 2023. [Online; accessed 6-September-2023].

[110] T. Harbert, "Here's how much the 2008 bailouts really cost." MIT Sloan School of Management, https://mitsloan.mit.edu/ideas-made-to-matter/heres-how-much-2008-bailouts-really-cost, February 2019.

[111] F. Mor, "Royal Bank of Scotland bailout: 10 years and counting." https://commonslibrary.parliament.uk/royal-bank-of-scotland-bailout-10-years-and-counting/, October 2018.

[112] G. Hiscott, "Fred 'The Shred' Goodwin amasses £17million pension 10 years after RBS crash that left millions £23k worse off," *The Daily Mirror, on-line,* September 2018.

[113] R. Tressell, *The Ragged Trousered Philanthropists.* Grant Richards Ltd., 1914.

[114] Wikipedia contributors, "Transport act 1947 — Wikipedia, the free encyclopedia." https://en.wikipedia.org/w/index.php?title=Transport_Act_1947, 2022. "Shares in the railway companies were exchanged for British Transport Stock, with a guaranteed 3% return ... repayable after forty years" [Online; accessed 6-September-2023].

[115] J. Stittle, "Nationalising Britain's railways is the only way to fix chronic problems – here's why." The Conversation, https://theconversation.com/nationalising-britains-railways-is-the-only-way-to-fix-chronic-problems-heres-why-88591, January 2018.

509

[116] A. Bowman, "An illusion of success: The consequences of British rail privatisation," *Accounting Forum,* vol. 39, no. 1, pp. 51–63, 2015.

[117] Y. El-Gingihy, "The great PFI heist: The real story of how Britain's economy has been left high and dry by a doomed economic philosophy," *The Independent, on-line,* February 2018.

[118] D. Campbell, "NHS hospital trusts to pay out further £55bn under PFI scheme," *The Guardian,* September 2019. Some trusts are having to spend as much as one-sixth of their entire budget on repaying debts due as a result of the PFI scheme.

[119] S. Youel, "Banking for People: Lessons from the UK's Girobank." Positive Money, https://positivemoney.org/2021/05/banking-for-people-lessons -from-the-uks-girobank/, May 2021.

[120] Wikipedia contributors, "Girobank — Wikipedia, the free encyclopedia." https://en.wikipedia.org/w/index.php?title=Girobank&oldid=11767727 48, 2023. [Online; accessed 17-December-2023].

[121] Z. Wood, "Debenhams 'never recovered from private equity ownership'," *The Guardian,* Dec 2020.

[122] D. Hussain, "How private equity fat-cats who rub shoulders with A-list celebrities and royalty triggered Debenhams' downfall by selling its stores and leasing them back before taking £1.2BILLION in dividends," *The Daily Mail,* Dec 2020.

[123] P. Comley, *Monkey with a Pin.* Pete Comley, 2012.

[124] M. Parietti, "This Is How Much Mutual Fund Managers Make," *Investopedia,* June 2020.

[125] J. Gray, "Number of DB pension schemes and members continue to fall." Pensions Age, https://www.pensionsage.com/pa/Number-of-DB-schem es-and-members-continue-to-shrink.php, December 2021.

[126] "DC trust: scheme return data 2019–20." UK Pensions Regulator, https: //www.thepensionsregulator.gov.uk/en/document-library/research-and -analysis/dc-trust-scheme-return-data-2019-2020, 2021.

[127] "Almost half of UK business owners have no pension savings." Actuarial Post, citing a survey by the Prudential, https://www.actuarialpost.co.u k/article/almost-half-of-uk-business-owners-have-no-pension-savings-3 554.htm. [Online; accessed 6-September-2023].

[128] Wikipedia contributors, "Financialization — Wikipedia, the free encyclopedia." https://en.wikipedia.org/w/index.php?title=Financialization&ol did=1153448096, 2023. [Online; accessed 6-September-2023].

[129] J. K. Galbraith, *The World Economy Since the Wars - A Personal View.* Sinclair-Stevenson, 1994. p234.

[130] "Why are interest rates high and when might they fall?." Bank of England Explainers https://www.bankofengland.co.uk/explainers/why-are-inter est-rates-in-the-uk-going-up, January 2024. [Online; accessed Jan-2024].

[131] S. Pittaway, "The Mortgage Crunch." The Resolution Foundation https://www.resolutionfoundation.org/publications/the-mortgage-crunch, June 2023.

[132] "Index of Private Housing Rental Prices, UK: December 2023." ONS http s://www.ons.gov.uk/economy/inflationandpriceindices/bulletins/indexo fprivatehousingrentalprices/december2023. [Online; accessed Jan-2024].

[133] S. Hunter, "Rising mortgage payments leading to higher rents warn landlords." National Residential Landlords Association, Industry News https://www.nrla.org.uk/news/rising-mortgage-payments-leading-to-h igher-rents, December 2023.

[134] "How increases in housing costs impact households." ONS https://www. ons.gov.uk/peoplepopulationandcommunity/housing/articles/howincrea sesinhousingcostsimpacthouseholds/2023-01-09, January 2023.

[135] F. Sosenko, M. Littlewood, G. Bramley, S. Fitzpatrick, and J. B. J. Wood, "State of Hunger. A study of poverty and food insecurity in the UK." The Trussell Trust https://www.stateofhunger.org/wp-content/uploads/201 9/11/State-of-Hunger-Report-November2019-Digital.pdf, 2019.

[136] A. Pratt, "Food Banks in the UK." House of Commons Library, Research Briefing https://commonslibrary.parliament.uk/research-briefings/cbp -8585, October 2023.

[137] "Supplemental Nutrition Assistance Program." U.S. Department of Agri-culture https://www.fns.usda.gov/snap/supplemental-nutrition-assista nce-program. [Online; accessed 2-Feb-2024].

[138] "Inflation rate, average consumer prices." IMF https://www.imf.org/ex ternal/datamapper/PCPIPCH@WEO/WEOWORLD?year=2024.

[139] "Unemployment rate." IMF https://www.imf.org/external/datamappe r/LUR@WEO/OEMDC/ADVEC/WEOWORLD?year=2024.

[140] "About Pay Review Bodies." GOV.UK https://www.gov.uk/governmen t/publications/pay-review-bodies-and-police-boards-introduction/an-i ntroduction-to-pay-review-bodies-and-police-boards, July 2023.

[141] J. Williamson, "All Aboard - Making worker representation on company boards a reality." Trade Union Congress, Economic Report Series https://www.tuc.org.uk/research-analysis/reports/all-aboard-making-worke r-representation-company-boards-reality, September 2016.

[142] L. Mishel, E. Gould, and J. Bivens, "Wage Stagnation in Nine Charts," *The Economic Policy Institute*, January 2015.

[143] "Bulletin of the Atomic Scientists." https://thebulletin.org/. Founded to warn humanity of existential risks, the Bulletin maintains the Doomsday Clock.

[144] "The Centre for the Study of Existential Risk." University of Cambridge https://www.cser.ac.uk/. Dedicated to the study and mitigation of risks that could lead to human extinction or civilizational collapse.

[145] S. Beard and L. Holt, "What are the biggest threats to humanity?." BBC, https://www.bbc.co.uk/news/world-47030233, February 2019.

[146] S. Pinker, *The Better Angels of Our Nature: Why Violence Has Declined.* New York: Viking Books, 2011.

[147] S. Pinker, *Enlightenment Now: The Case for Reason, Science, Humanism, and Progress.* New York: Viking Books, 2018.

[148] J. Diamond, *Collapse: How Societies Choose to Fail or Survive.* New York: Penguin, 2005.

[149] "It's 'now or never' to limit global warming to 1.5 degrees." UN News, https://news.un.org/en/story/2022/04/1115452, April 2022.

[150] G. Ceballos, P. R. Ehrlich, and R. Dirzo, "Biological annihilation via the ongoing sixth mass extinction signaled by vertebrate population losses and declines," *PNAS*, July 2017.

[151] "Revenue Statistics 2022 - the United Kingdom." OECD, https://www.oecd.org/tax/revenue-statistics-united-kingdom.pdf.

[152] A. Kamande, "Billionaires make billions, while billions get poorer," *Oxfam Views and Voices*, January 2022. The ten richest billionaires – all men – saw their wealth more than double from $700bn to $1.5 trillion between March 2020 and November 2021, according to calculations done by Oxfam based on Forbes billionaires.

[153] L. Hooker, "Millionaires at Davos say 'tax us more'." BBC, https://www.bbc.co.uk/news/business-61549155, May 2022.

[154] "In tax we trust. To our fellow millionaires and billionaires: ...." https://www.intaxwetrust.org/, January 2022.

[155] S. Crowther, "Henry Ford: Why I Favor Five Days' Work With Six Days' Pay." In an interview with Ford https://en.wikisource.org/wiki/Henry_Ford:_Why_I_Favor_Five_Days%27_Work_With_Six_Days%27_Pay, 1926. [Online; accessed 7-September-2023].

[156] Wikipedia contributors, "List of sovereign states by tax revenue to gdp ratio — Wikipedia, the free encyclopedia." https://en.wikipedia.org/w/index.php?title=List_of_sovereign_states_by_tax_revenue_to_GDP_ratio&oldid=1167665923, 2023. [Online; accessed 7-September-2023].

[157] Wikipedia contributors, "Reaganomics (debt and government expenditures) — Wikipedia, the free encyclopedia." https://en.wikipedia.org/w/index.php?title=Reaganomics&oldid=1171303739, 2023. [Online; accessed 7-September-2023].

[158] "Federal Debt Held by the Public." Federal Reserve Bank of St. Louis, https://fred.stlouisfed.org/graph/?g=k977, 2023. [Online; accessed 7-September-2023].

[159] M. Hellowell and A. Pollock, "Written Evidence to the National Assembly for Wales Finance Committee with Regards to its Inquiry on Public Private Partnerships," tech. rep., The Centre for International Public Health Policy, December 2007.

[160] S. Goodley, "P&O Ferries has paid some crew less than half UK minimum wage," *The Guardian*, March 2024.

[161] "P&O Ferries' sackings were appalling, says Sunak." BBC, 20 March 2022, https://www.bbc.co.uk/news/business-60812328.

[162] "UN Report: Nature's Dangerous Decline 'Unprecedented'; Species Extinction Rates 'Accelerating')." IPBES https://www.un.org/sustainabledevelopment/blog/2019/05/nature-decline-unprecedented-report/, May 2019.

[163] D. Goulson, "The insect apocalypse: 'Our world will grind to a halt without them'," *The Guardian*, July 2021.

[164] R. Bergl, A. Dunn, A. Fowler, I. Imong, D. Ndeloh, A. Nicholas, and J. Oates, "IUCN Red List assessment: Cross River Gorilla." https://www.iucnredlist.org/species/39998/102326240, 2016.

[165] H. Warwick, "Where have all the hedgehogs gone?," *The Daily Mail*, February 2013.

[166] D. Wembridge, "The state of Britain's hedgehogs 2011," tech. rep., British Hedgehog Preservation Society, 2011.

[167] "How many hours did people really work across human history?." https://www.lovemoney.com/gallerylist/84600/how-many-hours-did-people-really-work-across-human-history, 2023. [Online; accessed 8-Sep-2023].

[168] "Cars and Vans." International Energy Agency https://www.iea.org/energy-system/transport/cars-and-vans. 3.53 Gt CO2 emissions from cars and vans in 2022 [Online; accessed 26-March-2024].

[169] "Transport and environment statistics." UK Official Statistics https:// www.gov.uk/government/statistics/transport-and-environment-statistic s-2023/transport-and-environment-statistics-2023, October 2023.

[170] "Fast Facts on Transportation Greenhouse Gas Emissions." EPA U.S. Transportation Sector Greenhouse Gas Emissions 1990 - 2021 https:// www.epa.gov/greenvehicles/fast-facts-transportation-greenhouse-gas-e missions, June 2023.

[171] "United Nations Population Fund, World Population Dashboard." https: //www.unfpa.org/data/world-population-dashboard.

[172] "LowCVP study highlights importance of measuring whole life carbon emissions." Cited by Zemo Partnership, https://www.zemo.org.uk/news -events/news,lowcvp-study-highlights-importance-of-measuring-whole-l ife-carbon-emissions_1644.htm, June 2011.

[173] "Lifecycle Analysis of UK Road Vehicles." Report for UK Department for Transport https://assets.publishing.service.gov.uk/government/up loads/system/uploads/attachment_data/file/1062603/lifecycle-analy sis-of-UK-road-vehicles.pdf, November 2021. Estimates for 2020 that a typical battery electric car saves 65% GHG emissions compared to a petrol car. But that is for the UK electricity supply which already has a large wind and solar contribution and almost no coal.

[174] E. Commission, D.-G. for Climate Action, N. Hill, S. Amaral, S. Morgan-Price, T. Nokes, J. Bates, H. Helms, H. Fehrenbach, K. Biemann, N. Ab-dalla, J. Jöhrens, E. Cotton, L. German, A. Harris, S. Haye, C. Sim, A. Bauen, and S. Ziem-Milojevic, *Determining the environmental impacts of conventional and alternatively fuelled vehicles through LCA – Final report.* Publications Office of the European Union, 2020.

[175] M. Schoch, S. Kofi, T. Baah, C. Lakner, and J. Friedman, "Half of the global population lives on less than US$6.85 per person per day." World Bank https://blogs.worldbank.org/en/developmenttalk/half-global-pop ulation-lives-less-us685-person-day, 2022.

[176] "Household expenditure on motoring for households owning a car, UK: financial year ending 2021." UK Office for National Statistics, ref 15088. https://www.ons.gov.uk/peoplepopulationandcommunity/personalandh ouseholdfinances/expenditure/adhocs/15088householdexpenditureonmo toringforhouseholdsowningacarukfinancialyearending2021, September 2022.

[177] D. Carrington, "1% of people cause half of global aviation emissions – study," *The Guardian*, Nov 2020.

[178] "Aviation and Climate Change: Our Position." https://policy.friendsof theearth.uk/policy-positions/aviation-and-climate-change-our-position.

[179] F. F. Nerini, T. Fawcett, Y. Parag, and P. Ekins, "Personal carbon allowances revisited," *Nature Sustainability*, 2021.

[180] "Conraction & Convergence." Global Commons Institute (GCI), http://www.gci.org.uk/contconv/cc.html.

[181] "ZeroCarbonBritain." Centre for Alternative Technology (CAT), https://cat.org.uk/info-resources/zero-carbon-britain/research-reports/.

[182] "Global Footprint Network." https://www.footprintnetwork.org/. Compares the resource demand of individuals, governments, and businesses against Earth's capacity for biological regeneration.

[183] Wikipedia contributors, "Estimates of historical world population — Wikipedia, the free encyclopedia." https://en.wikipedia.org/w/index.php?title=Estimates_of_historical_world_population&oldid=1214044562, 2024. [Online; accessed 24-March-2024].

[184] Wikipedia contributors, "Roman egypt — Wikipedia, the free encyclopedia." https://en.wikipedia.org/w/index.php?title=Roman_Egypt&oldid=1201812522, 2024. [Online; accessed 25-March-2024].

[185] Wikipedia contributors, "List of countries by population in 1000 — Wikipedia, the free encyclopedia." https://en.wikipedia.org/w/index.php?title=List_of_countries_by_population_in_1000&oldid=1192145072, 2023. [Online; accessed 25-March-2024].

[186] Wikipedia contributors, "List of countries by population in 1800 — Wikipedia, the free encyclopedia." https://en.wikipedia.org/w/index.php?title=List_of_countries_by_population_in_1800&oldid=1214724970, 2024. [Online; accessed 25-March-2024].

[187] "The World Counts, Population of Egypt." https://www.theworldcounts.com/populations/countries/egypt. Estimates 10m in 1900, 20m in 1950.

[188] "China, voracious buyer of foreign agricultural land." France24 https://www.france24.com/en/20180225-china-voracious-buyer-foreign-agricultural-land, February 2018.

[189] F. Gale and E. Gooch, "China's Agricultural Investment Abroad Is Rising," *Amber Waves*, April 2018.

[190] Bloomberg, "China and US arable land per person." https://www.bloomberg.com/graphics/2017-feeding-china/, 2017.

[191] "How is China Feeding its Population of 1.4 Billion?." Center for Strategic and International Studies, https://chinapower.csis.org/china-food-security/. [Online; accessed 8-Sept-2023].

[192] S. Jennings, C. McCormack, and G. Stoll, "Thriving within our planetary means: reducing the UK's production and consumption footprint by 2030," tech. rep., WWF, June 2021.

[193] D. Colman, "Food Security in Great Britain: Past experience and the current view." Online, Kyushu University, Japan http://www.agr.kyushu-u.ac.jp/foodsci/4_paper_Colman.pdf, 2011.

[194] "Licensed vehicles at the end of the year by tax class." UK Department for Transport and Driver and Vehicle Licensing Agency (DVLA) https://assets.publishing.service.gov.uk/media/6489d029103ca6000c039ece/veh0103.ods. Great Britain from 1909; also United Kingdom from 2014.

[195] "Mid-1851 to Mid-2014 Population Estimates for United Kingdom." UK Office for National Statistics https://www.ons.gov.uk/peoplepopulationandcommunity/populationandmigration/populationestimates/adhocs/004356ukpopulationestimates1851to2014.

[196] S. Samir, "Food Security: How did Egypt achieve self-sufficiency in vegetables, fruits?," *Egypt Today*, May 2022.

[197] S. Asseng *et al.*, "Can Egypt become self-sufficient in wheat?," *Environmental Research Letters 13 094012*, September 2018.

[198] "Population Matters." https://populationmatters.org.

[199] R. Maynard, "Attenborough film: Saving our planet requires ending population growth." https://populationmatters.org/news/2020/10/attenborough-film-saving-our-planet-requires-ending-population-growth, October 2020.

[200] Wikipedia contributors, "Collapse of the atlantic northwest cod fishery — Wikipedia, the free encyclopedia." https://en.wikipedia.org/w/index.php?title=Collapse_of_the_Atlantic_northwest_cod_fishery&oldid=1174092342, 2023. [Online; accessed 8-Sep-2023].

[201] "The Collapse of the Grand Banks Cod Fishery." British Sea Fishing, https://britishseafishing.co.uk/the-collapse-of-the-grand-banks-cod-fishery/, 2022.

[202] J. Cooke, "IUCN Red List assessment: Antarctic Blue Whale." https://www.iucnredlist.org/species/41713/50226962\#assessment-information, June 2018.

[203] B. Coxworth, "Study suggests eating salmon-feed fish, instead of farmed salmon." NewAtlas, https://newatlas.com/environment/salmon-feed-wild-fish-human-consumption/, March 2022.

[204] Wikipedia contributors, "Fish meal — Wikipedia, the free encyclopedia." https://en.wikipedia.org/w/index.php?title=Fish_meal&oldid=1195862539, 2024. [Online; accessed 13-February-2024].

[205] "The Use Of Fish Meal In Animal Feeds." Advisory Committee On Animal Feeding Stuffs, ACAF/01/6, https://acaf.food.gov.uk/sites/default/files/mnt/drupal_data/sources/files/multimedia/pdfs/ACAF00106.pdf, February 2001. ACAF Secretariat, Food Standards Agency.

[206] J. Owen, "Farming Claims Almost Half Earth's Land, New Maps Show." National Geographic, https://www.nationalgeographic.com/history/article/agriculture-food-crops-land, December 2005.

[207] "Conservation successes overshadowed by more species declines – IUCN Red List update." IUCN Press Release, https://www.iucn.org/content/conservation-successes-overshadowed-more-species-declines-iucn-red-list-update, June 2015.

[208] R. Carson, *Silent Spring*. Boston: Houghton Mifflin, 1962.

[209] "Land use in agriculture by the numbers." UN FAO, https://www.fao.org/sustainability/news/detail/en/c/1274219/, May 2020.

[210] "Nature is Threatened by Unsustainable Production and Consumption of Soy." World Wide Fund For Nature (WWF), https://wwf.panda.org/discover/our_focus/food_practice/sustainable_production/soy/. [Online; accessed 8-Sep-2023].

[211] C. Brogan, "Best ways to cut carbon emissions from the cement industry explored." Imperial College, https://www.imperial.ac.uk/news/221654/best-ways-carbon-emissions-from-cement/, May 2021.

[212] "Make Listening Safe. Once you lose your hearing, it won't come back!." World Health Organisation https://www.who.int/docs/default-source/documents/infographic-safe-listening-2019.pdf, 2019.

[213] M. Winchcomb, "The Safety of Private E-Scooters in the UK." Parliamentary Advisory Council for Transport Safety https://www.pacts.org.uk/wp-content/uploads/PACTS-The-safety-of-private-e-scooters-in-the-UK-Report-5.0.pdf, 2021.

[214] S. Das and J. Ungoed-Thomas, "Child vaping risks becoming 'public health catastrophe' in UK, experts warn.," *The Guardian*, July 2022.

[215] "Ecodesign requirements for products with standby and off-mode." European Commission https://commission.europa.eu/energy-climate-change-environment/standards-tools-and-labels/products-labelling-rules-and-requirements/energy-label-and-ecodesign/energy-efficient-products/mode-standby-and-networked-standby-devices_en.

[216] "Letter to Mayor re tall buildings." London Assembly, see 'embodied energy' https://www.london.gov.uk/sites/default/files/final_tall_buildings_letter_to_mayor.pdf, March 2021.

[217] "High-rise buildings much more energy-intensive than low-rise." University College London https://www.ucl.ac.uk/news/2017/jun/high-rise-buildings-much-more-energy-intensive-low-rise, June 2017.

[218] "Circular economy: definition, importance and benefits." European Parliament, News https://www.europarl.europa.eu/news/en/headlines/economy/20151201STO05603/circular-economy-definition-importance-and-benefits, May 2023.

[219] R. Smithers, "England's plastic bag usage drops 85% since 5p charge introduced," *The Guardian*, July 2016.

[220] "The Citizens' Assembly, Republic of Ireland." https://citizensassembly.ie/.

[221] "Citizens' Assemblies in the UK." https://citizensassembly.co.uk/. See also: The RSA, Deliberative Democracy https://www.thersa.org/projects/deliberative-democracy, mySociety Research https://research.mysociety.org/publications/how-run-citizens-assembly.

[222] "Climate Assembly UK." https://www.climateassembly.uk/, 2020.

[223] "Doomsday Clock." Bulletin of Atomic Scientists https://thebulletin.org/doomsday-clock/.

[224] "Transition Town Network." https://transitionnetwork.org/.

[225] S. Bachra, A. Lovell, C. McLachlan, and A. M. Minas, "The co-benefits of climate action," tech. rep., CDP, 2020.

[226] A. Smith, *The Climate Bonus: co-benefits of climate policy*. Routledge, 2013.

[227] G. Zhang and R. Veenhoven, "Ancient Chinese philosophical advice: can it help us find happiness today?," *Journal of Happiness Studies 9, 425–443*, 2008.

[228] B. Russell, *The Conquest of Happiness*. Liveright, 1930.

[229] D. Nettle, *Happiness: The Science Behind Your Smile*. Oxford University Press, 2005.

[230] "Happy Planet Index." https://happyplanetindex.org/.

[231] "Building a wellbeing economy." New Economics Foundation, https://neweconomics.org/campaigns/wellbeing.

[232] "The Universal Declaration of Human Rights (UDHR)." https://www.un.org/en/about-us/universal-declaration-of-human-rights, December 1948.

[233] "The International Covenant on Economic, Social and Cultural Rights." https://www.ohchr.org/en/instruments-mechanisms/instruments/inte rnational-covenant-economic-social-and-cultural-rights, December 1966.

[234] "International Covenant on Civil and Political Rights." https://www.oh chr.org/en/instruments-mechanisms/instruments/international-covenan t-civil-and-political-rights, December 1966.

[235] "Badvertising." https://www.badverts.org.

[236] "Adfree Cities." https://adfreecities.org.uk/.

[237] K. Pickett and R. Wilkinson, *The Spirit Level: Why Equality is Better for Everyone.* Allen Lane, 2009.

[238] "The Equality Trust." https://equalitytrust.org.uk.

[239] B. Herre, F. Spooner, and M. Roser, "Homicides," *Our World in Data*, 2013. https://ourworldindata.org/homicides.

[240] W. Morris, *Signs of Change.* Longmans, Green and Co., 1896.

[241] K. Jeffrey, S. Mahony, J. Michaelson, and S. Abdallah, "Well-being at work - A review of the literature," tech. rep., New Economics Foundation, February 2014.

[242] E. Nova, "Demand for Populism as a Symptom of Learned Helplessness," *4liberty*, April 2016.

[243] E. MacColl, *Journeyman – An Autobiography.* Manchester University Press, 2009.

[244] B. Schwartz, *Paradox of Choice – Why More is Less.* Harper Perennial, 2004.

[245] A. Gorz, *Ecology as Politics.* South End Press, 1980.

[246] K. Wilson, "How small changes to prison food drastically cut inmate violence." BBC Science Focus https://www.sciencefocus.com/the-hum an-body/prison-food-nutrition-violence-mental-health/, April 2022.

[247] "Children who eat more fruit and veg have better mental health." Communications, Univerity of EastAnglia https://www.uea.ac.uk/news/-/ar ticle/children-who-eat-more-fruit-and-veg-have-better-mental-health, Sep 2021.

[248] "Global Obesity Observatory." https://data.worldobesity.org/rankings/.

[249] K. Douglas and J. Douglas, "Green spaces aren't just for nature – they boost our mental health too." New Scientist https://www.newscientist.c om/article/mg24933270-800-green-spaces-arent-just-for-nature-they-b oost-our-mental-health-too/, March 2021.

[250] D. Carrington, "Traffic noise slows children's memory development, study finds," *The Guardian*, June 2022.

[251] J. Wang, P. Sankaridurg, T. Naduvilath, W. Li, I. G. Morgan, K. A. Rose, R. Weng, X. Xu, and X. He, "Time outdoors positively associates with academic performance," *BMC Public Health*, April 2023.

[252] K. Loria, "Being outside can improve memory, fight depression, and lower blood pressure." https://www.businessinsider.com/why-spending-more-time-outside-is-healthy-2017-7, May 2023.

[253] F. Wheen, *How Mumbo Jumbo Conquered the World*. Harper Perennial, 2004.

[254] J. Haidt, *The Righteous Mind*. Penguin Books, 2012.

[255] R. Dawkins and Y. Wong, *The Ancestor's Tale: A Pilgrimage to the Dawn of Life*. London: Weidenfeld & Nicolson, 2004.

[256] T. Jackson, *Prosperity Without Growth*. London: Sustainable Development Commission, 2009.

[257] "The International Renewable Energy Agency (IRENA)." https://www.irena.org. IRENA drives the widespread adoption and sustainable use of all forms of renewable energy.

[258] "The Intergovernmental Panel on Climate Change (IPCC)." https://www.ipcc.ch/. IPCC is the UN body for assessing the science related to climate change.

[259] G. Thunberg, *The Climate Book*. London: Allen Lane, 2022.

[260] "Global Climate Change - Vital Signs of the Planet." https://climate.nasa.gov/. NASA information on climate change.

Index

Printed in Great Britain
by Amazon

44108028R00307